an introduction to folk music in the united states

by BRUNO NETTL

1962—Detroit

Wayne State University Press

Copyright © 1962 by *Wayne State University Press, Detroit 2, Michigan*
All rights reserved

Published simultaneously in Canada by Ambassador Books, Limited
Toronto, Ontario, Canada

Library of Congress Catalog Card Number 62-16346
Revised Edition with Index
Waynebook No. 7

For Wanda

PREFACE

During the past few years, folk music has become such a popular subject in America that hundreds of collections, printed and recorded, and dozens of descriptive books have appeared. Most of the latter concern themselves with special fields within American folk music, but, surprisingly, no over-all survey or summary of the subject in its entirety exists. The folk music of the non-English-speaking groups has been especially neglected in attempts to survey the field. This volume is intended, in an introductory and elementary fashion, to fill that gap. It does not pretend to be definitive or comprehensive nor to present new material. Based on previous publications by many authors, its purpose is to introduce the layman to the great variety of forms and cultures represented in the folk music in this country. Only a glimpse into each of the larger categories is offered, and many important song types, instruments, and ethnic groups are omitted. The emphasis is on the music; words are here a secondary consideration. I have tried to include such material on folk music in general as is necessary for understanding the material in this country (hence the non-American examples), and I have gone beyond what is usually included in folk music discussions in order to show the use of folk music in the modern city, in the professional singer's repertory, and in art music. But I advise the reader to continue beyond this introduction, which merely scratches the surface of the subject, into the fascinating world of folk music, a world to which the United States has made a unique contribution. The chapter bibliographies are included with the reader's further exploration in mind. Changes made in this revised edition are minimal. I have corrected obvious errors, and I have heeded some suggestions made by reviewers of the first edition. Also, I have brought biographical aids (p. 118–122) up to date, and I have added an index.

Finally, I am indebted to Richard M. Dorson for the idea of writing this book and for his valuable advice and suggestions.

BRUNO NETTL

CONTENTS

MUSICAL EXAMPLES

I

DEFINING FOLK MUSIC

The term "folk music" has been much used and abused in recent years, but it has been endowed with ever-increasing prestige. Indeed, much of the misuse of the term has been caused by a kind of veneration on the part of the public, which has been exploited by some individuals who use folk music in commercial pursuits, finding that their sales increase when the label "folk" is applied to their material. Sometimes they have used the term to cover music which under no honest definition could be accepted as folklore. Some of the confusion has indirectly stemmed from the inability of scholars to find a generally accepted definition.[1] I should like to show some of the diversity of opinion regarding such a definition and then adopt one as the basis of our further discussion.

There seem to be two main approaches to defining folk music. One is concerned with the properties of folk music as such, the other with its cultural milieu or background. For some people folk music must sound a certain way, it must be composed in a particular style and any music which conforms to this style is folk music. If one follows the other approach, one accepts as folk music all music produced by a particular group in society, which one calls and defines as the "folk."

Who the people included as "folk" are is something which folklorists have had considerable difficulty deciding, and nothing is better evidence of their lack of unanimity than the many definitions in the *Standard Dictionary of Folklore*.[2] Students of folk music must necessarily agree in their definitions with the folk-lorists at large, and they, too, have used many definitions of "folk." For Béla Bartók folk music was simply peasant music, or rural music.[3] For other scholars it has meant music especially characteristic of a given country or ethnic group, whether rural or urban. While most modern researchers agree with Bartók to some extent, many also tend to believe that folk music has existed in the towns and cities, at least under some circumstances.

The notion that folk music is very old has played a part in the problem of defining it. The idea that songs have always been with a people is a common feature in the creation myths of many primitive tribes, and the emphasis placed on tradition, the close identification of an entire people with its songs, has influenced research to the extent of causing the rejection of otherwise acceptable material simply because it lacked sufficient age. We must, however, distinguish between individual creations and the style in which they are composed. While a style may be very old, the songs composed in that style may be comparatively recent. Thus many folk songs are only a few decades old; although most of them are somewhat older, some may even go back many centuries. But many of the new folk songs are not appreciably different in style from those composed in earlier times. The opposite may also be true, however. A song may be old, but it may have changed in style over the years so that it bears hardly any evidence of its age. All of this shows us that, in contrast to cultivated music (music that is part of a culture through a written tradition), a folk song often has a life quite independent of its characteristic qualities, which is what we call "style."

There is also a strong belief that the origin of a piece of music determines whether it is folklore or not. A song composed by a trained, professional composer is not acceptable as folk music, but one created by an untrained musician is acceptable. Then again, we find the opinion that a song is a folk song even if written by a trained composer, as long as its origin is not known to the performers and hearers. The trouble with these definitions, however valuable in special cases, is that they depend on the gaps in our knowledge of folk song origins. If our information increased, the number of folk songs would have to decline. Although it has not changed in the process, a song whose origin is suddenly discovered would have to be reclassified.

Another basis for defining folk music is the manner in which it is transmitted. People learn some things through reading and other things by being told or shown. Political news which is read in a newspaper and a skill which is learned from a textbook are elements of culture which are transmitted in written tradition. Information which is passed from one person to another through speech is transmitted in oral tradition; songs, tales, methods of sewing, decorating, boat-building, beliefs, proverbs, riddles may be transmitted in this way, and if so, they are classed as folklore. Some cultures, like those of the American Indians, the African Negroes, and the Polynesians, make use of oral tradition exclusively; they are the so-called primitive cultures. But even the members of urban cultures, living in the centers of educated, literate society, learn some things by oral tradition, directly from other people, perhaps from their parents and childhood friends. Music of this sort can, with certain qualifications, be accepted as folklore. This is the most commonly accepted criterion today, and it will be ours in the following chapters.

School songs and religious music are often passed on by oral tradition, but they are rarely classified as folklore, for they are associated with institutions, like school and church, and they are composed, written, taught, and developed by professional musicians. Hymns and songs taught in school are usually passed on by printed media, and oral tradition enters only when a large mass of people learn them; of course this music is related to folklore, but we cannot accept it without qualification. On the other hand, some hymns do live entirely or largely in oral tradition, and these we distinguish by the term "folk-hymns."

A song may be a folk song at one time or in one place and an art song at a different time or place. Many songs begin in written form, created by a trained composer, and remain in the art song tradition. If, at the same time, they pass into the oral tradition for a sufficient time, they can also be considered folk songs.

The broad field of folk music is usually thought of in terms of two main subdivisions: folk music proper and primitive music. Folk music exists in certain segments of those cultures which have reading and writing, whereas primitive music belongs to the so-called pre-literate peoples. However, as a whole, primitive music is not really more primitive or more simple than folk music; indeed, it is often much more complex and highly developed. The difference between folk and primitive music is largely a reflection of the differences between folk and non-literate cultures; but we can also distinguish these two kinds of music by their styles, by the way they sound. Existing in literate societies, folk music is always in close contact with art music and popular music. There is always an interchange of musical materials and influence, and the folk music of a given country is bound to have many of the characteristics of the cultivated music of that country. Primitive music is less closely related to urban culture; it tends to sound strange to persons accustomed to hearing only cultivated music.

How and why does folk music come into being? This has been answered vaguely in many ways by many scholars, and only a few of the various kinds of theories can be touched upon here. An early one, propounded among others by the famous Grimm brothers, is that of the communal origin of folklore.[4] It maintains that all folklore, including folk music, is the expression of an entire people and that the whole ethnic group is the creator of each item of folklore. While this theory is credible in a rather indefinite and idealistic sense, it does not give due credit to the individual creators of folklore; indeed, it does not recognize them at all, and it is hardly accepted today.

Another theory, maintained by the Germans, Hans Naumann and John Meier, and slightly related to — but also distinct from — that of *communal creation,* states that an item of folklore, such as a song, originates in a sophisticated, urban society as art music, and is later taken up by lower social strata. It becomes *gesunkenes Kulturgut* (debased or lowered cultural elements).[5] For example, some songs by Franz Schubert, a member of a sophisticated musical culture, have passed into oral tradition and become folk songs in Austria and southern Germany. On the other hand, this theory does not admit that folklore and folk music could be created by the unsophisticated members of folk cultures. Like communal creation, it does not credit the individual in a folk community with any creativity.

The relationship between true folk songs, created by members of folk groups, and cultivated songs which pass into oral tradition has been used by Franz Magnus Boehme, an important pioneer in folk music research, to formulate a universal series of stages in the history of folk song.[6] He believes that true folk songs were created only before cultivated music came into existence. Later the sophisticated began to create songs which resemble folk music in their simplicity and their general appeal; these are called "*volkstümliche Lieder*" (popular or folk-like songs), and their appearance coincides with the division of society into cultivated and folk segments. Finally, in the third stage, even the folk have assimilated a good deal of sophisticated civilization. The true folk songs disappear and are entirely replaced by the folk-like songs. This theory is interesting and certainly contains some truth, especially if applied to German culture, but whether it is indicative of the history of folk music everywhere is something which we will never learn, just as a great many other questions basic to the entire field will always remain unanswered. One fundamental difficulty is that one can only rarely separate the true folk songs from the folk-like songs; for this reason we shall call both folk music without distinction.

There are no essential differences between the way cultivated music is composed and the methods used to create a folk song for the first time. The basic difference appears only *after* the initial creative act, when the task of the original composer himself is accomplished. A piece of cultivated music, for instance a symphony by Mozart, was performed in about the same way 150 years ago as it is today. True, changes in taste concerning tempo (speed) and size of the orchestra, etc., have taken place, but there would be no difficulty in identifying the two performances as interpretations of the same piece of music. The reason for this is that the symphony was learned by musicians then and now from the same printed sources, and thus both were equally close to the original composition. Individual pieces of music in written tradition do not change appreciably in their performance over the years; but pieces of folk music do, owing to the phenomenon of *communal re-creation.* This term, invented by Phillips Barry,[7] was coined to counteract the idea of communal creation, which assumes that an entire people create folklore, but is also supposed to indicate that many anonymous persons share in molding most items of folklore into the shape they have today. Supposing you look for a song like "Lord Randall" in a large printed collection; you are likely to find a number of different versions, all moderately similar, rather than one standard form. None of these versions, or variants, is the original. But all of them are descended from one or a few original versions which have been changed by all the persons who learned them or passed them on to others. Such changes come about for various reasons, including failure of memory and the desire to make changes and improvements. We have, then, a continuous line of changes and additions which sometimes alter the original beyond recognition. Although only one person created the first product, all of the people who have learned and retaught it have shared in re-creating it in its present form. Communal re-creation, the making of variants, is perhaps the greatest distinguishing feature in folk music as opposed to cultivated music. Oral tradition itself would not be particularly relevant or interesting if it did not result in this essential quality.

Singers tend to change songs for three reasons. One is forgetfulness. Another is individual creativity, the desire to improve a song, to change it according to one's own personal taste. A third is the tendency for a song to change in order for it to conform to the style of other songs in its environment. This is especially important when a song is passed from one country, culture, or ethnic group to another. We find that many tunes have variants in numerous European countries. But in each place the tune has taken on some traits of the local folk music style. If a Czech song is learned by Germans, it will in time begin to sound like a German song. All of this applies separately to melody and words; the two components may stay together or act independently.

Having discussed cultivated and folk music, we shall quickly mention a third, an intermediate category: the so-called popular music, which one finds in juke-boxes, on popular radio programs, and in sheet music publications. It is usually created by professionals, performed by professionals, and learned from the written page; it acts in this sense, therefore, like cultivated music. However, listeners often learn popular songs without having seen the written score. And occasionally a popular song, such as a song by Stephen Foster, passes into oral tradition and remains there even after it is no longer performed professionally.

I have outlined some of the basic characteristics of folk music in its social environment. Today folk music may seem a rather remote bit of culture, interesting perhaps for the antiquarian and the seeker of unusual entertainment. Yet folk music has played a part, and musically a very significant part, in almost everyone's life. There is no doubt that the songs learned in childhood, from one's parents, relatives, and friends, exercise a strong influence on a person's later musical development, and these songs are almost inevitably genuine folk songs. This, if nothing else, justifies an interest in the nature of folk music and of one's own particular traditions.

II

GENERAL CHARACTERISTICS OF
FOLK and PRIMITIVE MUSIC

In urban society, the listener takes little active part in music, for it is to him primarily a vehicle for aesthetic enjoyment, edification, and contemplation. But in folk and primitive cultures, music is almost always associated with an activity.[1] Integrated with active phases of life, it occupies a more prominent place in the community than does the music of Western urban civilization. It is true that in urban cultures, music may also be functional, whether it is religious music or dance music, a march or the accompaniment to drama; but the most significant musical creations in Western civilization are definitely "art for art's sake." In folklore, by contrast, the most important works of music are probably those which are especially closely tied to the culture and which therefore are the most accurate expressions of its nature and character.

There seems to be a considerable difference between primitive and folk cultures in the function of music. The folk cultures, after all, participate in some of the facets of urban cultures. Many folk songs are of city origin, and some are simultaneously art songs. In the degree to which it accompanies other activities, too, folk music occupies a kind of middle ground between the primitive and the cultivated, for primitive music does this most frequently, folk music somewhat less, but cultivated music only occasionally.

The most important single function of primitive music is a religious one and includes ceremonial material, corresponding roughly to our church services, as well as songs of magical and

8

charm significance. Most of the war songs of primitive peoples are not rallying or marching songs but are designed to solicit supernatural support in war. Many love songs are not personal, they do not usually address the loved one; they are not lyrical, but they seek supernatural aid in love. Gambling songs often ask divine guidance; and many dance songs, of course, also have religious significance, since dancing is the primary religious activity in many primitive cultures. This close relationship between music and religion in the world's simplest cultures stimulated the musicologist Siegfried Nadel[2] to formulate a theory that music must have begun as a special means for man to communicate with the supernatural.

Work songs are found in many primitive cultures, but not in the simplest of all. The theory of Bücher[3] that music must have begun with the recognition that rhythmic work, accompanied by singing, is especially efficient, is probably not justified. The world's simplest cultures, those whose technology is presumably closest to that of early man, do not have rhythmic group work songs, and perhaps this is one reason for their very simplicity. Those primitive cultures which are closest to urban civilization, such as the Pueblo Indians and many African Negro tribes, have work songs, as do many folk cultures.

The amount of non-functional music tends to increase as we move from simple to complex primitive cultures. In Equatorial Africa, for example, xylophone playing as an entertainment for the customers at village markets is a general practice. In folk cultures, the amount of music for entertainment is much larger yet.

An important function of folk music, but one which is rare in primitive music, is the accompaniment to narration. Songs which tell stories are common in the folklore throughout Europe and America, and these have aroused a very lively interest among scholars. Narrative songs are often not of folk origin; in many cases they were composed by sophisticated urbanites and trickled down into folk tradition, where they became rooted and acquired the essentials of genuine folk songs. The two important types of narrative song are ballads, which are relatively short, have a strophic form (divided into stanzas), and concentrate on a single event and its background; and epics, which are long, describe a series of events centering around a hero, and usually treat the individual line as the most important structural unit.

Many ballads and epics are based on historical events, and in some cases their function in the culture could be considered archival. But most members of folk cultures seem to consider them primarily as entertainment, and so it is possible to call this kind of folk music non-functional.

Some other functions of folk music are described specifically in Chapters V, VI, VII. There are dance songs, songs connected with special occupations, work songs, lyrical and love songs, religious and children's music. Although usually of city origin, hymns have become true folk songs in some areas, but elsewhere the members of folk cultures do not participate in religious folk music but sing only the hymns of the urban tradition. Related to hymns, however, are the calendric songs which are sung at various times of year and include such familiar types as Christmas carols and songs which are sung at specific times of the life-cycle, for instance at birth, at puberty, at marriage or death.

A measure of the function of music within a culture is the degree to which the members actually participate in it. In Western civilization music is a fairly specialized activity. There are a handful of composers and a few performers, who are usually professionals, and there are even specialized listeners (concert-goers and record-buyers). But in folk and primitive cultures this kind of specialization is much smaller, and professional musicians are almost absent. There are, to be sure, some individuals who concentrate on music, for example the shamans or priests, who often have the performance of certain music as a prerogative or duty. But there are at least some cultures in which composition is practiced by large segments of the population. Also, the members of a tribe or folk group participate equally in most of their music. All the people know most of the songs and are able to sing them, even though there are certain individuals in every group who are recognized as superior performers.

With a few important exceptions, a professional status for musicians is almost wholly missing in folk and primitive cultures. There are hardly any people who make their living by perform- ance or composition. They may be rewarded in small ways by gifts or money, but they earn their livelihood in the same way as their fellows, by hunting or herding, through agriculture or a craft. The most noteworthy exceptions are found in Negro Afri- ca, a continent classified as primitive because writing is absent, but one whose cultures and music are really very complex, ri- valling, with elaborate courts which sometimes include full- time musicians, those of the oriental high cultures. Whenever the chieftains of the Watusi in East Africa emerge in public, they must be accompanied by musicians playing different-sized drums. The Chopi of South Africa have professional composers and choreographers.[4] And the singers of the heroic epics in Yu- goslavia, Albania, and Bulgaria live from their earnings traveling from town to town as singers in cafes and other gathering-places.

But even these professionals lack the rigid, formal training which marks the musician in an urban culture. Primitive and folk groups do not have the elaborate systems of music theory and terminology for musical phenomena which tend to make the mu- sician and musical activity in our culture an esoteric matter. Most people know most of what there is to know about music, the music of the tribe is all theirs, and there is no distinction be- tween a "classical," esoteric music, intelligible only to the spe- cially trained, and a popular music for the rest.

Each country, each ethnic group and tribe has its own folk music with its own peculiar character and style. Yet all the bodies of folk and primitive music in the world have some common elements which make them, as a group, contrast with the music of urban civilization.

Folk music proper, whose provenience is Europe and the ori- ental cultures, is characterized by the resemblance it bears to the cultivated music with which it is associated. German folk music sounds a good deal like German art music; Italian folk music re- minds us of the Italian composers; and so on. And since most Western cultivated music is based on one musical system whose main property is the diatonic scale (which can be found by playing the white keys of the piano), it is not surprising that most European folk music also fits into this one system. Although it does not always exploit this system exhaustively, most European folk music can at least be fitted into the tonal patterns of Western cultivated music.

Primitive music is different, at least in its systems of pitch, scales, and tonal patterns. Since it uses no cultivated system as a model, primitive music is much more varied than folk music. Usually it cannot be played on the piano or on other Western instruments simply because the pitches which these instruments can produce do not fit the primitive pitch arrangements. There are, for example, intervals smaller than the half-tone, which is the smallest in Western civilization. There are other intervals intermediate in size between those of Western music, for example, a "neutral" third, half-way between a major and a minor third, found in many of the world's areas. Matters of pitch, however, constitute the greatest difference between folk and primitive music. Their other elements, rhythm, form, and polyphony, can be described with the same terms, there being a large degree of overlapping between these two bodies of music.

Singing predominates in both, and in both instrumental music is something of an exception. While there are cultures which stress instruments, there are others which have none at all. The amount of instrumental music tends to correlate roughly with the complexity of the culture involved, and with its technological development.

Most folk and primitive music is monophonic, or strictly melodic, without accompaniment or part-singing, and with only one pitch audible at a time. There are some cultures which have no polyphony or accompaniment, but all peoples have at least a sizeable proportion of their repertory in the monophonic style. It is interesting to find that the use of instruments tends to coincide with polyphony. Furthermore, there seems to be no essential difference between folk and primitive cultures in the extent to which they use polyphony; the influence of cultivated music may, therefore, not have been a very great factor in developing folk polyphony.

The compositions of folk and primitive music tend to be short, simple, and ofter very concise and concentrated. Length is usually achieved by verbatim repetition, and a great many of the compositions are strophic, that is, they are fairly short but are intended to be repeated a number of times. Often different words are sung with each repetition of the music. Generally speaking, everything in the music is equally important and basic. In most Western cultivated compositions we can distinguish themes, which are more important than the rest of the music because of their unique character and because other parts of the composition may be based on them. But in folk and primitive music, as well as many short forms in cultivated music, we cannot distinguish between themes and non-themes; for all of the material is equally thematic and primary. But of course this does not mean that the traditional music does not contain basic, germinal motifs which supply a sense of organization; these are certainly present. Indeed, compact and rigorous organization is a special feature of music in oral tradition.

Unity is created in ways also common in cultivated music; there is usually one main unifying element, an example of which is an isorhythmic pattern, a rhythmic formula which is repeated a number of times, each time with a different melody. Isorhythmic construction, which is found in many parts of the world, often breaks down near the end of a piece and is replaced by another common phenomenon, the tendency of units to lengthen and become drawn-out. (Example 28)

The melodic counterpart of isorhythmic patterning is the use of the same melodic phrase or line, each time at a different pitch level. This is called a melodic sequence, and it brings to a song a very strong kind of cohesion without resulting in monotony. Example 26 is made up entirely of a melodic sequence.

Simplicity itself may bring about unity. Thus, if a song is very complex and diversified melodically, a simple metric pattern may counteract the effect. A complex melody tends to be accompanied by a single, unchanging meter, and it may be a simple type such as 4/4, 3/4, or 6/8. (Example 1) on the other hand, a complex metric construction such as that in Example 31, which uses three kinds of meter (3/8, 2/4, 5/8) within a short space of time, may be accompanied by a simple melody, such as that in Example 31, which uses only three pitches.

A melodic contour (the term used for indicating the general movement of pitch, its ascent, descent, and overall pattern) can sometimes be used as a unifying element. For example, the songs of the Plains Indians often consist of two sections which have the same sharply descending, cascading contour, but which differ in other respects. (Example 18)

The relationship among the various sections of a composition is often important in establishing unity and variety. We can classify the forms of folk and primitive music in various ways, but one simple method is to indicate the presence or absence of symmetry. Symmetrical forms are quite common, but certainly not in the majority. One example is a type which consists of three parts, the first and last being identical, as ABA. Another, common in several styles of European folk music, is ABBA. The song in Example 27 even preserves symmetry within the sub-sections, so that the letter-scheme ABA C ABA applies.

Asymmetric forms may be more interesting. They can be analyzed most easily in pieces which can be divided into two main parts, one of which outweighs the other in length, range, or otherwise. In some songs, the first part is short, and the same material is elaborated in the second. Some Plains Indian songs use this arrangement, probably because the meaningful words appear only in the second part. (Example 18) The opposite arrangement, a condensing process, is found in Example 30, where the total form is $AB^1B^2AB^2$. The first part, $A\ B^1\ B^2$, is condensed to $A\ B^2$ by the elimination of B^1.

The over-all forms of folk and primitive music can also be described by indicating the relationship between a section of music and the one which follows it. Given one section, or phrase, the music can then go on to new material, bringing about a progressive relationship; repeat the section, creating an iterative one; or repeat material stated earlier, making a reverting one.[5] Although relatively few compositions fit exactly into any of these categories, one of these kinds of relationship is usually dominant. Entire repertories can be classified in this manner. For example, since most songs of the Indian tribes in the Great Basin area have forms in which each section is repeated, like AABB or AABBCC, their style is basically iterative. Many Anglo-American songs have the form ABBA or AABA, so their style is reverting. But all three of the mentioned principles are strongly entrenched in traditional music.

General simplicity correlates with simplicity in form. The form type found in the simplest styles consists entirely of the repetition, with some variation, of a single short bit of music. And although a long piece is usually nothing but the manifold repetition of a short one, variations are often introduced with the effect of lessening the monotony.

The melodic aspects of folk and primitive music are perhaps what is most interesting and distinctive about them; and at any rate they have been studied most thoroughly and perhaps emphasized disproportionately. That there is a basic difference between traditional and cultivated melodic systems has already been said. It remains to discuss briefly the specific nature of folk and primitive melody. The scale of a piece of music is an enumeration of the pitches which are used and a statement of the relationship between them. Most examples of folk and primitive music do not use as many pitches as do the compositions of cultivated music. One of the most common kinds of scale uses only five tones, such as g,a,b,d, and e, and their duplications at other octaves. (Example 1) This kind of scale, called "pentatonic," is common in many styles throughout the world. The very simplest kinds of music have scales with only two or three tones, such as g and a, or e, g, and a. Not confined to the simplest of the world's tribes, these scales are also present in many children's songs, lullabies, and gambling songs in European folk music.

The use of unessential tones, or ornaments, is common in many styles of folk and primitive music. They appear between the more important notes, taking up no specific amount of time, and their inclusion is often optional for the performer. (Example 7)

The melodic contour also tends to be a characteristic of each area or ethnic group. Some styles have undulating contours, others jagged ones; some have descending ones, others arc-shaped. Contours which only ascend are rare, possibly because of the difficulty of producing a rising melodic line with the human voice, for when a singer is exhaling, he finds descent much easier.

As already said, the rhythmic patterns of traditional music are often irregular, but nevertheless systematic. Meters change frequently, as in Example 31, or a song may consist of a pattern which, though repeated throughout the song, is in itself fairly complex. Meters such as 5/8, 7/8, 11/8, and 13/8 are found as well as the simpler types.

The rhythms and metric patterns in folk songs are often based on, or at least related to, the rhythm of the words. This is particularly true if the rhythmic aspects of the language are very pronounced. The rhythms of a musical style often reflect the characteristics of the language. In German, for instance, words often begin with unaccented syllables, and nouns are preceded by unstressed articles. In Czech, however, articles do not exist, and all words begin with stressed syllables. In some songs that have traveled across the German-Czech frontier we find the same traits: Czech variants often begin with stressed tones, and lack the so-called pick-up or up-beat, but German variants more commonly begin on the unaccented beats. We are not sure whether these musical traits originated along with those of the language because of some kind of aesthetic preference in the culture, or whether they are simply the result of tunes being set to specific words whose rhythm must be accommodated.[6]

The rhythmic structure of the text of a song seems to have other profound effects on the entire rhythmic structure of a musical style. For example, in most western European bodies of poetry the basic unit is the foot, which consists of one stressed syllable and one or two accompanying unstressed ones. We describe a line of poetry by indicating the type and number of feet. Thus, the foot arrangement in many of the Anglo-American ballads is iambic, 4,3,4,3. This rather regular alternation of stressed and unstressed syllables produces a fairly regular metric structure in the music. In most eastern European languages, however, metric feet do not exist in the poetry, and the basic unit is the syllable.

Rather than having feet whose numbers remain constant in a line, most eastern European poetry keeps the number of syllables constant. There are lines with seven, eight, eleven, and other numbers of syllables. The musical meter also tends to change even within the line, but there is more likelihood of a rhythmic unit, equivalent in length to a line of text, to be repeated with each line.

There is sometimes a close relationship between the melodic aspects and the words of a song. The most interesting examples of this come from the so-called tone languages, in which the pitch of each syllable, in relation to its environment, determines the actual meaning of the words. Such languages are common, and widespread, as proved by the fact that Chinese and many African and American Indian languages have tone systems. Songs in these languages must in some way account for the melodic aspect of the words. Even though the music does not always reflect the exact pitch pattern of the words, it usually does not violate it too flagrantly. And the drum and horn signals of many African tribes as well as the whistle-speech of several primitive cultures are based on playing the pitch-patterns of actual words. In order to understand this kind of signalling one must be able to recognize specific words simply from their speech melody.

Most polyphonic music in folk and primitive cultures is performed by more than one singer or instrumentalist; each plays or sings one "voice," and it is possible to describe the styles of polyphony in indicating the relationship among these voices. In many polyphonic styles the musical material in each voice is approximately the same. There may be simultaneous variation of the same music (heterophony), performance of the same music at different times (imitation), which often produces rounds, or at different pitch levels (parallelism). The distance in pitch between the voices in parallelism has a great influence on the total effect of the music. Parallelism is probably the most common kind of polyphony. Rounds (canons) are found in Negro Africa, Melanesia, and western Europe. Heterophony is especially common in many Asian styles. But to these three kinds of polyphony, in which the voices are approximately equal in importance, we should add a fourth, counterpoint, in which the voices perform different musical material. Counterpoint is not as common, however, as those types in which the same music appears in all of the voices.

Polyphony in which one voice predominates is also found in three main forms: one voice performs a melody while the other holds a single tone, called a drone, as with bagpipes; one voice performs a melody of some elaboration while the other repeats a short bit many times, called an ostinato; and one voice is accompanied by an instrument which produces a harmonic background, as in folk singing with guitar accompaniment.

Most, but not quite all, folk and primitive cultures have some musical instruments, and a few have a great wealth of them. The most common instruments are percussive; rattles and drums, notched sticks, bullroarers and buzzers are almost universal in their distribution. The melodic instruments are often exceedingly simple. The ancestor of all string instruments is the musical bow, shaped simply like a hunting bow whose string is plucked or struck and whose changes in pitch are produced by shortening the string. Some Pygmy groups in Africa use pipes which produce only one pitch each; the melodies are produced by having each player blow his pipe when its pitch is called for. There are single-keyed xylophones which evidently preceded the instruments with many keys.

Other instruments may be compounds of the simple ones. Panpipes, for examples, are series of simple flutes, each of which produces only one pitch, but which are arranged together so that melodies can be produced. The xylophone is a compound percussion instrument, as are panpipes, and, in a way, so are instruments with many strings. Many folk and primitive instruments, rather than being simply compounds of the simplest ones, are complex and rival those of urban cultures in technical perfection and beauty of sound. The harps and horns of Africa, the bagpipes, flutes, fiddles and dulcimers of Europe, the panpipes and mouth organs of East Asia are examples of this vast world. And although there are only a few basic categories of instruments, their varieties and sub-types throughout the world are innumerable.

Instrumental folk music usually differs from songs in the essentials of its style, being at least partially constructed on the basis of the technical possibilities and limitations of the instrument, with each instrument commanding a style of its own. But this should not be construed to mean that instrumental music and song do not influence each other. Quite the contrary, some cultures imitate the sounds of instruments in their vocal music, and many songs are assimilated into the instrumental repertories.

III

THE ETHNIC BACKGROUNDS of AMERICAN FOLK MUSIC

Folk music is often thought of as the expression of the spirit of a people, or a national or ethnic group, and in some ways this is certainly a valid definition. We know that a folk song, even though composed by a member of a given ethnic group, will not take hold in that group unless it conforms to the current aesthetic ideals. It may be rejected, or it may be accepted and then changed by the process of communal re-creation until it does conform. Consequently the material of an ethnic group tends to be fairly homogenenous and to express in some ways the character of that people. And especially in Europe and other parts of the Old World, where most ethnic groups have had long, continuous residence in the same geographic area, is the folklore rooted in the soil and the history.

In America, the rather different situation makes it necessary to think of folk music in a different way. Again, however, the folk music reflects the culture at large. The United States is a new country, consisting largely of English cultural traits which were modified to suit the specific requirements of America. Added to it were elements from many European countries, to greater or lesser degrees, and an important layer of African Negro culture. Underneath it all, relatively uninfluential but significant in certain isolated situations, is the culture of the American Indians. In recent decades, however, a merging of these diverse elements has taken place, creating a greater degree of unity. The ethnic composition of the United States has also changed because the proportion of immigrants from various European countries has changed periodically. In the middle of the nineteenth century a heavy influx of Germans gave a special color to the material; this was altered as many immigrants from Ireland, Italy, and eastern Europe followed. After the arrival of these groups, their continued flux from one region to another, the rapid urbanization of some districts and the isolation of others, as well as the phenomenon of the frontier, shaped the American civilization in certain characteristic ways.

We must remember that the United States has always been composed of combinations of ethnic groups, a situation which also occurs in European countries but in ways different from ours. In Europe, if several ethnic groups inhabit a nation, they are usually relatively isolated from each other. In Czechoslovakia, for example, the Czech- and German speaking inhabitants had little mutual contact, except among the intellectuals. Even in Switzerland, the German, French, and Italian groups have their own traditions and partake only to a small extent of a common folklore. In the United States, however, the various ethnic groups have tended to mix. There was no long tradition of cultural integrity in America, and practical considerations favored their becoming at least partially incorporated in the Anglo-American community. The German-American individual takes part in the traditions of both Germany and America, the Ukrainian-American in those of his homeland and the United States. There are, to be sure, a few enclaves of Europeans who preserve their old culture almost intact. But the majority of ethnic groups in America participate in a combination of traditions. Thus the Czech-American folklore is quite different from the original Czech, in content, form, and function; and the French-American contrasts with that of France.

Almost all bodies of folklore in the world are represented in America, but in making the transition, they sometimes lose their original functions. Thus, harvesting songs from Yugoslavia are not used for harvest here because the Yugoslavs in America are rarely farmers, and paddling songs in an African style are at times used simply for entertainment, as are Italian horse and mule calls. This change of function may change the character of the music and have a profound effect on its very existence.

The fact that the United States is largely an urban country also causes special problems for those dealing with its folk music. In most European countries, especially those of the eastern, central, and southern portions, the difference between urban and rural populations is considerable. But in the United States even the rural inhabitants share many of the urban culture elements, such as radio and television, newspapers and nationally circulated magazines, machinery, mechanical devices, and motion pictures. In contrast to most of Europe, the American rural population is quite mobile. People travel in automobiles much more than in Europe, and the migration between farm and city is steady and strong. There are relatively few individuals who have never lived in a city. Consequently we cannot, in this country, consider a rural environment as the chief feature of folk music, something which was often done by European students of folklore. American folk music lives at least partially in urban areas, and, in some cases, even in large cities, especially where European peasant groups have settled in industrial cities and have kept part of their heritage.

The concepts of nationality and national spirit, ethnic and cultural groups, social classes, and the rural and urban aspects of folklore show that American folk music is in many ways a very different phenomenon from its European counterpart, and that, from the point of view of some persons oriented towards European folklore, the American material is not folklore at all. Instead of taking such a point of view, however, let us simply say that these differences between American and European folk music are largely due to the different historical developments and contrasting cultural composition of the two hemispheres, and that both continents have a heritage which can be considered genuinely within the scope of folklore.

Besides indicating the basic differences between American and Old World folk music we must emphasize their common features. The United States is fertile soil for studying European folklore, and European folk song collectors have often come to America in order to round out the knowledge of their native traditions. They often find that America has preserved a great deal of European folklore which has disappeared in its original home. Early in the twentieth century (first in 1916) Cecil J. Sharp, a noted English folk song scholar, heard that the old English and Scottish ballads were still being sung in the United States. His resulting field trip to the mountain areas of Virginia, North Carolina, Tennessee, and Kentucky showed that the number of variants of these ballads current among the folk far exceeded that of present-day Britain; and he discovered some songs which had died out in British folk tradition.

Chapter VI describes the Amish, a Swiss-German farmer group of Protestants related to the Mennonites, who sing hymns in a style very different from anything else in American or European folklore, a style which seems to be distantly related to sixteenth and seventeenth century German cultivated music. This practice must have existed at one time in European folklore, but evidently it disappeared under the impact of urbanization. The survival of culture traits at the fringes of German or British culture, as indicated here, is explained by the theory of *marginal survivals,* which recognizes the fact that a trait often disappears in the original center of its geographic distribution (Germany and Switzerland, for example) but can survive and even flourish much longer in the outskirts or margins of that area, for example, among German-Americans. This theory helps to account for the great wealth of European folk music in America, a wealth which also makes it possible, at least in some ways, to study at first-hand the folk songs of most Old World cultures without leaving the United States.

IV

INDIAN MUSIC of the UNITED STATES

When the white man first came to the area which is now the United States, it was inhabited by fewer than one million Indians, who were organized in several hundred tribes of various sizes and languages. What we know about their culture and music five hundred and more years ago comes largely from investigating their life during the last hundred years, from the diaries and reports of early white travelers and missionaries, and from the artificial reconstruction of early conditions. Most scholars are pretty well agreed on the role of music in the aboriginal life of the Indians, and enough actual music remains in the Indian repertories today to give at least a fairly accurate indication of its scope and style before the discovery of America. Thus we are interested in two phases of Indian music, the aboriginal one, before contact between Indians and whites, and the acculturational one, including those very interesting developments in Indian music which occurred recently under the impact and influence of Western civilization.

Music was very important in the lives of the Indians, much more so than in the lives of sophisticated Westerners. The reason for this may be the mystical qualities with which the Indians believed music was endowed, their relative paucity of material culture, and the importance of dance. At any rate, in this respect their music closely parallels that of most of the other primitive societies in the world.

Religion is the aspect of Indian culture to which music was

most closely tied in the pre-contact period. Music dominated all
of the Indians' ceremonial life. They used music for ceremonial
dancing; they had songs for worship, corresponding somewhat
to our hymns; for war ceremonies, which tried to gain supernatural aid for victory; for healing ceremonies, in which songs were
used as magic; for love-charms and for many other functions.
Next in importance was music for social purposes: social dancing,
songs to be sung before and during battle, songs sung in connection with athletic contests and gambling games, songs which were
sung in folk tales. (Entire tales were sometimes sung in the Great
Basin area of Utah and Nevada.) And, of course, there were children's songs, lullabies, and, occasionally, work songs. Though
each tribe did not have all of these functions for music, it did
have most of them. Almost all of this Indian music was sung;
there was exceedingly little purely instrumental music.

Just as the cultures of the various tribes and sub-tribes were
different, the music differed also. There were areas in which
music was very complex and highly developed and areas where
it was exceedingly simple. Each area had a distinct musical
style. But in no case can Indian music be considered primitive in
an historical sense. Uninformed sources sometimes equate the culture of pre-literate cultures with those of early man. It is probable
that we can learn a great deal about early man from contemporary primitive cultures, and the same applies to music. But
this does not mean that primitive music, including American Indian music, has not changed immeasurably since its beginning,
and that it did not undergo processes of change and development
like those of cultivated music. Neither is it so simple as to warrant
comparison with infantile creations.

We tend to think of the songs of the Indians as having been
passed from singer to singer through many generations. But we
rarely think about the way these songs actually originated, and
we certainly don't visualize Indians as composers. However, the
songs had to come from somewhere, and indeed they were created by Indian composers; but these composers didn't work or
think quite like the masters of Western composition. We know
pitifully little about the methods and processes of Indian, or any

other primitive, composers, and probably tribal and regional differences are considerable. But there are at least two methods of composition in Indian life, and they correspond roughly to two important approaches among Western musicians.

Modern composers in Western civilization tend to fall into two main classes. Some consider the creative process something directly connected with the supernatural, with themselves merely the specially endowed mouthpiece, and with little direct responsibility for the shape and structure of the music. Others consider composition a craft, related to skilled labor or scientific thinking. One group believes in inspiration, the other in the mechanical accumulation of techniques. Among the Arapaho Indians of Wyoming and Colorado, I have found two analogous approaches to composition. One is intimately connected with religion; in fact, the Indian composer gets no credit for his work. It is a part of the "vision quest," one of the important religious practices of the Indians of the Great Plains and some other areas of North America.

Among the Arapaho most men are expected at some time in their lives to have a "vision." The following account of a vision is typical.[1]

A young man goes out into the wilderness, seeking a vision. He eats and drinks nothing and perhaps tortures himself in other ways. Finally, on the fourth day, the vision arrives. He faints and then sees and hears the following: a voice singing a song in the sky: "Man, look up here; it is I up here in the sky; I am the bird." At this point the visionary sees a large bird flying towards him singing the song. It lights and begins to speak to him, giving him advice about his conduct on his next war party. Then the bird says: "When you return to your people, teach them these four songs which I am going to sing to you." The songs follow, and the bird leaves. The young man returns to his band, meanwhile rehearsing and singing the songs which the bird sang to him. When he returns, he sings the songs for his associates, and, indeed, they are new songs.

From the Indian's point of view, the songs were a gift from the supernatural, the visionary's guardian spirit in this case. From a cynical point of view, we can assume that the young man composed the songs himself; yet he did not do so consciously. Indeed, we know of cases of Indians seeking visions unsuccessfully and falsely trying to make up songs, but Indians make a great distinction between these and honest visions. It may be that in the vision the young Indian was struck by some musical (and perhaps poetic) ideas and that he worked these out in detail while "rehearsing" on the way home. It should be mentioned that in some cases, "new" songs mean old melodies with new words. But often new melodies are learned in visions.

What does this tell us about Arapaho composers? First, there are no specialists in composition, although there may occasionally be some persons who are recognized for their excellence in this field. Second, a large proportion of the men, perhaps most, participate in musical composition at some point in their lives. Each man does not compose regularly or in great quantity, but many compose the few songs which they believe they have learned in visions.

Whereas this general approach to composition in primitive culture has been well known for some time, a more systematic and rational one has only recently come to light. Our example is again from the Arapaho tribe and is concerned specifically with the creation of the songs of the Peyote cult. This religion has come to the Indians of the United States only during the last two centuries; its music is nevertheless purely Indian, evidently without Western influence, but it is distinct in style from other Indian music. My Arapaho informant told me of two main ways of composing Peyote songs.[2] One is to take various sections of a number of old Peyote songs, join them together and perhaps add some original material, and end with the traditional formula which closes all Peyote songs. This method is eclectic and makes use of new combinations of material already in existence.

The other way of composing Peyote songs also makes use of old material. It is dependent on the fact that a great many Peyote songs are constructed in isorhythmic fashion, in which a rhythmic pattern is repeated several times, each time with a different melody. The composer of a new song sometimes takes an old one and adds to each section a bit of material, identical in each case, thus keeping the isorhythmic structure and the over-all form but creating a slightly different and more complex song. While we might think of these new songs merely as variants of the old, the Indians evidently think of them as separate creations.

Perhaps a word should be said about improvisation of music as a method of composing, that is, creating on the spur of the moment during performance. Some persons believe that the word "primitive" somehow implies spontaneous or unorganized creation. They consider the music of primitive cultures basically different from cultivated music because, they think, it adheres to no structural principles but is some kind of spontaneous outpouring of soul and culture. This is a generalization we cannot subscribe to, although a certain amount of spontaneity cannot be denied to any music in oral tradition. Some Indian and other primitive music is improvised, but this is true only under a few special conditions. There are certain structural principles in every Indian musical style, and a given composition retains its structure throughout many performances in spite of the fact that it is never committed to any permanent record.

Some evidence of the integrity and structural stability of most Indian music is given by the degree to which songs are rehearsed, and by the assertion of the Indians themselves to the effect that mistakes in singing are not tolerated. Systematic rehearsing of songs is found especially among the Indians of the Northwest Coast, Washington and British Columbia.[3] Here mistakes in songs are punished, and accuracy in performance is at a premium. Elsewhere, also, we hear of individuals practicing songs for specific performances. Since music is often assumed to have supernatural power, errors in performance obviously cannot be tolerated in certain rituals. Among the Navaho, for example, music is the main portion of some healing rituals which last several days. Theoretically, any error in the performance invalidates the ceremony and makes recovery impossible.[4] Of course, if the ritual fails to cure the patient, the failure can be blamed on errors in performance. Naturally some errors are unavoidable, and they sometimes result in permanent changes in the songs; no doubt many are due to the lack of a permanent written record against which one can check a performance. The errors are part of the process of communal re-creation, which is common to all music in oral tradition. However, such changes are only occasional and very gradual, and they do not alter the basic fact that Indian music exists in stable forms and not simply as a spontaneous torrent of emotion which could hardly be called art. Already the fact that the music can be notated (with some difficulties, to be sure) in the conventional Western system of notation is evidence favoring this view, and all conversation with Indian informants on the subject of music points in the same direction. The Indians that I have known have always referred to music as "songs," never as "music" or "singing" in the abstract.

According to George Herzog, Indians rarely speak (or think) of songs as "beautiful." Rather they tend to consider them as "good" or "powerful." This reflects the functional nature of Indian music, the fact that it is rarely, if ever, music for its own sake, but almost always an essential aid for other aspects of their culture. Herzog says that "good and beautiful may merge, and be expressed by the same word. This is the case with many tribes of the Southwest: the Pueblo, Navaho, Pima. The term is applied in many cases where 'good' or 'beautiful' alone would be meaningless; where undoubtedly the feeling for the ritualistically good and aesthetically pleasing is one and the same."[5]

What do Indians sing about? Paradoxically, many of the songs do not have meaningful texts. These songs do not have words but groups of meaningless syllables. Such syllables correspond roughly to the "la la la" found in many Western songs, but they are more complex and varied and, again, are not improvised but form an integral and fixed part of the song. Often they bear a close relationship to the rhythm and other musical features of the song.

But many of the songs do have meaningful texts, which, in many songs, do not take up the entire stanza. In such songs, the meaningless syllables tend to point out and emphasize the meaningful words. Although these texts can be considered poetry, usually they do not have the distinguishing marks which we ex-

pect of poetry in our culture. The texts are not divided into feet,
lines, or stanzas. They do not have meter or rhyme. They appear
very much like prose to us.

A typical song of the Plains Indians begins with a long sequence of meaningless syllables. The music to which they have
been sung is then repeated, slightly altered, with the entire meaningful text and a few meaningless syllables to fill it out. This
may take somewhat less than a minute, and since the song tends
to be repeated about four times, the entire rendition is likely to
take between two and four minutes. Many of the songs deal
with exploits in war, and the heroes sing about their own ad-
ventures. The first portion of the song is sung by the entire group
or audience; the second part, with the meaningful text, is frequently sung by a single performer who tells about his exploits
in texts like the following:

"The Ute Indian, while he was still looking around for me, I
swung him around."

Many Indian songs of the Great Plains had their texts changed
periodically in order to conform with current events and interests. The song about the Ute Indian (sung by the Arapaho) was
changed by Indians who fought in the first World War to deal
with a German soldier. A similar change must have produced the
following text:

"The German soldier fled and dragged his blanket behind."[6]
In order to give the reader a better idea of the Indian song texts,
I quote a number without detailed comment. The following are
Arapaho war songs:

> Soldier, have courage.
> Our flag has become famous.
>
> My relatives, gaze at our flag;
> it is waving in the skies.

The following are Arapaho vision songs:

> The star-child is here.
> It is through him that
> our people are living.

> Almighty, look down on me, have pity on me.

I am the crow. Watch me.

> Young man, be brave.
> You are going to a dangerous place.
> Your chieftainship will become famous.

Young man, it is good that you are going to war.

Birds, up there in the heavens, come down, have pity on us.

The following texts are from the Blackfoot Indians of Montana. Their culture is quite similar to that of the Arapaho, and so are text and musical structure.

> Woman, don't worry about me.
> I'm coming back home to eat berries.

This is sung by men going on a war party.

> White Dog [name of a Sioux chief],
> stay away from this tribe.
> You will cry when they scalp you.

The Indians of the Northwest Coast have more elaborate texts and fewer meaningless syllables. There is a considerable difference in subject matter and the way it is presented, when compared to the Plains songs. Frances Densmore recorded the following Nootka songs:

> Who is my equal or can compare with me?
> I have forty whales on my beach.[7]

> Do not think for a moment that you can defeat us,
> for we have slaves from all other tribes,
> even from the coast tribes to the north.[8]

These songs are part of the Northwest Coast complex of institutionalized boasting and threatening, a part of this highly competitive culture which has been presented to the general reader by Ruth Benedict.[9] The differences between Plains and Northwest Coast texts are also reflected in the music. While the Plains songs are sung in a relatively objective manner, all songs using roughly the same vocal style and having little emphasis on the words, the Northwest Coast songs are sung more expressively and boldly. Of course all the differences between these musical styles cannot be ascribed simply to general differences in outlook.

The Indians of the Southwest tend to have longer and more elaborate song texts, sometimes divided into lines, and more closely resembling Western types of poetry. Herzog gives the following texts from the Pima:

> Dragonfly got drunk
> Clasped hands with gigikukl bird
> Swaying they lurched along,
> Dragonfly untangled the songs (i.e.,
>   sang for the first time the songs he dreamt).[10]
> Where is the mountain?
> Yonder far away rises the mirage
> The dust raised by me rolls toward it
> Many people's yelling, between them I am moving.[11]

Many Indian tribes played gambling games, usually by hiding small objects, which were accompanied by songs. The team which was hiding an object sang songs whose texts mocked or ridiculed the opposing team, enabling the hiders to keep a poker face and thus avoided giving away the hiding place, and sometimes invoked supernatural aid for victory. Herzog quotes the following texts of gambling songs from the Navaho:

> Where is it going to be hidden (six times)
> Big turkey
> His wattle goes up and down.[12]
> The moccasins are laid out in a row (six times).
> It is going to be at the same place as before.[13]

This song refers to the fact that in the game a bullet is hidden in one of a row of moccasins. The song is evidently sung after the opposing team has made several unsuccessful attempts to find it.

Let us briefly turn to the structure of some of the meaningless-syllable texts. These, although they do not communicate anything specific, nevertheless leave an impression of rhythm and form which causes them to be remembered by the Western listener. They sometimes have about them a quality of rigidity and firmness as well as euphony which makes them an essential part of Indian poetry; and perhaps they correspond to Western poetry more closely than do the meaningful Indian texts. Because of their sensuous quality they can be enjoyed on an abstract level similar to that of music. I quote an example of a Shawnee Peyote song text:

> He ne ne yo yo (five times)
> He ya ne, he yo ea he ya ne (twice)
> Yo ho ho, yo ho ho, he ya na
> He yo wa ne hi ya na, he ne yo we.

The patterns and rhythms of this text correspond rather closely to the patterns of the melody. Peyote songs, as I have already said, are new to most North American Indians, and their music as well as their syllable sequences differ from those of other Indian songs. Most Peyote songs make use of syllables and groups of syllables similar to those in the text above, and certain characteristic meaningless "words" are found in many songs.[14] Among these are "he ya na," "yo wi ci ni," "he yo wi ci na yo." Most other Indian songs have their meaningless syllables restricted to the consonants y, w, h, and n plus a vowel. Still, there are always patterns which recur and, most interesting of all, the syllables remain the same from one performance to the next. Thus they must be considered essential parts of the poetry in spite of their lack of meaning.

Questions of text lead us to ask whether the music of Indian songs expresses anything of the subject matter, feelings, or emotions in the words. While this is a hard question to answer because informants do not ordinarily verbalize on the subject and, indeed, seem to believe it is irrelevant, it can be said that musical representation of a text does not ordinarily take place, and only a few isolated, even questionable, examples can be found. The closest thing to tone-painting yet found is the imitation of bird or animal calls in the songs. Sometimes these calls precede or follow a song, without forming a structural part of the music; these calls cannot be considered here. But occasionally the animal or bird call is obviously integrated into the song, fitting into the structure of its melody and rhythm. This is the case in a Shawnee song about the turkey, in which the last syllables, "tak tak tak," are said to be imitative of the call of the turkey.[15]

The influence of pitch patterns in language over those in music is relevant at this point. A number of Indian languages of the United States are tone languages. In an excellent study of the Navaho, Herzog[16] indicates that sometimes the pitch movement in the language influences the music while at other times the musical currents contravene the language. Of course it is theoretically possible for the words in a song to be misunderstood because their tone sequence is not paralleled by the music, but this rarely happens because the words are usually understood in their context. Arapaho is also a tone language, with two tones; and I have reported and described elsewhere results similar to those found for the Navaho.[17]

Most North American Indian instruments are of the percussion type: drums, rattles, notched sticks. There are some flutes, usually end-blown, like whistles and recorders. They are used to perform love songs which may be sung as well as played, so there is no special instrumental repertory. Practically all Indian music is strictly melodic (monophonic). There is no part-singing except in a few spots where local developments have taken place. There is no accompaniment except for the percussion, and only one pitch is heard at one time. Most Indian songs use a system of pitches which is more restricted than that of Western civilization and which is not too different from that of the other folk songs in America. But often the Indian pitches do not coincide with those of Western cultivated music, and thus it is not always possible to reproduce Indian songs on instruments like the piano. Most Indian singing would sound somewhat out-of-tune to un-sympathetic Western ears.

Despite the small number of Indians in the United States, the number of different musical styles is large. The Indians of the Plains sing in a tense, harsh, raucous way, and their melodies cascade down a series of terraces or steps, rarely moving up-wards. Their music sounds wild. The stressed tones are accented violently, and on the long notes the singers continue the rhythmic pulsations so that the music never comes to a rest. The melodies have large ranges with the singers beginning high, sometimes in a falsetto voice, and descending to a growling depth. Examples 18 and 23 represent the Plains style.

Some of the tribes of the Southwest, especially the Yumans of southern Arizona and California, have a different style. Their songs are relaxed; they give an impression of tight organization and rationality. This statement, however, should be interpreted not as an objective description but as an impressionistic expres-sion of the subjective reactions of a person of Western culture. The Plains songs are probably no wilder, in a real sense, than those of the Yumans; but we can judiciously use the term to de-scribe the music in a communicative way. The Yuman songs have small ranges, fairly simple rhythms, and an even flow. In contrast to them, again, the songs of the Southwestern Pueblos are complicated, consisting of several distinct portions, and often they are sung in a low, growling voice.

The songs of the Northwest Coast have considerable rhythmic complexity; the singer may perform rhythmic patterns quite dif-ferent from those of the drum or rattle accompaniment, some-thing rarely found elsewhere in the United States. The North-west Coast has a wealth of instruments and some part-singing, an unusual phenomenon among Indians. The desert tribes of Ne-vada and Utah, on the other hand, have a very simple kind of music. A distinctive feature is the repetition of each phrase so that everything appears twice. (Example 20 is in this style, even though it is from the Dakotas.) In eastern United States, one characteristic feature is the call-and-response pattern, performed by a leader and a chorus, in the social dance-songs. There are many other regional peculiarities; the picture as a whole evokes amazement at the creative genius of a people so small in number and with so simple a culture.

Just as there were areas in aboriginal North America which were characterized by a certain kind of culture, there were musical areas.[18] And these tend to coincide fairly well with the cultural ones, a fact which again demonstrates the close relationship between music and other activities of Indian life. We find also that in those areas in which the culture was especially complex, such as the Pueblos, the Northwest Coast, and the Gulf of Mexico, there also developed a more complex and varied musical style, and the invention of new stylistic elements, such as part-singing, rounds, and melodies of special length, occurred in these areas of complexity.

The coming of the white man had a considerable effect on the music of the Indians, just as it influenced all aspects of their culture. The whites brought on the second stage of American Indian music history, the acculturational one. It might be expected that a mixture of styles, partly European and partly Indian, would have developed in Indian music as it occurred in some parts of Africa. However, the differences between the European and Indian styles were evidently so great that in only a few isolated instances was such a mixture achieved. Indians today participate in two bodies of music, their old heritage and the white man's, but the two are not mixed to any great extent. The English language has made inroads; today, many songs in the old Indian musical styles have English words, such as the Blackfoot song in Example 23: "If you wait for me after the dance is over, I will take you home in my purchased wagon."

The white influence has made itself felt primarily by causing the Indians to unite, to lay down some of their tribal differences and to present a single cultural front to contrast with Western civilization. This was not done systematically and with political purposes. It is partially a result of the rapid and widespread migrations of many Indian tribes under white pressure, and of the forced amalgamation of tribes on special land reserved for Indians. Tribes who previously had had no contact with each other were now thrown together, and cultural interchange became inevitable.

One aspect of this pan-Indianism in music is the spread of two important religious cults through a large part of the United States. These cults made use of songs which penetrated the repertories of the tribes who took up the cults. One of them was the Ghost Dance religion, which arose after 1880 in the Great Basin area of Nevada and California. It was preached by a "prophet," Jack Wilson and held that if the Ghost Dance were performed, all dead Indians and buffalo would return to life and the white men would be pushed into the sea. Such ideas appealed especially to the Plains Indians, who were having great difficulties because their native food supply, the buffalo, was being eliminated by the whites. The religion was preached to them and they accepted it enthusiastically, learning with it the songs and the style, which had come from Nevada. These songs were quite different from those of the Plains, as we have seen in the descriptions of some styles above. The Ghost Dance was thought to be a military menace by the United States Army, and it was outlawed in 1890. But the songs have remained in the repertories of the Plains tribes, and thus we have at least two styles in each of them, the aboriginal one and the native style of the Great Basin.

Another style was soon to be added to these, that of the Peyote cult songs. The Peyote religion, based on the mildly intoxicating buttons of the Peyote cactus, originated in Mexico and reached the United States early in the eighteenth century. It was introduced to the Plains tribes during the nineteenth and twentieth centuries by way of the Apache, and its songs are related in a general way to the style of Apache music, which is again quite different from that of the Plains. Peyote spread much farther than the Ghost Dance, and it is the most important religious manifestation of the Indians today. The white influence, then, has tended to cause individual tribal styles to spread over vast territories and to create a variety of musical layers in these tribal repertories, which would otherwise have remained unified.

Another aspect of pan-Indianism in music is based on the prevalent idea of the character of Indian music held by the whites. Whites believe that Indian songs are wild-sounding, cascading, violently accentuated melodies, and indeed, this idea corresponds to the Plains and Pueblo styles. Since many Indians are dependent on tourists for a living, many of them have learned this style even though they live elsewhere. Consequently the Plains style has been replacing some native styles in other areas.

Although in some ways we tend to deplore the changes which have come about in Indian music through the influence of the whites, we must realize that this is only natural and inevitable. On the other hand, we must admire the resilience and flexibility of Indian culture, which has fashioned out of the white influence a kind of music which, although different from the older styles, is nevertheless a genuinely Indian contribution and a living force in the folk music of the United States.

V

THE BRITISH TRADITION

The oldest and fullest folk music tradition of the white Americans came from Great Britain. Many of the American songs came from England and Scotland, and upon them was superimposed a native body of folk song, created in American in the British pattern but endowed with many of the special qualities of American culture and personality.

Ballads are perhaps the most important songs within the British tradition. Today they are found primarily in the East and the South, especially in the relatively isolated mountain areas of New England and the Appalachians. Contrary to popular belief, however, the number of ballads current in the North is greater than that in the South. A great many English ballads were brought verbatim from the Old World, but since numerous variants were developed here, even more than in England in the case of some songs, British ballad scholars consider the United States very fertile ground for their studies.

Many of the ballads brought from England go back to the fifteenth and sixteenth centuries. It is unlikely that all of these were composed by members of folk groups, for their words as well as their music often show the impact of cultivated song. Nevertheless, these ballads passed into folk tradition even if they did not originate there, and they soon acquired the genuine characteristics of folklore so that today we think of them as typifying the field of folk music.

The words and the music of the English ballads are equally

interesting. By definition, a ballad is a narrative song with from five to twenty or more stanzas. Various kinds of poetic meter occur, but the most common kind, ballad meter, is an iambic stanza of four lines, alternating lines of four and three feet. The following stanza from "Sir Hugh" is typical:[1]

> As I walked out one holiday
> Some drops of rain did fall.
> And all the scholars in that school
> Were out a-playing ball.

Many ballads have refrains, some of which have little to do with the rest of the story, such as the refrain in "The Two Sisters":

          There lived an old lord in the North country
(Refrain) Bow down, bow down.
          There lived an old lord in the North country
(Refrain) Bow down to me.
          There lived an old lord in the North country
          And he had daughters one, two, three.
(Refrain) I'll be true to my love if my love will be true to me.

It is possible that ballads once served as accompaniment to dancing, as they still do in parts of Scandinavia and particularly in the Faroe Islands. If so, the refrain of "The Two Sisters" is perhaps a remnant of that practice; and "bow down" could be explained as referring to dance.

The stories of the ballads are often tragic, the most famous ones dealing with murder and death; but there are comic and even humorous ones, too. Examples of tragic ballads are "Barbara Allen," the most widespread in America, and "Lord Thomas and Fair Elinor," in which a young man marries a rich girl instead of his sweetheart. He invites his sweetheart to his wedding, but she insults the bride, who kills her, whereupon the groom kills both the bride and himself. In "The Two Sisters," a girl drowns her sister because of jealousy over a suitor. In "Edwin in the Lowlands," a tavern-keeper murders a guest for his money; but the victim turns out to be his prospective son-in-law. In "The Golden Vanity," the cabin-boy of a ship sinks an enemy vessel by swimming under it and boring holes in the hull. His captain, who has offered him great rewards in advance, now refuses to let him come aboard again, and the cabin-boy drowns. In some versions, however, the cabin-boy is allowed to return on board and then marries the captain's daughter despite parental objections. In "The Cruel Ship's Carpenter," also known in America as "Pretty Polly," a man murders his fiancée as they are out for a stroll and puts her in a grave which he has already prepared.

Sometimes the differences between the English and the American versions are considerable and reflect some essential traits of the two cultures. In the British version of "The House Carpenter," a man leaves his fiancée to go to sea, and drowns. His ghost returns years later and persuades the girl, who by now has married a house carpenter, to leave her husband and child and elope with him. At sea, when she begins to weep for her child, the demon in anger destroys the ship. But in most American versions, the supernatural elements are eliminated: the man simply returns from sea, finds his fiancée married, persuades her to go with him, and their ship sinks from ordinary causes. In "Sir Hugh," the basis of the plot is a medieval superstition dealing with the alleged killing of gentile children by Jews. A small boy is enticed into the Jew's garden and is murdered by the Jew's daughter. It is interesting that this superstition has disappeared in some versions, evidently because it meant nothing to the singers and listeners, and the Jew's daughter became the "duke's daughter."

Many British ballads also have happy endings. Lord Bateman, for instance, is rescued from prison by a Turkish lady, who finds him seven years later and marries him. In "The Gypsy Laddie," a woman leaves her aristocrat husband and elopes with a gypsy. The husband tries to persuade her to return, but she is adamant and presumably finds happiness in her new life. I suppose it is a matter of opinion whether this ballad is comic or tragic, depending on whose side one takes.

There are also some genuine humorous British ballads. In "The Wife Wrapped in Wether's Skin," a man who does not want to beat his shrewish wife finds a solution by putting his sheep skin on her and beating that. In "The Farmer's Curst Wife," the wife is fetched by the devil and taken to hell, but she is so difficult to handle that the devil returns her to her husband.

The stories — especially those of the oldest ballads — are told in an unique way. The narrator ordinarily takes no part in them, telling them with no signs of emotion, but remaining objective and detached, and in his singing not differentiating between a stanza which gives routine background and another which contains the dramatic climax. The musical aspects of the performance are equally austere and calm; they do not portray the dramatic and emotional impact of the stories. This might be considered detrimental to the total effect of the ballad, but in fact it seems to improve the performance, for the contrast between the dramatic tension in the plot and the quiet, detached delivery is in itself effective and helps to make the old folk ballads unique artistic phenomena.

The language of the ballads is a peculiar mixture of American colloquial speech and old English literary conventions. Along with such seventeenth century poetic expressions as "lily-white hand" and "milk-white steed," we find Americanisms like "Stay here you dear little babe and keep your pa company." ("House Carpenter").

The music of the older English ballads is in a style which seems to go back to the Renaissance and the Middle Ages. It has much in common with the folk music of other areas in Europe. Most of the tunes do not make use of the seven-tone scale, as do those of eighteenth and nineteenth century origin, but are restricted to five or six tones. Many of the tunes are modal; that is, they do not fit into the major and minor scales to which we are accustomed, and hence sometimes sound incomplete to our ears. The Mixolydian and Dorian modes are the most prominent after the major (Ionian) and the natural minor (Aeolian). In many of the tunes the melody rises to a peak about the middle and then descends slowly to its original level.

The rhythm of the ballads is largely dependent on that of the words. A line with four iambic feet may be set to a musical rhythm like the following, with all of the notes approximately the same length: ♩ | ♩ ♩ ♩ ♩ | ♩ ♩ ♩ Sometimes, however, the

second and fourth stressed styllables, which occupy final and semi-
final positions in the line, may have their accompanying notes
lengthened as follows: ♩ | ♩ ♩♩. ♩ | ♩ ♩ ♩ ♩. Examples 2a and
2b also illustrate this point. A third common rhythm accommo-
dates songs whose words are cast ♪ | ♫♪ ♫♪ | ♫♪ ♪
in dactyllic meters.

Some singers of old English ballads in America use a highly
ornate and embellished style of singing, which is evidently more
common among men in the North, and predominates among older
persons. The ornaments occur mostly on stressed or long tones, as
in Example 7. They consist of short, rhythmically insignificant
tones, and correspond to the "grace notes" of cultivated music.
But they are an essential part of the slow, declamatory way of
singing which America shares with several European folk music
styles and which is called the "parlando-rubato" style.[2] Resulting
in part from the tension on the vocal chords which some folk
singers produce consciously or unconsciously, this parlando-rubato
style is definitely a part of the older ballad style since it occurs
in that body of song frequently but only rarely in newer material,
even when both are sung by the same singer.

In the United States most ballad singing is unaccompanied. The
use of instruments is not nearly so common as is generally supposed, but some accompaniment does exist in genuine folk cultures. In some regions, indeed, accompaniment is taken for granted
— in some parts of Kentucky, for example, while in others, such
as the neighboring southern Indiana, it is quite rare.

The most common instruments in the United States are, of
course, the guitar, the banjo, and the dulcimer. Fiddles are used
for solo playing, and other plucked string instruments, such as the
mandolin, are frequently found. Since they are shared with urban
culture, most of these instruments are well known. The dulcimer
is perhaps the only one which has not penetrated cultivated music to any extent. It appears in various forms, but its simplest and
most characteristic shape is that of an elongated, thin violin which
lies on the player's lap or on a table while its strings are plucked

with a quill. There are usually three strings, the lower two providing a drone whose pitch never changes, but the highest string has frets under it similar to those of a guitar, and it carries the melody. Like most instruments, dulcimers are not standardized, for the instruments of folk culture behave like other kinds of folklore. Instrument making is governed by oral tradition and communal re-creation, and there are many variants of each basic type. Consequently, some dulcimers have string arrangements and shapes quite different from the one described here. The dulcimer is also found in northern and western Europe and it may have been brought to America from Scandinavia or Germany. Its somewhat artificial revival in America is paralleled in European schools and music clubs.

The drone principle, or accompaniment on the dulcimer, is quite important in American folk singing. When accompanied at all, most of the old ballads are set to a very simple arrangement of chords, often just a single chord, the tonic, predominating almost to the exclusion of any harmonic change. On the dulcimer this is inevitable, but it is also the practice on the guitar and the banjo. Even on the fiddle, open strings are often played along with the melody, producing an effect similar to that of the drone.

Many of the old English ballads were composed by professional song writers, printed on large sheets called broadsides, and peddled in the streets. These so-called broadside ballads often dealt with current events and news, and many passed into oral tradition. The early ballad scholars declined to include them with what they considered genuine ballads, which presumably had a popular origin. Thus an American scholar, Francis James Child, placed the British non-broadside material in a special category and gave each ballad a number.[3] Thus today, although the title for a ballad is not always fixed ("James Harris," "The Deamon Lover," and "The House Carpenter" are all variants of the same ballad.), it can always be identified by the number given by Child (243 for "The House Carpenter," 86 for "Barbara Allen," and so on). But the importance of the broadsides, often underrated in the past, is perhaps greater than that of the popular ballads, and this applies to America as well as Britain.

Well over two hundred broadside ballads of British origin are in circulation in the United States. About half of them deal in various ways with love, many are war ballads, some are about sailors and the sea, and a good many of them tell of crimes. There are also a number of humorous broadsides, but most are either tragedies or accounts of a hero's success despite obstacles. The attitude of the balladeer is rather conservative and even puritan, and the division of characters into good and bad is simple and standardized.

Most broadsides date from the seventeenth to the nineteenth centuries and give a good picture of popular taste of a period. Their interest is primarily textual, for the melodies were usually not printed in the original versions. Instead, a melody already popular was often named as the one to which the new words were to be sung. Thus we cannot speak of any real unity between words and music. A few tunes were used for a great many texts, and on the other hand, new tunes were frequently introduced by individual singers if they did not know the melodies originally intended for use.

Perhaps the British broadsides make up the largest single segment in Anglo-American folk song. At any rate, they have exercised a great deal of influence on the native American broadsides, many of which, indeed, are simply derived from the British ones. The stories of the broadside ballads are not as interesting, and not as well worked out poetically, as the popular ballads or the Child ballads. The recourse to clichés is greater, the events are more predictable and are usually of little psychological significance. For example, in "The Irish Mail Robber," a youth persists, despite his father's warnings, in drinking, gambling, and maintaining bad women. Convicted of mail robbery, he is imprisoned for nine years. In "The Bold Soldier" a father threatens to kill his daughter because she wants to marry a soldier. The soldier fights her seven brothers and threatens to kill the father, but the father agrees to the marriage and, after more pressure, gives the soldier all of his wealth. Many broadsides give accounts of actual happenings, such as crimes and accidents, and thus served to spread news and to keep a record of events.

A considerable number, perhaps as many as one-third, of the British broadsides are of Irish origin. Although in English, their style and their subject matter are different from the English and Scottish ones, and a larger proportion of them are in the humorous category.

Most of the native American ballads first appeared as broadsides and, typically, deal with real events. Their texts are similar to those of the British broadsides. They are presented in a more emotional, less detached manner, for the narrator sometimes takes part and often makes moral and ethical evaluations. In "Jesse James," for example, the refrain of each stanza condemns the hero's murderer:

> But that dirty little coward shot Mr. Howard
> And laid Jesse James in his grave.

The plots of the American and British broadsides are often much more complex than those of the British popular ballads. Often they have not been in oral tradition long enough to shake off the many secondary characters which have evidently disappeared in the older ballads. The broadside ballads do not always revolve around a single event as do the Child ballads. Some, like those dealing with Jesse James, John Henry, and even Franklin D. Roosevelt, are biographical and narrate several episodes. The order of events varies. Most of the American broadsides tend to emphasize a hero, praise his qualities and dwell on his deeds, including some which are not of primary importance to the main theme.

The music of the broadside ballads is sometimes in the style of the old English ones, but more often it is modern. It is usually based on a seven-tone scale and is in major or minor rather than in one of the other modes which are common in the older material. The rhythm is more varied than in the Child ballads, but it is usually cast in one of the standard eighteenth and nineteenth century meters, 3/4, 4/4, or 6/8. While the British material as sung in the Old World has a large proportion of triple meter, when these songs become established in American tradition, there tends to be a change to 4/4. Irregular musical meters, which we find in older songs, do not often appear in the broadsides. The poetic meters, however, exhibit more variety in the broadsides than in the Child ballads. The melodic contours and the over-all forms are more varied, and instrumental accompaniment is also more common. Indeed, the broadside tunes are constructed in the eighteenth and nineteenth century styles of popular music, which include an innate feeling for harmony, so that accompaniment is definitely called for.

Words and music in the ballads are not wedded to each other. Different texts may be found with a single tune, and one text is often sung to a number of unrelated tunes. If the singer forgets the tune of a song but knows the words, he may substitute another tune with the same rhythm. This is facilitated by the simple and stable patterns of ballad poetry. Sometimes a part of a tune is taken and given new words. This happened in the case of "The Pretty Mohee" (Example 9), originally a British broadside with four lines. The last two lines of the tune were separated and fitted to the text of "On Top of Old Smoky," an American folk song which subsequently became popular in the semi-folkloristic hillbilly tradition.

The specific relations between the words and the tune of a song are often intriguing. It goes without saying that the music must to some extent parallel the metric, rhythmic, and linear structure of the verbal stanza. The relationship often goes even further, however, to the extent of establishing parallels between the musical form and the content of the words. This should not be construed to mean tone-painting, or the use of musical imagery to represent words and ideas. Example 4, a version of "The Gypsy Laddie" collected in southern Indiana, shows what may occur in some cases. But other ballads have different kinds of text-music relationships, and we certainly cannot consider this example a representative one of general trends since this entire area of ballad study is still quite unexplored.

The musical form of this song could be described by the letter-scheme $A^1 \ A^2 \ A^1 \ A^{2L}$. The second and fourth lines are almost identical, the chief difference being the fact that the fourth line is an octave lower than the others. The verbal stanza is also divided into four lines whose contents can be interpreted in several ways, each with its parallel in the music: 1) The last line is the dramatic climax of the stanza, and its music is set off from the rest by being pitched an octave lower than the other lines. 2) The text can be divided into two equal parts, the first dealing with "last night," the second with "tonight." The music is also symmetrical, the second half being a repetition of the first, modified only by the octave transposition. 3) Lines 1 and 3 are united by describing the place in which "she" sleeps, lines 2 and 4 by indicating with whom. Again, this division is observed in the music, lines 1 and 2 being identical (A^1), and lines 2 and 4 being at least very close (A^2). Although this kind of integration of text and music must have been created unconsciously, it may nevertheless have been a factor in the survival of the ballad. While it is not evident in detail to the listener until after a detailed analysis, its effect may be felt subconsciously, and there may be aesthetic factors which direct a song towards this kind of integration. I should point out, however, that the parallels in this example occur only in the first stanza (which is repeated at the end) and that they are not followed through in subsequent ones.

Although the ballads are perhaps the most popular and best-known songs in the Anglo-American tradition, there are a great many other kinds, some brought from Britain, others native American, which live on in American folk culture. Many are associated with various occupations such as sailing, lumberjacking, cowpunching, mining, and farming. There are dance songs, play-party songs, and religious folk songs. All of these are closely related in musical style to the ballads, as are the love songs and the humorous songs which especially typify American folklore. Samuel Bayard[4] believes that most of the songs in the Anglo-American tradition are descended from about fifty-five tunes and thus belong to fifty-five "tune-families." If this is correct, American tradition has benefited enormously from communal re-creation, for the number of variants — some close to the original, some changed almost beyond recognition — of these few original tunes is today almost unlimited and constantly increasing.

The songs of cowboys, sailors, and other occupational types, being narratives, are often ballads, and many give accounts of disasters and other tragedies. Some have been considerably influenced by early musical comedy and vaudeville. Many miners' songs have been patterned after Negro folk music. Sailors' songs have also been adapted to tunes which originated in many European countries and the Americas, something not unexpected in a group which has had contact with cultures throughout the world.

The entire history of the United States has been illustrated in folk song. Among the ballads, particularly, but also in the lyrical songs, there are many which have historical content. We have songs about wars, giving the exploits of unsung and unknown individuals as well as accounts of world-famous events, from "Yankee Doodle" to the F.D.R. ballads. Peacetime history is narrated in songs about the frontier and the trials of Indian fighters, in songs of the industrial revolution and the labor movement, in the accounts of local incidents and biographies of folk heroes, criminals, gangsters, and benefactors of mankind. Even political subtleties like Jefferson's "Embargo" of 1808 found their way into the folk tradition, as indicated by the following song sung to the tune of "Yankee Doodle"[5]:

> Attention pay, ye bonny lads and listen to my Fargo
> About a nation deuced thing which people call Embargo
>
> > Chorus: Yankee doodle, keep it up,
> > Yankee doodle, dandy,
> > We'll soak our hide in home-made rum
> > If we can't get French brandy.

In Boston town the other day the people were all blustering,
And sailors too as thick as hail away to sea were mustering.

I asked the reason of the stir and why they made such pother,
But deuced a word they answered me or Jonathan my brother.

At last a man with powdered hair come up and said to me, Sir,

Why stand you gaping here, you rogue, come list and go to sea, Sir.

I've got a vessel at the wharf well loaded with a cargo,
And want a few more hands to help and clear the cursed embargo.

The song goes on to tell how the embargo was ignored by the American shipper, and that the narrator finds it unbelievable that "the Embargo's gone to sea, Sir."

There is a fairly large repertory of instrumental music, though it is rapidly disappearing, in Anglo-American folklore. Used largely for dancing and marching, it is played on fiddles, dulcimers, and fifes, and its style is closely allied to that of the songs. Many of the tunes are based on the song tunes; on the other hand, some of them have become songs through the addition of words.

The religious folk songs of the United States comprise a large body of music which has been gathered from many different sources: ballads and other folk songs, compositions by itinerant evangelists, patriotic songs, vaudeville and minstrel shows, dance tunes and marches, and old hymn tunes from urban churches. We find not only hymns sung at services but also camp-meeting songs and religious ballads. Most religious music is, of course, not folklore, but there are a number of Protestant groups in America who even today have little musical literacy and whose songs are transmitted entirely through oral tradition. Their hymns are folk songs, also, because many of them are variants of tunes current in other fields of musical folklore; like ballads and dance songs. Many of the folk hymns were printed in the shape-note system, a method of writing music which assigns a differently shaped note to each tone of the scale (do, re, mi, etc.). Of course the music printed in this way is not always real folk music by our definition, but there is usually a close relationship to folk music. Shape-note hymnals appeared during the nineteenth century throughout the North and the Southeast. It was especially strong in the nineteenth century South, and we know now, through the researches of George Pullen Jackson, that the Negro spirituals are closely related to, and often derived from, the so-called "white spirituals" of the Southerners of British descent. The Negroes have added much to the style of the spirituals and have made them essentially a Negro product, but the original material was usually taken from the folk hymns of the whites.

Among the religious folk songs we must also mention the carols, although the most popular ones ("Silent Night," "Adeste Fideles," etc.) should probably be excluded because they have become standardized and associated with school and church. In the areas where the British heritage is still living, there are also some folk carols which are generally unknown in the cities, such as "The Seven Joys of Mary," and the apocryphal ballad, "The Cherry Tree Carol." Many of these carols were discovered and championed by John Jacob Niles. Musically they tend to have the same features as the older songs in the Anglo-American tradition: they are modal or pentatonic, having relatively large ranges and sometimes irregular metric patterns.

Somewhat outside the Anglo-American tradition proper are a number of song types which are not very common in Britain but which have become typical of American folklore. Although their style is still close to the British, their content may be uniquely American, or at least it corresponded so well to the American culture patterns that it experienced a much greater degree of growth and diffusion here than in the Old World. The physical environment in America and the combination of the British and other cultures are responsible for some of the special American features in these songs.

Humorous songs are common in the American heritage, and they often follow the tradition of tall tales, which are regarded as the outstanding feature of American folk narrative. Some are about animals, such as the "Ram of Darby," which is as tall as the moon, one of whose locks is sufficient wool to make a gown, and whose butcher is drowned in its torrents of blood. Animal songs are generally popular in American folklore, with the animals the subjects of human-like exploits, being subject to praise or censure and giving advice to humans. Their tunes are also part of the same stylistic body as the ballads.

Unique among the occupational songs are the cowboy songs, many of which are partially sung in a falsetto voice and with yodeling of a sort. They serve as cattle calls and for communication over wide spaces. In some of them, the stanzas are followed by a falsetto refrain with meaningless syllables for a text. Others have no strophic structure but simply an alternation of a falsetto phrase with one sung with a normal voice.

Especially well collected are the coal miners' songs of Pennsylvania. Their subjects reflect pride in the mining trade and, frequently, discontent with the hard life and bad treatment of the miners in the late nineteenth and early twentieth cenuries. Musically, they exhibit many styles, some tunes being sung to the tunes of British ballads, others to modern broadside tunes especially composed for them, and still others to tunes brought from eastern and southern Europe by men who came to America to work in the mines and who sing (often in their native languages) of their homes, the families they left behind, their hopes and disillusionments in their new country, as in Example 28.

The love songs of the Anglo-American tradition are relatively few in number, compared to the other traditions of western Europe, and they are mostly sad songs of complaint, of lost love, or of anger at the beloved's infidelity. Some of their tunes are especially interesting examples of the old English ballad style. A common feature of the texts is the repetition at the end of the first stanza in a closed, cyclic form. Also relatively small in number are lullabies, whose musical material is sometimes identical with that of some love songs. Larger in number, and more lively in tradition, are children's game songs and counting-out rhymes, many of which go back to the play-party songs of Puritan New England, where they served as substitutes for dancing.

VI

IMMIGRANTS from EUROPE and AFRICA

The many groups of non-British immigrants to the United States have had a profound influence on our folk music culture, by diversifying the picture by the addition of new styles and the adaptation of their own aesthetic principles to British-American folk music. From a consideration of the ways their traditions have behaved, these immigrants can be divided into two groups: the Negro and the European.

Negro folk music, as well as some of the forms of popular music related to it, has commanded much attention among scholars, and the degree of relationship between the American Negro music and that of their African ancestors has been widely discussed and argued. Some students have asserted that American Negro music is simply African material,[1] while others have argued that it is an integral part of the British tradition.[2] One side maintains that it was borrowed from other cultures, and another that it has sprung from the unique position and history of the American Negro. Today it is generally believed that both of these views are at least partially right.[3]

The styles of African Negro music, although extremely varied, share a few general features. This is particularly true of West Africa, from which most of the slaves were brought. Much of their material is performed antiphonally, in call-and-response patterns, usually by a leader and a group. The phrases tend to be short, and the over-all forms of the songs are also short and simple but augmented by variations. Melodic development is not great, but rhythm is often very complex and syncopated, though the meters are simple and constant. The music is typically polyphonic, much more so than in most western European folk styles. Instruments, especially drums, rattles, and bells, but also horns, plucked string instruments, and xylophones, are prominent in number, variety, and function.

Some of these characteristics are present in the American Negro material. In the folk songs of those parts of the New World in which Negroes predominate, such as the West Indies, the African traits are easily discerned, but in the United States they are not as evident. Some songs which are still sung in Haiti were probably brought from Africa, but the United States seems to have no native African compositions because the Negroes have become Westernized. Even they, however, have not lost their African musical heritage completely, and it is specifically the surviving African traits which have made American Negro music so interesting to the white population.

The Negro spirituals are among the best-known products of Negro folklore. Although they were once believed to be the exclusive property of Negroes, they have now been shown to be closely related to the folk hymns of the Southern whites. George Pullen Jackson discovered most of these white spirituals published in shape-note hymn books of the early nineteenth century, and on this is based his conviction that the Negro spirituals are simply adaptations of the white hymns.[4] To be sure, if one examines the melodies of the spirituals on paper, they seem to fit the characteristics of Western hymnody. They have tunes which, although they could conceivably fit into some African styles, are definitely in the English folk song tradition or in that of urban hymn composition of the eighteenth and nineteenth centuries. They have pentatonic scales, the over-all forms usually consist of four phrases of equal length, and the rhythms are not essentially different from those of English folk songs. But if we listen to recordings of Negro spirituals sung by genuine folk singers, we find that a good many things occur which are simply not shown in the printed music. For although they are basically Western, the singers of the spirituals incorporate some of the special techniques which mark these songs as Negro property. It is not the nature of the songs themselves, but the way in which they are performed, which makes them a distinctive Negro contribution.

American Negro folk music, then, tends to consist of the superimposition of some performance traits originating in Africa upon music which is originally European in style. Those traits which are especially African, which have been developed to a high level in their original home, are carried over into American Negro music. The other traits, those whose development was neglected in Africa, tend to disappear and give way to their European counterparts. Negro spirituals, for example, are often sung polyphonically, more often than are hymns of the white people. To be sure, the kind of polyphony used is not African, but the very preference for it in itself indicates the presence of an African tradition. Many spirituals are performed in a call-and-response or "responsorial" manner. The freedom of the individual to deviate from the pattern as it is sung by the rest, and to introduce his own version, is probably an African survival, for improvising is a highly developed art in Africa. Syncopation and other features which create rhythmic interest, the use of percussive clapping and stamping, the use of dancing as a part of a Christian ceremony (in the ring-shouts, for example), can all probably be traced to the African musical traditions which the Negroes have carried with them, and whose stronger elements have survived in America in spite of the century-long acculturation of the Negroes to Western civilization.

We find these elements also in the non-religious Negro songs: ballads, blues, work songs, children's songs. Even in those children's ditties and counting-out rhymes which are not actually sung, but recited with established rhythm and intonation, we encounter some of these surviving characteristics.

The words of Negro folk songs are interesting because they often mirror the thinking of the people and their place in American culture. Thus the so-called "field blues" as well as the blues sung by city Negroes reflect dissatisfaction with their lot. Many of the work songs are songs of protest, as are some of the ballads and love songs. On the other hand, the content of many songs is similar to that of white people's songs. For example, John Henry, the steel-driving hero of a Negro ballad, is comparable to such a white ballad character as Jesse James.

The instruments of the Negroes were in some cases simply borrowed from the culture of the whites; they, too, use guitars, fiddles, mandolins, and dulcimers. But the Negroes brought some instruments from West Africa with them, modified them, and made them genuine members of the American family of folk instruments. The most famous, of course, is the banjo, originally the West African *bania,* the Negroes' favorite instrument for accompanying songs, which, with significant changes, has penetrated Anglo-American culture. Another is the "washtub," a string stretched vertically between an obliquely standing stick and a wash tub turned upside-down. It is evidently derived from a type of animal trap in which a skin is suspended over a hole by a string which breaks when an animal steps on the skin.

A subject which has commanded widespread interest and caused a great deal of discussion in recent years is the status of jazz in folklore. Jazz is obviously related to folklore, but the problem is whether it can actually be treated as folklore, whether it behaves like folk tradition.[5] There are a number of interesting aspects of this problem which bear discussion in a general book on folk music in the United States.

If we examine jazz as it is today, we find that it is composed and performed by highly trained, sophisticated, and even intellectual musicians in the cities and is hardly distinguishable from cultivated music, except by its popularity with the general public. And some of the most "progressive" jazz is not, in fact, popular. The usual justification given for calling it folklore is that much of it is improvised. This practice, however, is not really particularly characteristic of folk music, but it was a common phenomenon in various periods of cultivated music history. In the earlier periods of jazz, however, there were a good many elements found also in folklore. Many of the first jazz musicians were untrained or self-taught. They came from a tradition of genuine folk singers like Leadbelly and Josh White, singers who, in spite of their traditional background, composed songs and created unique, individual styles. These singers, although members of a folk culture, took on the specialization and professionalism characteristic of cultivated music and thus are in an intermediate position. It was through such in-between musicians that jazz rose to be a combination of folk and urban musical culture.

The older jazz, like Negro folk music, has some of the characteristics of African music. The emphasis on rhythm and rhythmic instruments, the theme-and-variation structure reminiscent of call-and-response patterns with variations, the improvisation of variants by individuals in the ensemble; all these tie jazz closely to Africa. And even though jazz is no longer folk music, even in the wider sense of the word, it can be understood only in its relationship to the folk music of the Negroes, both African and American.

The Negroes contrast with most other non-British groups in America because they introduced their native style into the songs of the British tradition. The immigrants from Europe, on the whole, brought their own songs from the old countries and kept them separate from the English ones. They learned English songs in addition to their own, but the two kinds of music usually did not mix. The musical elements of continental Europe, the complex rhythms of the Balkans, the polyphony of Russia, the florid style of Italian songs were not superimposed on British ballads and other music.

Most of the immigrants from Europe, especially those who arrived during the last eight or nine decades, settled in the cities. Some groups, however, settled in rural areas, especially the western and northern Europeans; Germans, Swedes, Irish, and French. And we must not forget the rich Spanish tradition which is centered in the American Southwest, a tradition which goes back several centuries before American domination of that region. We can mention only a few examples from many possibilities.

Some ethnic groups, the Amish, for example, live in virtual musical isolation, practicing ways of singing which seem to be totally different from those of other groups in their vicinity. The Amish are a Swiss-German religious group related to the Mennonites, who live in parts of Pennsylvania, Ohio, Indiana, and Iowa. They farm and, for religious reasons, live a life of considerable austerity, without mechanical appliances, education, or entertainment. Their only songs are hymns, whose tunes live only in oral tradition. The style of the hymns is extremely slow, melismatic, and rhythmically complex. Each word in the text takes up a good many notes, and it is not possible to discern a regular meter in the music. These hymns are always monophonic, for as a token of humility no part-singing or instrumental accompaniment is allowed. At first hearing, they make little sense musically and it is hard to believe that they are the product of a western European group. Indeed, there seems to be no trace of such a style in present-day Germany or Switzerland, nor is it reasonable to believe that the Amish learned it in America, or even in Russia, where they spent some time on the way to the United States.

In Chapter III, I pointed out that the Amish style is one of those peculiarly American phenomena, a marginal survival which seems to have disappeared in its original home, but which still exists on the fringes of its culture. And if the Amish tunes are taken apart it soon becomes evident that they are merely slowed down and highly ornamented versions of old German hymn tunes and that the embellishments themselves are retarded versions of some of the ornaments so characteristic of sixteenth and seventeenth century cultivated music. It is likely that the Amish hymn style is a survival of a way of singing hymns in rural southern Germany, a way which has since died out in its original home under the pressure of modernization.

Of the various ethnic groups in America, only a few have undergone thorough musical examination. We know a good deal about the music of the French-Americans, the German-Americans, the Spanish-Americans, but very little of other groups. In general, it appears that they all brought a sizeable portion of their Old-World traditions with them, that they practice these with considerable vigor, but that these traditions are nevertheless gradually diminishing and giving way to songs in English and to the abandonment of oral tradition in principle.

There are some instances of European songs merging with, or becoming incorporated in, the Anglo-American tradition. The German song, *Du, du, liegst mir im Herzen,* has become a part of the general American repertory, as have the French *Alouette* and *Frère Jacques.* Light, short children's songs or lyrical songs lend themselves easily to this inter-lingual exchange; ballads, because of their verbal complexity, usually do not do so, though isolated examples such as *Stenka Razin* do appear.

There are also some instances of melodies passing from one ethnic group to another. For example, the tune of a Pennyslvania German song about a house spirit, *Marjets wann ich uffschteh,*[6] is the tune of the children's song "Go tell Aunt Nancy the old grey goose is dead." There is a trend towards exchanging folk songs, towards the acceptance of English songs by ethnic groups, and the penetration of the British tradition by a few songs in foreign languages and styles.

It is impossible to go into the individual musical styles of the various ethnic groups in this short space; and such a procedure would not be proper here, since the musical styles of the ethnic groups are essentially those of their home countries. Thus, the best way to become informed on these styles and bodies of folk song is to study the music of the original homes of the various groups. For this purpose, a number of representative collections and studies of European folk styles are given in the bibliographical aids. In summary, however, we may be justified in saying that there seem to be at least three different modes of behavior among the folk styles which were brought to America by non-British immigrants. First, there are repertories in which the original stylistic elements alone survived and were imposed on a part of the British tradition. This mode obviously takes in the Negroes. In the second we include those repertories in which the European songs were brought over and which live side by side with the British songs, some individuals knowing songs from both traditions. Here the ethnic group retains some contact with a style existing in the Old World. The third mode are marginal survivals of styles which have completely disappeared in Europe or which are so different from the American development that the relation-

ship can no longer be recognized, like, for example, the hymns
of the Amish.

VII

FOLK MUSIC in the METROPOLIS

The study of folk music in the city is an integral part of American folklore research which has not yet been utilized exhaustively. Indeed, the picture of an individual city has not yet been presented in full, and the only raw material available is a few scattered and largely unpublished collections from individual non-English speaking groups and a collection of industrial songs from Pittsburgh. Most of this chapter, consequently, is devoted to a preliminary survey of the situation in Detroit, the only city for which even such a tentative report is available. But there is reason to believe that these findings would apply also to other American cities.

The folklore of the Detroit area has been extensively collected by Thelma G. James and her students at Wayne State University, especially in the field of oral literature and folk beliefs. Some collections and studies of music have been included in their project,[1] and in preparing the present chapter I have used these as well as material gathered by myself and by my students.[2]

Folk music of the city is interesting because it differs from rural folk music in structure and function. We would like to know whether it can be called folk music at all, whether it behaves like other folk music when it is transmitted, and whether it reflects the urban culture of which it is a part. We wish to know what kind of people participate in the folk music of the city, and what happens to songs which are brought from a rural into a city environment. We wish to explore the difference between

61

folk music in American cities and those of Europe, for in the an swer might lie a key to understanding some of the essentials of American civilization. I should like to discuss some of these ques tions and to suggest some possible answers which are based, how ever, only on material from Detroit and which cannot be con sidered definitive even for that city.

Whereas Detroit is a metropolis in the real sense of the word, it has become one only recently. As little as fifty years ago, its population was only one-tenth of its present two million.[3] This rapid growth is the basis of a specialized composition of the pop ulation, which is certainly a factor in the development of the musical folk culture — a rather different one from that of the countryside. In contrast to most large European cities and, to a smaller extent, cities of the Atlantic seaboard, which have grown more slowly and gradually, the new American cities have popu lations of which only small segments are descended from urban residents of long standing. By far the majority of the population is composed of individuals who themselves came from elsewhere to live in the city, or whose parents originated elsewhere. Thus the Detroiters have come from many different parts of the world, but most of them have come from the countryside of Europe or America.

I have already pointed out that folk music is usually considered essentially a rural product, and that some students of folklore do not admit the possibility of genuine folk music flourishing in the city. Accepting this statement, we can still consider the folk music of an American city genuine because the folk are only slightly removed from their rural roots. To be sure, most of this material was brought from the country in ready-made form. There is relatively little, if any, which actually originated in the American cities. But the rural music, once arrived, undergoes some important changes.

Again, using Detroit as an example, the native American popu lation which brought the Anglo-American tradition to the city has not kept this heritage as well as the later arrivals to America have kept theirs. Here Detroit contrasts with rural America. The English-speaking community from the South, composed of whites, tends to break down in the metropolis. Folk songs are not often passed from parents to children after the family arrives in the city. The musical life of the Southern whites in Detroit is taken out of oral tradition, it ceases to preserve the old folk songs, and it is removed from the hands of the family and entrusted to the tender care of the hillbilly disk jockey. And hillbilly songs (which are definitely related to folk music, but are not themselves folk songs) do not, as a rule, pass into oral tradition. The Southern white immigrants have left the tradition of active participation and have become spectators and listeners in the pattern of modern city entertainment. They know the hillbilly songs well, but they do not sing them or teach them to their children. Instead, they rely on the professional musicians in taverns, on radio and television, to propagate them. And when a song is dropped from these outlets of entertainment, it also dies in the minds of the Anglo-American viewers. The real folk songs, however, popular ballads, broadsides, and lyrical songs, seem gradually to disappear from the tradition, except for those kept alive by a few professional entertainers who make something quite different out of them because they were not originally intended for public entertainment.

The other English-speaking group which has recently arrived in the cities of the North, the Southern Negroes, seems on superficial examination to have retained only a little more of its rural folk tradition than the Southern whites. The Negroes seem to have kept at least a part of their religious folk song tradition, the spirituals, but their interest in secular folk songs has almost always been transformed into an interest in commerical Negro popular songs on records, performed by professionals who are objects of hero worship by both Negroes and whites. An interest in the folk blues has been turned into a love for the popular blues; the singing of work-songs has been replaced by listening to old-time jazz.

It is of interest, however, that the religious songs of the folk tradition flourish in comparison with the secular songs. There are several possible reasons. Some churches frown on the use of recorded material and radio, so that the spirituals must be passed on by oral tradition. Those Negroes whose family cohesion is strongest are usually the most devout; thus, since the family is usually an important unit in oral tradition, word-of-mouth transmission favors religious material. On the other hand, Negroes tend to prefer jazz and other popular music because it solidifies their urban status and is a field in which they, as a group, enjoy prestige among whites. The Negroes in industrial cities are avid record fans; the number of record stores in Negro residential areas is disproportionately great, even in the poverty-stricken districts. Negroes seem to have a greater desire to be urbanized than the Southern whites. The latter are often transient, returning periodically to the South, and they remain rural in spirit. Most Negroes in the North have no intention of returning to the South.

The non-English-speaking groups of the newer American cities are much more conscious of their folk music heritage than the native Americans. For them, folk music is a way of retaining the cohesion of their ethnic groups, but it is also a method of impressing and gaining the respect of other inhabitants of the city. While native Americans often scoff at the strange rituals, holiday observances, and accents of the immigrants, the European folk songs usually arouse their sympathy, warm interest, and even attempts at imitation. But in a foreign environment a European ethnic group must work hard to achieve this continuity. It does not usually trust to the usual channels of oral tradition to assure the survival of the songs. Instead, it organizes singing groups and clubs, it sponsors professional entertainers, it developes specialists. Folk music becomes the concern of the intellectual leaders of the ethnic groups. Thus, while folk music remains in the life of the ethnic group more fully than in that of the natives, it is changed under the pressure of Americanization and urbanization. It is probable that the folk music of immigrants from countries largely rural, from eastern Europe, for example, is greater in volume and more vigorous than that from the heavily urbanized and industrial countries of western Europe.

Nevertheless, the ethnic groups retain folk music in its most genuine form. They vary considerably in their use of folk music because of their original differences, times of immigration, and status in the New World. But oral tradition survives. A young Polish informant in Detroit, whose grandparents emigrated to this country over fifty years ago, knows many songs, all learned from his relatives, and he indicates that this is typical. Indeed, he believes that most of the second and third generation Polish-Americans know more folk songs than do those who have recently arrived in the United States. This fact is of great interest, for it reaffirms the theory of marginal survivals, and that the United States is one of their centers. We know that in many cases elements of a culture die out in the center of their distribution but survive longer at the margins. In this case, Polish folk songs have evidently decreased in number and strength at the center of their distribution, Poland, probably under the pressure of urbanization, industrialization, and political propaganda. But in the outskirts of Polish culture, among the Polish-Americans who left their homeland when folk music was flourishing, the songs have remained for a longer time and have been more vigorous.

A study comparing the songs sung by Puerto Rican children in New York with the versions sung in Puerto Rico yields interesting conclusions.[4] Gradual changes come about in the songs, the most recent arrivals in New York singing variants most closely corresponding to those collected in Puerto Rico. In the New York version, references to the rural life tend to disappear, English words and American place-names are introduced. The changes in the tunes are insignificant, and a vigorous folk song tradition seems to be evident.

The practice of general participation in folk song, one of the marks of most rural musical cultures, is of course weakened in the city. Whereas a large segment of the population still participates fully, there is a tendency to develop specialists in folk song, individuals who are not really professional musicians but who, because of their great knowledge of folk songs and their interest in them, are recognized as guardians of the tradition. Among the Polish, largest of the ethnic groups in the Detroit area, they are the cooks who cater at weddings and who also perform the musical parts of the marriage ritual. These cooks evidently know hundreds of songs, wedding songs and others, and they act as consultants in folk song and folklore.

Most of the ethnic groups have semi-official organizations which try to insure the preservation of the folk music heritage.[5] Choirs and bands are led by specialists in folk music who, although they participate in the folk tradition, are often trained professionally and have at least a semi-professional status and also specialize in teaching folk music. Thus, although they are instrumental in preserving the musical folk tradition, they are also responsible for some of the differences between rural and urban folk music.

Another aspect of most rural folk songs is communal recreation, the development of variants by creative change on the part of the singers. We are not at all sure whether communal re-creation operates in urban folk music. The indications are that it is weaker than in the country and that standardization is more general. A partial reason must be the rather frequent use of printed folk song collections, albums, and records. Another is the development of specialists who standardize their versions and develop conscious musical behavior.

Musical instruments tend to play a larger part in Detroit folk music than in the rural material, probably because of the preponderance of instrumental music in the city. The instruments themselves have not increased in number, but they are used often, both for solo and accompaniment, and proficiency on an instrument is demanded of most folk singers. The songs which must be sung unaccompanied tend to decline more rapidly than the others.

Most of the folk music of the ethnic groups seems to retain its original function to some extent. Wedding songs are still performed at weddings, dance songs are used for dancing, etc. However, the music of folk songs tends to become more important to the members of the ethnic groups than the song texts and their functions. According to some informants, the quality of a tune is a greater factor in the survival of a song in America than are its words. It is also interesting that folk dancing and knowledge of its details are more wide-spread than mere singing.

Individuals who speak a foreign language as well as English, and who are thus members of two folk cultures, at least potentially, usually do not participate in the musical folklore of both groups. Apparently they tend to take part in the folk music of the foreign-language group more commonly than in the Anglo-American material.

What kind of fate may the folk songs of the foreign ethnic groups expect in the future? It is possible that the songs will share the fate of the ethnic groups themselves. The latter have been decreasing in size and strength.

We can examine this same question from the point of view of individual informants. It appears, for example, that the oldest child in a family of Polish settlers knows more folk songs than the younger children. The extent of ethnic knowledge a Polish informant has seems to correlate with the amount of Polish he speaks. Doubtless the amount of music known by native members of the ethnic groups is smaller than that of their immigrant parents, and recent arrivals (as among the Puerto Ricans) are better versed than old-time United States residents. However, there is no doubt that some types of folk music, especially those associated with functions that remain in practice, such as dancing, survive for several generations.

The question also arises whether the new interest in folk music on the part of students and intellectuals is about to provide our cities with a new folk music. Certainly this interest is laudable, but if the essential components of folk music are kept in mind — oral tradition, development of variants — it is obvious that this new practice bears little relationship to folk music as classically defined. But the widespread singing of folksongs from the Anglo-American tradition in our cities is certainly affecting the people's attitude toward music, and while folk music itself may not strictly speaking be involved, there is no doubt that our musical culture as a whole is being vitally affected.

My final question, then, is: Is there any true city folk music in America? There seems to be little or none. Some institutions try to foist their songs on the population in order to achieve material results. For example, some labor unions try to fuse such songs as "Joe Hill," "The Union Maid," and "UAW-CIO" into oral tradition. Such attempts are usually failures in creating folk songs, granting some significant exceptions. Union members know these songs, but they learn them from the professional union song leaders at meetings and summer camps, and the latter, in turn, learn them from songbooks. The members themselves do not usually pass them on to their families, but there is reason to believe that these union songs may have been closer to folk tradition in the days when unions were first being organized. Similiar statements could probably be made about company songs, political songs, patriotic songs, and the like. Yet as the days of active strife and violence in labor relations gradually recede, there is a chance that a true body of traditional folklore in the labor movement is emerging in the cities of America.

Songs of complaint about the city, and particularly about industrial life, are evidently more common and are closer to being in a genuine folk tradition. A collection of Pittsburgh industrial folk songs[6] includes, besides a number of union songs, material which is not directly associated with union activity in spite of its pro-labor tone. Some of these songs are in the native languages of the foreign-born workers (Example 28), sung to eastern and southern European tunes, but others are in English and occasionally make use of the tunes current in popular and broadside balladry, such as the following text, which is sung to the tune of the well-known "Crawdad Song."

> Pittsburgh is a great old town, Pittsburgh;
> Pittsburgh is a great old town, Pittsburgh;
> Pittsburgh is a great old town,
> Solid steel from McKeesport down.
> Pittsburgh is a great old town, Pittsburgh.

Evidently, then, there seems to be little music of city origin which takes root in urban folk tradition. Just as a great deal of rural folk music seems ultimately to be of city origin and to trickle down to folk tradition, so we can say that the folk tradition within the city is dependent on material from the countryside. But the American city, in contrast to its European counterpart, is a storehouse of European folk music which is kept alive in the enclaves which perpetuate to a degree their original rural culture.

VIII

THE PROFESSIONAL FOLK SINGER

So far in this book we have discussed folk music as it exists in its natural environment, how it lives in its rural home, and something of its behavior when it migrates to the city from the countryside. And we have confined ourselves to the use of music by genuine folk cultures, whose property folk music is par excellence. But folk music has another side; it often penetrates the urban, sophisticated musical culture. Indeed, most readers have probably had their first contact with folk song from recordings made by professional folk singers rather than from material recorded in the field. Why is it possible and even necessary to separate these two ways of performing folk music? Because it usually undergoes some very fundamental changes when it becomes part of an urban and collegiate musical culture. Some of these changes are obvious, others subtle. But the lover of folk music should be aware of them, and be careful not to confuse the two modes of presentation. Their confusion has often resulted in misrepresentation of facts concerning the original, rural form; on the other hand, it has led to considerable abuse being heaped on the professional folk singer.

It is unfortunate to have this confusion. I recently suggested to a student that she collect some folk songs for a term project, whereupon she asked me whether I knew anyone who could get her a discount at a local record store. For her, folk songs existed only on commercial records, sung by professionals. She was unaware that she herself knew some folk songs, learned from her mother, and that folk music was at all different from cultivated and popular music. It is important to realize that what the professional folk singer is doing, is trying to do, and in fact is required to do is something quite different from what the member of the folk community does. And if we assume, as we have throughout this book, that a song may be folk music under some circumstances and cultivated music under other circumstances, it is possible that songs sung by the professionals are not, and cannot be, genuine folk songs at all. In order to solve this dilemma, we would have to decide whether a piece of music can exist in an abstract form, outside of a performance. This problem is outside our scope here, but I believe the answer in the case of folk music could easily be "no," since oral tradition is its primary distinguishing feature. Since folk music proper lives only in performance, we can judge it only within its medium of presentation.

There is much variety in a professional's degree of knowledge and first-hand experience in folklore. Some professionals are members of a genuine folk tradition, of families in which oral culture is well established. They usually embark on professionalism through urbanization, and they are affected accordingly. For example, a genuine informant who sang for Library of Congress collectors decided that he was successful enough among those learned gentlemen to go to New York and become a full-time ballad singer. Some other folk singers come from the cultivated musical field; they are trained concert artists who like folk songs and wish to bring them to their audiences. Others, again, are scholars with a knack for public performance and entertainment. Some professionals have a thorough knowledge of the fundamentals of folklore and the factors which separate it from other types of tradition; others constantly exhibit incredible naivete (or arrogance) and are willing categorically to call practically everything they wish to sing a folk song.

The presentation of folk songs by professional singers is a force to be reckoned with in today's urban musical culture. Its over-all influence has certainly been beneficial to the survival of folk music at large, in spite of the misunderstandings to which it has exposed its subject. It has caused a boom in the cities, which has in turn reached the country and persuaded the bearers of folk tradition to renew their waning enthusiasm. The purposes of professional folk singers are usually very laudable. The purposes are concerned with fostering a deeper understanding of folk heritage; they are educational and artistic. Too often, however, the professional has been propelled by political and nationalist ideas. In various European countries, especially Nazi Germany, Fascist Italy, and the Communist governments, folk music has been used to further the desires of the state, to underscore false scientific theories, and for other propaganda aims. Whether the actions of these governments are in themselves acceptable or not, this use of folk music has resulted in widespread misinformation about the nature of folklore and folk culture, and the song material itself has suffered from changes imposed by the state.

The American government has not participated in this subversion of folk music. But among the professional folk singers there are some who have used their material with such aims in mind. The use of folk music by professionals, and its appreciation by wide intellectual audiences, dates from the late 1920's, when songs were used to underscore the movements for social justice and to give emotional appeal to the arguments of labor. Later the use of folk music shifted from the "folks of the left" to those of "the right," and folk song became a patriotic and even nationalistic expression. Some folk singers tried to show the alleged superiority of Anglo-American folk songs as compared to those of other ethnic groups, and Americanization of minority groups via folk music was attempted.

Even when such motives are not involved, as in the majority of cases, it seems to be practically impossible for the professional folk singer to present his songs in a way which gives a true picture of the musical folk culture of the United States. After all, he is singing for the entertainment of an audience. In the folk culture the songs have a function beyond aesthetic enjoyment, but in the city this function is lost, and the folk singer must compete with Beethoven and Hoagy Carmichael for the favors of an audience. It is a sophisticated audience which knows what it wants. And it usually does not want folk songs served in the austere way of the countryside; it wants music which adheres to the prevalent tastes and fads, with a little of that folksiness and quaintness which the urbanites believe to be characteristic of folklore. The professional folk songer must cater to these wishes if he is to be successful. And from this need stem the various characteristics of professional folk singing, traits which are far removed from those of genuine folk music.

The professional folk singer inevitably accompanies his songs with an instrument, since cultivated music is prevailingly accompanied. But in order to give the appearance of authenticity, he uses folk instruments, or what resembles them. The guitar and the banjo are most common, and often they are perfectly in place. Only when the accompaniment takes on the character of a solo performance, when it is played with virtuosity, does it cease to sound like folk music. But sophisticated audiences are usually not content with simple accompaniments, restricted to prosaic strumming of two or three chords. They want some "razzle-dazzle" and the performer must supply it. Other folk instruments, the dulcimer, the mandolin or the zither are constructed and played with greater complexity than they ever are in a folk environment. Instruments of the Renaissance, the lute and the recorder, are resurrected, even though they were part of a sophisticated musical culture and are not folklore. All of this is good entertainment, even good music, but it certainly cannot be called folk music, and it gives the listener a completely false impression of what his folk heritage is like.

Perhaps the trap into which the professional folk singer most frequently falls is the individualization to which he must subject his songs and the attention which he must draw to himself as their interpreter. American folk culture does not admit much individuality. While songs do have interpretations which are characteristic of individual singers, a genuine singer in a folk culture tends to stick close to his tradition, in spite of the effects of communal re-creation. It is not his person which is the center of the listener's attention, for he is only the temporary mouthpiece of a long tradition in which the individual rendition is only incidental. The professional or collegiate folk singer must focus attention on himself because his audience insists on it. It wants to hear not a tradition but an individual, not the characteristics of a widespread style and its culture but the peculiarities and the mannerisms of an interpreter. Thus the professional must sing his songs in a very special, inimitable way, he must rehearse his peculiarities, and he must arrive at a distinct version of each song, a version which then has to ossify so that it will remain the same for years; if it does not, the audience will think that its hero is "slipping." He must practice his trademarks, his way of removing his coat, his talking to the audience. Obviously these traits are completely contradictory to genuine folk music. There is nothing wrong with them in themselves; indeed, they are the essentials of cultivated music, but they give a false picture of folklore and the listener should be aware of the discrepancy.

Genuine folk singers who become entertainers of urban civilization take on the characteristics of professionals even though they begin as members of a folk community. This is even true of some American Indian singers who entertain tourists; they begin to concentrate on one style of singing and on one kind of song, namely that one which the tourists find most appealing and believe to be most characteristically Indian. Folk singers select those melodies which allow them to exhibit vocal brilliance and virtuosity. The use of harmony and other kinds of part-singing in Anglo-American songs is common in the professional repertory but rare in folk cultures. There are many other ways in which professional singers change the musical characteristics of the raw material.

Perhaps their greatest offense is the introduction of songs into what the audience believes to be the folk repertory which are not folk songs at all, but cultivated or popular songs, or songs which the folk singer has composed himself. Why does he indulge in this? Again, because genuine folk songs may not be sufficiently entertaining and do not always conform to the notions of quaintness and folksiness which the city audience believes essential in folklore. The professional must supply the public's wants and has had to go far afield to find the right product. He has used cultivated medieval music which, so far as we know, was never a part of folklore. He sings patriotic songs, labor songs, work songs which were never in oral tradition. Finally, he is forced to compose songs himself and to hide his authorship. This must be particularly annoying to him, and it would not be necessary if it were widely admitted. But evidently the professional folk singer is committed to a career of mixed purposes, and the good, musical, and sophisticated arrangements which he makes out of folk songs, the interpretations which are often interesting and penetrating, must be presented as true folklore in the original version if it is to sell. A few professionals have solved this problem by calling themselves arrangers of folk songs, and some have tried to explain what they are doing in scholarly and objective terms. But most of them persist in defeating the educational aims to which they are devoted because they are not willing to tell their audiences what they are actually doing and how their versions differ from those of folk culture proper.

Professional singing is most common in the Anglo-American tradition, but it is also evident in American Negro music, and it has crept into the musical cultures of most ethnic groups. In the latter it is largely a method of preserving the songs and, more particularly, of fostering national pride and unity. Again, laudable as these aims may be in themselves, they do not give a true picture of folk music. Professional folk singing for entertainment is a great preservative, but it is also a catalytic agent. While preserving folklore it changes its very essence. But in order to find out about the true heritage of song in the United States we must go into the field, to the uneducated and often unmusical singer for whom folk songs are not only entertainment but also the expression of a way of life.

IX

COLLECTING and STUDYING
FOLK MUSIC

Research in folk and primitive music is part of several disciplines. The raw material is collected with the techniques of anthropology and classified with those developed by folklorists. It is then set down on paper and analyzed through methods developed by musicologists, but the results of the analysis are usually interpreted by means of anthropological theory. Thus the scholar who wishes to do a complete job of studying a body of folk music should be familiar with all of these fields. Let us outline the processes of acquiring information on folk and primitive music.

First comes collecting, which must be done with sound recordings since the members of folk and primitive cultures do not write music. Occasionally scholars have tried to write down the music as they heard it performed in the field, but this is usually so difficult that even several repeated hearings are not sufficient for an accurate notation. There is an amusing (though perhaps spurious) story about a great German anthropologist who was doing field work in Australia. He knew nothing about music, but he heard a native song which he thought interesting, and he wished that he could somehow transport it to his musicological colleagues. Since no recording apparatus was available, he proceeded to memorize the song. But his memory was poor, and he decided to rehearse the song every day so it would not disappear. By the time he returned to Europe and sang it for his colleagues, they laughed because it sounded like a German popular song.

Because he was not acquainted with the native system of music and perceived it only by comparing it with his own, he had gradually and unconsciously changed the song to conform to his own ideas and tastes and to what had been his musical experience.

Today's standard collecting equipment is the tape recorder; but in the past collectors have used Edison cylinders, some operated by a treadle similar to that of a sewing machine; then disks; and after World War II, wire. Tape recording did not become popular in the United States until very recently, although it has been used longer in Germany, where the first collection of folk music on tape was probably Dr. Fritz A. Bose's work in 1936 on German folk ballads.[1] Collecting is a rather arduous and specialized task, involving more than simply finding a band of Indians and switching on the current. It requires knowledge of the material which is to be collected, acquaintance with the culture of the informants, and a great deal of patience, understanding, and ability to handle people, resembling a combination of public relations and mental therapy. Having decided upon a group, a student must begin by reading the literature on the music and culture of the group, and considering the special problems facing a collector of its music. Collecting Indian music, for instance, involves careful selection of informants, for many Indians today do not know the old Indian songs and only a few remember them well. Let us consider ideal collecting conditions from the research scholar's point of view. Of course, the amateur collector need not feel that he must follow every point brought up here, but if he does, his collection will be more useful and worthwhile.

First, the collector must try to find an informant who is considered an authority on folk music in his community, if possible a person who has not spent much time outside his culture. He should be persuaded to sing as many songs as he knows, even if some are fragmentary. Often such a person is rather old and his voice will not be as good as in the past; but the fact that he knows much material and remembers a bygone era makes him a worthwhile informant. Then the collector should find others and collect from them whatever they know, especially including, if possible, the same material as that collected from the first informant. One should record the same songs from several people because there are slight differences among the various versions, differences which are important for a number of reasons described below and in earlier chapters. Finally the collector should return to all of his informants and ask them to perform again the material performed earlier. This is again necessary because there are slight but important differences between the versions, differences which are interesting from a number of points of view. For example, we may assume that certain things in a performance of music are significant, meaningful to the performer and listener, and others are insignificant and arbitrary, and might as well not be there. A performer usually leaves intact the significant things but he may change the insignificant ones. The study of various renditions of the same music by one or several performers may enable us to find out more about the essentials of that music, about what features are important in a given style and what are not.

Re-recording sometimes presents unforeseen problems. Some of the Plains Indian tribes, many of whose songs use meaningless syllables instead of words, do not identify the songs by name. As a result one cannot always ask a singer to perform a specific song. A song can be identified by its function; for example, it can be called a love song or a Rabbit Dance song, but these are categories and would make the singer think of a large group of songs. The collector can sing the beginning of the song one wants to hear, or play a bit of a previous recording, but this in a way defeats the purpose of re-recording because the informant's mind is directed to what he has just heard, and the dice are loaded in favor of that particular version. Since there is often no meaningful text, one cannot quote it to him. Sometimes the only recourse is simply to ask the singer to sing all or some of the songs he has sung before, and hope that he will faithfully do so. Even then it is a problem to unscramble the recordings, to identify the variants and the performances which go together, for in many tribal repertories all of the songs sound very much alike to Western ears; and two separate songs may sometimes seem closer to us than two versions of a single song. This is one of the many intricacies and fascinations of collecting folk music.

Perhaps a few words should be said about the recording media. Magnetic tape recording is of course the easiest from the point of view of convenience and is preferable for work in the laboratory. In studying a piece of music or trying to reduce it to notation, it is necessary to repeat short bits of it many times, a process which easily wears out a disk recording but not tape or wire. Wire, however, is prone to break under such strain and, once broken, ties itself into little knots which are almost impossible to handle. The result is a roomful of loose wire which can never be repaired, and often several minutes of music are lost in the process. Tape may also break, but it can be spliced very easily.

Tape should move as rapidly as possible on the recorder for best acoustic results. But speed could increase the cost of tape considerably. A rate of 7-1/2 inches per second is sufficiently fast, 15 inches practically ideal. For solo singing and some instruments, 3 3/4 is satisfactory and can be used for anything if necessary, but 1 7/8 is definitely too slow because it reproduces too few cycles. However, even at 7-1/2 inches per second tape is usually less costly than disks, so tape has all the advantages.

Besides making recordings, the collector should also assemble and write down a great deal of information about the music in order to make his collection of maximum usefulness. He must note what songs are sung by each informant, how often, and when. The types and functions of the songs should be reported, and if possible it should be ascertained where the informant learned each piece. Then there is much information about the musical culture of the group, something not directly related to the recordings, which helps nevertheless in their interpretation. For example, there is the question of composition, that is, who composes songs, and how. Furthermore, we are interested in standards of performance, for these, of course, vary from culture to culture. For example, the Plains Indians prefer performance by high voices, but the Pueblo Indians of the Southwest prefer a low, growling rendition. The collector should find out who the good performers in a community are and what, in the minds of

their compatriots, makes them superior. He should get information about musical instruments, their construction, use, and
tuning. For the latter, the recording machine can again be used.
It takes no technical knowledge of music to ask a performer to
play all the possible tones on a given instrument, and to record
them; but this procedure can be of tremendous importance to the
musicologist who studies the recordings. Other items could be
added, but let it suffice to say that any statements about music
made by native informants are welcome, important, and relevant.

Once the recordings are made, they pass into the hands of the
ethnomusicologist. His first job is to transcribe them into notation,
and sometimes this is his only objective — one valid task is simply
to present the raw material in notated form and make it available
for others to study. This transcribing of a piece of primitive music
into notation is a difficult job, and folk music is not much easier.
It is sometimes so time consuming that it is not uncommon for a
song which takes one minute to perform to be transcribed only
after an hour or more of work. Why should it take so long, if,
after all, first-year college music students can learn to write down
what they have heard repeated three or four times, in exercises
called "dictation"? The reason points up one of the most important and interesting facts about primitive and folk music, and
about the methods of studying it.

We should first realize that there are at least two ways of
reducing what one hears to notation. One can expect to hear music in a preconceived pattern, to which the music will adhere,
as in classes of music theory, where students are taught what to
expect and then to supplement what they have actually heard
with what they know should and will be played by the instructor.
But the student of primitive music has a different point of view.
He must try to write down exactly what occurs in the music;
he must not allow his hearing to be diverted by preconceived
ideas of what should take place. Otherwise what he writes down
will be subjective, influenced by the kind of music he has been
used to hearing, and he will "correct" what he hears in the light
of his previous listening, creating a transcription which would
obviously not tell us about the music itself, only about the stu-

dent's reaction to it.

We, as members of western European culture, have been conditioned since childhood to a type of music which is very complex and specialized, and whose accompanying theory tells us that it is the best and highest type of music. When we listen to the music of other cultures, our natural tendency is to compare it, at least subconsciously, to our own music and to correct in our minds the sounds which we hear with our ears, so that they will conform to our ideas. But the non-Western systems of music, and those of folk music, are often quite different from ours, with different patterns in melody, rhythm, harmony. Their pitches cannot always be reproduced on our instruments, for primitive and folk music tends to use different scales from ours. And since our system of notation has evolved to take care of Western music only, it is often difficult, if not impossible, to reproduce with it the music of other cultures.

I have said that the transcriber of primitive music must be objective; but this does not mean that he is to become an automatic gadget which simply records and which eliminates the human aspects of music. Humans do not make good gadgets, and there are some mechanical devices which are much more accurate than the human ear. These, however, are only good for giving us a partial insight into the music. Electronic apparatus gives us the acoustic aspects of music, shows us vibration rates and overtones, but it omits the emotional and communicative sides of music. But mechanical transcribers do have their value, and I shall describe the two most important ones here.

First is the oscillograph, which records all the pitches, overtones, etc., on a rotating drum with a stylus, much like a thermometer which records temperatures over a period of time. What it writes is very difficult to decipher because it includes so much more than the human ear can perceive. What it records must be re-transcribed into ordinary notation in order to be useful.

The stroboscope is more useful, but it does not really transcribe. It simply enables one to ascertain the exact pitch of a tone to a degree much more accurate than that of a human transcription. It is useful for finding out the scale of a musical style, but it would be an endless task to attempt to use a stroboscope for every single note in a song. Only for uncertain or especially interesting pitches and intervals is it of practical value.

Some attempts at an "instantaneous" music notator, into which recordings would be "fed" and digested into finished transcriptions of a highly technical nature, have not yet resulted in a model for general consumption. The most promising is one developed by Charles Seeger, designed, of course, to supplement rather than actually replace the human ear. Since music is, after all, performed by and for humans, the best instrument for recording it is, in spite of its limitations, the human ear and mind, even when a strange musical culture is involved. But the ear should be careful not to superimpose its own cultural and musical experience on what it hears. The transcriber has to be prepared to hear distinctions in pitch which do not exist, or rather, which are not significant in his own musical culture, and he must expect to hear rhythmic combinations and complexities which are beyond those he knows. In order to accommodate these differences between exotic and Western music, some special signs have been devised to help him reproduce what he hears in our system of notation, and yet to avoid violating the music. But in spite of all these aids, transcriptions are merely symbols, approximations of sound. It would be difficult for a Westerner to take such a transcription, to sing it, and have it sound at all like the original performance. Nevertheless, transcriptions are useful and necessary for learning about folk and primitive music, for we can only get a part of the picture from the sound recordings alone.

The following symbols are most frequently used to represent features in primitive and folk music foreign to Western notation:

+, ↑	slightly higher than notated
—, ↓	slightly lower than notated
(♩)	uncertain pitch
◻	indefinite pitch
✗	grace note, without rhythmic value
⨆,ǀ ǀ	weak tones
‛p̌‚	pulsations

⌒   strong tie
⌒̂   glissando
⌢   slightly longer than notated
◡   slightly shorter than notated

    Some of the schemes for notating exotic music modify the staff system in favor of a different arrangement of lines. The use of graph paper, which can show note length and pitch variation logically, seems promising for some purposes. Another method uses a conventional staff of large proportions, which enables the transcriber to place the notes at various points between the lines and spaces: Frances Densmore[2] has tried writing Indian songs in simplified form by representing only the over-all melodic contour. The difficulty with these methods is that most people learn with a certain amount of effort to read conventional music notation, after which they are not amenable to learning others. While these special schemes do have some value for presenting material to specialists and students, it seems best for the general reader and for educational purposes to continue with the conventional system aided by a few special modifications like those mentioned above.

    Classifying the recordings of folk and primitive music and making them available for study is an important aspect of research. This is especially true because one cannot positively identify a song in all its versions, and one does not always know whether two recordings are actually performances of the same song or not. Consequently, some special tune techniques of conservation have had to be invented. There are a number of important archives of recordings in the United States, the largest being the Archives of American Folksong in the Library of Congress, which specializes in American material. The Archives of Folk and Primitive Music at Indiana University has music from all continents and includes the world's largest collection of North American Indian recordings. The Laboratory of Comparative Musicology of Northwestern University is especially strong in African and New World Negro music, and there are smaller collections at various other institutions, including the Universities of California, Washington, and Michigan, and the Chicago Museum of Natural History. There are also some specialized archives such as the collection at Wayne State University, which is devoted exclusively to material collected in the Detroit area. All of these collections, however, share the job of preserving the folk music heritage of the world for times when it will have disappeared or will have changed beyond recognition. I should point out that they contain, for the most part, recordings which have never been duplicated in quantity or published. Since they often exist only in the original, they are usually not available to the public but only to students and researchers.

The analysis of folk and primitive music is a complex and difficult matter which requires much knowledge of basic music theory and which would take up more space in this book than can be allowed, were we to discuss it in detail. Among the basic principles involved, however, the following distinguish folk music research from that in other kinds of music. The scholar who analyzes folk music is usually working in a medium relatively distant from the music most familiar to him. Therefore he must be extremely careful, just as in transcribing, not to impose his own ideas and experiences on the music he is analyzing. He must not give way to the temptation of calling unusual intervals simply out-of-tune equivalents of their Western counterparts, or of calling complex rhythmic patterns "free" or "chaotic." He should abstain from criticizing and evaluating his material from an aesthetic point of view, since this is likely to distort the analysis and to produce an ethnocentric and thus irrelevant judgment. Finally, since most folk and primitive music consists of short, simple pieces whose structure does not approach the complexity of even the simple songs in Western music history, their description usually can and should go into greater detail than an examination of cultivated music. Analysis of folk and primitive music is expected to be more accurate and more objective than that of cultivated music.

The various fields of American folk music have not been evenly covered in research; some parts of it, such as American Indian music, are well known, but others, such as the music of the recent immigrants, have hardly been touched. Some, such as the music of the Negro, have been the subject of much theorizing with insufficient collecting, while elsewhere, as in the English tradition, there has been extensive collecting but little theoretical work. Although research in American folk and primitive music has been in progress only for about half a century, a tremendous amount of information has been accumulated. But much remains to be done; the musical folklore of the United States is still a wide open field for collecting, research, and publication.

X

FOLK MUSIC and CULTIVATED MUSIC

The use of folk music by the composers of cultivated or art music has been an important factor in the history of music. Composers have usually felt closer to and more familiar with folk music than have the historians of cultivated music, and, indeed, virtually all of our knowledge of folk music before the nineteenth century comes directly from sources of cultivated music rather than from theoretical and historical writing. In the early epochs of Western history folk and cultivated music were probably more similar in style and more clearly related in function than they are today. There was evidently a time in European culture when there was no essential distinction between the two types; the increasing degree of differentiation may have come about simply through the growing professionalism and specialization among the composers.

It is not the purpose of this chapter to cite the multitude of instances in which sophisticated composers have used folk music. I wish only to show some of the important types of relationship between traditional and cultivated music as shown in the works of these composers. The examples were chosen somewhat arbitrarily, for hundreds of others could have illustrated the points equally well; those given here are among the best known. Moreover, a complete survey of the compositions in which folk material appears is an impossibility, for the identification of this material is itself a difficult and problematic matter. Finally, I do not desire to evaluate the uses of folk music by cultivated composers, either from the point of view of the folklorist interested in presenting folk tradition in a pure form or from that of the music critic.

Historically speaking, the earliest type of relationship between traditional and cultivated music is probably that between the folk and the cultivated in an individual ethnic or national group. Professional composers seem to have begun using traditional elements unconsciously, without feeling that they were dealing with something foreign to their usual musical experience. They simply combined the similar styles used by the two groups without feeling that they were borrowing from one and adding to the other. The background for this similarity is usually the common musical heritage and experience of the two levels of the population and the existence of a common culture and possibly of similar personality types among both cultivated and folk composers. But the basic reason for this close relationship is probably much deeper and more elusive and cannot be described here any more than the question, why a given national group should have a particular musical style at all, can be fully answered. An historical approach to our problem would point to the fact that the cultivated music in a given country is descended from the same undifferentiated tradition as the folk music, which may be behind the relatively free and informal use of folk music by professional composers before the nineteenth century, composers who evidently considered folk music a part of their own tradition rather than a related but basically foreign one. Although the interest in folk music grew tremendously in the nineteenth century, at least on a conscious level, traditional material began to be set apart, so to speak, and treated in a special way, which was not the case in earlier centuries.

Since roughly 1800, professional composers have used folk and even primitive music, but they have viewed it as something exotic. They have not always really integrated such materials into their styles, but have simply added it as if it could be removed again without disturbing the results of their own personal inspiration. Their use of folk music can be arranged in three categories:

1. *Using folk music without essential changes or additions.* This usually consists of harmonizations of folk songs with an accompaniment sometimes designed to bring out the folk style, and at other times evidently composed so as to hide the peculiarities of that style and make the song conform to the standards of cultivated music. The former method is exemplified by the harmonizations of Hungarian, Slovak, and Rumanian folk songs by Béla Bartók; the latter by those of the Irish, Scottish, and Welsh songs by Beethoven. In all of these the original folk melodies have remained undisturbed in their original form, and the composer has contributed only a harmonic setting, inspired, in the case of Bartók, by the songs themselves, and in Beethoven's arrangements, by the composer's own style of harmony.

2. *Using folk melodies which have been changed somewhat to conform with the system and structure of cultivated music.* Examples of this category are rarer than of the other two. They are most commonly found where the traditional material is in a style considerably removed from that of the cultivated composer. In the American Indian songs used by American composers, for example, certain pitch differentiations can not easily be reproduced on European instruments. The original Indian material may then be changed so that it can be played by piano or orchestra. Changing the instrument without changing the music itself also comes under this category of arrangement. Similar changes may be made for rhythm and other elements of music. A famous example of this type of folk song use is the second theme of the first movement of Tschaikowsky's *Fourth Symphony,* based on a folk song, "The Beech Tree."

3. *Composing music imitating a folk style.* This category is probably of the greatest interest and may be the most common. Composition of folk-like music, often necessitating some kind of analysis by the composer, ranges from individual motifs and themes to full-length symphonies, as well as such short forms as songs and instrumental character-pieces.

For a professional composer to become something of a folk-composer, which is what happens in the latter category, involves either saturation with a folk style through long contact with the members of a folk group or musicological study. The results of such a use of folk music are varied. Some composers write melodies in the style of folk songs and fit them into an environment which bears little or no relationship to that style. This happened, for example, in Dvořàk's *Fifth Symphony (From the New World)*; the second theme of the first movement imitates an Indian song in a symphony which is otherwise not Indian in style. Another example is a theme in Aaron Copland's *Appalachian Spring* which sounds like an American fiddle tune. That these discrepancies do not inhibit the general effectiveness of the compositions goes without saying.

Less frequently, composers have taken certain characteristic elements of a folk style, such as a peculiar kind of tonal organization, a rhythmic pattern, or a kind of melodic contour, and used it, leaving other elements of the music in their non-folk style. An example is the violin solo from Rimski-Korsakov's *Scheherazade,* where the rhythmic monotony and the interweaving of a few tones, common in Arabic and Persian music, are taken over into a Western tonal and harmonic structure.

Finally, some composers try to reproduce the stylistic features of folk music even in those elements of their music which are not present in the folk style at all, such as harmony. This reproduction is usually accomplished by extending the patterns of the folk style, such as the use of a scale in the harmony which is already present in the melody. This manner of imparting the elements of a kind of folk or exotic music to the entire musical structure of a complex Western piece has been used by some modern composers, for example, by Bartók and Vaughan Williams in Hungarian and English folk songs.

The use of folk music has had several purposes. Occasionally it has been tried in order to create a light or gay mood. In music with a text or a program (representation of non-musical material), rustic scenes and peasants are sometimes characterized by folk-like elements. Various types of local color and geographic locations are indicated by folk or folk-like music. In the nineteenth century the main motivation for using traditional material seems to have been the growing national consciousness among those countries whose contribution to cultivated music had hitherto been small: Russia (whose composers Moussorgsky and Rimski-Korsakav along with many others, participated in the folk music movement), Denmark (Gade), England (Vaughan Williams, Britten), Spain (De Falla, Albéniz), Rumania (Enesco), Bohemia (Smetana, Dvořák), Hungary (Liszt, Bartók, Kodàly), and others; but it applies less to the centers of Western musical culture, Germany, Austria, Italy, and France. In the latter group, folk music was often used to illustrate the rural aspects of culture and to symbolize the foreign or exotic, a practice which has more recently become widespread. Thus we have the *Cappriccio Espagnol* of Rimski-Korsakov (which shows that he did not use Russian folk music alone), the use of Negro and Indian themes by Dvořák to show his reaction to America, and the use of Indian themes by American composers of English descent, and of Indonesian elements by Colin McPhee, an American.

In the late nineteenth and early twentieth centuries some composers used traditional music because it gave them opportunities to find new structural features and entire systems. Here the music itself often does not sound the least bit like folk music, but some folkloristic features are incorporated, as it were, abstractly. Modern composers, like the Czech Alois Haba, who use microtones and quartertones, were influenced by the small intervals of Near Eastern music. Bartók's compositions, again, contain some structural principles found in many Hungarian tunes, such as a characteristic type of symmetry in the tonal structure, even when the folk style is otherwise not evident.

Whereas European folk music, whose styles are closely related to Western cultivated music, has had an influence over the latter for centuries, the more remote styles of primitive and oriental music have become available to Western composers only recently. Nevertheless, they have exercised a considerable influence during the last few decades.

American composers have been concerned with the use of indigenous material because of their attempts to create some kind of national American music, a musical style which would distinguish them from the European composers.[1] As members of a

Western culture, they first thought of using the music in their own tradition, such as English and Scottish. But this did not distinguish them from their European colleagues, since this music is basically a European importation; so the American composers turned to those bodies of folk music which the United States shares with no other countries, American Indian and Negro songs. It is this material which predominates in American compositions.

One of the first among the composers interested in Indian materials was Edward MacDowell, often considered the greatest American composer. His *Indian Suite,* first performed in 1896, was, in the composer's own words, "suggested for the most part by melodies of the North American Indians."[2] The titles of the movements indicate some aspects of Indian culture: I. *Legend,* II. *Love Song,* III. *In War-time,* IV. *Dirge,* V. *Village Festival.*

Other composers who used Indian material are Arthur Farwell, Arthur Nevin, who composed an opera, *Poia,* based on a Blackfoot legend, Charles Ives, who experimented with many other stylistic innovations and folk styles as well, Frederic Jacobi, Charles W. Cadman, and Henry Cowell. The use of Indian elements is usually limited to certain simple melodies whose scales coincide with those of cultivated music. The rhythms and the over-all forms of Indian music are rarely used so that few of the compositions are in the first of the three categories of the cultivated use of folk music.

It was the Czech composer Dvořák who first popularized the idea of using Negro folk songs, especially spirituals, in cultivated music; and he had many American followers. The Negro songs combine the virtues of being fairly close to the style of cultivated music, having been derived from the white spirituals, and yet of being a unique American contribution to music literature. Before Dvořák, French Creole music from Louisiana was incorporated in the pieces of a Creole composer, George Moreau Gottschalk, who gained a considerable reputation in Europe. The English-language Negro songs have recently been the basis of arrangements for vocal soloists and choirs and as parts of instrumental pieces. The Negro composers, William Grant Still and Henry Thacker Burleigh, the latter a pupil of Dvořák's, are important in this field. The significance of Negro folk music in the development of popular music and jazz is obvious. Indirectly it has also been used by many prominent composers who assimilated the elements of jazz into more sophisticated compositions. George Gershwin is the most prominent American to have done so; Europeans, including such twentieth century greats as Igor Stravinsky and Darius Milhaud, have also contributed.

Anglo-American folk songs have not been entirely neglected. Charles Ives quoted them as themes in a number of his works, including his symphonies. He tried in several instances to convey the feelings and sounds of the simple musical performances which took place in his boyhood home in Danbury, Connecticut. Daniel Gregory Mason, too, experimented with folklore in some of his pieces, notably in a *Folk Song Fantasy*, which is based on the song "Fanny Blair." In more recent years, Aaron Copland and Roy Harris have used the British folk song style and incorporated some songs directly into their works. Their motive was, again, the creation of a distinctly American music. The folk music of other ethnic groups, however, has only rarely been absorbed into American cultivated music.

The United States has participated in the general revival of folk music as a source of inspiration for the composers of modern civilization. To be sure, a new, American style has not emerged from the revival, and it is unlikely that such a style could have been created simply through the use of folk music in a country whose musical traditions are so diverse and new. Nevertheless, the movement has contributed to the American people's awareness of their folklore, Indian, Negro, and British, and as such it deserves the attention of the student of folk music.

1

LADY ISABEL AND THE ELF-KNIGHT

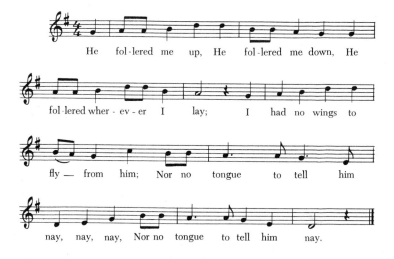

He fol-lered me up, He fol-lered me down, He fol-lered wher - ev - er I lay; I had no wings to fly — from him; Nor no tongue to tell him nay, nay, nay, Nor no tongue to tell him nay.

From George Korson, ed., *Pennsylvania Songs and Legends*
(Philadelphia: 1949, University of Pennsylvania Press), p. 30;
Collected by S. P. Bayard, 1943.

2

LORD BATEMAN

The Turks — they had but one lone daugh - ter, And she was of some high de - gree. She stole the keys of her fa - ther's dwel - ling, And

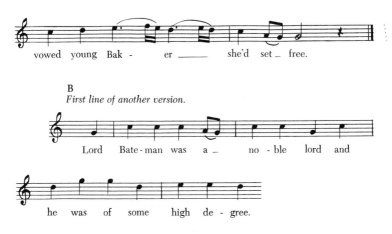

vowed young Bak - er _____ she'd set _ free.

B
First line of another version.

Lord Bate-man was a _ no - ble lord and

he was of some high de - gree.

Transcribed by B. Nettl, from Library of Congress record 1724B1;
Indiana.

3

GOLDEN VANITY

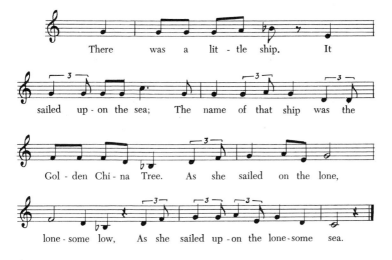

There was a lit - tle ship. It

sailed up - on the sea; The name of that ship was the

Gol - den Chi - na Tree. As she sailed on the lone,

lone - some low, As she sailed up - on the lone - some sea.

Transcribed by B. Nettl, from Library of Congress record 1740A1;
Indiana.

4

GYPSY LADDIE

Oh, would you for - sake your house and land, and would you for - sake your ba - by, And would you for - sake your own wed -ded lord to go with the gyp - sy Da - vy?

Transcribed by B. Nettl, from Library of Congress record 1750B1;
Indiana.

Variants of Gypsy Laddie

5

GYPSY LADDIE

Transcribed by B. Nettl; Collected by Richard M. Dorson in
Arkansas.

6

JUBILEE

Transcribed by B. Nettl, from Electra disk: *Jean Ritchie Sings.*

7

Tune for **THE LONESOME DOVE**

The words are not intelligible; the tune is illustrative of orna-
mentation in American singing.

Transcribed by B. Nettl, from Library of Congress record 1725A1;
Indiana.

THE JOLLY LUMBERMAN
Tune: "Canady-I-O"

Come all you jol - ly lum - ber -

men and lis - ten to my song, ———

— I'll tell you all my sto - ry ———

— and I won't de - tain you long. ———

— Con - cern - ing some hus - ky lum - ber -

men who once a - greed to go ———

— and spend a win - ter re - cent -

ly on Col - ley's Run - i - o. ____

From George Korson, ed., *Pennsylvania Songs and Legends*,
p. 343.

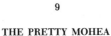

9

THE PRETTY MOHEA

As I was a - rov - ing for pleas - ure one day,

In self - re - col - lec - tion as the time passed a - way,

As I was a - mus - ing my - self on the grass

Oh, who should I spy but a sweet Ind - ian lass.

From James Harrington Cox, *Folk Songs from West Virginia*
(New York: National Service Bureau, 1939), p. 32.

10

WHEN I WAS A YOUNG GIRL
Play-Party Song

When I ＿＿＿ was a young girl, a

young girl, a young girl, when I ＿＿＿ was a

young girl, a young girl was I. It was

this way and that way, it was

this way and that way; When I ＿＿＿ was a

young girl, a young girl was I.

From Alton C. Morris, *Folksongs of Florida* (Gainesville: University of Florida Press, 1950), p. 204.

11

SOLDIER'S JOY
Fiddle Tune

From Samuel P. Bayard, *Hill Country Tunes* (Philadelphia:
American Folklore Society, 1944), No. 21.

12

BADUMA PADDLERS' SONG (Republic of Congo: Brazzaville)

From Rose Brandel, *The Music of Central Africa* (The Hague: Martinus Nijhoff, 1961), p. 200.

13

JOHN HENRY

From Alton C. Morris, *Folksongs of Florida*, p. 182.

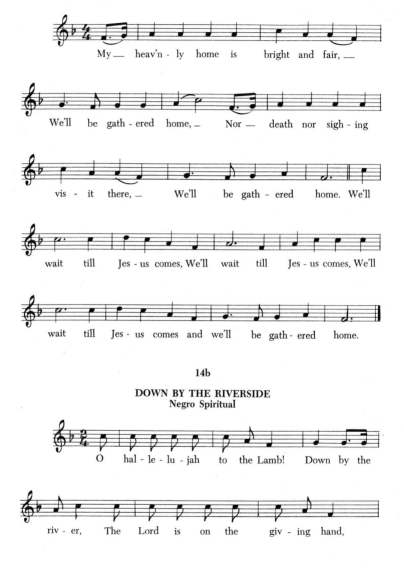

14a

WE'LL WAIT TILL JESUS COMES
White Spiritual

My — heav'n - ly home is bright and fair, —

We'll be gath - ered home, — Nor — death nor sigh - ing

vis - it there, — We'll be gath - ered home. We'll

wait till Jes - us comes, We'll wait till Jes - us comes, We'll

wait till Jes - us comes and we'll be gath - ered home.

14b

DOWN BY THE RIVERSIDE
Negro Spiritual

O hal - le - lu - jah to the Lamb! Down by the

riv - er, The Lord is on the giv - ing hand,

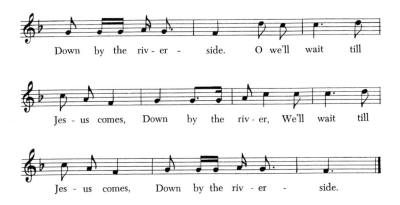

Down by the riv - er - side. O we'll wait till Jes - us comes, Down by the riv - er, We'll wait till Jes - us comes, Down by the riv - er - side.

From George Pullen Jackson, *White and Negro Spirituals* (New York: J. J. Augustin, 1943), pp. 192 and 193.

15

AMAZING GRACE
Negro Spiritual

A - maz - ing grace, how sweet the sound, I want to die a - shout - ing. I — want to feel my sav - ior near When— soul and bod - y's part - ing.

From George Pullen Jackson, *White and Negro Spirituals,* p. 173.

104

16

Makah Indian Song

Text translation: "Good-by, my sweetheart"

From Frances Densmore, *Nootka and Quileute Music,* Bulletin
124 of the Bureau of American Ethnology (Washington: Government Printing Office, 1939), p. 177.

17

Modoc Indian Song

From Jody C. Hall and Bruno Nettl, "Musical Style of the
Modoc," *Southwestern Journal of Anthropology,* XI (1955), 61.

18

Arapaho Indian THUNDERBIRD SONG

Transcribed by B. Nettl, recorded by Zdenek Salzmann, 1948.

19

Two Creek Indian Duck Dance Songs

From F. G. Speck, *Ceremonial Dances of the Creek and Yuchi*
(Philadelphia: University of Pennsylvania Museum, 1911), pp.
169-170.

20

Teton Indian Moccasin Game Song
(Associated with the Ghost Dance)

From Frances Densmore, *Teton Sioux Music* (Washington: Government Printing Office, 1918), p. 386.

21

Ute Indian Peyote Song

From David P. McAllester, *Peyote Music* (New York: Viking
Fund, Inc., 1949); Song No. 76.

22

Arapaho Indian Peyote Song

He ya   na hey   ney   ney,   He ya   na hey   ney   ney

He ya   na hey   ney   ney,   He ya   na hey   ney   ney

Hey ya·   na   he   he   ne   yo   we.

Collected and transcribed by B. Nettl, 1952.

108

23

Blackfoot Indian Song

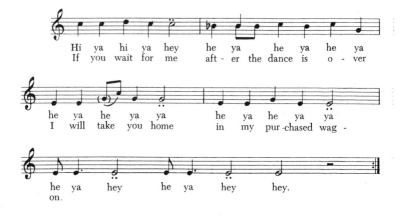

Hi ya hi ya hey he ya he ya he ya
If you wait for me aft - er the dance is o - ver

he ya he ya ya he ya he ya ya
I will take you home in my pur -chased wag -

he ya hey he ya hey hey.
on.

Collected and transcribed by B. Nettl, 1952.

24

SO WILL ICH'S ABER HEBEN AN

So will ich's a -

ber he - ben an

Sin - gen in Got - tes Ehr'

Transcribed by B. Nettl from Library of Congress record 1767A;
Indiana.

110

25

HRALY DUDY
Czech Song

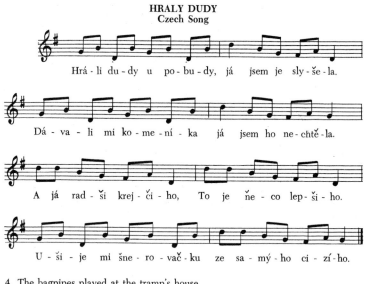

Hrá - li du - dy u po - bu - dy, já jsem je sly - še - la.

Dá - va - li mi ko - me - ní - ka já jsem ho ne - chtě - la.

A já rad - ši krej - či - ho, To je ňe - co lep - ši - ho.

U - ši - je mi šne - ro - vač - ku ze sa - mý - ho ci - zí - ho.

4. The bagpipes played at the tramp's house,
I listened to them.
They were marrying me to a chimney-sweep;
I didn't want him.
I prefer a tailor,
That is something better.
He will make me a corset
Out of foreign cloth.

From Bruno Nettl and Ivo Moravcik, "Czech and Slovak Songs
Collected in Detroit," *Midwest Folklore*, V (1955), 40-41.

26

ACH SYNKU
Czech Song

Ach syn - ku syn - ku, do - ma - li jsi?

Ach syn - ku, syn - ku, do - ma - li jsi?

Ta - tí - ček se — ptá o - ral - li jsi,

ta - tí - ček se — ptá, o - ral - li jsi.

Oh, son, son, are you at home?
Father is asking, have you plowed?

From Bruno Nettl and Ivo Moravcik, "Czech and Slovak Songs
Collected in Detroit," pp. 40-41.

27
OKOLO TŘEBONĚ
Czech Song

O - ko - lo Tře - bo - ně, o - ko - lo Tře - bo - ně
Až se mi na - pa - sou, Až se mi na - pa - sou

pa - sou se tam ko - ně. na pan - ském vý - ho - ně.
do - mů mě po - ne - sou do - mů mě po - né - sou.

Faster

Dej ko-by-lám, to ti po-ví-dám, dej ko-by-lám ov - sa.

Around Trebon, around Trebon,
Horses are grazing on the lord's field.
Give the horses, I'm telling you,
Give the horses oats.
When they have had their fill
They will carry me home.

From Bruno Nettl and Ivo Moravcik, "Czech and Slovak Songs
Collected in Detroit," pp. 42-43.

112

28

AJA LEJBER MAN
Slovak Industrial Song

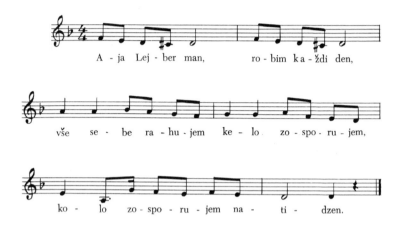

A - ja Lej - ber man, ro - bim ka - ždi den,
vše se - be ra - hu - jem ke - lo zo - spo - ru - jem,
ko - lo zo - spo - ru - jem na - ti - dzen.

I'm a labor man,
I work every day.
To myself I always figure
"How much am I saving,
How much am I saving each week?"

From George Korson, ed., *Pennsylvania Songs and Legends*, p. 436.

29

Ukrainian Polyphonic Song

Transcribed by B. Nettl; collected by Roman Rosdolsky and
Ossyp Rosdolsky.

Rumanian Christmas Carols

30

31

From Béla Bartók, *Rumanian Christmas Carols* (London: Boosey
and Hawkes, n.d.), p. 2.

32

PILL OLL HELLE
Estonian Song

Pill oll hel - le, pill oll hel - le hel - le pe - dä - jä - ne. Hoi, ma lel - los, _ Hoi, _ ma lel - los, ma lel - los, pe - dä - jä - ne jo!

The bagpipe sounds shrill,
The bagpipe sounds shrill,
Sounds shrill from pine.
Hoi, I would sing,
Hoi, I would sing
I would sing as if made from pine, yo!

Transcribed by B. Nettl; collected by B. Nettl and Raili Merivalja, 1956.

NOTES

Chapter I

1. Julian von Pulikowski, *Geschichte des Begriffes Volkslied im musikalischen Schrifttum* (Heidelberg, 1933) illustrates this diversity.
2. "Folklore," in Funk and Wagnall's *Standard Dictionary of Folklore. Mythology, and Legend* (New York, 1949), I, 398-403.
3. Halsey Stevens, *The Life and Music of Béla Bartók* (New York, 1953), pp. 21-27; Béla Bartók, *Hungarian Folk Music* (London, 1931).
4. Wilhelm and Jacob Grimm, *Deutsche Mythologie* (Leipzig, 1835).
5. Hans Naumann, *Grundzüge der deutschen Volkskunde* (Frankfurt, 1922).
6. Franz Magnus Boehme, *Altdeutsches Liederbuch* (Leipzig, 1877), pp. xii-xiii.
7. Phillips Barry, "Communal Recreation," *Bulletin of the Folk Song Society of the North East*, No. 5 (1933), pp. 4-6.

Chapter II

1. Theories on the functionality of folk and primitive music have been developed by George Herzog and are discussed in various papers mentioned in the bibliographical aids.
2. Siegfried Nadel, "The Origins of Music," *Musical Quarterly*, XVI (1930), 531-546.
3. Karl Buecher, *Arbeit and Rhythmus* (Leipzig, 1924).
4. Hugh Tracey, *Chopi Musicians* (Oxford, 1948).
5. These form types are introduced by George Herzog, "A Comparison of Pueblo and Pima Musical Styles," *Journal of American Folklore*, XLIX (1938), 305.
6. Bruno Nettl, "Stylistic Change in Folk Music," *Southern Folklore Quarterly*, XVII (1953), 216-220.

Chapter IV

1. From Arapaho informant William Shakespeare, 1952. See also A. L. Kroeber, *The Arapaho* (New York, 1902), pp. 418-421.

2. Bruno Nettl, "Notes on Musical Composition in Primitive Culture," *Anthropological Quarterly*, XXVII (1954), 81-90.
3. George Herzog, "Salish Music," in Marian Smith, ed., *Indians of the Urban Northwest* (New York, 1949), p. 107.
4. George Herzog, "Music in the Thinking of the American Indian," *Peabody Bulletin* (May, 1938), p. 4.
5. *Ibid.*, p. 5.
6. Frances Densmore, *Cheyenne and Arapaho Music* (Los Angeles, 1930), p. 40.

7. Frances Densmore, *Nootka and Quileute Music* (Washington, 1939), p. 185.
8. *Ibid.*
9. Ruth Benedict, *Patterns of Culture* (New York, 1934).
10. George Herzog, "A Comparison of Pueblo and Pima Musical Styles," *Journal of American Folklore*, XLIX (1938), 333.
11. *Ibid.*
12. George Herzog, "Speech-Melody and Primitive Music," *Musical Quarterly*, XX (1934), 460.
13. *Ibid.,* p. 461.
14. Bruno Nettl, "Observations on Meaningless Peyote Song Texts," *Journal of American Folklore*, LXVI (1953), 161-164.
15. Bruno Nettl, "The Shawnee Musical Style," *Southwestern Journal of Anthropology*, IX (1953), 284.
16. George Herzog, "Speech-Melody and Primitive Music."
17. Bruno Nettl, "Text-Music Relations in Arapaho Songs," *Southwestern Journal of Anthropology*, X (1954), 192-199.
18. Bruno Nettl, *North American Indian Musical Styles* (Philadelphia, 1954).

Chapter V

1. Variants of the ballads mentioned in this chapter can be found in the various collections listed in the bibliographical aids.
2. Béla Bartók, *Hungarian Folk Music* (London, 1931); George Herzog, "Song," in Funk and Wagnall's *Standard Dictionary of Folklore, Mythology, and Legend*, II, 1041.
3. Francis James Child, *The English and Scottish Popular Ballads* (8 vols.; Boston, 1857-59).
4. Samuel P. Bayard, "Prolegomena to a Study of the Principal Melodic Families of British-American Folk Song," *Journal of American Folklore*, LXIII (1950), 1-44.
5. From *Bay State Ballads*, LP Record Fp47/2, Folkways Records.

Chapter VI

1. Henry Edward Krehbiel, *Afro-American Folksongs* (New York, 1914).
2. George Pullen Jackson, *White and Negro Spirituals* (New York, 1943).
3. Richard A. Waterman, "African Influence in American Negro Music,"

in Sol Tax, ed., *Acculturation in the Americas* Chicago, 1952); Erich M. von Hornbostel, "American Negro Songs," *International Review of Missions*, XIV (1926), 748.
4. Jackson, *White and Negro Spirituals*.
5. Daniel G. Hoffman, "From Blues to Jazz," *Midwest Folklore*, V (1955), 107-114.
6. George Korson, ed., *Pennsylvania Songs and Legends* (Philadelphia, 1949).

Chapter VII

1. I am grateful to Professor Thelma James for permission to use a Serbo-Croatian collection. In addition, I have used a Master's thesis by Helen Goranowski, *An Analysis of 65 Polish Folk Songs*, Wayne University, 1951. An important publication resulting from the collecting program at Wayne is Harriet M. Pawlowska, ed., *Merrily We Sing; 105 Polish Folksongs* (Detroit, 1961).

2. This includes recorded songs and written song-texts, in original as well as translation, with background information on songs and informants. The following ethnic groups were included: native white and Negro, German, Polish, Czech, Italian, Armenian, Scottish, Greek, Albanian, Russian, and Hungarian. The only part of this material published so far is by Bruno Nettl and Ivo Moravcik, "Czech and Slovak Songs Collected in Detroit," *Midwest Folklore*, VI (1956), 37–49.

3. All statements of population growth are based on Albert Mayer, *A Study of the Foreign-Born Population of Detroit 1870–1950* (Detroit, 1951), mimeographed.

4. Shulamith Rybak, "Puerto Rican Children's Songs in New York," *Midwest Folklore*, VIII (1958), 5-20.

5. These groups are listed among the official and semi-official organizations of the ethnic groups in a detailed listing by Albert Mayer, *Ethnic Groups in Detroit: 1951* (Detroit, 1951), mimeographed.

6. Jacob A. Evanson, "Folk Songs of an Industrial City," George Korson, ed., *Pennsylvania Songs and Legends* (Philadelphia, 1949), pp. 423-466.

Chapter IX

1. Fritz Bose, personal communication in 1955.

2. Frances Densmore, *Teton Sioux Music* (Washington, 1918).

Chapter X

1. The material in this chapter is partially based on two important general histories of American music, which also include thorough bibliographies: John Tasker Howard, *Our American Music* (New York, 1939) and Gilbert Chase, *America's Music* (New York, 1955).

2. Howard, *Our American Music*, p. 331.

BIBLIOGRAPHICAL AIDS

Suggestions for further reading and study.

CHAPTER I

There are not many books about folk music in general or about the definition and the concept of folk music. Several of the articles, especially that on "Folklore," in Funk and Wagnall's *Standard Dictionary of Folklore and Mythology* (New York, 1949), can be recommended. The research side of folk music is explained in Charles Seeger, "Systematic Musicology: Viewpoints, Orientations, and Methods," in *Journal of the American Musicological Society*, IV (1951), 240–248, and in Bruno Nettl, "Historical Aspects of Ethnomusicology," in *American Anthropologist* LX (1958), 518–532.

A number of important bibliographies, which list collections and studies, have been published. Among them should be mentioned Charles Haywood's *Bibliography of North American Folklore and Folksong* (New York, 1951), which lists materials in Anglo-American, Indian, Negro, and all other groups; also Bruno Nettl, "Musicological Studies in American Ethnological Journals," *Notes*, XIII (1955), 205–209. *A List of American Folksongs Currently Available on Records* was published by the Archive of American Folksong, Library of Congress, Washington, in 1953.

The standard bibliography of non-Western music is Jaap Kunst, *Ethnomusicology*, 3rd ed. (The Hague, 1959). A bibliography of current publications appears in each issue of *Ethnomusicology*, journal of the Society for Ethnomusicology.

CHAPTER II

The function of folk music in society is discussed by George Herzog in the articles, "Song," in Funk and Wagnall's *Standard Dictionary of Folklore and Mythology* (New York, 1949) and in a series by Bruno Nettl in the various issues of *Etude*, 1956–57. A short book by Russell Ames, *The Story of American Folk Song* (New York, 1955), gives a picture of American history as it appears in folk songs but deals only with the British tradition and makes little mention of the musical side of folk songs.

The variety and the common features of musical structure in European folk song are illustrated in an anthology, *Europäischer Volksgesang*, by Walter Wiora (Cologne, 1953). There is no book in English which discusses the musical aspects of folk music in detail; in German there is one, though it is already somewhat obsolete: Werner Danckert, *Das europäische Volkslied* (Berlin, 1939).

Primitive music has fared better, for there are several general accounts which cover all of the world's areas. Marius Schneider, "Primitive Music," in vol. 1 of the *New Oxford History of Music* (London, 1957) and Bruno Nettl, *Music in Primitive Culture* (Cambridge, Mass., 1956) illustrate two opposing viewpoints. Several books by Curt Sachs contain large sections on primitive music which show a third approach and tie their subject matter to European cultivated music in a unique way: *The Rise of Music in the Ancient World* (New York, 1943); *Rhythm and Tempo* (New York, 1953); and *World History of the Dance* (New York, 1937), which also, of course, discusses the relationship of primitive music to the dances of non-Western cultures.

Theories on the origin of music, relevant to a study of primitive music, are discussed in Siegfried Nadel, "The Origins of Music," *Musical Quarterly,* XVI (1930), 531–546. A survey of primitive and folk instruments is included in Curt Sachs, *The History of Musical Instruments* (New York, 1940).

CHAPTER III

Alan P. Merriam, "Music in American Culture," *American Anthropologist* 57:1173–78, 1955, surveys briefly the unique structure of our musical life. Alan Lomax, *The Folk Songs of North America in the English Language* (New York, 1960) is mainly a collection of songs but includes important introductory comments about the nature of American folk music.

CHAPTER IV

Several survey studies of North American Indian music have been published. Helen H. Roberts, *Musical Areas in Aboriginal North America* (New Haven, 1936) and Bruno Nettl, *North American Indian Musical Styles* (Philadelphia, 1954) are the most recent. Among the collections of music without musicological discussion are *The Indians' Book* by Natalie Curtis-Burlin (New York, 1907) and the many books by Frances Densmore published by the Bureau of American Ethnology. The most important of Densmore's books are *Chippewa Music* (Washington, 1910); *Choctaw Music* (1943); *Northern Ute Music* (1922); *Papago Music* (1929); and *Teton Sioux Music* (1918). These also represent five distinct musical styles.

Among the studies of individual tribes, styles, and aspects of Indian music, the following are representative: Alice C. Fletcher, *The Hako* (Washington, 1904); George Herzog, "A Comparison of Pueblo and Pima Musical Styles," *Journal of American Folklore,* XLIX (1936), 283–417, and "The Yuman Musical Style," *Journal of American Folklore,* XLI (1928), 183–231; David P. McAllester, *Peyote Music* (New York, 1949); Bruno Nettl, "Musical Culture of the Arapaho," *Musical Quarterly,* XLI (1955), 325–331, and "The Shawnee Musical Style," *Southwestern Journal of Anthropology,* IX (1953), 277–285; Helen H. Roberts, *Form in Primitive Music* (New York, 1933); and Edward Sapir, "Song Recitative in Paiute Mythology," *Journal of American Folklore,* XXIII (1910), 455–472.

The relationship of music to other aspects of culture is discussed from various points of view in the following: George Herzog, "Music in the Thinking of the American Indian," *Peabody Bulletin,* May, 1938, pp. 1–5, and "Plains Ghost Dance and Great Basin Music," *American Anthropologist,* XXXVII (1935), 403–419; David P. McAllester, *Enemy Way Music* (Cambridge, Mass., 1954); and Willard Rhodes, "Acculturation in North American Indian Music," Sol Tax, ed., in *Acculturation in the Americas* (Chicago, 1952). Willard Rhodes, "North American Indian Music, a Bibliographic Survey of Anthropological Theory," *Notes,* X (1952), 33–45, classifies the many ways in which Indian music has been approached.

CHAPTER V

The ballad texts are listed, described, and annotated in four standard bibliographic works: Francis James Child, *The English and Scottish Popular Ballads* (5 vols. in 3; New York, 1957); Tristram P. Coffin, *The British Traditional Ballad in North America* (Philadelphia, 1951); Malcolm G. Laws, Jr., *Native American Balladry* (Philadelphia, 1951) and *American Balladry from British Broadsides* (Philadelphia, 1957).

A large number of printed collections are available; only a few are mentioned here, some of which contain material outside the Anglo-American tradition, particularly Negro folk songs: Benjamin A. Botkin, *The American Play-party Song* (Lincoln, Neb., 1937); Byron Arnold, *Folksongs of Alabama* (University, Alabama, 1950); Phillips Barry, Fannie H. Eckstrom, and Mary W. Smith, *British Ballads from Maine* (London, 1929); Samuel P. Bayard, *Hill Country Tunes* (Philadelphia, 1944), a collection of fiddle and fife tunes; Arthur Kyle Davis, *Traditional Ballads of Virginia* (Cambridge, Mass., 1929); Helen H. Flanders, *Ancient Ballads Traditionally Sung in New England* (4 vols., *Philadelphia,* 1960–); Emelyn E. Gardner and Geraldine J. Chickering, *Ballads and Songs of Southern Michigan* (Ann Arbor, 1939); George Pullen Jackson, *White Spirituals of the Southern Uplands* (Chapel Hill, 1933); George Korson, *Coal Dust on the Fiddle* (Philadelphia, 1943); John A. and Alan Lomax, *Cowboy Songs* (New York, 1938); Vance Randolph, *Ozark Folksongs* (Columbia, Mo., 1946–50); Franz Rickaby, *Ballads and Songs of the Shanty-Boy* (Cambridge, Mass., 1926); Ruth Crawford Seeger, *American Folk Songs for Children* (New York, 1948); and the most important, Cecil J. Sharp, *English Folk Songs from the Southern Appalachians* (London, 1932).

Much has been published in the way of criticism, analysis, and theory. Only a few items, indicating the different directions of research, are given here: Phillips Barry, *Folk Music in America* (New York, 1939); Samuel P. Bayard, "Decline and Revival of Anglo-American Folk Music," *Midwest Folklore,* V (1955), 69–77, and "Prolegomena to a Study of the Principal Melodic Families of British-American Folk Songs," *Journal of American Folklore,* LXIII (1950), 1–44, both of which approach the entire body of Anglo-American folk music and treat it as a musical unit; Bertrand H. Bronson, "The Morphology of the Ballad Tunes," *Journal of American Folklore,* LXVII

(1954), 1–14; Sigurd B. Hustvedt, *A Melodic Index of Child's Ballad Tunes* (Berkeley, 1936); Bruno Nettl, "The Musical Style of English Ballads Collected in Indiana," *Acta Musicologica*, XXVII (1955), 77–84; Cecil J. Sharp, *English Folk Song, Some Conclusions* (London, 1907); Evelyn Kendrick Wells, *The Ballad Tree* (New York, 1950). By far the most important study of the music of British ballads is Bertrand Harris Bronson, *The Traditional Tunes of the Child Ballads* (Princeton, N. J., vol. I, 1959).

An excellent survey of collecting and scholarship is D. K. Wilgus, *Anglo-American Folksong Scholarship Since 1898* (New Brunswick, N. J., 1959).

CHAPTER VI

A large body of literature on American Negro music exists, but much of it cannot be recommended from the point of view of authenticity and scholarship. Among the collections, Edward A. McIlhenny, *Befo' de War Spirituals* (Boston, 1933), N. I. White, *American Negro Folk-Songs* (Cambridge, Mass., 1928), and George Pullen Jackson, *White and Negro Spirituals* (New York, 1954) are useful. In the field of description and theory, these are representative: E. M. von Horbostel, "American Negro Songs," *International Review of Missions*, XV (1926), 748ff.; George Pullen Jackson, "The Genesis of the Negro Spiritual," *American Mercury*, XXVI (1932), 243–248; Guy B. Johnson, "The Negro Spiritual, a Problem in Anthropology," *American Anthropologist*, XXXIII (1931), 157–171; Guy B. Johnson and H. W. Odum, *The Negro and his Songs* (Chapel Hill, 1925); Henry E. Krehbiel, *Afro-American Folksongs* (New York, 1914); Rudi Blesh, *Shining Trumpets* (New York, 1946); Richard A. Waterman, "African Influences on American Negro Music," in Sol Tax, ed., *Acculturation in the Americas* (Chicago, 1952), and "Hot Rhythm in Negro Music," *Journal of the American Musicological Society*, I (1948), 24–37. Bruno Nettl, *Music in Primitive Culture* (Cambridge, Mass., 1956) includes a chapter outlining the relationship between African and New World Negro music.

The literature on the folk music of other immigrant groups to the United States is much smaller. George Korson, *Pennsylvania Songs and Legends* (Philadelphia, 1949), includes some relevant material. A few publications are entirely devoted to non-British European immigrants: C. G. Peterson, *Creole Songs from New Orleans* (New Orleans, 1909); Bruno Nettl and Ivo Moravcik, "Czech and Slovak Songs Collected in Detroit," *Midwest Folklore*, V (1955), 37–49; and Bruno Nettl, "The Hymns of the Amish, an Example of Marginal Survival," *Journal of American Folklore*, LXX (1957), 323–328, which also gives other literature on German-American folk music.

CHAPTER VII

The following important collections of European folk music are perhaps relevant to his chapter: Béla Bartók, *Hungarian Folk Music* (London, 1931); Béla Bartók and Albert B. Lord, *Serbo-Croatian Folk Songs* (New York, 1951); Franz Magnus Böhme, *Altdeutsches Liederbuch* (Leipzig, 1877);

Ludwig Erk and Franz Magnus Böhme, *Deutscher Liederhort* (Leipzig, 1859–1872); Eleanor Hague, *Latin American Music, Past and Present* (Santa Anna, Calif., 1934); Boris Kremenlief, *Bulgarian-Macedonian Folk Music* (Berkeley and Los Angeles, 1952); Ilmari Krohn, *Suomen Kansan sävelmiä* (Helsinki, 1893–1912); A. E. Launis, *Lappische Juoigos-Melodien* (Helsinki, 1908); Elsa Mahler, *Altrussische Volkslieder aus dem Pecoryland* (Basel, 1951); John Meier, ed., *Deutsche Volkslieder mit ihren Melodien* (Leipzig, 1935–); Felipe Pedrell, *Cancionero musical popular español* (Barcelona, 1948).

Chapter VIII

This field has hardly been touched in theoretical and scholarly literature. Some statements by professional folk singers are relevant here, however: T. Anthony and Burl Ives, "Wayfaring Minstrel," *Etude,* LXIII (1945), 688; and John Jacob Niles, "My Precarious Life in the Public Domain," *Atlantic,* CLXXXII (1948), 129–131. Biographical information on folk singers is available in Ray M. Lawless, *Folksingers and Folksongs in America* (New York, 1960).

Chapter IX

The methods of studying folk and primitive music are outlined by Jaap Kunst, *Ethno-Musicology* (The Hague, 3d ed. 1959), and in Chapter 7 of Glen Haydon, *Introduction to Musicology* (New York, 1941), also in several of the descriptions of primitive music listed in Chapter II. Some special problems in this field are treated in Bertrand H. Bronson, "Mechanical Help in the Study of Folk Song," *"Journal of American Folklore,* LXII (1949), 81–86; George Herzog, "Speech-Melody and Primitive Music," *Musical Quarterly,* XX (1934), 452–466, and "Musical Typology in Folksong," *Southern Folklore Quarterly,* I (1937), 48–55.

Collecting techniques are discussed by Bruno Nettl, "Recording Primitive and Folk Music in the Field," *American Anthropologist,* LVI (1954), 1101–1102; and in several short publications by the International Folk Music Council: *Memorandum on Cataloguing and Classification of Sound Recordings of Folk Music* (London, 1955) and *Manual for Folk Music Collections* (London, 1951). The I.F.M.C. has also published a pamphlet, *Notation of Folk Music* (London, 1952), which surveys the available methods and makes recommendations. A guide to general research materials is Bruno Nettl, *Reference Materials in Ethnomusicology* (Detroit, 1961).

Chapter X

A scholarly survey of the uses of folk music in cultivated music is Walter Wiora, *Europäische Volksmusik und abendländische Tonkunst* (Kassel, 1957). A famous composer's view is presented in Ralph Vaughan Williams, *National Music* (London, 1959).

INDEX

The fact that in the United States the top 6% of wealth-holding families own 57% of the total net family wealth seems to run counter to the American ideal of equal opportunity. Ronald Chester's pertinent and provocative advocacy of wealth taxation reform addresses such important issues as economic growth, fairness, and the redistribution of wealth, and often challenges the assumptions of Reaganomics.

In *Inheritance, Wealth, and Society* the author's insights on inheritance as a legal institution emerge from a consideration of the principles of classical and contemporary theorists. In his review of the historical foundations of the subject in England and the United States, Chester demonstrates that the native roots of a critical appraisal of inheritance can be found in nineteenth-century political and economic writings. He then proceeds to evaluate inherited wealth in terms of its costs and benefits to society and to assess the impact of inheritance on charity, creditors' rights, and criminality. In discussing the effect of the institution of inheritance on property crime, Chester develops the concept of "perceived relative deprivation" and suggests measures to diminish it, including changes in the tax and transfer payment systems.

Finally, the author discusses the reconciliation of the redistribution of wealth with economic growth. He points out that while many inheritance taxes have high nominal rates, their effective yields have been relatively low, reducing their usefulness as a distributive device. A form of wealth transfer taxation is cautiously proposed as a more effective and equitable solution. "The rich rather than the middle class should bear the brunt of redistribution aimed at reversing the trend toward greater inequality," Chester forthrightly asserts. "Within this group, the increased tax burden should fall to the extent possible on inherited rather than earned wealth.... The wealthy must realize that unless they, like the rest of us, are ready to accept reasonable sacrifices, even a modified capitalism may not survive."

Inheritance, Wealth, and Society is a closely reasoned, original contribution to the debate on wealth and poverty in America.

INHERITANCE,
WEALTH,
AND SOCIETY

INHERITANCE,

WEALTH,

AND SOCIETY

Ronald Chester

INDIANA UNIVERSITY PRESS
Bloomington

Portions of this book are based on articles that originally appeared in
Indiana Law Journal, Crime and Delinquency, and *Rutgers Law Review.*

Manufactured in the United States of America

Library of Congress Cataloging in Publication Data

Chester, Ronald, 1944-
  Inheritance, wealth, and society.

  Bibliography: p.
  Includes index.
  1. Inheritance and succession. 2. Inheritance and
succession—United States. 3. Wealth. 4. Wealth—
United States. 5. Liberalism. I. Title.
HB715.C48   330'.16   81-48082
ISBN 0-253-33009-2   AACR2
1 2 3 4 5 86 85 84 83 82

To Charles G. and Mary Carol Chester,
Nia and Caben Chester, Hazel H. Young, and to the
memory of Clarence P. McClelland.

Contents

Preface

My first eighteen years were spent in Republican Illinois where I was raised on comfortable bourgeois notions of property, inheritance, and individual rights. The last eighteen have been spent largely in the Eastern cities, where the struggles of America's disadvantaged are every day apparent. This book is an attempt to reconcile the intellectual conflicts such a juxtaposition produces and to establish a new liberal synthesis for an age of scarcity. It is also an attempt to reconcile what I now know about America with the dream of a free and open society on which I was raised and whose appeal I still cherish.

The institution of inheritance involves one of the most emotional and characteristic processes of family life—the gift of one generation on earth to its children. At the same time, it seems unfair that some children should be born so much more privileged than others. Despite my concern with this structural inequality in American life, I realized in writing this book that overall equality of result, promoting as it would a "gray" society, is not the answer. America's equal opportunity ideology is a powerful one despite the woeful gap between the nation's professed ideals and the reality of its people's lives.

In approaching the problem of wealth concentration through inheritance, I relied heavily on my training and exprience in American intellectual history. Thus, this is chiefly a book examining the expressed attitudes of literate elites. My background left me confident that the notions of these elites were mirrored both in social thought and in political action. Whether such ideas were causative in any sense, or merely reflective of the ideas of mass society, seems relatively unimportant in the long run. Rather, their importance lay in the attempt to articulate society's internal divisions over these controversial topics. Whether it leads or follows popular opinion, such an articulation organizes strands of social thought into the coherence necessary for effective political action.

Even without examining in detail the link between theory and particular actions, writing the intellectual history of an institution over centuries imposes a substantial burden on the historian. Since he will be generalizing from self-selected sources, the historian must be aware not only of his own intellectual framework, but also of the implicit goal of his labors: why he wrote the book.

The framework from which I write is not one suspicious of generalization. In fact, like Morton Horwitz and Lawrence Friedman, I believe generalization is what gives history meaning. My own belief, moreover, is that history is an art: an imaginative recreation of the past from glimmers of what people have thought and done. I leave detailed examination of discrete subjects to the social scientists.

In essence, my goals are relatively straightforward. I want America to move decisively toward fulfilling the bourgeois ideology that gave its institutions meaning: one that moves toward insuring equal starting places for its children. This is a centrist goal, positioned between libertarianism on one hand and ends-egalitarianism on the other. Whether, as I hope, I state these views fairly before critiquing them, only the reader can ultimately judge. In any event, I do not believe history requires an objectivity that takes no position.

As I wrote the book, my conviction grew that that history was a particularly good way of illuminating the matrix of problems enveloping inheritance. Because the institution has not been rigorously questioned since the Great Depression, my discovery of earlier generations' profound ambivalence toward inheritance should serve as a reminder that our current notions about the institution may have no more permanence than any others. When one discovers that an important American intellectual tradition considered inheritance dispensable at legislative whim, one is apt to view the current enthusiasm for the institution both with caution and with deeper understanding.

Acknowledgments

The story of this book begins in 1969, a year in which America, including Columbia University and its students, was in turmoil. In this year, among other things, I was swept up in the Columbia "bust," worked for a major Wall Street law firm, and married my wife, Nia. At Columbia, I saw the fabric of my safe society tearing, while on Wall Street, I tried to concentrate on improving the language of $50 million trust funds.

At Columbia, two teachers helped me piece together what I was seeing. The first was George Cooper, a provocative estate and gift tax teacher who always asked "why" instead of merely showing me "how." The second was Leon Radzinowicz, the British criminologist who indulged my interest in the anthropology of crime and invited me to Cambridge, England, for a fellowship year upon my graduation.

At Cambridge in 1971, I made an early attempt to draw connections between inherited wealth and crime in the paper required for the Diploma in Criminology. A few years after returning to the States, I found myself in law teaching, a profession which gave me the opportunity to write down more of what I was thinking. Two articles in *Crime and Delinquency* spun out my Cambridge work, while two later articles in law reviews helped me synthesize my ideas about inheritance itself. When I was asked in 1979–80 to visit Indiana University Law School, Bloomington, as Foskett Professor of Estates and Trusts, I saw that it was time to make a final synthesis of my work to date. The Law School kindly provided me with research assistant Mark Smith and the light second-semester teaching load necessary to get the project under way. The outstanding Indiana University library provided sources as the project progressed.

As this brief narrative indicates, a number of people and institutions helped nurture and sustain me while my ideas developed. I would here like to thank some not already named. These include the Ford Foundation for my year at Cambridge, and the National Endowment for the Humanities for a year of research and study as Fellow in Law and Humanities at Harvard early in my teaching career. The Harvard University Libraries were a source of continual replenishment. The New England School of Law assisted me in ways too numerous to count, always encouraging my writing, despite its non-traditional nature. New England Law also provided me with an excellent research assistant, Glenn Nathan Solomon, whose intellectual courage and critical skills made this a better book.

At Indiana, I received a splendid, almost line-by-line critique of my introduction from legal historian Dirk Hartog and additional help from Associate Dean John Baker. At home my talented wife, Dr. Nia Lane Chester, gave unstintingly of her love and understanding when my own courage failed. She and my delightful son Caben provided the happy family life without which truly reflective work is nearly impossible. Of the numerous typists who have helped me, Pamela Lane at Indiana, and Brenda Hunt and Paula Flanagan at New England deserve special mention.

I hope the quality of this book in some way reflects all the kindness and assistance I have received; those who offered this help are, of course, in no way responsible for any errors I have made. Finally, I hope readers will indulge my use, in general, of masculine pronouns for simplicity, though pronouns of either gender would do as well.

INHERITANCE,
WEALTH,
AND SOCIETY

1

Introduction:
Inheritance and Wealth in America

Inheritance—the process of succession to real and personal property at its holder's death—is an institution common to all Western societies. As an ordering of the intergenerational transfer of wealth, it often helps stabilize families and groups. So long as the uneven distribution of wealth which inheritance encouraged was associated with the political legitimacy of chiefs, kings, and lords who offered governance and protection in return for its privileges, the institution could also be viewed as a stabilizing force in society as a whole.

This book focuses on both the tensions and opportunities associated with the continued tolerance for inheritance as a concentrator of wealth, following the triumph of Western capitalism in the nineteenth century. Once wealth became concentrated in an economic elite without the legitimizing cloak of political power, the transmission of wealth between generations of elite families raised new and markedly different issues. This concentration created private centers of power which could avoid direct political accountability for the ways in which their wealth was used. On the other hand, freedom from public political pressures allowed this elite to use inherited wealth for socially beneficial ventures like charity without fear of political crosswinds.

This book is aimed primarily at America's public decision- and policy-makers: judges, legislators, administrators, politicians, and their assistants. In writing it I have assumed a "best case" hypothesis:

that the majority of these decision-makers are receptive to ideas about social change, provided they receive adequate and convincing information. Though there are often connections between wealth and political power, countervailing democratic pressures also exist in the decision-making process. These pressures can probably be brought to bear most effectively where the legitimacy of the wealth involved is most questionable. Since inheritance is chief among these areas of questionable legitimacy, it was chosen as the focus of this book.

Since many in my audience may be American lawyers and other technocrats uncomfortable with long-term planning, I might be expected to present them with discrete problems for technical solution. Quite to the contrary, my hope is to provoke these public elites to engage in an analysis of the institution of inheritance in all its aspects. By identifying and defining the parameters of this institution and then by examining effects that a projected change might have at points where it interacts with other social institutions and groups, we can make rational choices in society's policies related to inheritance. Once we discern the scope of the American institution of inheritance and decide to change certain of its characteristics (through legislation, regulation, judicial decision, or executive fiat), we should examine the effects these will have *wherever* this institution intersects with other aspects of American life. Thus if we wish to change a section of the federal estate and gift tax code, we should examine not only its effects on capital formation but also its less obvious relationships, such as with property crime.

Admittedly, institutional analysis in this broad sense is not a style comfortable to many of my target audience, particularly its lawyers. Many lawyers in my experience seek to narrow a problem through abstract formulation and to apply their skills to its technical solution. This book provides a different way of thinking about problems, though not anything really so neat and simple as a model. It is not a book chiefly about solutions, but rather about a far greater difficulty in our pragmatic, technocratic society— it is a book about getting the questions right.

INSTITUTIONS AND THEIR EFFECTS

A working definition of institution is the first step in our journey. A straightforward one which may serve is "Institutions are only ways of doing things."[1] More precisely, one must focus on the clusters or groups of complex behavior patterns within a culture which together make up the social structures of the society.[2] If one of these clusters has a high degree of specificity and internal cohesiveness—thus becoming an established practice, law or custom—it is an institution.[3]

Institutions are the *relational* patterns manifested by groups. Thus in abstracting the institution from the group which contains it, one can discover the common pattern displayed by an indefinite number of groups. If we are interested in a common institution like inheritance, we can observe its manifestations in a vast number of family groups. One may look at the larger society, therefore, as a system of such institutions, forming the basis for a complete way of life.[4]

An institution itself is a system; individuals, social groups, their artifacts, and typical behavior are the sets of variables constituting it. Together with its environment such a system forms what sociologists call an absolute system. This absolute system can only affect things within its "reach," within what sociologists call its available environment. Two relevant available environments exist for the institution of inheritance: the society of which an institution is the most complex part, and the culture within which both are immersed.[5]

This book studies the institution of inheritance in its evolutionary, dynamic state: in the changing ways that it organizes folkways and laws into systems serving a variety of social functions. At different levels of abstraction, both inheritance and the subsystem of probate courts that administer it are institutions. For purposes of clarification, however, one might term the probate courts a subinstitution of inheritance, just as Harvard University is a subinstitution of education.[6]

When considering change, one must first consider the effects of a change in a subinstitution on its parent, on other subinstitutions of the parent, and on its own subinstitutions, if any. When the new status of both parent institution and its component parts is thus defined, one can look at the effects of this changed status on other institutions in society. For example, one might look at the effects that altered housing patterns would have on the family or on education possibilities in the community.

Economists tell us that economic institutions such as inheritance are revised when it appears desirable for individuals or groups to undertake the costs of such changes; they hope to "capture some profit" which is unattainable under the old arrangement. Thus we change an institutional arrangement if the expected net gains exceed the expected costs.[7] With respect to inheritance, under the approach used in this book, we should consider gains and costs not only for related institutions (such as those involving property rights and capital formation) but also for all the institutions making up the rest of the available environments for inheritance, including those associated with crime and social unrest.

INHERITANCE AND WEALTH DISTRIBUTION IN THE UNITED STATES

It is no surprise to thoughtful people that the United States has a highly unequal distribution of wealth, at least as compared with the egalitarian components of its social ideology. Recent estimates indicate that the top 6% of wealth-holding families own 57% of total net family wealth, while the lowest 28% own very little indeed.[8] Further, the top 1% of wealth-holders held about 27% of this wealth in 1972, a figure which has remained nearly constant in the postwar years.[9] Analysts have recently admitted, moreover, that the figures for those in the top 1% are substantially underestimated due to the exclusion from estate tax returns of most wealth held in trust.[10]

Since World War I there has been some consensus in America that inheritance is responsible for much of this concentration of wealth and that such concentration has bad effects as well as good.[11] The result has been estate and inheritance taxes at both the federal and state levels.[12]

While many of these taxes have high nominal rates, their effective yields have been relatively low, nullifying their usefulness as a device to redistribute wealth.[13] Economist Lester Thurow has suggested that this gap is politically motivated, at once salving the popular demand for high taxes on inherited wealth and the demands of the politically powerful rich that they should not be forced to reduce their capital holdings substantially.[14] James Brittain of the Brookings Institution has established a statistical connection between inheritance and unequal wealth distribution, thus illuminating the need to raise the effective rates of inheritance tax toward their nominal levels if we wish to alter this inequality.[15]

Even assuming the nexus between inheritance and unequal wealth distribution, we are faced with at least two questions: first, is it desirable to remedy this unequal distribution, and if so, are once-in-a-lifetime death taxes the way to accomplish the change?

Richard Wagner is a leading foe of Brittain and Thurow on such issues. While freely admitting inequalities of wealth and income, he believes that since people often choose benefits other than material ones, wealth distribution figures overestimate the actual inequalities in life. Presumably, he is talking about forms of "psychic income." He also notes that the figures leave out wealth implicit in such schemes as Social Security. Moreover, he assumes that a degree of material inequality is inevitable and even desirable: the "focus of concern" should be not the amount of inequality, but the rate of mobility on the income scale.[16]

Wagner argues that much of the support for wealth transfer taxation, including that on inheritance, has been stimulated by the belief or fear that a market economy tends naturally to produce a cumulative concentration of wealth because of the compounding of interest. This belief stimulates a demand for the estate tax to offset a concentration process in which "the rich get richer and the poor get poorer." Wagner believes that since fortunes accumulate at more than the average rate of return for the economy, the compound-interest explanation is invalid. Furthermore, such taxation, while putting some penalty on existing wealth-holders, puts a more serious obstacle in the path of those who are poorer but might want to become wealthy. In short, Wagner assumes, these individuals will not take the risks necessary to become wealthy because high progressive taxation of both estates and income stymies their incentive.[17]

The Wagner thesis rests on several challengeable assumptions. His belief in the freedom of individual choice within a highly developed economy is based on the classical economic assumption of a free and competitive market. Wagner's intellectual ancestors are Bentham and Ricardo; as Veblen cautioned at the nineteenth century's close, such model-building is a lifeless abstraction, divorced from human experience. It is a priori and theoretical, rather than a posteriori and empirical.

One may fairly raise the following questions with Wagner: Considering their subsistence needs and their often poor education, are those in lower socioeconomic classes in a position to make such choices as Wagner suggests? By contrast, are the middle and upper-middle classes, with their emphasis on personal achievement, actu-

ally deterred from taking risks by high progressive rates of taxation?
If so, are high nominal but low effective taxation rates a disincentive?
And even if progressive income taxation did stymie incentive, is an
achiever and risk-taker truly concerned by *death* taxes?

Again, Wagner is disregarding experience; it seems naive to
assume both that the lower socioeconomic classes can take the risks
necessary for wealth accumulation and that high death tax rates,
which exist only on paper, will deter those who can take such risks.
What empirical evidence there is suggests that the potential middle-
class risk-taker is influenced far more by the achievement that his
lifetime wealth accumulation represents than by the wealth itself.[18]
Finally, the successful risk-taker seems relatively unconcerned by
the effects of taxation upon his accumulated fortune at death; if a
prime motive of wealth accumulators had been to leave more property to their successors, history would have revealed far more lifetime transfers before 1976, when the gift tax rate was substantially
lower than the tax rate on estates.[19] Thurow argues that, despite the
classical model, the accumulation of large fortunes is largely accidental. High rates of return may persist in a given market over time
because of business biases toward internal investment. Thus, contrary to free market theory, the goal of profit maximization is subser-
vient to that of maintaining economic power by direct control over
investment assets. For this reason, capital invested in a market in this
sort of disequilibrium may produce more than a 30% rate of return.
Since there is imperfect information available to secure an expected
rate of return on an investment within each risk range, the selection
of an investment, according to Thurow, simulates a lottery. Investors
"bet" on some nonquantifiable factors of an investment, with some
"winning big" and others "losing big" in a random way.[20]

If Thurow is correct that the accumulation of wealth by a given
individual is largely accidental, an annual or semiannual tax on net
worth is as acceptable a way of taxing this "luck,"[21] as the death tax
is of taxing the luck of inheritance. Since economists agree that a
periodic net worth tax is a more efficient way of taking wealth from
top wealth-holders than the once-in-a-lifetime death levy, the acceptance of Thurow's philosophical basis for the taxation of wealth, if
given effect, could move significantly toward reducing inequality to
a politically desired level. While effective in redistributing wealth,
the net worth tax, unlike the death levy, taxes directly those

"earned" assets which are left after imposition of the income tax. Perhaps it is the unwillingness to impose a double levy on annual earnings which has caused the United States to avoid such a tax, although many Western European democracies have already imposed one.[22] If all Western nations come to view the accumulation of wealth as accidental in the same way inheritance is, then those desiring wealth redistribution might concentrate on the most effective tax to remedy such an imbalance, without concern for the possible disincentive effects of taxing a given revenue source. A 2% net worth tax on the $2 trillion dollars of privately held wealth in the United States in 1976 would have produced $40 billion for the Treasury, compared with about $5 billion produced by estate and gift taxes. If directly redistributed, this revenue would have been more than enough to raise all families above median wealth figures.[23]

TOWARD EQUALIZING LIFE'S STARTING PLACES

Clearly, strengthening inheritance taxes and/or imposing a net worth tax would produce substantial additional revenues, which could be used to redistribute wealth. Even if this revenue were used elsewhere, such taxation could begin to equalize starting places for the new generation's children. But is it necessary to take from the rich in order to allow mobility under the American system? Will not our present economic mobility, as Wagner suggests, allow those individuals desiring and deserving of wealth to acquire it?

In a recent study for the Carnegie Council on Children, Richard DeLone focused on "a simple but far-reaching idea: that children have been assigned a key role in dealing with the deepest tension in American life, the conflict between economic and political liberalism."[24] Since economic liberalism led to concentrations of wealth and power for the successful, those less successful could realize the credo of political liberalism—that there should be the greatest possible equality—only through their children. This of course was an evasion and a pipe dream, putting pressures on the young to achieve what is often unachievable.[25]

According to DeLone, the promise of a more equal society implicit in the ideology of equal opportunity has not been fulfilled. Not only has the inequality of income and wealth remained stable since the founding of the Republic, but the American social structure seems no more fluid than that of other industrialized nations. Correspondingly, as Stephen Thernstrom found among the "other Bosto-nians," inequalities in the life chances associated with social class have displayed a "remarkable, almost eerie continuity" since the nation's early days.[26]

Mobility, within an individual's career as well as between gener-ations of a family, does not mirror what is "depicted in our social mythology." Thus, the probability that any single individual below the top 1% of wealth-holders can move into the top 1% is less than .00002,[27] and when mobility by individual effort is the criterion, only 20% of American males exceed the status of their fathers.[28] Most of this 20%, moreover, do not climb "many rungs up the social ladder,"[29] rendering it almost impossible to make the top 1%.

Sociologist Christopher Jencks put the issue directly in 1979: "If we define 'equal opportunity' as a situation in which sons born into different families have the same chances of success, our data show that America comes nowhere near achieving it."[30] On the other hand, "relatively few people seem to care whether sons born into different families have different chances of success." This contrast becomes an issue only "if the reasons for such differences are judged 'unfair or unjust.' "[31]

Jencks's analysis indicates a central reason for focusing on inheri-tance, despite other factors associated with both unequal opportu-nity and inequality of end result: inheritance is a philosophically vulnerable contributor to these social phenomena. As Jencks says, "[I]n contemporary America . . . inequality between families or indi-viduals [and thus inequalities in their life chances] is acceptable so long as it derives from 'merit' of some sort." He finds, however, little if any correlation between merit and individual or family success.[32] This is a suggestive conclusion for those intrigued by the association between unmerited inheritance and inequalities in life chances.

If unequal starting places, encouraged by the free inheritance of wealth, are associated with low levels of mobility, it seems only rea-sonable to inquire whether more equal starting places, occasioned by diminished inheritance, would better serve the desire for more equal outcomes without sacrificing the liberty of the competitors. In exam-ining this question, I will attempt to show that inheritance, a recog-nized hindrance to egalitarianism, is not even a necessary ingredient of libertarian society.

CONTENTS AND DIRECTIONS

Certain troubling effects of allowing substantial inheritances thus begin to emerge. The institution in its American form is intimately involved with the great disparities of wealth in the United States. It helps provide uneven starting places for our children, which are in turn associated with low social and economic mobility. As DeLone says, the "dynamics of our social structure are not likely to produce more equality of opportunity unless there is more equality to begin with."[33] This of course is the egalitarian perspective.[34] Economists like Wagner and Gordon Tullock[35] think Americans do not want or need equality; they are supported in this position by political philosophers of reputation, such as Friedrich Hayek and Robert Nozick.[36]

In the tradition of Veblen, I believe that we must first understand the historical, evolutionary form of an institution in order to establish an empirical baseline for prospective changes.[37] Thus chapter 2 will trace the development of the institution of inheritance before the twentieth century in Western European thought; chapter 3 will do the same for America. Chapter 4 examines in detail the twentieth-century debate about the fairness and utility of the institution.

Chapters 5, 6, and 7 examine the effects of inheritance as it presently exists on other institutions in American society. Though this impact is felt on many institutions, three are used as examples: charity, creditors' rights, and criminality. Chapter 5 deals with the impact of inheritance on charitable institutions. This is followed by an analysis of how "dead hand control" of these institutions can be modified by judicial means: the application of funds of a failed charitable trust or corporation to an allied charitable purpose through use of the *cy pres* power. In chapter 6 the impact of inheritance on creditors' rights is outlined: judicial and legislative changes are suggested for the "spendthrift trust" and associated doctrines that have sought to preserve family dynasties despite the legitimate claims of the beneficiaries' creditors.

In chapter 7 the book turns to broad, horizontal considerations which I feel should draw the attention of policy- and decision-makers: the effect of relatively untrammeled inheritance on institutions not usually associated with inheritance—criminality and the subinstitutions structured to cope with it. This chapter develops the concept of perceived relative deprivation and its effect on property crime. The final chapter recommends directions which legislators and administrators might take if they wish to reform inheritance laws in light of the problems raised in this book. These include changes in death taxation.

2

Inheritance in Western European Thought

Thinking about an institution requires both a working definition of it and an understanding of its place in the evolving cultural matrix of society. By inheritance I mean the process of succession to the property of a decedent, whether by operation of law or custom, or pursuant to the decedent's power to leave property by will. An heir's right of succession by law or custom is an ancient and powerful right rooted in kinship ties. It was an attribute of European feudal life, allowing family members to share that portion of their property vacated by a kinsman's death. The right of beneficiary to take property under a will is dependent on the legal power or right of the decedent to will this property to him. This latter right was recognized relatively recently in Western thought and has often been regarded as having been created for society's convenience.

The right of bequest was symbolic of the shift from feudal to individual conceptions of property in Western society. The will was by no means a universal institution, being unknown to the early law of Greece, India, Egypt, Babylon, and Israel. The testamentary conception built on by the Europeans had its origins in Roman law and was resurrected after feudalism through the influence of the Church.[1]

In England the customary right of testamentary disposition was recognized in very early times, but land—the main source of wealth

—could not be willed until after the Norman invasion and the establishment of feudal tenures. The Statute of Wills (1541)[2] declared the right of an individual to leave real property to whomever he pleased via a duly executed will. This statute confirmed a customary right long recognized for personal property.

Once established, the right of an individual to leave property outside the family and the right of the beneficiary to succeed to that property necessitated legal protection for disinherited family members. In Britain, primogeniture protected the eldest sons of landed decedents into the nineteenth century. Common law rights of dower and curtesy for surviving wives and husbands also existed; these eventually spawned statutory shares of the property for the surviving spouse. Children who were left out of wills were not protected directly, except those benefiting under primogeniture; however, wills of their parents were scrutinized strictly to ensure that they had not been left out unintentionally. One English rule derived from Roman law even stated that to cut off an heir "without a shilling" raised a presumption that the testator was legally incompetent to make a will. Thus conceptions of the family's right to the property of one of their dead were protected not only when the testator died with no will (intestate), but also in certain circumstances when he did express his last will. The right of the family or the beneficiary of a will to take the property of the dead in either of these situations is termed the right of inheritance in this book.

If the foregoing contributes to an understanding of how the term inheritance is used in this book, the task remains of placing the institution within the context of Western thought. It is not surprising that the weaving of this context begins with a look at the root institution of property; in any reasonable schema, inheritance must be seen as ancillary to property. It is ancillary because the ability of the property owner to control the devolution of property after his death (either via his presumed intent to benefit relatives through intestate succession or through his expressed testamentary intent) is not a necessary attribute of his right to enjoy that property while alive. Since Americans tend to entangle inheritance rights and property rights, it is worthwhile to remember this subordinate status for the former as the historical narrative that follows unfolds. One important point which emerges is that the more modern Western philosophers and legal thinkers have treated the two institutions quite differently;

they have with near uniformity provided property rights of the living far greater protection.

The remainder of this chapter attempts to explain how the institution of inheritance was conceived by Western European thinkers from the seventeenth through the nineteenth century. The treatment is necessarily selective, reviewing chiefly those writings that have significantly affected the American experience with inheritance. A few additional contributions have been included for contrast. The discussion begins with those thinkers who are most clearly post-feudal and modern. British thought is emphasized because of its direct influence on America. The chapter concludes with European thought of the nineteenth century, after which time America had clearly chosen its own course, and—for better or worse—was less subject to influence from abroad.

THE FOUNDATIONS OF PROPERTY AND INHERITANCE IN POST-FEUDAL BRITAIN

British notions of property in the seventeenth century were crystallized in the works of John Locke (1632–1704), particularly the *Two Treatises of Government* (c. 1690). Locke is generally credited by scholars with having developed the theory of revolutionary change used by the Whigs in the Glorious Revolution of 1688 and by the American colonists in the revolution of 1776. The Whigs employed the *Second Treatise* to establish the dominance of their Protestant bourgeois ideal over James II, whom they accused of violating the social compact with his people; Jefferson would use it likewise for the Americans against King George.[3]

Every man in Locke's view had an aboriginal right to the fruits of his own labor; his right was thus a natural one, ungrounded in social utility. The right to property possessed by man in the "state of nature" was not a civilly created one; it was a God-given right, in the exercise of which the individual *ought* to be protected from his neighbors so long as he did not unduly impinge on their property rights. Through a social contract between individual and state, Locke argued, people established a ruler to protect this and other fundamental rights.[4]

Some scholars have noted that the Protestant commercialism of his day influenced Locke to put the natural right of property on a higher plane than the right to life itself. This may have been to defend the legitimacy of existing institutions and the gains of the middle class against the social claims of radical democrats. On the other hand, he was affirming the social functions of individual property and labor being stressed by the rising bourgeoisie against the Church and nobility.[5]

Locke's concern with the inalienability of material property appears to have carried over into inheritance rights: "Every man is born with . . . a right," he wrote, "to inherit with his brethren, his father's goods." Thus a conqueror could not upsurp either the "property rights" or "descents" of those conquered, unless the conquered consented to this arrangement via a new social compact.[6] The status of "right" was not extended, however, to the English practice of allowing the first son to inherit all his father's land through primogeniture.[7] Nor was it extended to the power of bequest. However, there was recognition of a power to dispose of property as one wished "when his children are out of danger of perishing for want."[8]

When referring to rights associated with inheritance, Locke was clearly speaking of natural rights just as he was with lifetime property. He did not view inheritance rights as in any way less fundamental than other property rights. Thus the right of children to inherit their father's goods was not due to "common tacit consent" (which had neither been asked nor given), because this would make the right merely a positive and not a natural one. Since God planted in men a strong desire of propagating their kind and continuing themselves in their posterity, this gives the children a title to share in the "property" of their parents and a (natural) right to inherit their possessions. Likewise, the universality of the practice of inheritance makes it "reasonable to think the cause is natural."[9]

The strength of Locke's natural rights views of property and inheritance were amenable to notions widely held by the gentry and commercial classes of his century. Frank Coleman posits that Locke, associated as he was with these classes, used the language of natural law rhetorically to support their property rights. These classes had become comfortable with the language of natural law and used it indiscriminately to justify their wealth, both inherited and acquired.[10]

The foregoing is consistent with Locke's belief that the social compact assumed substantial social inequities. Those who sustained political institutions in Lockean society were the landed gentry, owners of enclosed land, and wealthy men of commerce. They were not, it appears, groups like "the Levellers," small freeholders and tradesmen who sought an enlarged sphere of political and religious liberty, a redistribution of the land of the gentry and nobility, and a shift of the burden of excise and land taxes from yeoman to landed gentry.[11]

Locke, however, was attempting to justify Whig views against attacks from both the nobility and the workers. Thus his views were not entirely consistent. Though preservation of an individual's property was the chief end of Lockean government, this was true only where "there is enough, and as good left in common for others." One would like to carry this argument further: if undue concentrations of wealth (via inheritance) eliminated such remaining "good property," the "established, settled, known law" could intercede to protect "the common good."[12] Though there was a natural right of property for those who attached their labor to it, if their leaving it to whom they pleased at death were to impinge on the acquisition of such property by others, Locke's concept might seem to require civil regulation of the right by which such property was acquired.

Locke wrote about civil limitations on inheritance itself in sections 72 and 73 of the *Second Treatise.* In these passages, Locke first addressed the father's power (not natural right) to pass property to the children, whether in the portions established under intestacy customs, or in those reflected in his expressed will. Thus the "possession of the father [was] the expectation and inheritance" of the children. However, the inheritance of an estate reached only those who would take it upon the conditions annexed to the land by the father in his contract with civil government. Thus it was "no natural tie or engagement, but a voluntary submission" to civil control. If the children were to "enjoy the inheritance of their ancestors," they had to submit to these civil conditions.

Still, we are carrying Locke too far if we attempt to see him as favoring wealth redistribution. Writing before the Industrial Revolution, he seems to have had little appreciation of the inordinate political power the possession of great wealth can give. Otherwise he would scarcely have placed political control in the hands of a property-owning minority, expecting them to exercise it impartially in the interests of all. If, as J. W. Gough writes, this part of his political theory seems by modern standards "naïve and inadequate," it was still "no more so than that of his contemporaries." Though contemporary Levellers like Rainborough were more consistently "modern," it was only in the second half of the nineteenth century that the importance of the economic factor in politics came generally to be understood.[13]

Even if Locke's occasional references to limits on property rights can be seen as political offerings to groups like the Levellers, they do leave a legacy with which Western Europe and America have felt it necessary to deal. In fact, much of the inconsistency in modern American thought may be traced ultimately to Locke's seeming ambivalence about limits on property. While C. E. Vaughan may be right that Locke believed redistribution of property to be "the grossest of usurpations, the most flagrant of wrongs,"[14] this must be read alongside Locke's view that if some persons were left with an insufficient amount of property, hoarding and amassing of fortunes might conflict with the law of nature.[15] Likewise, while asserting that "the Supreme Power cannot take from any man any part of his property without his consent," Locke approved taxation, apparently by viewing the consent of the majority as involving the tacit consent of the individual.[16]

Despite inconsistencies, Locke's essential views of property can be clarified by comparing him with other thinkers not subjected to the catalyst of the Industrial Revolution— men like St. Thomas Aquinas and Jean Jacques Rousseau. The former was much more explicit than Locke in showing that private property was not an ultimate category and that, whether it was the product of personal labor or the result of occupancy, it must be limited or conditioned by the needs of others.[17] Likewise, Rousseau moved beyond Locke by stating that there can be no genuine right of property (as distinguished from possession) except in the civil state. Further—and more radically—property must then be held on *whatever* conditions the state imposes. While Locke's main emphasis was on the political rather than the economic rights of man, Rousseau argued that man must submit to the direction of the general will in matters of property as in everything else.[18]

Locke's use of natural law to protect property against the state can be seen largely as a political reaction to the turmoil of the period. His occasional intimations of a civil right to control property raises for us the question of whether Locke considered inheritance a necessary institution for all time. Philosopher John Rawls thinks not.

Though the social contract in Locke's Britain had permitted the institution, this did not mean that future contracts had to. Apparently, any social contract was acceptable to Locke unless it was irrational or in violation of a duty to self or others. Thus a contract barring inheritance, if we take Locke at face value, might be fully as agreeable as the one that then existed; either could be seen as rational.[19]

Given his social class and the times, Locke apparently saw no need to draw out some of the implications about inheritance which his *Treatises* suggested. His juxtaposition of natural rights with those created by the social contract with civil government was essentially ambiguous. Certainly, it left room for his successors to divorce inheritance from property rights, rendering the former a civilly created adjunct of the latter. One matter that remained for later thinkers to resolve was whether, under a social contract permitting inheritance, the Lockean limits of rationality and adherence to duty were sufficient to prevent wealth accumulations that hindered equal opportunity.

EARLY MODERN BRITAIN: INHERITANCE AS CIVIL RIGHT

Writing at the turn of the eighteenth century, Jeremy Bentham, the first prominent Utilitarian, professed great esteem for Locke, seeing the calculus of "good" and "evil" in his moral philosophy as equivalent to the Utilitarian concepts of pleasure and pain. In political philosophy, however, Locke had (according to Bentham) "no clear view" of the "greatest happiness" principle.[20] Besides, Locke had professed natural rights views, which Bentham emphatically did not share.

Actually Thomas Hobbes is generally considered to have had more effect on the Utilitarians than Locke himself. Though believing, like Locke, in the natural right of property, Hobbes stated more clearly that *each* individual could bargain with government as to the protection of that right. Individuals, Hobbes thought, were essentially hedonistic egoists, and harmony of their interests could be created only through the discipline of centrally imposed (positivistic) law. This Hobbesian harmony of interests, which could only be achieved by central government, became the guiding principle of Utilitarianism: public happiness, or "the greatest good for the greatest number."[21]

Bentham, however, eschewed the natural rights rhetoric of both Hobbes and Locke. He began his philosophical career in 1776 with a stinging attack on the vague references to the "law of nature" in William Blackstone's *Commentaries on the Law of England* (1769). These were ways, says Bentham, "of intimating that a man is firmly persuaded of the truth of this or that moral proposition, though he either thinks he *need not*, or finds he cannot, tell why." Bentham's argument emphasized how particular interests had dictated the various formulations of the "law of nature," which when made concrete, were often flatly contradictory.[22]

Blackstone's preference for the general principles contained in the law of nature or in the common law, led him to use syllogisms and deductive logic to arrive at truth. Bentham, on the other hand, professed to prefer the scientific method of Newton, inducing general principles from the empirical data of experience. He, like the other Utilitarians, was not truly empirical, however. Seeing a correspondence between the laws of the natural and ethical world, Bentham assumed that value-free outcomes would arise from the working of the utility principle. In doing so, he was abstracting from experience instead of using it, constructing an a priori model whose invisible workings would dictate result regardless of the social conditions of the moment.[23] While one might argue that the principle of utility was based on the experience of Bentham's own era, it was hardly empirical to project the theory's usefulness into the future as a guiding principle for all time.

Very early in his career, Bentham made a vigorous attack on the ethical justification of the institution of inheritance and insisted upon the "unburthensomeness" of even heavy taxes upon it.[24] Later, in the *Principles of the Civil Code,* he summarized his position:

> When property by death of the proprietor ceases to have an owner, the law can interfere in its distribution, either by limiting in certain respects the testamentary power in order to prevent too great an accumulation of wealth in the hands of an individual; or by regulating the succession in favor of equality in cases where the deceased has left no consort, nor relation in the direct line, and has made no will. The question then relates to new acquirers who have formed no expectations; and equality may do what is best for all without disappointing any.[25]

While Bentham sought philosophical consistency in a neutral principle remote from the moral trappings of natural law, he in fact flirted with a "natural law" of utility. Blackstone, on the other hand, had no quarrel with natural law; in fact, he argued it was the basis on which the English common law stood. More particularly, he viewed property itself as a natural right, predating all civil institutions.[26] He sharply distinguished, however, the institution of inheritance, which he considered civilly created. By doing so Blackstone etched in the common law of both Britain and America the distinction toward which Locke had been groping.

Since Blackstone felt actual possession and the intention of keeping possession of property ceased at death, the property itself, which was based on such possession, also ceased at this time:

> For naturally speaking, the instant a man ceases to be, he ceased to have any dominion: else, if he had a right to dispose of his acquisitions one moment beyond his life, he would also have a right to direct their disposal for millions of ages after him: which would be highly absurd and inconvenient. But as [not allowing inheritance] would be productive of endless disturbances, the universal law of almost every nation has either given the dying person a power of continuing his property, by disposing of his possessions by will (or by succession).[27]

Blackstone's statement of the law was not only the cornerstone for British interpretations of the common law in the nineteenth century; it had a profound effect on American perceptions as well. Thus when Blackstone emphasized that the permanent or continuing right of property in the ancestor, as distinguished from his occupancy-derived lifetime right, "was no *natural,* but merely a civil right," this was to set the baseline for the discussion of inheritance in Britain and America for generations to come. Despite Western tolerance for the institution, we have never quite forgotten Blackstone's dictum: "Wills and testaments, rights of inheritance and succession, are all of them creatures of the civil or municipal laws, and accordingly are in all respects regulated by them. . . ."[28]

It is worthwhile noting, then, that while Bentham and Blackstone started from widely different conceptions of property, both considered inheritance a civil right, subject to government regulation. While both split off the right of inheritance from that of property in the tradition of Locke, Blackstone at least kept it an "important" right stressing the inconvenience of its removal. Bentham himself was clearly less impressed with the institution's utility, perhaps because he did not consider its parent institution, property, as natural or fundamental.

As British philosophers tore inheritance loose from its moorings in the right of property, their economist counterparts were free to consider both the practical effects of the institution and whether certain types of taxation or regulation were economically sound. Adam Smith, a contemporary of both Bentham and Blackstone, bore more relation to the great jurist than to the philosophical patriarch of classical economics. Many have seen his espousal of the "invisible hand" of the Free Market as simply another evocation of natural law. He certainly differed markedly from Bentham, claiming that "the care of universal happiness" was only the "business of God and not of Man."[29] Though he was early indoctrinated with the natural law philosophy of Francis Hutcheson and many of his discussions center around the "natural course" of specific economic activities, Smith was chiefly a moralist and liberal reformer.[30] Thus his adherence to natural law theories was sporadic.

Smith's chief contribution to economic philosophy was the discovery of an orderly and beneficent system operating behind the often cruel and haphazard society of eighteenth-century Britain. Natural laws which governed this "market" were those of individual enlightened self-interest and competition, which if allowed to operate freely would be harmonized by the "invisible hand" for the good of society. Thus every man, as long as he did not violate the laws of natural justice, was free to pursue his interest in his own way.[31]

Adam Smith accepted the basic property relations of British society. He did not feel that private property was fundamentally wrong; thus the institution could be tolerated, though reforms had to be undertaken to ensure its more equal distribution. For example, Smith proposed an end through civil law to the primogeniture and entail aspects of English inheritance which "beggared" the younger children in a landed family in order to keep the estate intact.[32]

While he did not desire to level all differences between social classes, Smith did feel it would be expedient and just to reduce the fortunes of certain individuals if the well-being of the majority could thereby be enhanced. Inheritance, as the product of impersonal market forces, could be regulated by a tax on the heir if it resulted in overenrichment of the few. Such a tax was sound because it did not hinder the ability of the beneficiary to pay the tax; however—and this reveals Smith's ambivalence about the institution—it would also diminish the capital necessary for the maintenance of productive labor.[33]

David Ricardo, the first prominent classical economist of the nineteenth century, was in fundamental disagreement with Adam Smith. He was very much in the Benthamite mold, analyzing society in a static, rather than dynamic, state. Thus the historical, sociological, and political discussions which fill the *Wealth of Nations* were missing in his works. While Smith had few rigid elements in his theoretic structure, Ricardo was a conceptualist, studying like a mathematician the economic mechanisms of society. Whereas Smith was empirical, looking chiefly at the society he knew and considering it as neither natural nor normal, Ricardo, like the early Utilitarians, tried to fashion abstract "laws" for all time.[34]

Ricardo's views on inheritance were typical of classical and neo-classical economic theory. He felt that taxing the institution dissipated capital wealth and checked its further accumulation:

> It should be the policy of governments to encourage a disposition to [increase their capital and income], and never to lay such taxes as will inevitably fall on capital: since by so doing, they impair the funds for the maintenance of labor, and thereby diminish ... future production.... In England this policy has been neglected, in taxing the probate of wills, in the legacy duty, and in all taxes affecting the transference of property from the dead to the living.[35]

Still, he was arguing against the utility of such taxation here, not whether taxing the institution through civil law would violate a natural right.

The individualism and conceptualism of both the Benthamites and the classical economists made them indifferent to social class. To these thinkers, competing individuals and not rival groups made up society. Social phenomena were thus explicable through the a priori logic of an individual, rather than through observable social fact. In this view social institutions like inheritance were contrivances to satisfy individual human wants; they had no life of their own. Society for Bentham as for Ricardo was a market, satisfying as many desires as possible at the least cost.

CONTINENTAL CONCEPTIONS OF PROPERTY AND INHERITANCE

The British Utilitarians proposed the greatest happiness principle—or utility—as the way to escape the belief that the laws of nature and normative principles were one. This stance, however, necessitated the abandonment of natural law as the ideal or "right," a position Immanuel Kant of Germany was plainly unwilling to take. Instead, Kant took a middle position, in which not all positive laws were "good" (natural) laws; until they were so rendered, however, they nonetheless had to be obeyed.

In concentrating on Kant's view of property and inheritance in this section, I realize that I am giving more credence to Kant as a political philosopher than have most scholars, at least in English-speaking countries. Apparently, the lack of importance attached to his political writings is connected with the awe in which his critical philosophy—as expounded in his three *Critiques*[36]—is generally held. As Hans Reiss writes, this encourages the greatly mistaken belief that his political philosophy is not crucial to Kant's thought. Not an "accidental by-product of his thought," Kant's political writings in fact "grow organically out of his critical philosophy."[37]

It may be going too far to call Kant the philosopher of the French Revolution, but his political thought, molded in part by the American Revolution, had a substantial impact on the French crisis. By asserting the independence of the individual in the face of authority, he placed the general concern of both revolutions—the problem of human freedom—at the very core of his thought.[38]

Kant was profoundly excited by the idea of the French Revolution. A portrait of Rousseau, the thinker who taught Kant respect for the common man, was the only adornment permitted in his house. Still, he differed with Rousseau in his interpretations of both "nature" and the "general will." In addition, it was his stated belief that his less cosmopolitan and decentralized fellow-countrymen were not ripe for a revolution such as Rousseau had inspired.[39]

If he was ultimately hesitant about revolution (except in the abstract), this may have been because Kant, like Locke, wrote before the Industrial Revolution. Thus he concentrated in a like way on the question of political equality, with little attention to its economic underpinnings.[40] In Kant's view, the uniform equality of human beings as subjects of the state was perfectly consistent with the utmost inequality in the degree of their possessions (including fortuitous external property). He saw nothing wrong with the dependence of the poor on the rich in a society where all were "equal as subjects before the law."[41]

Thus, Kant's thought had clearly not progressed as far as that of Rousseau concerning the connections between economic and political equality. However, Kant's strong influence on Hegel, and through Hegel on Marx,[42] carried his notions of individual freedom forward to the period when economic rather than political equality became paramount.

Kant's political theory was based on the assimilation and criticism of many thinkers other than Rousseau; these include Machiavelli, the natural law theorists, Locke, Hume, and Hobbes. His relation with Hobbes, the fount of Utilitarian thinking, is particularly interesting. He agreed with Hobbes, and not Rousseau, that the "state of nature" was the "war of the all against the all," not a state of perfection. Thus society civilized man. However, Kant rejected Hobbes's authoritarian view of sovereignty, his rationalism, and his belief that the cement of society was the common fear of sudden death. Yet, the political problem was the same for both—to turn a state of war into a state of order and peace through a rigorous argument based on an appeal to reason, unhampered by tradition.[43]

Both Kant and Hobbes believed that law is a command and must, by necessity, be enforced. However, in contrast to Hobbes, Kant is indebted to natural law and he believed in an immutable standard of right. It should be noted, however, that his view of natural right was more radical and revolutionary than that of traditional natural rights thinkers like Samuel Pufendorf.[44]

In emphasizing the rights of the individual, Kant set himself against every form of Utilitarianism. These rights—rather than social utility, the general happiness, or the common good—provided the foundation for morality and law. Insofar as any action, public or private, conflicted with these rights, Kant thought it was wrong *ipso facto,* regardless of how much good might result from it.[45] Thus Kant's principles of morality were formal, ruling out all references to the consequences of actions such as the attainment of happiness. If, for example, the pursuit of happiness is made a maxim of our actions, the human will is not autonomous—an insupportable proposition to Kant.[46]

To Kant, justice, or *Recht,* was known a priori by every individual. This differentiated his natural law philosophy from those who found natural law not within the self, but in God or Nature. Further, Kant's *Recht* did not stand for law in general, but only *right* principles of law—just principles providing the very basis for law and politics:[47] "Every action which enables the freedom of each individual's will to coexist with the freedom of everyone else in accord with a universal law is *right.*"[48]

Law to Kant was a part of morals. Thus positive laws had to be based on principles of justice, or natural law. One ought to obey them even if they were "bad" laws because they represented the duties of justice. The "letter of the law" represented what was actual law and had to be obeyed; this was distinguished, however, from the spirit of the law, which represented the legal ideal for which one should strive.[49]

Kant also found a duality between the ideal and the observable in the thought process itself. He described the two objects of thought as phenomena (those coming through the senses) and noumena (the objects of understanding). Thus objects like ethical, legal, or political thought, insofar as they were not matters of empirical knowledge (phenomena), were noumena. The faculty principally concerned with noumena, that is, with normative rather than descriptive thought, Kant called "pure practical reason." It made nonempirically based evaluations of what "ought to be," but had to share the mind with the sensible faculty, collecting the data of experience. Thus the mind of Kant was neither wholly Locke's *tabula rasa,* passively collecting the experience of the senses, nor that of idealists like Hegel or the American Transcendentalists, who believed that mind was the only reality, creating its own world regardless of experience.[50] Instead the Kantian mind had a balance of these qualities.

In line with this dualism, Kant saw possession of externals as of two different types: sensible (factual) and intelligible (normative). The latter—possession in the de jure sense—was what man called "property."[51] Inheritance was the transfer by the testator of this property to a survivor, through the consent of the will of both. The exchange of "Mine" and "Thine" took place "just when the Testator [ceased] to be."[52]

But how could there be a transition of property to the other person in the very moment the testator ceased to be? Certainly the property was not at that moment in actual, common possession.

What the successor had, said Kant, was not the property itself but the *right of choice* as to whether he would actually make the estate his own; thus his will as well as the testator's was involved at the moment of death. The successor had acquired no property *in fact* from the testator, but was in *juridicial* or *rational* possession of it. Since this possession was never interrupted, "the proposition *testamenta sunt juris naturae* [was] established beyond all dispute."[53]

However, the validity of testaments by natural right was capable of being sanctioned by the civil state, whenever such was instituted: "For," said Kant, "it is only the common will in the civil state that maintains the possession of the inheritance or succession, while it hangs between acceptance or rejection and specially belongs to no particular individual."[54] This transmission of possession of the property from the hand of the dead "does not alter the possibility of acquisition according to universal principles of Natural Right, although a civil constitution must be assumed to apply them to cases of actual experience."[55]

Rights like inheritance—external rights from our noumenal selves (in contrast to possession)—were possible only in civil society.[56] Thus this society could regulate the right, through compulsory taxation,[57] for example. In relation to external property, "the will of the legislator cannot be reproached."[58]

Kant was strongly against hereditary political privilege since it stood in the way of "talent, industry, and good fortune."[59] He also believed that government was justified in compelling prosperous citizens who had submitted to civil society to provide the means of preserving those "unable to provide themselves with even the most rudimentary necessities of nature."[60] It is not a difficult leap from these positions to one sanctioning redistribution of inherited economic privileges.

Kant's conception that inheritance was a natural right recognized and sanctioned by the civil state predominated on the Continent during the nineteenth century. Thus in France the Orthodox economists, including Maréschal and Stourm, ignored the view of the Utilitarians that the dead have no rights, asserting that the transmission of property by bequest or succession was an exercise of the will of the living. The Orthodox economists, however, were not above borrowing a page from Utilitarianism when it suited their purposes. One of their number, Faucher, argued that if the institution of inheritance did not exist, it would be necessary to invent it because it maximized happiness.[61]

René Stourm was typical of the Orthodox school. In 1893, his work on taxation took issue with John Stuart Mill and Sir William Harcourt, Chancellor of the Exchequer, on the very point of whether the dead had rights. If they did not, argued Stourm, it was of little consequence since in enforcing inheritance one was protecting the actual or presumed will of the *living* testator. Thus if the state could forbid inheritance it could forbid lifetime gifts as well. Besides, though the drafters of the French code were equivocal about the institution, they did agree that it was an invocation of the law of nature.[62]

Stourm's chief target was the Utilitarians. Mill had been joined by "the followers of Saint-Simon" in France in arguing that unearned income was unjust and that redistribution of wealth should be undertaken to provide for the greater good for the greater number. Stourm put forward several practical reasons why the institution should be maintained. First, he did not believe social goals should be obtained at the expense of established legal principles. Besides, the alternative social goals of work and savings were fostered by the institution itself. Since people wanted to leave their earnings to their children, they strove to accumulate wealth, thereby providing a stimulus for others to do so. In this way the capital of the nation was produced and maintained.[63]

UTILITARIANISM AND SOCIAL DARWINISM
IN LATE NINETEENTH-CENTURY BRITAIN

American ideas about inheritance, however, did not follow the French course as the nineteenth century wore on. Instead they adhered more closely to the sophisticated Utilitarianism of John Stuart Mill. Mill had been influenced by the Kantian movement away from the obsessive rationalism of the Enlightenment; this caused him to rebel against the barren, calculating model building of Bentham and his own father, James Mill.[64]

This rebellion, however, did not lead him into the acceptance of an Orthodox natural rights stance. Instead he developed a more positive, complex, and flexible brand of Utilitarianism. In doing so, he rejected not only natural rights, but also the a priori and dogmatic thinking of Hegel, the later Comte, and other Continental idealists who invariably cited the nonempirical character of logical and mathematical truths. By showing the purely inductive basis for deductive logic, he propounded a philosophy of experience to test truth.[65]

In his defense of liberty, Mill fashioned perhaps the most powerful argument ever made for the ideals of an open society and individual self-development. He believed social progress was possible only in a society in which no person, however humble, was precluded from making his contribution. A proponent of laissez-faire economics and positive government, he railed against the Continental intuitionists and idealists, with their dogmatic group-consciousness.[66] Viewing society as an atomistic aggregation of individuals, Mill had no use for the social compact. He considered it a fiction theorists used from which to deduce social obligations; still, if one received benefits from society, Mill felt one owed society a return.[67]

Like the Bentham of a half-century earlier, Mill believed that truth lay in the Utilitarian calculus of pleasure and pain, though unlike Bentham he felt the need to test his models and alter them as experience dictated. To both, property was a means to an end, not the end itself. Thus, it was an institution civilly created as a means toward the end of happiness.

Mill's rejection of natural law is worth repeating in some detail, in view of its frequent use as the basis of property rights. Mill crisply differentiated between the physical laws of nature such as motion or gravitation and the laws of land, of nations, or of morality. Among these latter, Mill noted, "is dragged in, by jurists and publicists, something they think proper to call the law of Nature. . . . To bid people conform to the laws of nature . . . when it is a physical impossibility for them to do the smallest thing otherwise than through some law of nature, is an absurdity." Thus, though all conduct is in conformance to the physical laws of nature, "all conduct is not grounded on knowledge of them," nor is all intelligence "directed to attainment of purposes by means of them."[68]

Thus, despite the fact that nature was a poor guide to action in the particular case, there were "those who talk of *jus naturae* even as [positive] law, fit to be administered by tribunals and enforced by sanctions." Though intelligent action was in conformance with natural laws, right action must mean something more. On the other hand, "That a thing is unnatural . . . is no argument for its being blamable."[69] Clearly, Mill saw the natural world and civil law as occupying different spheres; human institutions like property and inheritance were to be governed by the latter.

In Mill's eyes, the duty of man was not to follow nature, but to use it for his own purposes. Thus Mill felt the instinct for things natural should be subordinated to reason and that reason should bend to the task of living rather than to learning, in unknowable detail, the designs of Providence. "What good nature brings to men," he wrote, "is mostly the result of their own exertions."[70]

How did the two aspects of inheritance, bequest and succession, stand up in the face of this practical liberalism? Not entirely well, it appears. Building on Bentham's notions, Mill argues that the right of bequest was by implication an attribute of private property, though the right of succession by law or custom was not. Nonetheless, "like all other proprietary rights and in even greater degree than most, the power of bequest may be so exercised as to conflict with the permanent interests of the human race."[71] His philosophy of experience led him to question the observable phenomena of private and charitable wealth held in near perpetuity by means of various estate-planning devices. Thus, the "unearned advantage of those who inherited savings of others should be curtailed, as much as is consistent with justice to those who thought fit to dispose of their savings by giving them to their descendants."[72]

In the feudal family or clan, Mill continued, "exclusive individual property, in the modern sense, scarcely entered into the ideas of the time; when a clan member died, he really left nothing vacant but his own share in the whole, which devolved on the member of the family who succeeded to his authority." He noted that bequest itself was seldom recognized in a feudal society.[73]

Mill continued:

> But the feudal family, the last historical form of patriarchal life, has long perished, and the unit of society is not now the family or clan, composed of all the reputed decendants of a common ancestor, but the individual; or at most a pair of individuals, with their unemancipated children. Property is now inherent in individuals, not in families: the children when grown up do not follow the occupations or fortunes of the parent: if they participate in the parent's pecuniary means it is at his or her pleasure, and not by a voice in the ownership and government of the whole, but generally by the exclusive enjoyment of a part. . . .[74]

Mill then discussed what degree of succession should be allowed in a society so constituted. As to collateral heirs, he agreed with Bentham: "Mr. Bentham long ago proposed, and other high authorities have agreed in the opinion, that if there are no heirs either in the descending or in the ascending line, the property in the case of intestacy should escheat to the state." The claims of children he viewed quite differently. They should get a "reasonable amount," considering both the interests of individuals and society; the surplus "could rightfully be appropriated" to the general purposes of the community. If parents want to leave their children more than they have a moral right to, "the means are afforded by the liberty of bequest."[75]

Mill considered the question of whether the power of bequest should itself be subject to limitation "an ulterior question of great importance." Unlike inheritance *ab intestato,* the power of bequest was a property right; also, it "may be so exercised as to conflict with the permanent interests of the human race." Recognizing this, Mill favored restrictions. However, he preferred to restrict, not what anyone might bequeath, but what anyone should be permitted to acquire by bequest:

> Each person should have power to dispose by will of his or her whole property; but not to lavish it in enriching some one individual, beyond a certain maximum, which should be fixed sufficiently high to afford the means of comfortable independence. . . . I see nothing objectionable in fixing a limit to what anyone may acquire by the mere favour of others, without any exercise of his faculties, and in requiring that if he desires any further accession of fortune, he shall work for it.[76]

Additionally, Mill felt the testator should be forced to provide for those who would otherwise become a burden to the state in an equivalent amount to what the state would have to provide.[77]

Using the key Utilitarian argument of the decreasing marginal utility of wealth increments, Mill declared, "it must be apparent to everyone, that the difference to the happiness of the possessor between a moderate independence and five times as much, is insignificant when weighed against the enjoyment that might be given, and the permanent benefits diffused, by some other disposal of the four-fifths."[78] Mill perceived that if the restriction could be made practically effectual, the benefit would be great:

> Wealth which could no longer be employed in over-enriching a few, would either be devoted to objects of public usefulness, or if bestowed on individuals, would be distributed among a larger number. While those enormous fortunes which no one needs for any personal purpose but ostentation or improper power, would become much less numerous, there would be a great multiplication of persons in easy circumstances, with the advantages of leisure, and all the real enjoyments which wealth can give, except those of vanity. . . .[79]

Clearly, Mill did not see this group as entailing all the citizenry; rather it would compose a new leisure class whose work, or at least the tone it set for the rest of society, "would be rendered in a much more beneficial manner than at the present."[80]

Somewhat later in the *Political Economy,* Mill directed his attention more specifically to the taxation of large legacies:

> It is not the fortunes which are earned, but those which are unearned, that it is for the public good to place under limitation. . . . [I]f all were done which it would be in the power of a good government to do, by instruction and legislation, to diminish inequality of opportunities, the differences in fortune arising from people's own earnings could not justly give umbrage. With respect to large fortunes acquired by gift or inheritance, the power of bequesting is one of those privileges of property which are fit subjects for regulation on grounds of general expediency; . . . as a possible mode of restraining the accumulation of large fortunes in the hands of those who have not earned them by exertion, a limitation should be made of the amount which any one person should be permitted to acquire by gift, bequest or inheritance. . . . I conceive that inheritance and legacies, exceeding a certain amount are highly proper subjects for taxation. . . .[81]

Further, Mill felt that though graduated taxation was generally objectionable (presumably because it hampered the efforts of those who earned a living), it seemed to him both "just and expedient as applied to legacy and inheritance duties."[82]

Mill's balanced approach to inheritance remains an eminently sensible one for Western democracy. Although influential in both Britain and America, his discussions of the institution were not happily received by most of these nations' plutocrats. Rather than sophisticated arguments based on social utility, they sought a theory of society which would defend the legitimacy of the dynasties they were building. They found it in the theory of evolution of biologist Charles Darwin.

Darwin died in 1884, just as Herbert Spencer and others were adapting his theories to society. Had he lived to see the ends to which his discoveries were finally put, Darwin would very likely have been aghast. "Survival of the fittest" in nature meant that those species best adapted to produce offspring in a changing environment would survive. It had nothing whatever to do with the struggle for money and power among men, as Spencer and his ilk claimed. Nonetheless, the "Social Darwinists" (as they were called), used the theory as justification for the huge disparities in wealth associated with maturing capitalism. In Britain, the plutocracy embraced the ruminations of Spencer as evidence that, by an iron law of nature, they had "survived" best because they were morally and intellectually "fittest." Nowhere in Spencer's publications do we find a direct explanation of how the fittest could be determined in a society where inherited concentrations of wealth made starting points so unequal. At the end of the century, Britain, like America, was hardly in a "state of nature," where each individual could fight the social struggle on relatively equal terms.

Spencer's failure to discuss inheritance and its effects directly stemmed from his unconscious wedding of existing social advantages with nature.[83] Being himself an heir of substantial wealth, Spencer wrote:

> We have to accept ... the established constitution of things, though under it an inferiority for which the individual is not blamable, brings its evils, and a superiority for which he can claim no merit, brings its benefits. ... But while it does not devolve upon me to defend the order of Nature, I may say again ... that only in the virtue of the law under which every creature takes the good and bad results entailed by its inherited organization, has life advanced to its present height and can continue to advance.[84]

Like the nineteenth-century society of which Spencer was a part, such blasé acceptance of the order of things was doomed to extinction.

CONCLUSIONS

Admittedly, the foregoing is a quick ride through Western European intellectual history of the seventeenth through the nineteenth century. Nonetheless, I think it sufficient to provide the reader with an understanding of the backdrop against which the drama of inheritance in America has been played.

Certain characteristics of inheritance had been well delineated by European thinkers; in the main these left the institution vulnerable to civil control. John Locke, the first prominent figure of the Enlightenment in Britain, had foreshadowed this vulnerability when he suggested civil limitations on the natural rights of property and inheritance. By the time Blackstone wrote his *Commentaries* in the mid-eighteenth century, the two rights were clearly separated in Britain, with property a natural right and succession to property its civilly enacted adjunct. Still inheritance rights, though not inalienable, were of great importance and were not easily changed.

Bentham's iconoclasm did away with both fundamental rights like those of lifetime property and rights important for other reasons. In fact, by Bentham's calculations it was idle to talk of rights at all; every institution had to be tested for its social utility, which might change and uproot any individual's expectations. It remained for John Stuart Mill to temper this barren calculus and to test its computations by experience. This produced a balanced and sophisticated view of the inheritance problem.

Mill's emphasis on experience had clearly been influenced by Kant's break with the Enlightenment, but he did not go so far as to ally morality with law and the institutions it protected. Kant's genius, on the other hand, was sufficiently flexible to allow the natural and moral right of inheritance to be regulated by civil law, because civil law was conceptually necessary to the transfer of property from decedent and successor at the moment the former's dominion ceased. Unfortunately, this bargain with experience was lost on the Orthodox economists in France, who took an untempered natural rights view of inheritance in their own struggle with the Utilitarians. Finally the Social Darwinists like Spencer found it unnecessary to discuss the institution of inheritance at all; in their rigidly deterministic view, whatever survived was best and right; and by 1900, inheritance had not only survived but prospered.

Within the institution itself, certain adjustments had been made by European thinkers. In the matured view of Mill, bequest, though of more recent vintage than intestate succession, was the more important right. Indeed, Mill like Bentham did not regard succession by collateral heirs as a right at all and recommended its abolishment;

children, likewise, had only a limited right to a reasonable amount of inheritance.

By contrast, the greater protection Mill afforded the right of bequest was related to the expectations of those involved. He who had bequeathed property had mixed his labor with it during life under the expectation he could continue his power over it, even beyond the grave. Those who could "come into" property through intestate succession had formed no such legitimate expectations in the property, divorced as it was from the sweat of their brows. Those who took by will, by contrast, took under color not of their own rights but those of the expectant testator.

Despite these differences, Mill was a practical man. Though succession was not strictly a property right, Mill felt children should be able to succeed to a reasonable though not lavish amount of property. While making this concession to the social necessity of family maintenance on the one hand, he decided on the other that even the property right of bequest could be limited so as not to enrich the few. Whether property right or not, each aspect of inheritance rose or fell on its own social utility.

If a generalization about inheritance can be teased out of pre-twentieth-century Western European thought, it is that the institution was, in all its guises, in no sense immutable; thus, it was subject to civil control. Watching this concept develop from across the Atlantic, nineteenth-century America would apply it in a dynamic situation where "dead hand control" of property often conflicted with the desire for a competitive, expanding economy.

3

Inheritance in Early American Thought

While it would be inaccurate to view the mind of post-Revolutionary America as a vast *tabula rasa* awaiting the imprint of notions from abroad, it was at least ready to experiment with many of these ideas in light of American conditions. The American acceptance of European views on property and inheritance showed a significant lag. Partially, this was due to the fact that the industrial revolution occurred in America somewhat later in the nineteenth century than it did in Europe.

In mid-nineteenth-century Britain, with its industrial revolution accomplished and opportunities for new land closed, one can sense the political climate in which John Stuart Mill could argue for strong limitations on inheritance. Such a discussion in America would have to await the events of later in the century: urbanization, heavy industrialization, and the closing of the American frontier. For most of the century, America seemed a nation without limits, which made it far more concerned with economic development than with philosophical speculations about wealth redistribution.

The problem of organizing for the reader a period in which ideas from abroad mixed like quicksilver with native hopes and dreams is a formidable one. The approach taken is to use Jefferson as the root for ideas about property and inheritance much as Locke was used in chapter 2. From Jefferson's philosophy it is possible to trace lines of thought leading on one hand to the rational, aristocratic jurists like James Kent and Joseph Story and on the other to the democrats with their preference for popular legislation. Finally, the century culminates in the American version of Social Darwinism, which, somewhat surprisingly, proves to have its own roots in Jeffersonianism.

THE JEFFERSONIANS

To Thomas Jefferson, property was made for the use of the living by the operation of natural law. However, specific lands were owned by particular individuals only by virtue of society's laws. These laws decreed that after death no man could control by natural right the lands he had occupied.[1] "For if he could," Jefferson wrote Madison, "he might during his own life, eat up the usufruct of lands for several generations to come, and then the lands would belong to the dead. . . . Earth belongs in usufruct to the living; the dead have neither powers nor rights over it." Thus, the portion occupied by an individual ceases upon death "and reverts to society."[2]

Although one can see in these ideas the economic instrumentalism necessary for the development of the new nation, they also demonstrate that distinction between natural and civil rights which is so basic to Jefferson's philosophy. Jefferson believed that the essential natural freedoms of man were political and personal, and did not include unbounded use of property. As Thomas Paine put it, natural rights were those "of personal competency," such as thinking, speaking, forming and giving opinions.[3] Civil rights were rights derived from the social compact which secured to individuals personal protection for acquiring and possessing property. In response to Madison's urging, Jefferson admitted that this compact was founded on utility as defined by each new generation, rather than on natural law.[4]

Paine mirrored Jefferson's belief that the earth belonged to the living, who could change the dead's rights. He wrote "[No] generation [has] a property in the generations which are to follow. . . . It is the living and not the dead that are to be accommodated. . . . When man ceases to be, his power cease[s] with him."[5] Others of his circle, such as Jefferson's personal physician in Paris, the influential Dr. Gem, had urged him that "the dead and those who are unborn can have no rights of property."[6]

Jeffersonian philosophy of natural rights was not the abstract and metaphysical doctrine natural law later became. It was instead an operational approach to establish sound conditions for human security and growth. "Rights" to Jefferson and Paine had to listen to "Reason"; "Reason" itself had no quarrel with "Utility."[7] At the heart of Jefferson's economic philosophy was a notion that distinguished him from Adam Smith: the recognition that economic institutions might change and that no one was wise enough to fix perpetual laws of property that would serve the needs of posterity.[8] Jefferson viewed man and his institutions in an evolutionary, naturalistic context; they fit into the whole framework of nature, struggling for survival among myriad other species.[9]

In addition to its elements of natural rights theory and pragmatism, Jeffersonian philosophy was not immune from Bentham's utilitarianism. "So invariably do the laws of nature create our duties and interests," said Jefferson, that when they seem to be at variance, "the fallacy is in human intellect and reason." It was inconceivable to Jefferson that the Creator had failed to calculate utility when He originally shaped man's moral faculty; mastery of the utilitarian calculus was attributable only to God. Since the orderly benevolence of the Creator and intrinsic perfection of the natural process bound reason and morals, Jefferson believed the solution of moral problems lay in the successful life of action.[10]

Jefferson's belief in the morality of the results of the natural struggle for survival was to become an uncomfortable companion of his emphasis on the rights of each new generation. To reconcile these beliefs, this natural struggle would have to be rendered fair in each generation; as the frontier closed and concentrations of wealth grew, inheritance of property would stand squarely in the path of the American self-made man.

Perhaps Jefferson had begun to see this problem in his later years. His last words on the consequences of earth belonging to the living appear in a letter to Thomas Earle in 1823. In it, he addressed the institution of inheritance directly: "for the sake of convenience and the encouragement of industry the laws of civil society . . . give the property of the parent to his family on his death," and in "most civilized countries permit him even to give it, by testament, to whom he pleases." Since "habit alone confounds what is civil practice with natural right," the insitution's existence does "not lessen the right of the majority to repeal it whenever a change of circumstances or will calls for it."[11] Jefferson's developed notion of the rights of a new generation to alter civil institutions like inheritance entered his own state's jurisprudence some thirty-five years later in the decision of *Eyre* v. *Jacob,* [12] a leading precedent sustaining the powers of the several states to tax inheritances.

In *Eyre* the plaintiff had challenged the constitutionality of the state tax on inheritances. Judge Lee, speaking for the Court held that the tax was not a tax on property but on the process of passing the estate from the dead to the living; the ability to take property in this manner was not a right, but "a benefit or privilege" of citizenship.

Judge Lee then set down in a single paragraph a strong vindication of the legislature's power to regulate and tax the "civil right" or "privilege" of inheritance:

> The right to take property by devise or descent is the creature of the law and secured and protected by its authority. The legislature might if it saw proper, restrict succession to a decendent's estate . . . or it may tommorrow, if it pleases, absolutely repeal the statute of wills and that of descents and distributions and declare that upon the death of a party, his property shall be applied to payment of his debts and the residue appropriated to public uses.[13]

Stated thus boldly was the power of legislatures to confiscate inheritances — a power affirmed by the United States Supreme Court and good law to this day.[14] As Lee concluded, it was difficult to see how the legislature "possessing this sweeping power over the whole subject" of inheritance, could be challenged on its right to appropriate "a modicum of the estate, call it a tax or what you will." This appropriation was simply the condition upon which those who took the estates were "permitted to enjoy it."[15]

THE RISE OF LEGAL RATIONALISM

The Jeffersonians had no quarrel with natural reason, that intuitive sense of right and wrong functioning automatically within every human being. When cultivated, this sense of reason could be relied on to decide moral questions by affirmative, logical choice. The Jeffersonians soon found themselves confronted with a variant of this rationalism, however: the new legal elite.

The new rationalism of aristocratic lawyers like James Kent, John Marshall, and Joseph Story differed from both the popularized law of nature so important to the democrats and the purely philosophical rationalism of the eighteenth-century Enlightenment. Still these "rational jurists," in their drive to make law and lawyers autonomous from politics and politicians, exhibited traces of both traditions.[16] While they staunchly defended property, their conclusions on inheritance (if often kept to themselves) differed little from those of the Jeffersonian judge in *Eyre* v. *Jacob*.

Though their conservative views on property and social structure were in eclipse by the 1850s, the elite jurists succeeded in establishing an autonomous legal profession. Their bible in this triumph was William Blackstone's monumental *Commentaries on the Law of England,*[17] which had been completed in 1769. This work, so influential both in Britain and America, provided the very synthesis of legislative, natural, and common law which the rational jurists needed.

Blackstone had built on the twin bases of Hobbes and Locke. While both men identified sovereignty with the power to make and enforce laws, Hobbes saw the content of laws as essentially arbitrary. Thus, legislative choice operated within a very wide range: the state not only ordered the society, but also had created it. Locke argued, by contrast, that the state existed solely to enforce the law of nature by resolving disputes about its definition and ensuring its impartial execution: the order which the state imposed pre-existed it.[18] Though some scholars have thought Locke's use of natural law was chiefly rhetorical,[19]—a conclusion which would bring him much closer to Hobbes—this was true of many who used the concept, probably including Blackstone himself.

In any event, Blackstone adopted both the Lockean natural rights view and the Hobbesian notion that Parliament represented an absolute and uncontrollable sovereign power. He did not regard the rules of property, for example, as merely a positivized, state-enforced version of the law of nature; this depended on whether the particular right involved was God-given or merely "neutral." As explained in the previous chapter, this led to his distinction between the natural right of lifetime property and inheritance, its civil or neutral adjunct.[20]

The connection Blackstone fashioned between natural law and the common law of England was slippery yet useful to the American rational jurists. He conceived of the common law historically, as a statement of immemorial custom. As to precisely how the hetero-geneous common law managed to declare the homogeneous princi-ples of natural law, Blackstone was vague; what had to suffice was his observation that the law of nature, dictated by God himself, was an obligation superior to any other. "It is binding all over the globe in all countries, and at all times; no human laws are of any validity, if contrary to this." Having said this, he exhorted the readers of his *Commentaries* to learn with particularity common law principles (however these might appear to conflict with nature and reason) as examples of the sound maxims of natural law.[21]

This attempt was enough for American lawyers like James Wil-son of Philadelphia and Nathaniel Chipman of Vermont, who quickly picked up natural law as a basis for positive law in the new republic. In doing so they gave natural law, in Perry Miller's words, "a quite baffling comprehensiveness." Their construct included not only the law of physical objects, but "the moral law of the Bible, the innermost promptings of natural conscience, a calculus of the benefits of or-dered social exchange and a vision of the perfection to which Amer-ica could aspire."[22] Still, the American natural lawyer could not escape the fact that common law *had* grown up by accident, and was not, until Kent and Story molded it, in any sense a systematic wis-dom.

Building his thought on a Blackstonian base as adapted by the American natural lawyers, James Kent was the chief architect of the new American jurisprudence. Jurist, law professor, and politician, Kent surpassed even John Marshall and Joseph Story in influence due to the popularity of his *Commentaries.* More so than even his fellow jurists, he carried a solid remnant of Enlightenment rationality into the Romantic cauldron of early nineteenth-century America. By ex-pressing his conception of universal order not merely in ad hoc judicial decisions but in his systematic compendium of legal learning, Kent guaranteed that the Republic would preserve its sanity in the midst of swirling enthusiasms like Revivalism and Transcendental-ism.[23]

The cornerstone of Kent's jurisprudence was the right of prop-erty. His conception of the right was based on the natural law/com-mon law synthesis of Blackstone, by now accepted and free from the arbitrary grasp of legislative power.

The attachment to the natural right of property went very far indeed with Kent. He turned to Blackstone to free American lawyers from the notion that property rights derived from the Lockean social compact or that they must depend on society's *recognition* that the owner had made something his own by mixing his labor with it. In Kent (as in Blackstone), the concept of property existed before there was any society at all. It was to protect the individual in this right, vested in him by the immutable law of nature, that governments were created.[24]

In flat contradiction to Jeffersonianism, then, Kent's law would not authorize the least violation of property even for the general good of the community. Contrary to the natural law concepts of Locke, Grotius, and Samuel Pufendorf, Kent's notion of private property was suggested first to the mind of man by reason and nature: prior to the U.S. Constitution, state constitutions, enumerated bills of rights, and above all prior to the demagoguery of the Jacksonians.[25]

Despite his adherence to the natural right of property, Kent was muddled on the subject of inheritance: he had difficulty divorcing this civil institution from its natural parent. Perhaps, at the moment of writing what follows, the weight of all the traditions he was trying to fuse into an American common law became too great, particularly in light of his fondness for property and hereditary aristocracy.

Kent began by admitting that since title to property rested originally in occupancy, "that title ceased, of course, upon the death of the occupant." He then began to extricate himself from the thought of his intellectual mentor:

> Sir William Blackstone considers the equally political institutions and creatures of the municipal [civil] law, and not natural rights; and that the law of nature suggests, that on the death of the possessor, the estate should become common, and be open to the next occupant. He admits, however, that, for the sake of peace and order, the universal law of almost every nation gives to the possessor the power to continue his property by will; and if it be not disposed of in that way, that the [civil] law steps in, and declares who shall be the heir of the deceased.[26]

Next came the heresy, albeit cautiously framed: "As a mere speculative question, it may well be doubted, whether this is to be a perfectly correct view of the law of nature on this subject." Then came a puzzling phrase: "the right to transmit property by descent, to one's own offspring, is dictated by the voice of nature" (citing Grotius).[27]

Did Kent mean, as some later claimed,[28] that the "voice of nature" was different from "the law of nature"? Apparently he did not, although he was indirect in saying so:

> The universality of the sense of a rule or obligation, is pretty good evidence that it has its foundations in natural law. It is in accordance with the sympathies and reason of all mankind, that the children of the owner of property, which he acquired and improved by his skill and industry, *and by their association and labor* [emphasis added] should have a better title to it at his death, than the passing stranger.[29]

The reader may find interesting Kent's attempt to give the heirs a labor-derived natural property right in the phrase emphasized above; likewise his attempt to fashion this right through "association" with the occupant. If this failed to convince, Kent claimed that the "better title of the children has been recognized in every age and nation, and it is founded in the natural affections," which were the outgrowth of "domestic ties and the order of Providence."[30]

Having discharged all this artillery without directly terming inheritance a natural right, Kent retrenched a bit to conform to the overwhelming tide of British thought on the subject:

> But the particular distribution among heirs of the blood, and the regulation and extent of the degrees of consanguinity to which the right of succession should be attached, do undoubtedly depend *essentially* upon positive [civil] institution. [emphasis added][31]

After such a smoke screen, the reader may still be left wondering whether Kent believed in the natural right of inheritance; at best his explanation is evasive.

Kent seemed eager to pass this point and to discuss his views of the law in the area of inheritance. There followed praise for the American adaptation of the institution:

> [European] entailments have been effectively removed in this country; and the right . . . to devise, and to transmit property by inheritance to one's descendants in regular order and succession, is enjoyed in the fulness and perfection of the absolute right. Every individual has as much freedom in the . . . disposition of his property, as is consistent with good order, and the reciprocal rights of others.[32]

With the liberty of the individual safe, Kent could mouth his disapproval of the state of equality desired by his democratic opponents:

> [This] is impossible to be maintained, for it is against the laws of our nature; and if it could be reduced to practice it would place the human race in a state of tasteless enjoyment and stupid inactivity. . . . [33]

In place of this dull equality, Kent postulated a laissez-faire utopia which would have made Adam Smith content: "When the laws allow a free circulation to property by the abolition of perpetuities, entailments, claims of primogeniture, and all inequalities of descent, the operation of steady laws of nature will of themselves preserve a proper equilibrium. . . ." This was the conservative jurists' notion in all its glory, but Kent felt it necessary to add a teaser for the democrats: the automatic functioning of this system would, he postulated, "dissipate the mounds of property" as fast as they accumulated.[34]

Supreme Court Justices John Marshall and Joseph Story were somewhat more restrained in their enthusiasm for property than was Kent. Marshall's social thought rested on the assumption that man brought certain inalienable rights with him into society. Unlike Jefferson, though in accord with Kent, he felt that these included property and that society existed not to circumscribe these rights, but to preserve and promote them. Unlike Kent, however, he was less likely to posit that the right to hold and enjoy property was absolute; in fact on specific occasions it could be interfered with, depending on whether this promoted natural rights in the aggregate.[35]

Marshall felt that the English, in coming to America had brought their natural rights with them. When they codified certain rights for themselves in the Constitution, however, American citizens had not given up those other rights conferred on man in his original state. Hence those property rights Marshall considered "vested" were protected from state interference not only by the Constitution, but also by their permissibility in a state of nature.[36]

Specifically, this meant that property rights were to be protected if they symbolized freedom to make use of one's acquisitive skills, but not if they represented simply the fruits of inheritance. Thus institutions like primogeniture could be abolished summarily by the new nation, while the right to make use of the fruits of one's labor could not be so easily curtailed.[37] Marshall, unlike Kent, seemed to have little trouble with the power of government to modify and adapt inheritance.

Like Kent, Joseph Story was a jurist, treatise writer, and law professor waging the battle for autonomous law, made by judges, against the legislative legions of Jacksonianism. His *Commentaries on the Constitution,* completed four years after Kent's great treatise, shows a development of the theoretical basis Kent had constructed for natural rights.

Kent's thought was in transition from an occupancy-derived basis for natural rights, protected under the social compact, to a historical view of these rights. This movement was in part to demonstrate that the historical and evolutionary character of the common law made it particularly appropriate to America, where this form of law could develop along with a rapidly changing society. By the time of the Story treatise in 1833, the development of the theoretical basis was complete: no longer was the social compact the basis for rights and government, but rights were seen as evolving historically, confirmed by a constitution declaratory of them.[38]

Another of the "rational jurists," Lemuel Shaw of the Massachusetts Supreme Court, expanded this historical notion. Even more so than Story or Kent, he presented the common law as the very opposite of a series of detailed, practical rules perhaps more attuned to the peculiarities of the British experience. Rather, Shaw's common law consisted of "a few broad and comprehensive principles founded on natural justice and enlightened public policy modified and adapted to the circumstances of all particular cases which fall within it."[39] Likewise, Theodore Dwight, in his law lectures at Columbia in 1858, sought to demonstrate that the common law was not an artificial invention of man, but was wholly "natural" and thus suitable for transplantation to the American landscape.[40]

Kent and Story found that natural law, along with its synthesis with common law, could easily be reconciled with Bentham's proposals. In fact, they argued that Bentham's utilitarianism had nothing in it except his calculus of pains and pleasures, which was not in the utilitarian natural law that went before him. As Roscoe Pound later reminded us, the rational proposition that the end sought by man is happiness can be traced back to the natural law theories of Samuel Pufendorf.[41]

Imbued with a rather more flexible view of natural law and rights than Kent, Story found little difficulty in extricating the civil right of inheritance from property rights, which could, he found, be viewed in both an historical and utilitarian way. Therefore there

> must be many cases in which the interests of parties may be directly, greatly and injuriously affected by mere legislative action in entire conformity with the principles of civil liberty.... Nothing, therefore can be clearer than that the rules of descent are subject to be changed by legislative authority.... [42]

Despite this recognition of civil authority over inheritance, the rational jurists were not prepared to abandon willy-nilly the rights and prerogatives of the propertied classes. In fact, Story and Kent clearly saw the elite lawyers "as sentinels on the walls and at the gates," striving to drive back the Jacksonian torrent that threatened "destruction equally to public liberty and private property."[43] As Story himself wrote in the Providence Bank case, "That government can scarcely be deemed free where the rights of property are left solely to depend on the will of a legislative body, without any restraint."[44] This restraint of course was to be judicial authority.

A commentator in the *American Law Magazine* in 1843 put frankly the issue bothering the rational jurists: "The real concern of society is the protection of property," which "stands in need of every paper barrier.... Democracy is incurably hostile to the possessions of a few" and the Constitution gave property "insufficient protection."[45] As Maine Probate Judge David Bronson declared in 1857 "if the legislature can take the property of A and transfer it to B, then "they can take A himself and either shut him up in prison or put him to death."[46]

It must be understood that these fierce judicial defenses of property were being voiced before great concentrations of family wealth were built up in the late nineteenth century. Thus in 1834 Boston Judge Peter Thatcher could still explain the inequality of wealth and condition among men with the observation that mankind was "divided into the provident and the improvident, the idle and the diligent."[47] Meanwhile, Story expressed the prevailing view of the jurists that a strong defense of property would not lead to distortions of the social structure: experience in America had already shown, he said, that property did not stay long in any one family, and the nation need not fear a permanent plutocracy.[48] At least in this respect, one cannot call Story prescient.

Given their strong defense of property rights and their grudging recognition of the civil nature of inheritance, it is not surprising that the rational jurists were not the first to announce the possibility of confiscating inheritance in a Supreme Court opinion. Instead this task fell to Jackson's appointee as Chief Justice, Roger Taney, Story's *bête noire* in the famous Charles River Bridge case.[49] The case was *Mager* v. *Grima,*[50] decided in 1850 without dissent.

Perhaps out of caution Taney chose the case of an alien, not a citizen, to announce the doctrine Europe had developed, Jefferson had adapted, and even Story had accepted. The inheritance tax in question was, wrote Taney:

> [N]othing more than an exercise of the power which every state and sovereignty possesses of regulating the manner and term upon which property real or personal within its dominion may be transmitted by last will and testament; and of prescribing who shall and shall not be capable of taking it. . . . We can see no [constitutional] objection to such a tax, whether imposed on citizens [or] aliens . . .[51]

This was "a plain case" to Taney. A state, "if it may deny the privilege [of inheritance] altogether," may, "when it grants that privilege, . . . annex any conditions which it supposes to be required by its interests or policy."[52]

By the time of *Mager,* the conservative jurists had established an elite legal profession and were in political retreat before the democratic tide. Thus they often acquiesced in the numerous state and federal decisions which supported the constitutionality of inheritance taxation (and even confiscation) during the next half-century. While admitting legislative power over inheritance, they continued to hope that judicial review might save them if democratic legislators became too extreme in their demands for the redistribution of wealth.

THE TRANSCENDENTALIST RESPONSE
TO RATIONAL JURISPRUDENCE

The lawyers' rationalism had to contend for a time with a philosophical movement that claimed its roots in Kantian notions of the ordering power of the mind. Transcendentalism was a philosophy born in the drawing rooms of the New England aristocracy, but with Democratic party connections which disturbed the rational jurists. If the jurists were heirs of the rational side of Jeffersonianism, the Transcendentalists found succor in Jefferson's naturalism and his preference for democracy.

To Ralph Waldo Emerson, mind was the only reality, of which men and all other species in nature were better or worse reflections. He had no respect for labor or its product, property, otherwise than as a symbol, a faithful rendering of the details of the laws of "being." Emerson and his associates were reacting to the skeptical philosophy of Locke, which insisted that there was nothing in the intellect that was not in the senses. Like Kant, they believed there was an important class of ideas or imperative forms which did not come by experience, but through which experience was acquired. Unlike Kant, they gave these intuitions or transcendental forms absolute hegemony.

Emerson viewed man as a creature of nature, deriving from its powers both individuality and freedom. He had as little use for scientific empiricism as he did for the organized religion of the day. The curse of science was its isolated dependence on the intellect. "Pure intellect," said Emerson, betraying his view of the eighteenth century Enlightenment, "is the pure devil."[53] Thus internal feeling was as important as intellectual analysis in understanding nature; though science had significance, nature could teach more than Newtonian materialism.[54]

Emerson was the supreme individualist, rejecting at once the material spirit of his day and the experimental collectivism of Brook Farm. It was the individual human in whose heart the Over-Soul dwelt who was of transcendant importance: "I am the transparent eyeball; I am nothing; I see all; the currents of the Universal Being circulate through me; I am part and parcel of God."[55]

Around Emerson, the rough egalitarianism of the frontier was passing and wealth was beginning to concentrate in the hands of the few. Both he and Thoreau believed in a law of nature which left all men free to pursue transcendence; they hoped abstractly that a democracy embodying this concept would triumph over the materialism and mean-spiritedness of the day. "The philosopher," wrote Emerson, "will wish to cast his vote for the democrat . . . for facilitating in every manner access of the young and poor to sources of wealth and power."[56]

Theodore Parker, a Unitarian minister and associate of Emerson and Thoreau, left perhaps the most complete philosophical delineation of Transcendentalism. He contrasted it with the "sensationalism" of Locke which "knew nothing of" absolute right or absolute justice. He took the political outcome of Lockean thought to mean "there is no right but might,"[57] though one may argue that this is far closer to Hobbes than to Locke himself.

Parker thought that sensationalism was based only on human history. It showed only what had been, not what should or would be. Further, the "aim of sensationalist politics" was the greatest good for the greatest number. To Parker's dismay, such ends could be obtained only be sacrificing the greatest good of the smaller number, the sacrificing of any individual, or the sacrificing of absolute good.[58]

Bentham, to Parker, represented the sensationalist morals of politics. To Bentham, Rousseau, and others, "society has no divine original, only the social compact; there is no natural justice, natural right . . . no greater good than the Utilitarian calculus." To that end, the sensationalist politician would sacrifice anything: this led such men to defend a constitution rather than the ideal of justice.[59]

Mind, to Parker, was far more than the *tabula rasa* of Locke; since man had faculties which transcended the senses he sought neither their origin nor their proof there. Knowledge, then, was chiefly a priori. The working of God transcended our experience, telling us the absolute right of the situation, not the *relatively* right.[60]

For Parker the Declaration of Independence embodied three simple ideas which showed how transcendental philosophy worked. The first was that man is endowed with certain inalienable rights; the second, that with respect to these rights all men are equal. Both of these were "ontological facts" existing in the human consciousness. The third—that a government is to protect each man in the enjoyment of all of these rights—was to Parker a synthetic a priori judgment, not learned from sensationalist experience. Never in history had a government fulfilled these ideals. Each of the first two ideas transcended history: every inalienable right has been alienated and still was being alienated; no two men had been equal in actual rights. Yet Parker asserted that the ideas themselves were true.[61]

He thought that America was an attempt to prove by experience the transcendental proposition, to organize the transcendental notion of politics. This could only be done by a democracy, what Parker considered a form of government by natural justice. In a pure democracy, conscience transcends experience, putting "natural right and natural duty before all institutions, all laws, and all traditions."[62] In the Jeffersonian mold, Parker and the Transcendentalists confined natural rights to those of free expression, ignoring Kent's and Story's attempts to include property.

The Transcendentalists were essentially offshoots of the German idealism of Hegel, though nature rather than society formed their ideal. No matter how they attempted to rationalize their emotions or appeal to experience in the fashion of Kant, the point of departure for their argument was the ability of each individual to attain natural divinity. In most Trancendentalists this translated into an aloofness from law and politics, though they professed admiration for the principles of the Democratic party. Emerson spoke for them when he complained rather lamely that "of the two great parties . . . one has the best cause and the other [the Whigs] contains the best men."[63]

For two of the Transcendentalists, however, the relations between democracy and their philosophy seemed close and vital. To historian George Bancroft and editor Orestes Brownson, the Jacksonians were carrying on the same revolt against the "dead hand" of Locke in politics as the Transcendentalists were waging in religion. This revolt stressed the rights of the free mind against the pretensions of precedents or entrenched institutions. I planted the individual squarely on his instincts, responsible only to himself and to God.[64]

Bancroft sought directly to reconcile transcendent individualism with the claims of Jacksonian democracy. He modified transcendentalism by adding that the collective sense of the people provided an indispensable check on the anarchy of individual institutions. "If reason is a universal faculty," wrote Bancroft, "the decision of the common mind is the nearest criterion of truth."[65] Thus democracy perfected in practice the philosophical insights of his circle.

Another Transcendentalist who refused to eschew the hurly-burly of politics was Orestes A. Brownson, editor of and chief contributor to the *Boston Quarterly Review*. This publication made itself notorious in 1840 by attacking not only organized Christianity and the penal code but also the institution of inherited wealth. Brownson's analysis of the latter parallels Mill's in depth and scope, if not in ultimate direction. Though it was not as politically acceptable as Mill's analysis, it is worth repeating in detail for the expression it gave to notions about the institution of inheritance, which—though not those of the American majority—survived well into the twentieth century.

Brownson agreed with various authorities that man has a natural right of property, based either on the labor theory of Locke or on the occupancy theory of Blackstone and Kant. Man also has title by dictate of civil law, he wrote, which "may not be good in morals, but is in general good against society itself, at least as concerns the present proprietor." To Brownson, man's right to property was coupled with a right, *within the limits of the moral law,* to do what he wanted with it.[66]

Though admitting man's right to the property formed by his labor, Brownson added "this is not the only property to which he has a natural right." Brownson also modified the theory of first occupancy: "according to both Christianity and democracy, every man had a right of property to a portion of the whole, equal to that of every other man ... provided the claim thus acquired [did] not stretch over more than, in an equal division of the whole, would have fallen to the occupant's share." The right to property by dint of civil law was likewise qualified: "Society is under law and ... has no right to enact what rests not on a higher law than its will—the law of Nature or God."[67]

As I have attempted to show, there were numerous authorities for Brownson's next and crucial point that, however acquired, all property had to cease at death. Kent, Blackstone, and Jefferson served as direct examples for this argument; Bentham and Locke agreed by indirection. Bentham, wrote Brownson, proposed that property and law are born together and die together; by denying all natural right to property, he left the subject of inheritance to whatever devices might be judged "most useful." Locke, by founding property on primitive contract, made that contract "of course alterable by consent of the contracting parties."[68]

Where Jefferson would have let the portion of property occupied by the decedent revert to society upon death, Brownson proposed that society "dispose of it by some equitable law, for the use of the generation that takes its place." Jefferson "merely declared what was natural law on this subject." Brownson now demanded "that the actual arrangements of society be conformed to that law." If man's natural right to property ceases at death, Brownson continued, then "he has no natural right to dispose of it by will or testament, to be effective after his death."[69] Citing Jefferson, Brownson noted that the legatee takes "by the law of the society of which he is a member, and to which he is subject." According to Blackstone, any other theory would make the right of bequest "absurdly inconvenient."[70]

Next Brownson inquired whether the children or relations of the decedent had a natural right to the decedent's property. Blackstone, Jefferson, and Montesquieu had said no. Brownson interpreted Kent's comment that they take "by the voice of nature" to mean not by natural right, but by natural familial concern. If children and other relations took by natural right, Brownson concluded, this would preclude the testamentary right of the decedent to devise to those of his choice.[71]

Thus far Brownson's argument had been carefully based; now it was time to spring his plan. Though Blackstone and others had defended the civil right of inheritance on the grounds of wisdom and convenience, Brownson countered that society had to obey the law of nature, which in this case dictated equal property division. Thus "the child of the decedent stands in the same relation to the property as any other child," and therefore natural justice demanded the abolishment of hereditary property and its equitable disposition "for the use of the new generation."[72] This of course is the great leap that American society has repeatedly refused to take.

Brownson knew at this point in his argument he must appeal to the pragmatic side of his countrymen concerning "equitable disposition" of property. As property became "vacant," he wrote, "it should be reappointed to individuals of the new generation in order eventually to give each individual an even start in life." In order to decide the proportion due to each, a general valuation of all property of the commonwealth would need to be made. A "simple rule of division" would then determine how much was "the portion of the new occupant."[73]

In theory his argument was in perfect harmony with the nation's professed belief in equal opportunity and individual enterprise. Brownson was not "contend[ing] against the inequality of property," but asking that all inequalities of property depend "not on unequal reappropriations of what comes down from another generation," but "on the personal character and exertions" of the new owners.[74] This argument for equality of means rather than ends remains the strongest in the arsenal of those who want to restrict or even end the institution of inheritance in America.

Practical problems aside, the scheme faltered on what I call the "lottery" phenomenon: the strong desire of the majority of Americans to have a chance to "win big" by inheriting wealth, thus vaulting without exertion above the mass of men. Brownson recognized both this yearning and its near relation: the hope of leaving a windfall to one's children. "We say to these workingmen, your children have a natural and indefeasible right not to the little you can save out of your necessities to leave them," but "to an equal portion with the children of the rich." Under his plan the children of the rich would inherit less than usual, but the children of the hard-working poor would "inherit more."[75]

Whatever the logical merit of his proposal, Brownson knew that he would be swamped by pragmatic dissents; these he attempted to answer. First, he tried to refute the argument that a confiscation of inheritance would simply shift gift giving to lifetime (*inter vivos*) transfers. To this he responded that (1) man rarely knows the precise hour of his death and will hang on to his property so as not to be dependent in his old age; and (2) gifts which are *causa mortis* (in anticipation of death) as opposed to truly *inter vivos* transfers should not be permitted by the law.[76] That is, those gifts which were designed to continue the donor's dominion after death should be banned, while those made to transfer control completely during life should be permitted.

To the argument of the Orthodox economists that inheritance confiscation would destroy capital formation, Brownson made a politically unfortunate response which may have betrayed his affinity for the utopians of Brook Farm: he proffered the notion that to lessen capital accumulation would be good for society. Wealth would soon cease to be sought "for the distinction it confers." This would be true, Brownson thought, in a society where "fortunes were nearly equal" and all children were brought up "in the same way and at the same schools," having the "same general manners, cultivation and refinement."[77]

It is obvious from the remainder of his argument that Brownson was under attack, expecially by members of his own social class, for his ideas about wealth redistribution: his argument was largely defensive and has little present value. He felt his new system would not only improve the repute of labor (since all would have to work) but that—and here he contradicts himself—the accumulation of wealth would actually become much greater: there would be less waste, more skillfully directed labor, and all laborers would be thoroughly educated. He ended with the unhappy political message that because the privileged would resist his plan, he was ready for class war.[78]

AMERICAN THOUGHT IN THE LATE NINETEENTH CENTURY

Perhaps Brownson's apocalyptic vision was prompted by the realization that his idealist notions were doomed by the tide of materialism. What sway he and his fellow Transcendentalists had was finally crushed by the machine of the Civil War. From then to the end of the century, what passed for philosophy could be found in the writings of British sociologist Herbert Spencer and his American populizer, William Graham Sumner. It was the age of biology adapted to society, of so-called "Social Darwinism."

Social Darwinism was a significant variant of Jeffersonian naturalism, but it was only a variant. There was less a difference between the philosophy of the Age of Jefferson and that of the "Robber Barons" than a difference in stages of development of the same philosophy. The Darwinists widened the focus of Jeffersonian naturalism on man's natural struggle against other species to include the struggle for survival against those of his own species. This shift in emphasis was understandable in the context of the late nineteenth century, when an individual's prosperity depended less on his ability to master Nature than on his cunning in outwitting (or defeating) his neighbor.[79]

In sum, Jeffersonian naturalism was a period of promise and prophecy; Spencerian naturalism was one of retrospect on material accomplishment. Whereas Jefferson, facing the boundless opportunities of an open continent, could optimistically tie prosperity with virtue, those who looked back at the century's end were faced only with the grim facts of social struggle, unfiltered by the prism of dreams.

In an 1887 article, William Graham Sumner took the familiar Social Darwinist position on inequality of wealth. "Whether there are great extremes of rich and poor in society is a matter of very little significance," he wrote. Furthermore, reformers who wanted repartition of property were consumed by envy, which should not be the basis of social philosophy. Taking an empirical approach, Sumner argued that if an examination of the laws and institutions of society hindered anyone "from fighting out the battle of life on his own behalf to the best of one's ability," then reform should be attempted, "especially if [these laws and institutions] hinder one to the advantage of another."[80] If examination of the social organism showed no such unfair operation of laws and institutions, however, inequality of achievements would show social health rather than disease.

Sumner's a posteriori look at the American social struggle clearly did not discern disease. Even if it had, a reform like wealth redistribution was not one Sumner wished to consider. In a rather simplistic passage Sumner argued that "forcible repartition of wealth" would, like the extant system, produce "wide grades of inequality." His concern was that taking from the rich and giving to the poor would make both extremes rich, squeezing out the vital middle class and leading to socialism. As the rich used trickery to avoid much of the redistribution, and the poor received all the redistribution actually made, the middle class would thus fight a losing struggle for survival.[81]

Sumner revealed, albeit dimly, in this excerpt a central dilemma in the Social Darwinist view of inheritance: if the free evolution of society produced great inequalities of wealth, his favorite, the self-made man, might have to fight the "battle of life" from an extreme competitive disadvantage. Turning hastily from this perception to his worries about socialism, Sumner ignored the idea that redistribution might be used creatively to make life's starting places rather than its end results more equal.

Sumner's failure had its roots deep in liberal political theory. Ostensibly, his theory of "natural selection" and "survival of the fittest" was derived from Spencer's *Social Statics,* which was in turn based on biological science. Actually, the pre-formation of national consciousness by liberal ideology instilled in him a Hobbesian taste for notions of competitiveness, struggle and isolation. Sumner's individual, like Hobbes's, had the unlimited right to employ whatever aids proved necessary in his egoistic struggle for existence.[82]

For both Hobbes and Sumner, the state must provide man with equal opportunity in service as a tribute to the worth of each individual; it does so, however, without imposing an ideal pattern of life. Sumner's historical problem was that the Hobbesian construction of liberal institutions had come increasingly into conflict with political realities. A cluster of wealthy men by the 1890s employed the power of the state to augment their already disproportionate share of capital. While such millionaires were consistent with his liberal ideology as products of "natural selection," these plutocrats plundered the state for subsidies, contracts, tax write-offs and tariff protection. Of what use were exhortations to "Get capital!" when cumulative disparities were infringing on the relative opportunities of individuals to obtain it?[83]

Sumner's contemporary, steel magnate Andrew Carnegie, perceived both the inheritance portion of the equal opportunity problem and its solution more clearly than Sumner. "Why," asked Carnegie, "should men leave great fortunes to their children?" He insisted that the answer lay in "misguided affection" and that the evils of the institution of inheritance were greater than its benefits. He advocated a progressive federal inheritance tax that would confiscate all of a decedent's estate except a moderate allowance to immediate heirs.[84] Charles Bellamy, a Utopian socialist writing in 1884, had been somewhat more moderate. He suggested limiting the amount any individual might receive by inheritance or bequest to a sum whose income would be ample. In addition, he favored limiting the total amount that might be distributed by will.[85]

Carnegie believed that since the accumulation of great wealth came only from value produced by society, the return of the bulk of it was but a just redistribution. Since "equality of opportunity" and democracy were important American ideals, he thought that institutional burdens to individual achievement should be lifted; the disinherited heirs of the fortune should not complain, since their opportunities would still be greater than those of laborers' sons. Carnegie scoffed at the notion that such a confiscatory tax would check initiative, since the captains of industry, in his view, did not accumulate great fortunes for the sake of posterity so much as for their joy in the struggle for accumulation.[86]

Carnegie had a purpose for this position—his promotion of philanthropy as the proper way for the rich to use their wealth:

> By taxing estates heavily at death, the state marks its condemnation of the selfish millionaire's unworthy life. It is desirable that nations should go much further in this direction ... until of the millionaire's

unworthy hoard, as of Shylock's, at least — 'The other half / comes to the privy coffer of the state.' This policy would work powerfully to induce the rich man to attend to the administration of wealth during his life.[87]

Thus Carnegie saw the rich man as trustee (above the moderate wants of his family) for the public, spending money for its benefit. It was better in his view to spend sums for public purposes "from which the masses reap the principal benefit" than to scatter money among them through the course of many years so that the poor might waste it "in indulgence of appetite."[88] Touting his plan as an antidote for the unequal distribution of wealth and as a balm for the reconciliation of rich and poor, Carnegie must be credited with at least a portion of the inheritance tax movement, though both his naïveté and his paternalism would ultimately make his redistribution scheme unworkable.

The inheritance tax movement itself took place in an era when the courts had begun to limit quite carefully what popularly-elected legislatures could do. This was an outgrowth of the long struggle between the rational "common lawyers" and democratic legislators. The issues involved were put most clearly by an Illinois justice in 1848, who agreed with the rational jurists that the common law originated in natural law, but complained that, as so conceived, it became clay in the hands of the courts, to be shaped by their will. Unless the American common law could be regularized and declared to all through codification, this judge worried that, far from being enslaved to Jacksonian "pettifoggers" as Kent and Story feared, democracy would be captured by "professional intellectuals" like the rational jurists.[89]

Though systematic codification of the common law failed and jurists continued to hold the key to its mysteries, legislatures were not afraid to pass laws, even controversial ones. For instance a number of inheritance taxes were levied during the period from the Civil War to 1900, due generally to revenue needs during wartime, but in some measure they were a result of the Utilitarian concern for legislated social progress. Inheritance taxes and a probate duty enacted during the Civil War were repealed in 1870 and 1872 respectively. In 1874, the Supreme Court held the former constitutional in a decision ignoring the natural right/civil right distinction.[90]

By the 1890s the Supreme Court majority combined a hostile attitude toward government infringements of what they considered "natural" economic rights with a conception of the appellate judiciary as an active check on the legislature. Ignoring the distinctions between natural rights and constitutional principles acknowledged even by Kent and Story, they merged the two into a governing concept. By allying a constitution written by men, with rights declared by nature and interpreted by them, the majority strengthened the autonomous role posited for the judiciary by the rational jurists. The essence of this role was to act as a buffer between the people and their government.[91]

In this context, the approach the Court took toward inheritance and its taxation was surprising. Instead of lumping inheritance with the inalienable right of property, it followed the line taken in Europe, by Jefferson, and in the Court's own precedents. Clearly separating the civil institution of inheritance from property itself, the Court affirmed that the institution was subject to governmental control. In the Court's view, taxes on inheritance were not direct taxes on people's property, but indirect duties on the *process* of transferring that property from the dead to the living. I have chosen as examples of this position two decisions of the period—one upholding a state inheritance tax, the other the federal inheritance tax occasioned by the Spanish-American War.

In *Magoun* v. *Illinois Trust & Savings Bank* (1897), which considered the validity of an Illinois inheritance tax, Justice McKenna, writing for the Court, put the matter directly:

> The right to take property by devise or descent is the creature of the law, and not a natural right — a privilege, and therefore the authority which confers it may impose conditions upon it.[92]

Next McKenna began to maneuver between this widely accepted principle and the sentiment of the Court and the times. Refusing to take a stand either on the State's argument that its power "could be exerted to the extent of making the State the heir to everybody," and the appellant's claim that children have a natural right to inherit property, McKenna noted cryptically that despite his claim, appellant had "conceded that [both] testamentary disposition and inheritance were subject to regulation."[93] Apparently, then, appellant did not take his own natural law argument very seriously. He may have gotten the idea from a maverick distinction attempted by Justice Brown in *United States* v. *Perkins* the year before, that though bequest was a civil right, the inheritance of children was a natural one.[94]

In any event, Justice McKenna was treading more orthodox paths, citing *Mager* v. *Grima* as authority that both rights were civil in nature.[95] Also cited was *United States* v. *Fox* where the court had declared that, as to real property, "the power of the State to regulate ... the rules of its descent, and the extent to which a testamentary disposition of it may be exercised by its owner, is undoubted."[96] Surpisingly, McKenna then cited *Perkins* at length and without direct comment, including the passage trying to distinguish the rights of bequest and inheritance. Perhaps he felt no need to divorce himself from Justice Brown's comments about the natural right of inheritance since Brown had decided that the tax involved in *Perkins* was on the power of bequest—thus rendering the point about children mere *dicta* (without value as precedent). Perhaps Justice Brown had confused the social need for family maintenance with natural right.

If doubt remained on whether the Court entertained a natural right for children to inherit, the leading case of *Knowlton* v. *Moore* (1900)[97] dispelled it in a decision upholding the Spanish-American War federal succession tax as constitutional. Citing *Mager*, *Magoun*, and *Eyre* v. *Jacob*, Justice White reiterated the *Magoun* principle that "The right to take property by devise or *descent* [emphasis added] is the creature of the law, and not a natural right. . . . "[98] Though *Perkins* was also cited for this general proposition, no mention was made of its natural rights attempt; after all, the twentieth century had begun.

With the question of civilian control decided, Justice White turned to the tax itself, in a statement which remains good law until this day:

> The thing forming the universal subject of taxation, upon which inheritance and legacy taxes rest is the transmission or receipt [of property]. . . . Although different modes of assessing such duties prevail, and although they have different accidental names, such as probate duties, . . . taxes on . . . the act of passing of an estate or succession, legacy taxes, or estate taxes, . . . tax laws of this nature in all countries rest in their

essence upon the principle that death is the generating source from which the particular taxing power takes its being. . . . [99]

As Jefferson had said at the century's beginning, "earth belongs to the living;" thus, in White's words, taxation could justly fall on the "power to transmit," or the "transmission from the dead to the living."[100]

CONCLUSION

By the close of the nineteenth century, growing inequities in American social and economic conditions provided the basis for a serious discussion of the institution of inheritance. The natural right to property was no longer the vague weapon of the rational jurists, but had been reduced to its specific enumeration in the Constitution and Bill of Rights. The Fifth and Fourteenth Amendments, for example, guaranteed that property could not be taken without due process of law, including compensation. Bequest and succession, however, were specifically guaranteed neither in these amendments, nor in the Constitution as a whole. America thus entered the Progressive Era with some of the philosophical barriers to a comprehensive federal estate tax removed; it became increasingly likely that this and other redistributive measures would be enacted by Congress and legislatures, without the interference of the courts. Still lurking in the background, however, was the courts' insistence on the vested right to property during life—a concept encouraging the nation's profound ambivalence about ancillary rights like inheritance.

4

Inheritance in Twentieth-Century American Thought

This chapter has two main aims. The first is to tie together previously discussed strands of Western thought about inheritance as they emerged in the context of early twentieth-century America: these strands produce a principle for reforming inheritance laws which might be used today. The second aim is to inquire whether philosophical and political bases exist for acting upon such a principle. In this context, the modern debate about inheritance and inequality is presented, suggesting answers to libertarian concerns about egalitarian limitations on the institution.

PART I. THEMES OF EARLY CENTURY

As the twentieth century dawned in America, little doubt remained that the institution of inheritance was a privilege permitted by the state, subject to its control in a far broader sense than the parent institution, private property. During the Progressive period early in the century, it appeared that state control might substantially curtail the institution through use of the taxing power. That this did not occur was due in large part to the ingenious arguments used by the privileged to defend their wealth. These arguments, in turn, flourished in a climate of opinion characterized both by the notion that the individual should be allowed to control property after death and the hope of winning the "inheritance lottery."

EQUAL OPPORTUNITY AND SELF-HELP

Equality of opportunity and self-help are ideas that give direction to an important side of the movement for American inheritance reform. The attitude toward inheritance of Theodore Roosevelt and Andrew Carnegie, both rugged individualists, neatly captures American expressions of these notions early in the century. Roosevelt, Progressive son of a wealthy New York family, was being entirely consistent with his "trust-busting" philosophy when he proposed in 1906 to provide equal opportunity for individuals as well as businesses. In that year he proposed an inheritance tax, "so framed as to put it out of the power of the owner of one of these enormous fortunes to hand more than certain amount to any one individual."[1] In his presidential message on December 3 of that year, Roosevelt suggested that Congress pass a heavily progressive inheritance tax.[2] However, conservative opposition halted his drive against accumulated fortunes, and no substantial new attempt was made to impose a federal inheritance tax until the urgent need for war funds produced the estate tax of 1916.[3]

There was a strain of Andrew Carnegie in Theodore Roosevelt and to understand it fully one must consider the influence of their Protestant Christianity. The established Protestantism of the time had given its assent to Spencerian Social Darwinism in political economy; its concept of charity, unlike that of the Catholics, was directed only to the deserving poor. Help would be given not to all who requested it, but only to those willing to "pull themselves up by their own bootstraps."[4] The attitude of Carnegie and Roosevelt toward inheritance should be seen in light of their firm belief in self-help; their goal, like that of contemporary Protestant reformers, was to make the "game of life" fairer, not to dictate its results. Theirs was a defense of individualism in an era when concentrations of personal and corporate wealth blocked many people's mobility within the social system.

The clamor for breaking up the huge individual fortunes of this period was intensified by the ostentatious consumption of the new industrial and financial elite. Reacting to this phenomenon in 1907, an American economist drew on the themes of self-help, equal opportunity, and Protestant charity to the deserving poor:

> [The] social including both the moral and political, influence of so high a degree of concentration of riches at the present is, on the whole evil. Some inequality is inevitable and also highly desirable. But inequality of natural endowment will, under any probable circumstances insure all the economic inequality that is needed. [The] inequalities in men to which inequality of property should correspond are not of mere capacity to acquire wealth, but of capacity to use it well. We have too much concentration of riches. It threatens that equality of opportunity, and that spirit of individuality and self-reliance which are essential to democracy.[5]

On the eve of the adoption of the 1916 estate tax by Congress, economist Irving Fisher picked up this "self-made man" theme by remarking that "Americans still admire" this sort of individual compared to the man "whose wealth came to him through no merit of his own, but merely by accident of birth." Thus, "the real menace from great wealth to democratic ideals" is "the danger of an hereditary plutocracy" which the estate tax might help to alleviate.[6]

The self-made man theme and fear of plutocracy also marked Harlan Read's book, *The Abolition of Inheritance.* Appearing in 1919, this tract reiterated a theme of my previous chapters—the civil rather than natural character of inheritance as a basis for its confiscation. Read felt the vast disparities of wealth which characterized the twentieth century dictated the use of civil power to destroy inheritance, the critical ingredient in wealth concentration. Removing the institution would eliminate the ethical incongruity of its nurture by a society which believed in equal opportunity.[7]

Read's notions bore political fruit in the postwar period when the battle was once again joined over whether a wartime death tax should be continued as a permanent part of the American fiscal system. In a special conference on the federal estate tax, preceding the regular meeting of the National Tax Association in 1924, inheritance tax expert John L. McMaster, amid the discussion of various technical aspects of the tax, presented a capable philosophical defense of estate taxation. Commenting favorably on Read's "important book" which had "attracted considerable attention," McMaster outlined the self-help and equal opportunity themes in the work of both Mill and Carnegie. Finally, he described the contemporary "Cleveland Declaration" of the Progressive party, which advocated a large increase in inheritance and estate tax rates in order to break up concentrations of wealth and equalize opportunity.[8]

EQUALITY OF ENDS: EUROPEAN SOCIALISM AND ITS AMERICAN ADAPTATION

1. THE RIGNANO PLAN   "Equal starting places" in life was a concept amenable to American values; this was not true of "equality of end results," a socialist notion aimed at eliminating the individual's right to rise above his brother through the efforts of a lifetime. As we saw in chapter 2, even Orestes Brownson, when presenting the Platonic idea that inheritances should be split up among all children of a generation rather than simply among the heirs of the rich, was talking about equal opportunity, not forced egalitarian results.[9]

Still, America was not immune to socialistic notions spawned by the triumph of Russian Communism and the terrible economic conditions of postwar Europe. These factors had induced European socialists, notably Eugenio Rignano of Italy, to consider the philosophical basis of inheritance in ways that filtered back to America during the Great War and its aftermath.

Rignano's plan was anchored in the belief that property rights (including inheritance) should be restricted to that historical period strictly necessary and sufficient to guarantee the maximization of labor and saving. Rignano based his view on the Utilitarian principle of Bentham and Mill that the justification of all human institutions should be sought exclusively in their social utility; the social utility of inheritance had, to Rignano's mind, vanished by the 1920s. Now that Western nations had accumulated the necessary capital, Rignano wanted to act decisively to stop its further concentration, rather than waiting, like the pure Marxists, for the forces of history to displace the system which had created it. One can see in his scheme a desire to defuse the revolutionary pressures of the immediate postwar period via a gradual though ultimately confiscatory use of taxation.

Though Rignano aimed for eventual state control of capital, he sought to preserve bourgeois incentives for production at the same time. Fearing a violent confrontation between the classes in the economic crisis following the war, Rignano sought a "pacific and legal transformation of the economic system—radical though gradual—which would tend to modify the distributive system in the direction of greater justice, without causing violent and disastrous crises in production."[10] This could be done by "leaving the production of commodities and the accumulation of new capital to individual initiative, and by enabling "certain property or instruments of production—those most suitable for public management—to pass gradually, by a steady and automatic process," to the nation.[11] By graduating inheritance taxation according to the number of transfers which different parts of an estate had previously undergone, Rignano hoped to accomplish this transformation without "violent revolutionary expropriation" on one hand, or "a system of compensation" on the other.[12]

Rignano hoped to reconcile "certain unassailable truths of orthodox economic doctrine" with socialistic critiques of capitalism relating to justice and social welfare.[13] His perspective, however, was different from that of the American "equal opportunity" theorists. Rignano cared less for individuals than for the ultimate good of the state. He wanted to leave "unhampered individual enterprise" and "free competition" in place as they then existed in order to maintain and expand the national capital so ravaged by war.[14] Unlike Roosevelt, Carnegie, and Read, he was not interested in making the game of life fairer for those who would help themselves, but in allowing those who had produced to continue that production along the slow route to state socialism.

Certain parts of the Rignano scheme, however, were adaptable to the American experience. The principle of destroying wealth concentration through taxation graduated by number of transfers could be used to unlock social mobility in America, rather than to concentrate all wealth in the hands of the state. Rignano suggested that assets be completely confiscated by the state upon their third intergenerational transfer, a plan which would eventually eliminate all private capital, save that being accumulated at any time by the living. In the American setting, application of high, but nonconfiscatory tax rates on successive transfers, coupled with redistribution of these revenues to the relatively disadvantaged, would tend to equalize the economic opportunities of individual citizens rather than fill the collective purse of the state.

Specifically, Rignano would leave intact inheritance taxation graduated by size of estate and degree of relation of heirs, but then graduate it according to the number of transfers (by way of hereditary succession or lifetime donation) which different parts of the estate had undergone before coming into the decedent's possession. In other words, the rate Rignano wished to impose varied markedly with the relative "age" of the particular assets involved. Once an estate was divided into what the decedent himself had earned and what he had received by transfer, the state would first tax the earned portion at normal rates. Then it would impose a much heavier levy, say 50%, on the portion which came directly from his donor, typically the father. The portion which had passed through the father from the grandfather would be very heavily taxed, possibly at a rate of 100%.[15]

Rignano saw the state, therefore, as co-heir to accumulated fortunes; under his system, the state would gain control of more and more of the country's capital.[16] His scheme offered some protection to individuals by allowing an exemption of $10,000 in assets, except for presently due inheritance tax. Also, certain parts of the estate that might be of sentimental value, such as the paternal house or a piece of land, could be protected by paying the state their value out of current income. For example, a house valued at $50,000 could be protected against 100% confiscation upon passage to the grandson if the grandson had accumulated $50,000 of new earnings to pay the state in its stead.[17] Rignano thought this feature would be an inducement to earnings on the part of these heirs who had little or no incentive to work and accumulate under the existing system.[18]

Much of the conservative response to Rignano's plan centered on the disincentive effects of eventual inheritance confiscation on saving and capital formation. Thus, Rignano was careful to explain that his system would *stimulate* savings, since each sum an individual saved would have much greater after-tax value for death transfer purposes than property he had himself inherited.[19] However, Rignano refused to spend much time on the savings-disincentive argument, since:

> It skillfully draws attention to certain sentimental archaic and arcadian aspects of the capitalist regime but ... forgets altogether to point out the ugly and unjust miseries, the too numerous exceptions to (the) ideal

of patriarchial family life which this regime permits or causes and the inadmissible privileges it implies for parasitic and useless individuals who otherwise would be condemned by nature to be replaced by others more worthy than themselves.[20]

This condemnation of the unworthy rich by the laws of nature likely struck a responsive chord in those sympathetic to Social Darwinist elements of the American inheritance reform movement. However, it is important to note that Rignano was not talking about the replacement of these "parasites" with more economically productive individuals; rather he was referring to the managers of state capital who would come to power under socialism. As these managers, operating in the name of the collective, came to control most capital after three generations, individual citizens would become much more equal materially. The differences in individual lifetime accumulations of private property would become relatively unimportant since control of the means of production would have passed to the state itself. The rough equality of end result that this system would enforce among its people was not a goal congenial to American values.

2. A BRITISH ADAPTATION IN THE EQUAL OPPORTUNITY VEIN   Rignano's principles were popularized with substantial modifications by British Liberal economist Hubert Henderson and by American economist William Shultz. Henderson, a student of John Maynard Keynes at Cambridge and his colleague on the Council of Liberal Summer Schools, expressed strong ethical reasons for restricting inheritance in explaining his adaptation of Rignano's principles. He saw extreme inequality in wealth as the main source of social unrest, "that condition of latent class-warfare which is the note of modern industrial communities."[21] Solutions such as better housing and reduced unemployment were mere palliatives: "We deceive ourselves if we imagine it is possible by such means to extirpate social content, so long as wealth is distributed as it is today"[22] The contemporary social system had, Henderson believed, "accentuated initial inequalities in a cumulative way. A chief contributor to this system was the influence of 'dead hand' control over property; social justice demanded a constant erosion of accumulated fortunes to limit this influence."[23]

Henderson also saw the effects of what I have called elsewhere the phenomenon of perceived relative deprivation. An increased perception of wealth differentials by the poor had in his view caused an envy which had to be assuaged:

> So long as superiority of persons was associated with superiority of culture, intelligence, capacity and public spirit, so long as those in the humbler walks of life felt, however resentfully, that their more fortunate fellow-citizens were in a real sense their "betters." The contrast between riches and poverty did not rankle. It is because so much has been done to spread knowledge, to widen horizons, to raise moral standards, to supply the great mass of people with the conditions that make for self-respect . . . that the inequality in the distribution of wealth stands out today [1926] as a gross and undefensible anomaly. [Britain's] inequality is too gross to be defended . . . The man who maintains that the graduations of wealth which prevail in Britain today reflect and measure, however roughly and imperfectly, corresponding differences in the value of services rendered to society is not a realist, but a poet.[24]

The plan devised by Henderson to alleviate social unrest used Rignano's generational approach to wealth redistribution, but was devoid of its suggestion of eventual confiscation. First, he would have deducted the regular British estate tax duty (say £20,000) from A's £100,000 estate. One quarter of the remaining estate (£20,000) would then be paid to the state, which would pay an annuity from this to the heirs.[25] Assuming the heirs were four children receiving equal shares, each would thus be paid the income on £5,000 for life, plus a £15,000 share of the legacy itself. The annuities would cease upon the death of each child with capital escheating to the state.[26]

Assuming child B increased his holdings to a total of £25,000 during life, his estate would first be subject to the normal estate duty. Then, B's children (assuming they were heirs), would each be assessed a "re-inheritance duty" on their legacies. This duty would thus fall on each grandchild of original decedent A, but would be graduated by the size of the legacy which constituted the first inheritance (£15,000) not according to the amount each such grandchild received. Thus, each of the four family "trees" in the second generation would be taxed equally. Otherwise, a family with five children each receiving £3,000 would pay less total tax than the family with three children each receiving £5,000 legacies which are taxed at higher rates.[27]

Henderson noted that making the amount received by B the basis for taxation would also diminish the indirect capital reduction problem which economists felt fear of death taxation would produce. "So long as the benefit which an heir's *children* will derive from his savings is not diminished (by the re-inheritance duty), his incentive to save will not be greatly weakened by curtailing the benefits his *grandchildren* will derive."[28] Henderson's argument did not deal, however, with the direct reduction in private capital produced by this added tax; perhaps he assumed it would be redistributed into other private hands. After all, unlike Rignano, Henderson was not suggesting either that all inherited capital should be taxed or that the duty itself should eventually confiscate all such property for the state. Clearly, some rearrangement of private ownership of capital had greater appeal in Britain than did state socialism, however gradually that might be reached.

3. THE AMERICAN RIGNANO PLAN   As Rignano's American interpreter and translator, William Shultz recognized not only the Italian's desire for state socialism, but also his hope to lessen the distinction between capitalists and wage earners "as the latter received through their cooperative associations an ever-increasing share of this nationalized wealth."[29] Shultz knew it was necessary to put aside such elements of the plan because of their offensiveness to most Americans and Britons. However, they "would rally eagerly to the support of a fiscal measure, however radical, that gives promise of lightening tax burdens in other directions and that can be proved noninjurious to economic progress."[30] In favor of what he called his "minimum program," Shultz noted that "the economic democratization [that] would result through even a moderate revision of the privilege of inheritance would be a notable step in the direction of greater social justice."[31]

Shultz would have estimated the decedent's tax under the normal progressive estate tax structure and then quadrupled it if the decedent's estate had been transmitted to him in its entirety. If the decedent's estate were one-half earned and one-half inherited, the estimated tax would be doubled instead of quadrupled. Such a reform would not lead to the gradual nationalization of all means of production advocated by Rignano, but would, besides preparing legislators for future uses of the Rignano principle, commit the nation to a practical and just program of shifting some of the tax burden from incomes and indirect levies to inheritances.[32]

Shultz felt he had to deal with the telling argument of the fiscal economists that income and customs duties levy only upon the current income of the nation, while heavy inheritance taxes absorb its capital wealth. "They argue that if the burden of taxation be shifted to inheritances, the economic foundations of our industrial society will be weakened."[33] Though recognizing the possibility that the capital fund would not be increased as rapidly as it had been without severe inheritance taxation, he answered that this would not be an "unmixed evil." Besides, accumulation would not be substantially decreased since "remission of other taxes would relieve industry of a great burden, and would also result in saving and accumulation by a great many individuals who today find themselves unable to do so because of (e.g., income) tax burdens."[34] Thus, the capital fund would be built up:

> (N)ot so rapidly, perhaps as at present—by the small contributions of a great many people intead of by the huge fortunes of relatively few individuals—and surely this wide dissemination of title to the capital fund would be a closer approach to social justice than our present system. Moreover, so long as the tax demands of the government are moderate, [capital-reduction] dangers hardly exist; they would only become imminent when inheritance tax rates become confiscatory. There could be no reasons for making the rates confiscatory unless the government planned to enter upon a program of nationalization; . . . under these conditions the capital fund would be preserved not only by individual contributors but to a large extent by the government itself.[35]

Thus described, Shultz's vision sought equal material opportunity for the many rather than for the few, leaving the question of state control for the future.

Considering the narrow orthodoxy of current American tax policy, one might think that a tax such as Rignano and Shultz were proposing could never have received substantial enough political support to be taken seriously. Yet it is worth remembering that the war and postwar climate was an extraordinary one, giving rise to notions of reform which strike us as radical in the modern context. Following are several examples representative of this climate.

In August of 1915, the *Chicago Tribune,* then as now no radical sheet, editorially declared that a sharp limitation on inheritances would be salutary and intimated its approval of the recommendation of the Federal Commission on Industrial Relations that a million dollars be that limit.[36] The following month, John R. Montgomery of the Chicago Bar referred to this editorial in presenting a paper to the Law Club of that city describing the increasing threat to inheritances.[37]

Montgomery was concerned mainly with the state's power to confiscate inheritances either totally or those over a certain limit. While the right of the federal government was based solely on its right to levy excise *taxes* on privileges, the power of state governments included not only this right, but also the right to *regulate* the entire process of passing or receiving property by will or inheritance. Montgomery explained that though the federal government might at any time levy an inheritance tax, even a very large one, it would never attempt to take any considerable portion of a decedent's estate because its right depended solely on the taxing power and it had never asserted its right "to confer, revoke or regulate [such] state-regulated privileges." Though admitting that the "power to tax involves the power to destroy," Montgomery declined to believe that the federal government's taxing power "involves the right to destroy or confiscate the property of every citizen of each state at his death, and thereby to nullify the power reserved to the several states to confer, revoke or regulate the right of inheritance." However, if the Illinois legislature attempted limitation or even confiscation, the courts would have to uphold it.[38]

Montgomery pointed out that a special commission of the Illinois Bar Association had introduced an inheritance limitation bill into the Illinois legislature as early as 1887. This bill, which had not passed, would have limited inheritances by individuals in a direct line to $500,000 and among collateral heirs to $100,000. He noted this was in accord with the ethical notions expressed by the great philanthropist, Alfred Noble:

> Experience has taught me that great fortunes acquired by inheritance never bring happiness, they only dull the faculties. Any man possessing a large fortune ought not to leave more than a small part of it to his heirs, not even his direct heirs—just enought to make their way in the world.[39]

Expressing his concern that the worldwide struggle between the proletariate and the Establishment would bring limitations on American inheritances in the near future, Montgomery ended by proposing a constitutional amendment to restrict the power of the legislatures to limit inheritance to a set amount.[40] Although the political process ultimately made such amendments unnecessary, the limitation debate was being joined in other states as well.

In 1919, the Mississippi State Tax Commission openly approved of an inheritance tax for the purpose of equalizing wealth and suggested an estate duty absorbing the amount by which any estate exceeded $5,000,000.

> There are many millionaires in the Union with but few heirs at law. Such estates have been accumulated out of the pockets of the citizens of the several states. . . . Where profits are so enormous, they cease to be profits simply, but they are nothing other than a tax. The citizenship, that has paid them, is more entitled to the benefits than the heirs at law.[41]

As is suggested by such state attempts to limit inheritances, plans like Rignano's had an acceptable basis in American law. Shultz was careful to make the point that civil control over inheritances was settled law in the Supreme Court. Since this facet was taken up in detail in chapter 3, Shultz's argument is only highlighted here.

Citing *Magoun* v. *Illinois Trust and Savings Bank,*[42] Shultz noted that the right to take property by devise or descent was a creature of law, not a natural right. It was therefore a privilege upon which the authority which conferred it might impose conditions. Still American "states'-rights" arguments like those of attorney Montgomery had to be considered because the "success of Signor Rignano's program would only be possible if applied to a *national* inheritance tax. *State* inheritance taxes could only be supplementary to his project."[43]

Thus, though the "right of the nation to levy an inheritance tax has been securely upheld in court decisions" like *Magoun,* "it has only been under the assumption that this tax is not a property tax but an excise upon the right to transmit property at death."[44] If not an indirect excise, the federal inheritance tax would violate the constitutional requirement (Article I, §8) that a direct tax be equal in its burdens and uniform in its application, and be divided among the states in proportion to their population.[45]

Characterization of the tax as an excise was also important to guard it from possible application of the Fifth and Fourteenth amendments to the Constitution. The first of these provides that private property cannot be taken for public use "without just compensation" and the second that "no state shall deprive any person of . . . property without due process of law; nor deny to any person . . . the equal protection of the law." Of course, even careful characterization of the tax as one on transfer rather than on property itself might not save from violation of these amendments a confiscatory inheritance tax which would in reality prevent any transfer of money between the generations.[46]

With only the extreme measure of confiscation subject to constitutional question, it is not surprising (given the postwar climate) that the Under Secretary of the Treasury publicly suggested the Rignano principle at the 1924 National Tax Association Conference in St. Louis:

> Perhaps if taxes were levied lightly on the result of a man's own efforts and heavily upon his inherited assets, they would not destroy the initiative to produce and the government would still get the maximum revenue out of death duties. It has been accordingly suggested that a light tax be levied on what the decedent himself made, a heavier tax on what his father left him, and still heavier tax on what remained of his grandfather's estate. Such a policy would meet the wishes of those who believe that artificial means are necessary to prevent the continued existence through generations of large fortunes and at the same time would not penalize the initiative which is characteristic of progress.[47]

SHULTZ AND RIGNANO FROM THE
PERSPECTIVE OF AMERICAN VALUES

The Shultz adaptation of Rignano's program seems to have both logic and appeal for those who earn a living. To Shultz, the lowering of income taxes made possible by increased inheritance taxation would allow the "Horatio Algers" of the nation to same more money, thus supplanting to a large extent the reduction in saving and accumulation which stiffened inheritance taxation might cause among the wealthy.[48] However, an argument can be made that dispersion of capital in this manner, though perhaps productive of greater opportunity, would not necessarily lead to savings by the many equivalent to the savings no longer possible for the wealthy.

In the first place, conspicuous consumption, which has constantly been paraded before the relatively disadvantaged by advertising and the media, has not produced a psychological climate conducive to saving the added assets that reduced income taxes would make available. Thus many people would be tempted to consume rather than to save this extra money.

This psychological effect would be augmented by the differing impact that added dollars have on the rich and relatively poor. Since the typical wage earner "consumes" a much higher percentage of his total assets than a wealthy person, he will have a smaller percentage of these assets available for saving. Thus, a given amount of capital taken from the wealthy and given back to the wage earner through reduced income taxes would not produce the same total savings. According to orthodox economic theory, this would result in lessened capital formation.

A third problem is that dispersion of wealth into the hands of the many probably results in less efficient investment of capital than its concentration; this effect cannot be mitigated without massive financial education of small investors and group investment.

These factors might be counterbalanced to some extent if reduced income taxation increased productivity, so that the small investor would now have a relatively greater asset base upon which these negative effects could operate. The problem here is that we are not now, if we ever were, a nation of Horatio Algers, ready for economic success if given the chance. As technology moves us further and further away from the day of labor-intensive industries, we are faced with expanding legions of the unemployed and functionally unemployable. Thus, an increasing percentage of our citizens have no chance to establish an economic base upon which they can hope to build themselves into even small investors. As a result, some of the revenue gain from stiffened inheritance taxes would most likely have to be redistributed directly to those who have no meaningful income,[49] either just to keep them alive or to bring them into the free enterprise system. This would lessen the amount we could redistribute through reduced income taxes to those already in a small way a part of that system.

If Rignano's state socialism is inimical to basic American values, and Shultz's adaptation of his plan is incomplete in solving problems of redistribution and capital formation, the basic idea of graduating taxes according to the number of transfers still can be fitted within the American framework of self-help and equal opportunity.

In the final chapter, the taxation aspects of inheritance reform are considered more fully, including a suggestion that a consumption tax be used to help solve the capital reduction effects which might accompany stiff Rignano-based inheritance taxation. These technical questions of tax policy await the resolution of more fundamental ones: Would the severe restriction on inheritance (and, to some extent on all personal wealth) be both just and politically feasible in a democracy like America? Assuming that such a scheme is technically possible, would Western philosophical and political traditions, particularly in America, *permit* its implementation?

PART II THE MODERN DEBATE: IS INHERITANCE JUSTIFIED?

After the 1920s produced a permanent federal estate tax with nominally high and progressive rates supplemented by universal state inheritance taxation, agitation for inheritance reform nearly ceased. Had the American public been misled by this apparent solution, as economist Lester Thurow has suggested,[50] or are there sound reasons for not addressing the persistent inequalities associated with inheritance? Answering these questions has been made easier by a good deal of recent literature on inheritance, written mainly by economists and suggestive of reborn interest in the topic.

James Brittain has written two important monographs on inheritance since 1976. His work appears to occupy the central ground in the rekindled debate between Lester Thurow, on the left, and more orthodox economists like Gordon Tullock and Richard Wagner, on the right. For this reason and because of my belief in its basic soundness, Brittain's argument is carefully considered in what follows, as are its connections with studies by other "equal opportunity" economists. The remainder of the chapter summarizes the other positions in the debate insofar as they relate to the practicality and fairness of severe inheritance restriction. Finally the evolving equal-opportunity position is examined from the perspective that it presents the best chance of resolving the conflict between liberty and equality in the inheritance field.

THE EQUAL-OPPORTUNITY POSITION:
BRITTAIN, THUROW AND OTHERS

Brittain hypotheses that American society tolerates substantial inequality of individual rewards largely because of the belief that the greater the variation in reward, the greater the competitive effort and productive efficiency of individuals will be. However, "the suspicion persists that the material inequality generated by the American economic system could be greatly reduced without a significant loss of efficiency."[51] In addition, it has been shown that inequality of material wealth may be due in large measure to the inheritance of not only "pull, superficial characteristics and productivity,"[52] but also of wealth itself. Since material wealth is the component of inheritance over which society can exert the most control, it is emphasized in the discussion which follows.

A central premise of the equal opportunity position is that bequests of material wealth play a major role in the persistence of economic inequality, especially in the maintenance of the wealth and income shares of the very wealthy. The inequality generated by material inheritance is widely viewed, furthermore, as a philosophically "more fitting target for redistribution policies than inequality due to independent individual performance."[53] However, as suggested in chapter 1, "through New Deal, Fair Deal, New Society, Great Society, and the War Against Poverty," the relative gap between rich and poor in America has remained substantially impervious to egalitarian public policy.[54]

Inheritance merits the attention of American public policy precisely because it may create an "unfair" head start—a handicap. Even orthodox economists feel uncomfortable "with the transmission of rewards so unrelated to the recipient's efforts."[55] Like Brittain, they are puzzled by the lack of public support for more progressive and effective taxes on inherited wealth than those on earned income. Instead, public acquiescence in the low effective rates of American death taxation would have satisfied even those, like industrialist Andrew Mellon, who feared that heavy taxation of inherited capital would eliminate all private property in a few generations.[56]

Brittain suggests that the reason for this lack of popular support stems from intense public attachment to the right of bequest, even among those with no reasonable expectations of becoming either a significant donor or heir. He points to the "national cry of outrage" that greeted Senator George McGovern's proposal during the 1972 presidential campagn to place much stiffer taxes on inheritance: "This reaction may have reflected an impression that the right to bequeath itself was challenged by an early McGovern proposal with confiscatory rates." Brittain feels that if stiffer inheritance taxes could be presented as levies, not on the estate but on the individual heirs, analogous to the tax on the income stream from employer to employee, then "they would enjoy greater public acceptance." If framed in this way, "it seems highly likely that the public would accept much higher tax rates on completely unearned inheritances than on earned incomes."[57]

There is reason to doubt this hypothesis. Certainly interference with the right of bequest would be viewed as just another government intrusion on our individual prerogatives; in that respect it is indeed suspect. People after all are reluctant to give up dead hand control over property, the secular equivalent of eternal life. Despite Jeffersonian promptings, they probably prefer this measure of post-mortem control to a society belonging *entirely* to the succeeding generations. Still, unlike the federal government, most states do levy taxes on the individual beneficiary's inheritance rather than on the estate, and there is no evidence that this type of tax is any more popular than the estate tax. Finally, though the analogy of inheritance flow to income flow might seem persuasive to the well-informed, such fine points would inevitably be lost on the public at large.

One suspects moreover that people feel at least as strongly about the right to inherit as they do about the right to bequeath. Even the vast majority, who can expect little or nothing from this right, want the *chance* to inherit. A Brittain footnote seems to admit the power of this lottery phenomenon, but does not pursue its implications for his method of gaining inheritance tax support:

It is possible, of course, that people may be so enthusiastic about their own (or others') chances of receiving windfalls such a lottery payoffs, that they may wish to leave the outcomes undisturbed by public policy. This would be consistent with the . . . opposition to Senator McGovern's inheritance tax proposals in 1972.[58]

One need only consider the enormous popularity of games of chance in our society to understand the part the inheritance lottery could have played in stifling McGovern's proposals. Many Americans want to "strike it rich;" if this cannot be accomplished through their labor, then they will take a chance on football, horse racing, slot-machines, dice, or a game of cards. Whatever the rationality of arguments about fairness or probability, many Americans prefer to flirt with the irrational chance of success at inheriting wealth. Since being "above the crowd" is a vital part of the American Dream, many prefer the chance of gaining that distinction through an inheritance windfall to the movement toward real equality that might be made through elimination of that chance.

Thus, with all respect to Brittain, the answer to public resistance to inheritance tax reform does not seem to lie in a hair-splitting definition of where and on what the tax actually falls. Whether public hopes for a windfall are strong enough to block stiff taxes on the inheritance recipient, whether desire for dead hand control is similarly strong, and what is the relative strength of these two phenomena—all are vital questions inviting empirical research. Otherwise, we will remain unsure of Brittain's conclusion that severe inheritance restriction will please the public if not couched as an incursion on the individual's right to bequeath.

Another empirical issue is whether, regardless of the answers to these questions, the majority of Americans really want greater equality: the recent popularity of Ronald Reagan among the working class, for example, may suggest that they do not. Brittain himself is only willing to go so far as to say that an "overwhelming majority of the population appears to favor at least some modification of the inequality that emerges in the marketplace."[59] Even American intellectuals, who presumably contribute to the shaping of popular opinion, are ambivalent about equality, at least equality of ends. Many are caught in the Jeffersonian paradox of wanting both an aristocracy of the intellect and greater equality; their desire to be singled out is not, furthermore, lost on the people who do favor greater equality.[60] If both society and the intellectuals move—and there are signs they are —to a position of clear preference for individualism over equality, the paradox will of course be solved. Then, however, reforms such as I propose for inheritance would have little apparent impetus.

Assuming however, that Brittain's conclusion about inequality modification still holds for the majority, the next question might be the one discussed in chapter 1: the extent to which lack of equal opportunity and low social mobility are effects of a high degree of wealth inequality. Such effects may in turn relate to a problem only alluded to there: interference of the wealthy with the democratic political process. As Brittain notes, extreme concentration of material wealth "may confer power on a few that is hazardous to democratic institutions."[61] This power has feedback effect as well; it may be used to block the very changes which would increase equal opportunity and social mobility.

Attitudes toward wealth inequality depend not only on such probable effects, but on public views of its causes. If it could be shown, for example, that unequal wealth was due mainly to unequal income, then wealth inequality could simply be treated as a facet of income inequality. The basic approach to that problem would be to equalize income opportunities. If, on the other hand, the primary cause of wealth inequality is a factor like material inheritance, one would look for ways to redistribute wealth directly.

Since it is unlikely that public policy will intervene more forcefully in the inheritance process without suggestive evidence of the link between material inheritance and the inequality of wealth, forging that link is attempted in the paragraphs that follow. In considering the argument, the reader should be mindful that intergenerational transfers of "human wealth" or earning power may play just as big a role in maintaining unequal economic status. The issues raised by the transfer of such "human wealth" are outside the scope of this book.

Though it has long been suspected that intergenerational gifts and inheritances are a major factor in perpetuating economic inequality, the strength of their effect has been subject to widely divergent estimates. For example, a seminal 1929 study by British economist Josiah Wedgwood found that "in the great majority of . . . cases, the fortunes of one generation belong to the children of those who possessed the large fortunes of the preceding generations," and that "rich men who have sprung from poor parents are in the minority."[62] In contrast, articles in America's *Fortune* magazine over the last twenty years suggest that about one-half of the very wealthy have been self-made men.[63]

Before investigating the issues these quotations pose, I should say a word about the available data. The only official estimates of the distribution of shares of national net worth are those of the Internal

Revenue Service, derived by the "estate-multiplier technique," which applies mortality rates to the distribution of decedents' estates.[64] This method greatly underestimates the assets of wealth-holders, because of the exclusion from estate tax returns of most assets held in trust— a very popular form of holding wealth in the top group. The beneficiaries of trusteed wealth are limited in their access to these assets but they receive much the same security from this capital as do outright recipients. They typically receive the income from this property, and can have the capital invested for their benefit if necessary; likewise, most outright recipients of capital live off the income and invade principal only when necessary. The great under-statement of wealth and security that this lack of trust data allows, is only partially balanced in the inequality calculus by another form of wealth not counted by the I.R.S.: the accrued pension claims of workers.

In 1962, Robert Lampman used I.R.S. data to estimate the share of the national wealth held by the top 1% of living individual wealth-holders. His analysis suggested that a high (22%–38%) and relatively stable share of wealth was held by this group, despite some cyclical swings.[65] A later study by Smith and Franklin shows a remarkable stability in the share of the top 1%, varying between 26% and 27% during the 1958–1972 period.[66] In light of these studies and others discussed in chapter 1, it is evident that the nominal estate tax rates established in the 1930s have had little or no effect in diminishing wealth inequality—any such downward trend, as Brittain suggests, would certainly have shown up by the 1970s.[67]

To assess directly what portion of these persistent inequalities are due to inheritance, one must divide present wealth into its inherited and noninherited components. A. B. Atkinson has argued that the latter rivals inheritance in the amassing of large fortunes; however he stressed that great new fortunes grew out of extraordinary returns in a small minority of capitalist ventures, rather than from gradual saving by the average earner.[68] Economist Lester Thurow later elaborated on Atkinson's views.[69]

The Atkinson-Thurow view of wealth accumulation contrasts with the view of neoclassical economists that fortunes accumulate gradually over a lifetime and then decumulate as the individual invades capital after retirement; this is generally known as the "life-cycle" hypothesis. Their notion is that fortunes cannot grow out of routine saving and that wealthy people continue accumulating in their old age for the sake of economic power, despite tax incentives to make lifetime gifts to their children.[70]

Thurow points out that great wealth is often made by operating in financial markets to take advantage of "disequilibrium in rates of return on capital investment money used to purchase a business's plant and equipment." To illustrate: suppose an entrepreneur figures he can build and equip a plant to build widgets at a cost of $10 million and that he will be able to sell them at a price guaranteeing a return of $3 million a year, or a 30% rate of return. If other forms of capital investment are yielding returns that average 10%, the widget manufacturer is in an above-average disequilibrium situation. Since at the average 10% rate of return it would take a capital investment of $30 million to produce the $3 million return, it becomes possible to sell shares in ownership of the widget plant for $30 million, even though it cost only $10 million to build. The entrepreneur has suddenly added $20 million to his wealth.[71]

Because business managers prefer to plow earnings back into their businesses, capital does not flow efficiently to these high-yield industries, and there is a chronic disequilibrium in financial markets. This disequilibrium has permitted the continuing acquisition of enormous fortunes by those operating in these markets. While this explains the existence of instant fortunes, it does not explain how these fortunes are allocated to individuals.[72]

The answer is found in the "random walk" theory. This theory recognizes that since all information about a corporation is quickly capitalized into the price of a share, it is of no value to the investor; he may as well invest at random. Some investors pick losers, others obtain average yields, and a very few may buy "a Xerox" and become very wealthy. Since, upon capitalization of the information, all investments look equally good, those who pick a winner simply win a lottery. Since these winners are not unique in any way, the result is a highly skewed distribution of wealth which is much more unequal than the distribution of talent, effort, or any other productive input into the economy. Furthermore, "there is no feedback principle in the random walk that tends to equalize the distribution of wealth once it has become unequal."[73] The standard pattern is to make a great fortune and then settle down to earning the market rate of return.[74]

Thurow estimates that, at any one time, half of the fortunes over $1 million are the result of inheritance. Despite the random walk, however, independent accumulation still has *some* relation to productivity, whereas inheritance has none whatsoever.[75] Thus to the extent that tax policy favors wealth associated with one's own contribution, lifetime accumulation should still be taxes less than inheritance.

In looking more closely at the relative importance of independent accumulation and inheritance, Brittain (unlike Thurow) takes issue with the conclusion of the *Fortune* studies that about half of top wealth holders "inherited the bulk of it." Apparently, the ad hoc surveys used by *Fortune* treated inheritance as an "either-or" proposition. Since the ratio of the original value of inheritance to total current wealth is "a gross understatement of the role of that inheritance" (due to compounding of interest, inflation, etc.), Brittain concludes that far more than half of current fortunes were heavily influenced by receipt of an initial inheritance.[76]

As Brittain indicates, there are methodological difficulties with even more scientific sampling surveys on the subject.[77] The most recent, by Lebergott,[78] tries to demonstrate the prevalence of upward social mobility and the creation of a newly rich group even more substantial than that suggested in the *Fortune* articles. For example, Lebergott uses mortality rates to estimate those top wealth-holders in 1922 who survived until 1953. He then looks at top wealth-holders at least 71 years old in 1952, assuming that they consist only of survivors of the 1922 rich, plus those in lower wealth classes in 1922. Estimating that there were 62,000 survivors from this top group in 1953 among the total of 255,000 derived by Lampman,[79] he concludes that the remaining 193,000 are newly rich. Brittain points out, however, that there are many objections to Lebergott's reasoning, the most notable being that many of these newcomers are the children of the 1922 rich. As their wealth grew with age and inflation, children of the estate return files in 1922 who had not yet inherited, or had inherited perhaps only $40,000, could appear in large numbers among wealth-holders in 1953 with gross estates of $60,000 or more. They need only to have increased their wealth from this $40,-000 figure to $60,000 in 31 years to be classed as *nouveau riche!* Furthermore, the number of $60,000 wealth-holders had grown from 255,000 in 1953 to 1,392,000 in 1969. It is not surprising, then, that this method finds many in the newly rich category. As Brittain concludes, Lebergott's approach seems to exaggerate greatly the number of the newly rich and to discount unduly the role of inheritance in the generation of wealth.[80]

Brittain himself presents new evidence derived from I.R.S. estimates of the distribution of net worth by age, sex, and marital status. Part of his argument is based on the patterns of inheritance by both sexes revealed by secondary analysis of data collected for 1964–65 decedents in the Cleveland area by Sussman, Cates and Smith. He finds that gifts and bequests, on the average, account for half or more of the net worth of very wealthy men and for most of the net worth of equally wealthy women. He weights this finding against the suggested alternative that wealth simply increases with age, producing a relatively "benign" form of inequality at any given time. He concludes that, based on statistics, the age-related component of accumulation accounts for relatively little inequality and is a far less important factor than intergenerational wealth transfers. Further, he agrees with Thurow that the prospect of heavy transfer taxes far in the future has little effect on the career behavior of the parent generation. "Wealthy retired persons tend to continue accumulating wealth until death."[81]

THE LIBERTARIANS

Those economists and philosophers who oppose incursions on the institution of inheritance do not usually argue with the links Brittain and Thurow develop between the persistence of the institution and continued material inequality. Instead, the chief thrust of their opposition focuses on the fairness and utility of inheritance, regardless of its consequences for equality. This group may be characterized as the "libertarians," because of their accent on the complete freedom of the individual; they are generally labeled conservatives politically. Libertarians point to Mill's distinction between the production and distribution functions of the economy, saying that giving separate status to the latter (instead of leaving it to the market) has encouraged governmental "meddling" in the market economy, such as the imposition of progressive estate and inheritance taxes. Richard Wagner, writing for the conservative Free Enterprise Institute, feels that Mill's problem was in regarding benefits from production as an artificial creation manipulated by the state.

Mill's view was a sharp break from that of Adam Smith[82] and runs counter to the libertarian views of the neoclassical economists.

Milton Friedman is the intellectual leader of these economists, who are also known as "the Chicago School." Lately Friedman expressed his views on the PBS television series, "Free to Choose," which was broadcast concurrently with the publication of his book of the same name. His show on "Inequality" contained a number of generalizations useful in framing the discussion that follows.[83] Friedman's view is that the greatest source of inequlity in our society is government or governmental privilege. Pointing to the British experience with its "vast redistributions" of wealth, Friedman notes that the result has been not greater equality, but the formation of different privileged classes like trade unionists and bureaucrats. It is a myth, he says, that the rich benefit at the expense of the poor. Instead the "free market" produces a smaller gap between rich and poor than does one marked by government intervention—traditional capitalist society "gives poor kids the best chance."

Friedman believes that "equality of ends" is at war with human nature. He says that he wants people to start equal rather than to end that way and thus is a believer in equal opportunity. In Friedman's view: "Put freedom before equality and you'll get more of both . . . Individual decisions, not societal ones will produce the outcomes most of us want."

Of course, things are seldom as simple as libertarian economic models may make them seem. Since concentrations of wealth invitably arise from allowing economic liberty, it is hard to understand how "letting the free market work" will provide the equal opportunity we have been discussing. Apparently, Friedman believes that the tendency of large fortunes to decumulate over time continues to open up opportunity for the relatively disadvantaged. Based on the studies discussed, all one can say is that this has not happened. In fact, the persistence of both inequality and low social mobility prompted one of Friedman's panelists to note why some modern egalitarians have become "result" rather than "means-oriented." The continued lack of access to such benefits as equal housing and education has caused equal opportunity itself to become, in her words, "empty."

Friedman's attempt to justify inheritance proceeds from the analogy between inherited talent and inherited property. Showing children of famous musicians practicing in an elite music school,

Friedman remarks that since society does not try to stop the biological inheritance from which these children benefit, neither should it try to stop material inheritance. It struck this viewer that the inheritance of "musical genes" was not the issue in the scene. Rather we were witnessing the ability of successful parents to pass on special educational opportunity to their children—a phenomenon generating inequality enough and one which arguably should not be augmented by material inheritance.

But the libertarians are not concerned by this augmentation. Friederich Hayek, recognizing that inheritance is "unquestionably one of the institutional causes of inequality" feels that the question which requires answering is whether "people ought to be free to pass to children or others such material possessions as will cause substantial inequality." He agrees with philosopher Robert Nozick that there is "no greater injustice involved in some people being born to wealthy parents than there is in being born to kind or intelligent parents, and that both situations are of equal advantage to the community." Thus, there is sensible ground for harnessing the "natural instincts of parents" to equip the new generation with material benefits "when there is no such limitation on nonmaterial ones."[84] Further, it is relatively inexpensive for society to give the outlet of inheritance to those wishing to provide for their children, since, for example, increased nepotism might follow confiscation of inheritance. Alternative forms of parental beneficence are the pattern, remarks Hayek, "in all societies in which inheritance of property does not exist, including the Communist."[85]

While it is true, as Friedman also asserts, that there are all kinds of ways to pass on wealth, such as providing the "human wealth" of education to children, material wealth is more easily subject to government control. Moreover, forms of human wealth like education, attitudes, or lifestyle encourage emotional bonding through family traditions, while material wealth is value-neutral. Since human wealth consists also of biological inheritances like intelligence and good looks one may agree with Nozick that these forms are no more unjust than material inheritance.[86] However, they are not presently subject to societal control; even if they were, it is likely that society would not choose to exercise this power before it regulated material wealth.

Friedman also presents the inheritance lottery argument, which as I have suggested has an observable basis in behavior. Thus many people would put primacy on the right to have a chance to inherit. While it is true that people are "always gambling" and like lotteries,[87] this penchant (which has always been treated with ambivalence by the law) does not provide a sound ground for public policy.

In Nozick's view, both the freedom to inherit and freedom of bequest are essential aspects of the absolute liberty which should be accorded to each individual. Thus, as to property, Nozick writes:

> From each according to what he chooses to do, to each according to what he makes for himself . . . and what others choose to do for him and *choose to give him* of what they've been given previously (under this maxim) and haven't yet expended or transferred . . . (or, in sum) from each as they choose, to each as they are chosen.[88]

Though this sentiment will strike many as reasonable, leaving it to the market to *determine* the just results of such liberty seeks to produce free will via determinism: this paradox leads one to ask whether the libertarians really believe in individual freedom or merely use the concept of liberty to veil a selfish egoism: one which shirks moral responsibility for the impingement that a laissez faire system inevitably makes on the freedom of those not favored by the market.

The libertarians of course admit no such thing. Most solve the paradox by allying themselves with so-called "soft-determinism" allowing the market to determine overall choices and the individual to make limited decisions within the scope of these choices. This would seem to provide true freedom for only a few.

LIBERTARIAN OBJECTIONS TO INHERITANCE REFORM Libertarian views of both the philosophical soundness and practicality of severe limitations on inheritance can be briefly summarized.[89] Their philosophical ideas include these:

1. Inequality may be unjust in the extreme, but it has been overestimated by looking at only its material aspects.

2. Society needs a certain amount of material inequality because this increases (through efficient saving and investment) the wealth of both rich and poor. Progressive wealth taxation is thus a form of "masochism" for all.

3. Inherited material wealth itself is legitimate, or at least no less legitimate than other forms of wealth.

4. Envy of another's inherited wealth is not a sound basis for stiff limitations on it. This imposes a direct penalty on the rich, and (see 2 above) it also hampers the poor.

Neoclassical economists generally take Mill's position that legitimizing envy is inconsistent with a free society: that merely to be emotionally affronted by someone is not good grounds for legislation if a free society is to survive. Though Wagner admits that if inheritance were abolished, some envy would perhaps be assuaged and Pareto-optimality attained.[90] Nevertheless he finds the practical results of abolishing inheritance or heavy taxation on it more compelling.[91] Also, as Gordon Tullock writes, the inheritance tax cannot efficiently be set higher than the rate which would produce the maximum revenue yield, whether or not this would reduce envy.[92] He assumes that at some level, total revenue will decline because of the resulting disincentives to leaving a substantial estate.

"Welfare economists" such as Thurow and Kenneth Green, however, take the position that since many are envious of those who inherit wealth (while few are envious of those who "earn" their wealth), Pareto-optimality requires that this envy be assuaged through stiff inheritance taxation. As Green writes:

> It seems likely that an individual will resent much more another's income if it is generated from inherited wealth rather than from some other source. The student of human capital and the behavioral psychologist may argue that such attitudes are irrational, that the ability to earn income by one's own efforts is no less inherited than a trust fund, but this does not mean that these attitudes do not exist . . . [Thus if people's] envy of inherited wealth is stronger than their envy of other forms . . . a move from a world of permitted inheritance to one where it is prohibited is not necessarily . . . as Tullock contends . . . Pareto inefficient.[93]

Green in effect is arguing that by reducing envy in a Pareto-efficient way, society may still have made a rational choice in setting the tax above that rate which would produce the maximum revenue yield; increasing revenue is only one way of maximizing societal utility.

The libertarians also have numerous practical objections to inheritance limitation. These include:

1. Reduction in charitable giving and the centers of distribution, like foundations, which it creates.

2. Forced liquidation of closely-held corporations and family farms.

3. Stifled incentive for the successful, causing hard work to have less "survival value" than characteristics like pleasing superiors and appearing personable in public.

4. Weakening of intergenerational bonds.

5. Nepotism in occupations.

6. Reduction of mobility between and among income levels because investors will be less likely to take chances if they know they cannot leave money as they wish to.

7. The tendency for wealth accumulators, barred from leaving substantial inheritances, to put their money in annuities in exchange for a steady lifetime income, and to consume their capital within their lifetime.

8. Increase of "deadweight" loss to the economy because of costs for estate planning to avoid heavy taxation.

9. Reduction of savings and capital formation.

10. The inefficiency of confiscatory inheritance taxes in equalizing income since they may fall on heirs already "not too well off."

11. Loss to society of the great contributions of men like Sir Robert Boyle, whose large inheritance allowed him to pursue his investigations in chemistry and physics.

These arguments can be answered in the following ways:

1. *Charitable giving:* This will be investigated in chapter 5, which concludes that present levels of charitable giving can be maintained under properly designed limitations on inheritance.

2. *Closely-held corporations and family farms:* Real estate in both types of organization is amenable to special treatment via technical manipulation of the estate and gift tax laws, to the extent that freer inheritance of these forms of wealth is seen as necessary or desirable. The chief problem which needs to be addressed is the illiquidity of assets in such farms and businesses, not whether they should bear a tax.

3. *Incentive:* It is just such characteristics as hard work that Carnegie *et al.* think would be strengthened by severe restrictions on inheritance that Wagner *et al.* think would be weakened. Surely, those born with the proverbial silver spoon would have more incen-

tive to produce under a reformed system; on the other hand, there is no solid evidence that their parent accumulators would cease accumulating if reform were enacted.

4. *Weakening of intergenerational bonds:* The oft-told stories of the damaging effects of material wealth on family relations indicate that affection can be more usefully shown through nonmaterial means.

5. *Nepotism:* This exists already to the extent that institutions will allow it. I can see no reason for those institutions that often prohibit it (because it reduces efficiency and may be unfair) to allow it free reign if material inheritance were curbed.

6. *Reduction of mobility through lower risk-taking:* In practice, the risk-taking entrepreneur of neoclassical legend is dead. Much great wealth is held in trust form and trustees are generally conservative institutions or individuals, further blocked from taking risks by conservative legal standards of fiduciary investment discretion. To the extent that risk-investment still takes place, it is often done to symbolize achievement, usually by those with an already comfortable life. As a policy matter, we should really not be too concerned with mobility at the extreme top of the economic range; even if we were, the specter of future inheritance taxes has had little or no demonstrable effect in reducing such risk taking.

7. *Annuities:* Again, the evidence is that wealth accumulators eschew the purchase of annuities in favor of the power conferred by wealth held in more traditional forms.

8. *Deadweight losses in estate planning:* Much of the attention of death tax reform now centers on the very loopholes which keep estate planners employed. A truly high, progressive, and effective tax would convince taxpayers that they could pass on only a relatively small, relatively certain, amount; estate planners would thus become much less useful.

9. *Saving and capital formation:* The old capital-reduction argument is without substantial modern support. Even if capitalists would save and accumulate less for fear of heavy death taxes (in itself a doubtful proposition), this traditional way to material wealth may be less important than random strokes of enormous good fortune. To the extent that disincentive effects can be established, they can be remedied by a progressive consumption tax such as is presented in the final chapter.

10. *Effect on poor heirs:* One surmises that Tullock sees testators as private distributors of wealth, often making choices in favor of the relatively needy. While there is no reason to doubt that many testators do take account of the material circumstances of various heirs in making their bequests, for the most part these heirs are not likely to be "poor" on any absolute scale. Whatever they get from inheritance is still a windfall, putting them in a relatively better position than those poor who are not heirs.

11. *Great contributions of those with inherited wealth:* One has sympathy with the desire to free certain talented people from the burdens of economic necessity. However, one may be even more sympathetic with a general reduction in economic burdens across the social spectrum. Tax reforms and redistribution of wealth as discussed in this book can be expected to remove a number of institutional barriers to individual expression. As an American sociologist puts it, in a country where special privilege and worker alienation are allowed to exist side-by-side, "a great deal of individual talent remains forever dormant [due to] lack of opportunity for the vast majority of . . . people, who live in limited material and spiritual circumstances."[94] Alleviating this lack of opportunity would not only provide greater social justice, but also might have a fortuitous political effect: to freshen the sagging appeal of Western ideology in a competitive world.

CONCLUSION: THE EGALITARIAN SEARCH FOR LIMITS IN INHERITANCE REFORM

The libertarian urge for society where the individual is paramount to the state and where each may pursue his own will to the ultimate good of the collectivity likely has its roots in Jeffersonian idealism. Certainly, it strikes a sympathetic note with many intellectuals who dislike the vision of a dreary and initiative-stifling equality of ends such as has been pursued in China. However, libertarianism tends to emphasize production in the economy rather than distribution, and many modern thinkers have lost faith in the free market's capacity to distribute fairly. Thus, though many intellectuals value personal freedom, they have become convinced that government interventions are necessary in that market to keep opportunity relatively equal. It is the complex task of this group, as it is in a small way of this book, to face the question of just how much intervention will produce the "greatest good."

The material presented thus far in support of the equal opportunity position has indicated that inequality, both of ends and starting places, is far more pervasive than the libertarians care to admit. Further, as Brittain and Thurow note, severely restricting inheritance would fairly reduce inequality of opportunity without sacrificing economic efficiency. To the extent that capital is generated not by random strokes of fortune, but by providing incentives to capitalists, the prospect of future death taxes does not significantly reduce its production. The primary reason for accumulating money is, as economist Thomas Ireland notes, not to leave wealthy heirs but to attain the "status and social power inherent in holding a variety of wealth forms."[95] As to the justice of singling out this form of wealth for strong government intervention, one important view is that of egalitarian philosopher John Rawls. He agrees with the libertarians that this form is no more unjust than other forms of wealth, material or human, though he notes that "it is presumably more easily subject to social control." This inherent fairness means inheritance is "permissible," but only if "the resulting inequalities are to the advantage of the least fortunate and compatible with liberty and fair equality of opportunity."[96] To Rawls, fair equality of opportunity means:

> A certain set of institutions that assures similar chances of education and culture for persons similarily motivated and keeps positions and offices open to all. . . . It is these institutions that are put in jeopardy when inequalities of wealth exceed a certain limit; and political liberty likewise tends to lose its value, and representative government to become such in appearance only. The taxes and enactments of the distribution branch are to prevent this limit from being exceeded.[97]

How should society judge where this limit lies? Rawls would leave it to "political judgement guided by theory, good sense and plain sense."[98] On the other hand, Alan Tait feels that "since many alternative sources of revenue exist," the political decision to tax wealth must "ultimately be based on ethical grounds." If we single out inheritance, we are thus saying that the distribution of such wealth is unfair and that society can order distributions in a more equitable manner. Then, as Tait remarks, we are making the judgment that some forms of luck (such as the inherited intelligence which produces wealth) are more worthy than others like material inheritance.[99]

Rawls' pragmatic search for limits on inheritance may simply postpone the ethical question until wealth inequalities become too great. On the other hand, the "theory" he asks politicians to apply may just be a form of Utilitarianism: he may want them to limit inheritance only when the relative social disutility of the institution outweighs its benefits. Since Tait believes that material inheritance is inherently unjust, he might go further in limiting it than would a follower of Rawls. Whether the philosophical basis of the search is unfairness or disutility, it seems that the concept of "envy" holds the key to setting inheritance limitations.

As Wagner himself admits, Mill may have been incorrect in his prognosis that policy based on envy of the lot and choices of others is inconsistent with the maintenance of a free society.[100] I see no reason why dislike by the majority of the advantages of a minority cannot serve as a basis for social policy. This is true whether such envy is styled as Pareto-inefficient or as the outcome of a situation which is ethically unfair. Since there is strength in the argument that material inheritance is only one form of unfairness, those seeking to limit inheritance taxation are seemingly on firmer ground analyzing the Pareto-utility of reducing envy rather than inheritance's relative "fairness."

5

The Impact of Inheritance Reform on Foundations

This chapter examines the impact of institutional reform of inheritance on another important American institution—charitable foundations: if inheritance law is reformed to provide more equal starting places, what role should these organizations play in the new system? Two types of reform are discussed. The first type has been already suggested: changes in the federal estate tax; the second is the use of the judicial doctrine of *cy pres* to save a foundation whose original purpose has failed. The initial step in the analysis concentrates on the connections between inheritance and the establishment and operation of foundations.

INHERITANCE AND FOUNDATIONS

It is a common assumption that foundations are by and large the stepchildren of inherited wealth. Though this is substantially true, the situation is more complicated than may first appear. We begin with data compiled by the Peterson Commission on Foundations showing where the assets of selected foundations originate (see Table 1).[1]

Though the figures are not recent, they are based on scientific sampling of 186 foundations. The results are suggestive: foundations receive slightly less than one-quarter of their assets directly from bequests. What then is the original source of the approximately half

TABLE 1

Percentages of Foundation Assets from Specific Sources, 1968

	Under $200,000	$200,000– $1 million	$1 million– $10 million	$10 million– $100 million	$100 million+	$100 million+ excluding Ford	Total
Contributions by living donors and gains therefrom	66	65	38	49	63	76	47
Contributions from estates and gains therefrom	28	14	54	46	14	24	23
Corporate and other contributions	6	20	8	5	23	1	31

(47%) of foundation assets derived from the lifetime contributions of individual donors?

The Peterson Commission states:

> Today, as in the past, philanthropy depends heavily on the generosity of the well-to-do. The commission, faced by a paucity of data on charitable giving, was unable to get a precise estimate of the extent to which total charitable giving is concentrated among the wealthy. Yet experience says that it is the large gift which raises the sights of the philanthropic enterprise, sets the pace for fundraising, and enables new philanthropic organizations to take root.

This phenomenon stems from the fact that "the wealthy have surplus resources beyond those used to maintain a desired standard of living."[2]

Estimates vary on how many of the fortunes of the wealthy are chiefly based on inheritance. If we take the conservative Wagner-Thurow estimate of 50% (which Brittain thinks is quite low), lifetime contributions from those who inherited their wealth would be half of 47% or 23.5%. Adding this figure to the 23% coming directly to foundations via charitable bequests, we find that nearly 50% of foundation assets are due to individual contributions stemming from inheritance. This compares to less than 25% coming from lifetime gifts associated with lifetime earnings. Thus, while changes in the federal estate tax or other inheritance reforms might affect only about 25% of foundation assets directly, they would ultimately affect one-half (or more, if we believe Brittain) because of lifetime gifts to charity by individuals whose wealth is associated with an original inheritance.

What, after all, *are* foundations? Legally, they are usually established as trusts or non-profit corporations (occasionally unincorporated associations). Functionally they serve as intermediaries between donors and ultimate charitable beneficiaries: that is, they both receive and make donations. One group consists of company-sponsored, family, and community foundations. These are generally small and tend to make gifts to established religious and welfare organizations. Another consists of what Milton Katz calls "general philanthropic foundations"; these are usually larger, and tend to concentrate on research and innovation in education, science and health, and the arts.[3]

The Peterson Commission made a most careful attempt to define which organizations which fall into these groups should actually be termed foundations. Its definition excluded organizations that are broadly supported by the general public. According to the I.R.S. definition, those excluded would receive one-third of their support (exclusive of capital gains) from the public and less than one-third of their income from investments. Unlike the I.R.S., the Peterson Commission excluded "operating charities" like schools, churches, and hospitals. They included only those entities that devote most of their funds to making grants rather than to the direct conduct of charitable activites. Also excluded were so-called "feeder" organizations which support only a single charity.[4]

Many of the small foundations are family and community ones established during the life of the donor for tax reasons. Federal tax laws allow the donor to set these up free of gift tax and with up to 50% of their value deductible from income tax; if he waits until death, the donor gets the unlimited estate tax charitable deduction, but no income tax break. Many of these small foundations disappear at the donor's death, or if he is a testator, at the death of the close friends and relatives who direct its use; in either case, no one is left to manage the assets.[5] Such small foundations are in the majority. In 1977–78, of 21,505 foundations, those with less than $1 million in assets (or $100,000 in yearly gifts) totalled 18,367.[6]

Our main concern here is with foundations with more than $1 million in assets. Though they numbered only 3,138 in 1977, they held 93% of all foundation assets and made 92% of all foundation grants.[7] Unlike the smaller foundations, these larger ones often have sufficient assets to continue operations after the death of the donor and his associates.

While the small foundation is usually either company sponsored or family controlled, the large foundation is often independent with a significant endowment of its own. In 1978, for example, the Ford Foundation had assets of nearly $2.3 billion, while fourteen others had assets of over $200 million, including two near the $1 billion mark.[8] According to Katz, general philanthropic foundations (which he subdivides into general purpose foundations like Ford and special purpose ones like the American Cancer Society) make 66% of all grants for foundations of over $1 million in size; the remainder are made by the larger family, corporate, and community foundations.

Because of the giving patterns of the general philanthropic foundations, a larger proportion of foundation giving goes to education,
health, science, and the arts and humanities then goes to religion. It
is in these areas that foundations pose significant alternatives to federal endowments for science, the arts, and humanities.[9]

The mixed public/private character of the large foundations has
received considerable attention. A foundation is public because it
devotes its resources to charitable purposes; it is private because its
make-up is nongovernmental and it derives its resources from gifts
(or income from the investment of such gifts) from private donors.
It is a privately organized public institution.[10]

THE PLACE OF FOUNDATIONS IN AMERICAN SOCIETY

American foundations, as we now know them, began to emerge
in the post-Civil War period; they multiplied most rapidly after
World War II. It is possible to trace the modern foundation's precur-
sors to the charitable trusts which gradually gained acceptance during the 1800s. Later the corporate form of foundation, governed by
much the same laws as these trusts, became popular.

To appreciate the new nation's antipathy toward bequests in this
form, one must understand, as legal historian Lawrence Friedman
put it, that "in the early nineteenth century, charity was associated
with privilege, with the dead hand, with established churches, with
massive wealth held in perpetuity."[11] On the practical side, what
legal historian Morton Horwitz calls a "flexible, instrumental conception of law"[12] was proving necessary to promote the transformation
of the post-Revolutionary American legal system. Land bequeathed
by testators which was to be held in perpetuity by churches could not
be improved by individual entrepreneurs. This hindered the economic development so vital to an expanding nation.

The situation came to a head in 1819 when the Supreme Court,
per Chief Justice Marshall, voided all English statutes, including the
Statute of Charitable Uses, in *Trustees of Philadelphia Baptist Ass'n.
v. Hart's Executors.*[13] The court erroneously found that the English
equity courts had no inherent jurisdiction to sustain charitable
trusts.[14] It was not long, however, before influential elements of the
new society discovered that restrictions imposed by this case complicated the legal status of religious bodies. Moreover, by hamstringing

gifts intended for education, poor relief and other necessary social services, these restrictions proved costly to society as a whole.[15]

Judges such as Henry Baldwin and James Kent began arguing for a pragmatic, permissive legal doctrine which would take account of contemporary practice. To those who countered that law had always been suspicious of perpetuities and that charitable trusts were indeed perpetual (as were charitable foundations), these judges replied that the public received sufficient benefit from charitable bequests to warrant liberal interpretations. Moreover, they stressed the legal right of testators to control property beyond the grave, claiming that the power to make charitable bequests with the expectation that they be faithfully executed was within an individual's property rights.[16]

Still, opposition to philanthropy persisted among an influential group of judges and legislators. For example, St. George Tucker, James Madison, Thomas Jefferson, and other secular-minded and progressive Virginians felt charities symbolized advancing clerical power in society, threatening the rights of future generations.[17] Justice Story believed that charities trampled individual rights by depriving heirs of their property. He complained of the lack of safeguards, such as the mortmain statutes in England,[18] against the making of unwise charitable gifts. "We are in some danger," he felt, "of having our most valuable estates locked up in mortmain, and our surplus wealth pass away in specious or mistaken charities, founded upon visionary or useless schemes. . . ."[19] Coupled with the fear of clerical control and the power of the dead hand to pass property away from the living, was a fear of trusts and corporations in general, because of their impersonal nature and perpetual life.[20]

While fear of the consequences of permitting property to pass from general circulation into the hands of perpetual charitable associations argued against permissive charity policy, religious teachings, humanitarian and social needs argued for it.[21] Since charitable trusts might violate legal rules against perpetuities and indefiniteness of beneficiary, they were more apt to be struck down on legal technicalities than were charitable corporations, whose impersonal nature and perpetual life were settled. The time when the balance turned in favor of the charitable trust is generally marked by the case of Stephen Girard's will, *Vidal* v. *Girard's Executors*,[22] in which Supreme Court support for charitable trusts was finally affirmed. While the majority of states were happy to embrace this judicial blessing of the charitable trust, a more restricted attitude toward the device remained important in states like Virginia, New York, and Maryland.[23]

Later, as the paper fortunes amassed in the industrial revolution began to accumulate and the need for effective mechanisms to control the use of new forms of wealth became manifest, charitable trusts slowly gained favor. In the main, this was because courts saw that by encouraging private contributions they were reducing the expenses of government.[24] Thus courts began to declare charitable trusts "favorites of the law" and they employed liberal rules of construction to support them.[25] Still, this was the era of "rugged individualism" and the intent of the donor was paramount. Charitable trusts were construed by detailed inquiries into the state of the testator's mind and his wishes at the time of the making of the gift, instead of being seen in light of changing social conditions.

The charitable trust had one more hurdle to pass in late-nineteenth-century New York. When Samuel J. Tilden, Democratic candidate for President in 1876, left a portion of his millions to fund a public library for the City of New York, the New York Court of Appeals in *Tilden* v. *Green*[26] struck down the trust for want of definite beneficiaries.[27] Because of the public outcry at this outrageous decision, remedial legislation for such gifts was passed by the New York legislature in 1893.[28] What changed minds in New York was the realization that, when the Tilden trust failed, "no dead hand became richer [though its relatives did]; but the city itself was the poorer."[29] Gifts like Tilden's could be used to reduce government expenditures; shopworn legal doctrines would have to give way to practical reality.

Despite occasional *Tilden*-like decisions by a grudging judiciary, something fundamental had changed in American social thought by the beginning of the twentieth century. Faced with the grim misery of the industrial slums, thoughtful individuals began to realize that the free market was not working for all, nor in fact for the majority of people in this new urban society. As legal philosopher Roscoe Pound noted, "the problem, therefore, of the present is to lead our law to hold a more even balance between individualism and collectivism. Its present extreme individualism must be tempered to meet the ideas of the modern world."[30]

In philanthropy, Andrew Carnegie had already met the challenge Pound was setting for law. He gave credence to the notion that great wealth was a public trust to be administered not for the excessive benefit of private heirs but for the good of the worthy public.[31] Though the courts were somewhat tardy in applying collectivist ideas in the field of philanthropy, their first use of the public trust theory can be seen just after World War I.[32]

The Depression years of the 1930s brought the added realization that it was in the pragmatic interest of society to defuse revolutionary pressures by using great wealth for the public benefit. One court noted, for instance, that in a society with a sense of personal responsibility for wealth "there is little temptation to violent explosions" so prevalent in other lands.[33] Another opinion, written near the end of the Depression, speaks of the necessity of relying on private beneficence to meet some of the needs of these "troubled times."[34] Saved from the Depression by the necessities of war, the Americans emerged from that conflict into the greatest business boom in their history. Part of the 1950s business orientation focused on the "business" of organized charitable giving: from 1948 to 1960 the number of foundations grew from 899 to around 12,000.[35]

FOUNDATION ABUSES

During the reform-minded 1960s, a " cluster of questions, apprehensions, suspicions, and perplexities" emerged amid the burgeoning of foundation activity. According to Milton Katz, two lines of concern were expressed: one involving issues of tax avoidance and evasion; the other, alleged concentrations of financial power. Additional, less explicit themes also emerged. For example, there were doubts about the validity of institutions apparently subject to neither the competitive discipline of the marketplaces nor to control by popular suffrage. Another concern was the perpetual, impersonal, and secretive nature of foundations.[36]

1. TAX AVOIDANCE AND EVASION   In 1964, the Treasury sought to identify which of the expressed public concerns about tax avoidance and evasion were well-founded. It found some evidence of foundation tax abuses, which its report divided into six categories. To the extent that they occurred, these tax abuses subordinated the interests of philanthropy to the personal or commercial advantage of individuals or corporations. In some cases the objective was tax evasion under the guise of philanthropic activity. In others, the sheltered tax position of a philanthropic organization was misused to furnish a competitive business advantage.[37]

One of the major abuses was self-dealing. Although trustees and directors of charitable foundations are prohibited under state law from such activities, prior to the 1969 Tax Reform Act, foundations lost their tax-exempt status only if the trustees engaged in specified and limited self-dealing transactions. Not being subject to close state audit because of the inattention of state attorneys general, the foundations felt they were governed by the more lenient standards of the Internal Revenue Code. Thus, a charitable foundation could be established in which the donor himself was able to borrow back his contributions.[38]

Despite its finding of such abuse, the Treasury emphasized its conclusion "that the preponderant number of private foundations perform their functions" properly. Reaffirming the "special and vital role" played by private philanthropy in our society, the Treasury promulgated its recommendations to the Senate in order to end "the diversions, distractions, and abuses" in the tax field, while continuing "to stimulate and foster active pursuit of charitable ends."[39]

This Treasury report ultimately provided the basis for the foundation provisions of the Tax Reform Act of 1969. The act classified organizations which receive donations from few sources as "private foundations," distinguishing these from ones that are "publicly supported." A 4% excise tax (later reduced to 2%) was assessed on the net investment income of the former group. The act also created a number of substantive rules governing their operations.[40]

For private foundations, the act's prohibitions against self-dealing were more stringent than under state law. In addition to prohibitions on accumulation of yearly income, these organizations must invade and expend principal in any year that their investment income is less than a federally-defined minimum investment return. State laws defining permissible investments are now superseded by a rule preventing private foundations, together with their "disqualified persons," from holding more than 20% of a single corporation or of the financial interest in a business entity. A new federal "prudent man" rule was also enacted to determine when an investment manager was acting in violation of the foundation's tax-exempt purposes.[41]

Congress likewise prohibited certain types of charitable activities once considered proper. The act prohibits expenditures for lobbying, influencing elections, and making certain types of grants to individuals and other foundations. Violation of these provisions can lead to imposition of excise taxes on the foundations, and in some cases, on its fiduciaries, principal donors, the families of both groups or their business interests. Loss of tax-exempt status now results in taxation at individual or corporate rates and perhaps imposition of a (confiscatory) tax on the foundations's net assets. Disclosure is also important: severe penalties can be imposed on the foundation and its managers for failure to make timely and proper reports. Notice is to be given to the state attorney general of all charitable organizations (not merely private foundations) that have been refused tax-exempt status or have had their tax-exemptions revoked. Also, state authorities are permitted to inspect the tax returns of charitable organizations.[42]

Another reform was made in the way charitable trusts could be established. Under the old law, testator could establish a testamentary trust under which, for example, income was to be paid to his sister for life, with remainder to the American Cancer Society. Under such a "charitable remainder trust," testator's estate would receive the charitable deduction for the present discounted value of the remainder left to the foundation. However, the trustee could be given wide discretion in his power to invade the trust corpus, and could thus deplete it for the benefit of the beneficiary during her life, leaving little or nothing for the charity, despite the deduction gained. Under the new forms of "trust" permitted by the 1969 Act, valuation of the charitable remainder is simplified, and trusts in which the trustee is given power to invade principal are prohibited from taking the deduction.[43]

Merrimon Cuninggim, president of the Danforth Foundation, claimed in 1973 that "on balance," the 1969 Act was "strong and useful legislation." Despite his pleasure with the "full-disclosure" aspects of the act, he complained about its failure to go far enough in requiring uniform standards of financial reporting. Most of the act's bad effects, in Cuninggim's opinion, were more psychological than substantive. This stemmed from the feeling in many foundations that the entire industry had been scapegoated by Congress due to the abuses of a few of their number.[44]

In any event, the Tax Reform Act of 1969 served as a safety valve for much of the attention which had been focused on foundations during the 1960s. The general effect of the legislation was probably to doom many of the smallest foundations which could not, after donors and friend died, hire managers to comply with the professional standards demanded by the act. Meanwhile, the larger foundations were forced to perfect the financial standards that had been evolving in their organizations; remaining public concern could now focus more clearly on the second of Katz's themes—the concentration of financial power these larger foundations represent.

2. CONCENTRATION OF FINANCIAL POWER   If one looks at the figures, it is hard not to conclude that the size and financial power of medium and large foundations has been overrated. Fifty years ago foundations spent more money in education than the federal government. Now federal spending for education amounts to several times the total of foundation spending for all purposes.[45] In 1971 federal programs for education totalled $6.5 billion, while foundations gave less than 6% of this, or $343 million.[46]

In other areas, the decline in the relative proportion of foundation to federal giving has been just as marked. Richard Friedman points out that in 1961 the federal government spent $3.5 billion, or 16 times the foundations' total of $218 million, in human services; in 1971 the federal government spent $15.3 billion in this area, or 23 times the foundations' $673 million.[47] In 1979, foundation giving of about $2.25 billion was 1% of GNP, down from slightly over 1% in 1978.[48] In asset size, the over-$1-million foundations had $32.4 billion in 1978, which was less than one-sixth of government outlays in that single fiscal year in the areas of health, education, and welfare alone.[49]

From these figures, it is easy to see the foundations' size is relatively unimportant—and increasingly so—when compared to that of the government. Within their relatively small share of the giving "market," however, it is possible to discern another possible reason for public concern. The largest ten foundations in the over-$1-million category held nearly $8.7 billion in assets, or 25% of the total for all foundations in 1978. Since there were over 3,100 other foundations in this category, the figures do show a degree of concentration of wealth and power within the foundation industry, whatever the relative importance of foundation and government giving.[50]

The size of the top ten and other large foundations provides benefits as well as disadvantages. Though they are unable to provide a substantial alternative to government assistance for private universities or health and welfare agencies, these foundations can offer alternative sources of support for particular requirements. The existence of other sources of funds for the same need can relieve the officer of a private university or hospital from the sense that he must accept whatever is offered by the government, regardless of the terms. Even *with* such alternative sources available, however, non-profit educational, scientific and medical organizations find it hard to maintain their independence from government.[51] Reducing foundations' strength further would thus make this difficult situation even worse.

3. OTHER CONCERNS   As to the *implicit* public concerns mentioned by Katz, the most important appears to be the lack of incentive and market discipline for foundations. In fairness, the claim that foundations suffer no penalties in the marketplace for bad judgment can be applied to many arms of government, including the military and career foreign and civil services. It is thus a problem well-known to many American organizations—a problem whose solution lies in the creation of internal standards, self-discipline, and a well-founded *esprit de corps.* Since foundations as we now know them are barely a century old, Milton Katz believes their officers will come increasingly to think of themselves as a professional corps. As foundations begin fully to understand their own roles the public will come to better understand them.[52] Whether this professionalization will outstrip that in similar governmental institutions is an open question since government bureaucracy is held politically accountable by the budgetary process.

Developing a sense of professionalism appears to be a more politically acceptable answer than limiting the existence of any philanthropic foundation to a term of years fixed by law. One such proposal was made by the foundations' *bête noire* during the 1960s, populist Representative Wright Patman of Texas, Chairman of the House Select Committee on Small Business. He proposed in 1962 that foundations ought to go out of business in twenty-five years.[53] In the work of the Senate Finance Committee preceding the Tax Reform Act of 1969, Senator Albert Gore finally succeeded in getting a forty-year limitation, after failing at limits down to twenty years. Whether through lobbying by foundations and their friends or through simple Senate dislike of the proposals, however, the Senate soundly defeated what Senator Mondale called the "death sentence amendment."[54] Whatever echoes of the hoary legal doctrines of mortmain and perpetuities still bothered the public, Congress was sufficiently convinced of the foundations' utility to continue their "eternal life."

Another difficulty with foundations, which opens these institutions to charges of political bias was pointed out in a 1968 issue of *The Nation*: "The influence of the rich in philanthropy focuses on the established institution, tends to maintain the *status quo*. It is rare, indeed, that major donations are made to encourage basic change, or even minor dislocation of any aspect of established society."[55] Or, as Merle Curti noted in a 1962 issue of *Foundation News*: "Philanthropy on the whole has avoided controversial issues, the very issues, perhaps, that offer the greatest challenge and that point to the greatest need."[56]

Cuninggim tiptoes around this issue, putting most of the blame on small family or corporate foundations. He cites the report of the Peterson Commission which asked foundation officers whether they considered any of their projects in the past three years "controversial" or "particularly unpopular." Whereas only one percent of all foundations said yes, 38% of foundations in the $100-million-plus category said yes.[57] If this self-report is to be taken at face value, the general philanthropic foundations often do take chances. However, what is controversial to a McGeorge Bundy may not be considered controversial by, for example, a community worker.[58]

The problem of Establishment funding policies is related to a self-perpetuating, narrow base of representation within the governing structure of foundations.[59] According to a president of the Spencer Foundation, studies have revealed that the typical foundation trustee is in his sixties, is the graduate of a private college, a WASP, and a moderate Republican; moreover, two-thirds of trustees in the twenty-five largest foundations were from the business, banking, or legal professions.[60] The effect of this socioeconomic homogeneity can be seen in the context of foundation funding of women's programs.

As Bob Gangi, program director for the John Hay Whitney Foundation, noted: "Since most foundations are run by white, upper-class men, that would be [a] factor in the lack of responsiveness to women's issues."[61]

An increase in the currently small number of women trustees, board and staff members of foundations was cited in a 1977 study by the National Committee for Responsive Philanthropy as crucial to progress on women's issues. After examining those women's programs that did receive grants, this study (itself funded by the Ford Foundation) found that "a catalyst in many programs was the presence of a woman in a position of power who helped mobilize the effort." Still, out of more than $2 billion in private foundation grants in 1976, only six-tenths of 1% went to women's programs; however, this did represent an increase in funding levels from $1.7 million in 1971 to some $12 million in 1976.[62]

Perhaps the homogeneous backgrounds of those who run foundations is a function of the lack of political accountability in these organizations as compared with government. In fact, however, the National Endowment for the Arts and the National Endowment for the Humanities, far from avoiding the white, upper-class leadership of the foundations, have reportedly relied on this same group for much of their own expertise. The result, as a 1980 article in *Harper's* points out, may be a sort of "high society" approach to government in these areas, with public funds being used to finance "galas" for artists, scholars, and their patrons.[63] When seen in this light, the supposedly competitive features of foundations in the area of giving is more apparent than real. With government and large foundations constantly exchanging personnel who believe in the same types of projects, the "alternative" provided for the recipient may be less a choice between different viewpoints than simply another source of funds used to finance the same viewpoints. To the extent that these funds might be made up by the government in the absence of foundations, even this advantage would be lost.

DONOR CONTROL OF FOUNDATIONS

An area of concern linked to the discussion of broadening foundation boards has been that of donor control; the discussion also raised questions of social equity since the public treasury subsidizes the foundation's choices. As the Peterson Commission suggested, the strongest attraction for establishing a foundation is that the donor can obtain charitable tax deductions for his contribution while retaining a limited but substantial control over these assets. This differs markedly from making direct contributions to operating charities, "where at the time the contribution is made, the property passes out of the donor's control." Traditionally, after the foundation is established, the giver plays an active role in its running or, if the foundation is originated by a bequest, the testator's family and associates play such a rule, guided by his instructions.[64]

Because of the wish for direct donor control (which, however, is limited by the Tax Reform Act of 1969), the majority of foundations are established during life, though they may receive additional funds via the donor's will. As the Peterson Commission notes, many donors who want to support operating charities after their death do so by direct testamentary bequests. Still, a number do not want to give their entire contribution at this one time or for one purpose. These testators, reports the Commission, actually are not exercising the dead hand control that might otherwise result. Their motive in establishing a foundation as a conduit for their bequest—particularly one with a broad mandate—may stem from the realization that a foundation provides flexibility to meet changing social needs.[65]

As previously indicated, at least 50% of foundation assets can ultimately be traced to inherited wealth, whether or not the foundations themselves were established during the donor's life. Therefore the problems of both donor control during life and dead hand control are germane to a book on inheritance. Because bequests from estates (rather than lifetime gifts) most directly involve the inheritance process, what follows is a discussion of the degree to which this form of gift exercises dead hand control over foundations.

First, I should emphasize what type of institutions are most likely to be influenced by this control. As John Nason has suggested, the 1969 Tax Reform Act may encourage the dissolution or merger of small foundations. "Family foundations may die a natural death; they may at some future date receive a life sentence; or like so many organizations in which people's emotions are centered, they may exhibit a remarkable capacity for survival. In any event," writes Nason, "they represent too small a segment of the foundation world to justify concern over their natural tie to donors and to donors' families." The issue of control thus "focuses on the middle-sized and larger foundations, those with assets of $1 million or more."[66]

Next is the issue of who are the testators who are funding these foundations. It cannot be denied that the very wealthy exercise most of the control over the tax subsidy provided by the government for charitable bequests. In 1973, estates over $5 million as a group gave $125 million to charity for every $100 million to individuals. In the same year the wealthiest 2% of estates large enough to require an estate tax return (less than two-tenths of 1% of all estates), took 63% of all deductions for charitable bequests.[67] There are no similar figures for bequests to foundations alone. Reason, however, would dictate that the very wealthy exert an even greater influence in that area.

The argument can be made that allowing such a degree of control by the very rich over foundations is consistent with the principles of estate and inheritance taxation: it keeps great wealth out of private hands in the next generation. As Franklin Roosevelt urged in 1935, a heavy estate tax should be used to prevent the accumulation of static wealth in private hands. However, such a tax need not prevent the active use of such wealth for the public good, even if this use is guided by a wealthy hand.[68]

FOUNDATIONS FROM THE PERSPECTIVE OF INHERITANCE REFORM

I have spent some time in this chapter considering the pros and cons of foundations because of their intimate connection with inherited wealth. In weighing possible changes in the institution of inheritance, their impact on foundations ought to be considered. Should the policy-maker try to keep bequests to foundations at current levels, or decrease these levels? On the other hand, should he be indifferent to such effect due to their relative unimportance?

1. SHOULD FOUNDATIONS BE SAVED?   The picture sketched thus far is certainly mixed. On one hand, it does not go as far as Waldemar Nielson did in his book, *The Big Foundations.* Nielson looked at the 33 largest foundations in 1970, those with assets over $100 million, and found them to be sick institutions, with little hope of recovery. After a suitable grace period, Nielson felt, society should simply let them expire. Laying much of his criticism at the doorstep of donor control, Nielson nonetheless described various instances where tightly controlled foundations have produced highly productive programs.[69]

Most of the literature on the other side assumes a crisis in foundations and argues for saving them. The reports of the Peterson Commission (1970) and the Commission on Private Philanthropy and Public Needs (1975) should be seen in this light. More recently, John Nason's *Trustees and the Future of Foundations* (1977) argues that foundations are important as an interface between those who want stability and those desiring change; they are also tremendously influential for the size of their assets. Since Nason also feels that foundations are in danger, he focuses on the responsibilities of trustees for the reforms necessary to save these institutions. Many of the suspicions surrounding foundations Nason dismisses as a "tempest in a teapot."[70]

Fritz Heiman, former executive director of the Peterson Commission, also argues for saving the foundations and does so in an important way. Recognizing that most are—and even at best, will continue to be—institutions of modest and limited resources, he sees flexibility as their main asset. Since they are not politically accountable, they can try an experimental project in one community without being politically pressured, as government is, to give equal treatment to other communities. Likewise, they can, if they choose, fund only the best institutions without worrying about equal treatment. This flexibility, this ability to be adventuresome must, however, be utilized. If foundations support only what is popular with politicians, their role will become insignificant because such projects have access to much larger government funds. On the other hand, if they limit grants to charitable instutitions already supported by direct individual giving, foundations become "unnecessary middlemen."[71]

Perhaps the argument about foundations boils down to whether individual preferences—liberty—should continue to have a significant say in the distribution of assets that might otherwise be geared to equality. While libertarians like Wagner argue for greatly increased incentives for charitable bequests and for an increase in the role of foundations, there has been enough egalitarian pressure against charitable deductions and on the foundations themselves to halt any such increase. Thus, at least until the appearance of the Reagan administration, the desire to preserve minority preferences (and perhaps efficiency) by fostering competition between charitable foundations in providing services has not been strong enough politically for foundations to expand their role.[72]

What the effect of Reagan administration policies will be is presently unclear. The early successes of the administration in reducing social spending by the government would seem to stimulate the demand for a greater role by foundations in such areas. Yet Congress's substantial weakening of the estate tax in 1981 at President Reagan's request, will likely reduce gifts to charitable foundations. Indeed, such organizations lobbied heavily against the changes which were made. As amended, the law seems to work against either the government or foundations providing grants to the poor.

It is easy to predict an egalitarian backlash against these policies, but exactly when and in what form it will appear is difficult to know. Certainly, foundations will be under pressure to expand their role, if not over all, at least in areas affected by federal budget cuts. The discussion that follows, however, focuses on ways egalitarian inheritance reform can be accomplished while preserving present levels of funding for such centers of nongovernmental largesse. While the current political situation might argue for increasing these levels, reality suggests maintenance of the status quo as a first step. Besides, if the people ultimately turn their backs on President Reagan's policies, present levels of funding for foundations are about right.

Assuming that the backlash occurs and causes an estate tax increase, the first way to stem the negative effects of such an increase on charitable bequests is to cut other estate tax deductions and exemptions. The second is the greatly expanded use of the judicial doctrine of cy pres to save failing charitable organizations for public purposes similar to those for which they were formed.

2. THE EFFECTS OF ESTATE TAX REFORMS ON FOUNDATIONS At present, §2055 of the Internal Revenue Code allows a deduction, in determining the taxable estate, for the amount of all bequests to a charitable corporation or a trust, order, or association organized for religious, charitable, scientific, or educational purposes. To the extent that the activities supported by deduction-induced contributions provide benefits or services that otherwise would have to be financed by government, the deduction serves to reduce the cost of government and the state forgoes the amount of the revenue which would come to them if the contributions were included in the taxable estate. Though libertarians have argued the point, most view the deduction as a government subsidy for charitable activities.

As I have discussed, the subsidy is particularly useful for the very rich. Compare two testators, one in the 30% tax bracket and the other in the 70% bracket. For each dollar transferred to exempt institutions by the decedent with the smaller estate, his tax liability is reduced by thirty cents. By contrast, the richer testator is able to secure a seventy-cent reduction in tax liability for each dollar transferred. Thus the charitable deduction allows private testators to direct the expenditure of what may be regarded as public revenue. It also allows richer testators to exert a disproportionately large influence over the use of such diverted revenue.[73]

The libertarian position is that if we increase estate tax rates while leaving the charitable deduction as is, charitable bequests will decrease. Richard Wagner provides a simplified example of how this works in his monograph *Inheritance and the State*. Wagner's basic hypothesis seems reasonable: in planning his estate, the testator will first establish a target level of wealth for the family, leaving any balance for charity. Suppose that after tax free bequests to his wife, funeral and administration expenses, and disposal of the standard exempt amounts (which will rise to $600,000 by 1987), he leaves an estate of $1.0 million to be divided between charity and family members. Then suppose testator wants to leave $300,000 to family members and is willing to pay a certain tax cost to do so. At a 33 ⅓% rate of tax, Wagner assumes this cost will be $150,000, meaning he must leave $450,000 to the family, with $550,000 left for charity.

Wagner's example next considers the effect on this estate of a rise in estate tax from 33⅓% to 50%, an increase in magnitude reasonable under the argument developed in this book. This rate change would raise the tax cost of the $300,000 bequest to $300,000 reducing to $400,000 the amount available for charity. Since I propose to keep charitable bequests at current levels, my reform would have to make compensatory alterations elsewhere in the tax in order to balance the negative effects of the rate increase.

In order to show how this can be done, it is necessary to take a more complete look at the situation of the testator than Wagner does. Although they would have to be subtracted before reaching a $1.0 million figure, tax-free amounts covered by funeral, administrative, and casualty loss deductions, the now-unlimited marital deduction, and the tax credit (equal in 1982 to a standard exemption of $225,-000) are not mentioned in Wagner's example.

Thus we are really dealing with a much larger estate than Wagner's example shows. Given the actual situation, where a testator can pass, tax free, unlimited amounts to his wife and $225,000 to family members and others, and where he typically gives much less to charity (average of 5-6.5%)[74] than Wagner's figure (55%),[75] we might have a $2.0 million estate which could be distributed as follows:

TABLE 2

Modified Wagner Model of Estate Distribution

Items Not Considered in Wagner's Example:

1. §2053 and §2054 deductible expenses (funeral, casualty)	$	25,000
2. "Exempt" property to non-family members		225,000
3. Non-taxable property to wife (marital deduction)		1,150,000

Items Considered by Wagner:

4. Tax-free amount to charity (reduced to realistic figure)		150,000
4a. Subtotal		1,550,000
5. Amount remaining for family members ($2.0 million minus 4a)		450,000
6. Tax on amount in #5 at $33\frac{1}{3}$ % rate		150,000
7. After-tax amount to family members		300,000
Total Estate		$2,000,000

One can readily see that under Wagner's assumptions, which for simplicity include zero elasticity of demand, a move to the 50% tax rate would—in our model—reduce charitable bequests to zero because of the doubled tax cost. (The reduction would probably be somewhat less because of greater elasticity of demand in an actual situation.) What reforms can be made to keep this from happening?

At first blush, the new unlimited marital deduction (which testator could have taken for all of his property had he bequeathed it to his wife) seems a likely candidate for reform. Prior to the 1981 act, the size of the marital deduction was meant to provide equity between the tax treatment of estates in common law and community property states in pursuit of the reasonable social policy of protecting the spouse. In the eight community property states (which include California and Texas) one-half the marital property is automatically that of the surviving spouse and cannot be taxed in the testator's estate. Instead, this one-half is not taxed until settlement of the surviving spouse's estate, which is substantially the same situation the Code mandated for the 42 common law states by giving the testator a deduction on one-half his estate if this is bequeathed to his wife. In both situations, the surviving spouse got the use of her one-half of the estate tax-free until her death.[76] Prior law thus seems to go far enough in protecting the spouse.

In our example, another change which would help restore charitable bequests involves the "standard exemption" of $225,000. I see no sound reason to allow such a large exemption, particularly where this allows the testator to make sizeable tax-free bequests directed neither to his wife nor to charity. "Family protection" is more than amply provided by the marital deduction. If we want to leave testator *some* tax-free leeway aside from spousal bequests, I would suggest a smaller amount like $75,000, for example. The problems such a small exemption raises for real estate held by family farms and closely-held businesses can be solved, *inter alia,* by valuing such property at less than its maximum value, as is provided in both the 1976 and 1981 reform acts.

In the example, lowering the standard exemption to $75,000 while raising tax rates from 33⅓% to 50% would exactly restore the amount lost to charity under the rate hike alone. Thus, the distribution of the estate would look like this under my plan:

TABLE 3

Modifications Necessary to Maintain Same Bequest
to Charity at 50% Tax Rate

Items in the distribution:

1. §2053 and §2054 deductible expenses	$ 25,000
2. "Exempt" property to non-family members	75,000
3. Non-taxable property to wife (marital deduction)	1,150,000
4. Tax-free amount to charity	150,000
4a. Subtotal	1,400,000
5. Amount remaining for family members ($2.0 million minus 4a)	600,000
6. Tax on amount in #5 at 50% rate	300,000
7. After-tax amount to family members	300,000
Total Estate	$2,000,000

Since it has been estimated that at least 50% of charitable bequests are due to the charitable deduction,[77] it takes little extrapolation from Table 3 to understand that current levels of charitable bequesting could not be maintained in the absence of the deduction, whatever other manipulations were tried. Elimination of the deduction would drop charitable bequests to $75,000, with the remaining $37,500 going to family at a tax cost of $37,500.

As can be seen, we have doubled the estate tax revenue while leaving intact the gift to the spouse and the current level of charitable bequests, all without altering Wagner's basic assumptions about testator priorities. As mentioned in chapter 4, this additional tax revenue can be redistributed at least two ways: (1) by decreasing taxes on earned income and (2) by direct grants to the poor. Since wealth redistribution must be sold to wage and salary earners, a reduction in their taxes would be politically necessary. Perhaps the additional revenue could be split evenly between the two purposes.

Estate and gift tax revenues have made up approximately 1% of total federal receipts for each year in the past decade. Lately this has been about the same amount as is collected from the alcohol excise tax. Estimates for 1980 showed total federal receipts of $523.8 billion, while estate and gift and alcohol excise revenues were put at $5.5 and $5.6 billion respectively. In 1981 estate and gift taxes continued to produce about 1% of Federal revenues or about $7 billion.[78]

These figures show that the estate and gift tax has been a suprisingly small source of revenue. Under the 1981 Tax Reform Act it will become a substantially smaller source unless the act is amended. However, assume for a moment that the government changes course and gears the tax to double estate tax revenue as I did in my example. Using 1981 figures, this would allow $3.5 billion extra to be used in direct government grants (largely to the poor) and a similar amount for the reduction of the personal income tax.

Though I have proposed that we keep foundations operating at least at current levels, the extra amount available for government grants after doubling estate tax yield would slightly reduce the foundations' proportionate share of grant-making. Since foundation giving is so small a share of government grant-making anyway, this would not, however, significantly shift the ratio between foundation and government giving that now exists. Of course, if *all* additional estate tax revenue were used to reduce the income tax (a popular move in today's political climate), the balance would not be altered at all. Given the critical needs of the poor, however, it would seem preferable to split the benefits of the new revenue between the needy and those who pay the income tax.

Whatever allocation is made of the additional estate tax revenues, the result will hardly be a substantial redistribution of wealth. If, however, the Rignano principle is applied to successive transfers, this will produce a more substantial redistribution over the next several generations. In addition, the final chapter suggests that a net worth tax be enacted; this too will aid the process of slow redistribution that seems necessary. In order to be politically acceptable, inheritance reform must be approached gradually and from a number of angles. Immediate, massive redistribution would surely occasion widespread tax evasion and might even lead to revolution. Gradualism in this matter neither unfairly shatters the expectation of those who are relatively wealthy, nor unduly raises the present expectations of the relatively poor.

3. CY PRES AND FOUNDATIONS   In the last section, we have seen how the estate tax can be manipulated to keep charitable bequests at current levels, despite a significant rate increase. This is important to foundations because they ultimately receive around 50% of their assets from this source.[79] However, in 1977–78, about 85% of all foundations had assets of less than $1 million.[80] As mentioned, these foundations are in grave danger under the Tax Reform Act of 1969: they may not have the funds necessary to perform their charitable purposes under the standards required. Thus the Peterson Commission concluded that either remedial legislation "or a broad use of judicial cy pres" would be necessary to save their funds for charitable purposes. Since foundations may fail for other reasons than financial (e.g., their charitable purpose becomes obsolete), such curative steps may also be necessary for some of the larger ones.

Cy pres (a French legal term meaning "so near") is a doctrine used to reform charitable trusts whose purposes have become impossible to accomplish. It does so by applying the fund to a similar charitable purpose. In the modern context, it can be used to channel the funds of failed charitable trusts and foundations to serve redistributive functions which promote equal opportunity.

Today charitable bequests other than direct gifts establish entities ranging from a small trust to provide a scholarship at a named college to a large, multi-purpose foundation. When a donor desires to accomplish a single purpose through his foundation, or has only limited funds for charity, he will likely use the simple trust form of foundation. When channeling a substantial amount of wealth into a broad spectrum of public objectives, with specifics to be determined in the future by the fund's managers, he will probably establish a nonprofit corporation. Both forms of foundations are generally subject to the same legal rules.[81]

This similarity of treatment is particularly notable where a gift is made to a nonprofit corporation for a specific purpose; the corporation is then subject to the same rules as a trust, whether or not it technically holds the property in trust. As the *Restatement of Trusts* states, though the property of a charitable corporation is not held in trust, it must be used like trust property in accord with the restrictions on the gift.[82]

Likewise, corporate foundations are subject to "traditional trust doctrines such as cy pres". However, the problem of failure of trust purpose which triggers the doctrine is minor in the larger foundations, which are usually in corporate form: a board of directors is charged with the details of management, and in the usual case the articles of incorporation show a broad corporate purpose. Nevertheless, a great number of foundations have been affected by legal changes in the 1969 Act and require a compensating reform of the cy pres doctrine to save them. The excursus to follow demonstrates that a reform the courts might have treated directly as a matter of social policy has instead involved considerable manipulation of legal doctrine.

a. Cy Pres Development   Before the 1850s very few charitable trusts were created in the United States and fewer still had been allowed to stand; thus, there was only the most occasional demand for the application of cy pres.[83] When the demand arose, the courts of most states were extremely hostile to the doctrine. Of the fifteen states which had had occasion to consider cy pres by 1860, the courts of ten states had either condemned or repudiated its use.[84] One cause of this antagonism was the early and mistaken notion that the doctrine could be exercised only by means of the uncontrolled prerogative of the sovereign.[85] Thus, the use of this so-called prerogative cy pres was heartily resisted in a new nation fresh from a triumph over monarchial authority. In fact Chancery had long exercised an equitable or judicial cy pres which attempted to effectuate the intent of the donor rather than the arbitrary wishes of the sovereign.[86] It was this judicial cy pres power which eventually found root in America.

American use of the doctrine springs from the case of *Jackson* v. *Phillips.* Francis Jackson died in 1861 leaving money in trust to be used to create a public sentiment that would put an end to Negro slavery; the trustees were to use another part of the fund for the benefit of fugitive slaves. Since slaves had been legally freed as a result of the Civil War, by 1867 these objectives could not be carried out. Despite the demands of the settlor's heirs, the court refused to dismantle the trust and directed the cy pres use of the fund for welfare and educational work among freed slaves and other New England blacks.[87]

According to historian Lawrence Friedman, this case gave the old English doctrine "a new and different life, as an adjunct of the law of dynastic charities." Friedman feels that cy pres is actually a facet of dead hand control: charitable trusts "allow a childless settlor to fund a bloodless dynasty" and cy pres prevents "destruction of the [dynastic charitable] trust," which would scatter fragments of the corpus among unintended beneficiaries. Thus, though not fulfilling the founder's specific intent, cy pres allows "substantial fulfillment" of this intent and the perpetuation of the donor's memorial.[88]

Although the possibility was raised of saving gifts through finding a general charitable intent as in *Jackson,* the finding of such intent was rigidly circumscribed, in the name of protecting the testator's wishes. Since most men were regarded as selfish profit-maximizers out for their own family's private gain, the abiding spirit of the times was suspicious of benevolence operating for the public good.

Typical of this spirit was the decision in *Harvard College* v. *Society for Promoting Theological Education.*[89] The Theological Society brought an equitable action requesting that donations made to Harvard for theological instruction and held in trust by the college be transferred to the society or an independent board of trustees. The court held that it could not substitute a new scheme merely because the trustees believed it would be a better or more convenient one than the settlor's. As a later Connecticut court wrote: "No public benefit, no increased beneficence, no advantage to religious activity can justify a court in making over the wills . . . of men, in the conviction that changed conditions make this . . . highly desirable."[90]

The Progressive era and the Depression years of the 1930s saw a gradual change in such judicial attitudes. Fear of revolution[91] and recognition of the need for private funds to serve critical public needs[92] were key factors.

It was during this period when "individualism" gradually lost ground to "public welfare," and "the clasp of the dead hand was loosened, that the cy pres doctrine began to be freely applied by the courts."[93] When faced with a great increase in the amount of charitable trust property—a phenomenon which had been encouraged substantially by favorable tax treatment for charitable giving—the courts began to apply the cy pres doctrine liberally. During the period 1900–1950, twenty-one jurisdictions expressly applied cy pres for the first time, and many statutes were passed by state legislatures expressly giving the cy pres power to courts.[94]

Over the years, three primary requirements had developed for the application of cy pres. The first of these—that a valid charitable *trust* has been created—crumbled quickly during the 1900–1950 period: courts applied the doctrine whenever a charitable gift had been made, either directly, in trust, or to a charitable corporation. The second—that the original bequest must have become impossible or impractical to apply—retreated before the courts' increased willingness to discover "impossibility" when confronted with what they considered a much better use of the bequest.[95]

Still, the troublesome requirement remained that, in order to apply cy pres to a charitable bequest whose specific purpose had failed, the court was required to find that the testator also possessed a more general charitable intent.[96] Though this requirement was abolished by statute in Pennsylvania in 1947,[97] elsewhere it remained: courts refused to apply cy pres in the absence of general charitable intent, especially where a "gift over" to another party was provided by the instrument in the event of the gift's failure.[98]

b. The Current Status of Cy Pres Since the history of cy pres in America has been one of slow but steady expansion of the doctrine, one might have anticipated the virtual elimination by modern times of all the technical requirements for its application, just as Edith Fisch proposed in the 1959 *Cornell Law Quarterly.* According to Fisch, the prerequisites for applying cy pres serve "no useful end":

Their elimination ... would not only render unnecessary the present circumlocutions employed to take cases outside the orbit of cy pres but would facilitate the preservation of charitable gifts since the only question ... would then be the proper exercise of the court's discretion [in requiring] a different mode of operation or choice of operation or choice of another charitable purpose.[99]

G. G. and G. T. Bogert, in their treatise *Trusts and Trustees,* have likewise called for the removal of the troublesome "general intent" rule. In their view, the rule causes many unnecessary claims by heirs or next of kin of the settlor and much expensive and time-consuming litigation:

[I]t would seem preferable either to provide that the charitable intent shall be presumed to be general unless the settlor expressly negates the application of cy pres or to follow the Pennsylvania statutory precedent [*supra* at note 97] and make cy pres application [in absence of such a direction] whether the settlor's charitable intent is found to be general or special.[100]

To these calls for elimination of the "general charitable intent" rule, which would make the application of cy pres virtually automatic in the event of a failed charitable trust, the courts have turned a deaf ear. Though "impossibility" has become easier to find, and neither undesignated charitable beneficiaries nor the styling of the bequest as a gift rather than trust now hinder application of cy pres, the dead hand of the settlor still controls the fund through the courts' observance of his or her intent.

A possible reason for the continuation of dead hand control lies in one of the dilemmas of American democracy—the conflict between individual control over property and the use of that property for the common good. Courts may be reluctant to assume a direct role in reallocating charitable funds for public purposes precisely for fear of taking one more step toward the obliteration of individual will in an increasingly socialist world. As this modern dilemma is examined, one may ask whether individual control, however important to our system during an individual's life, should extend beyond the testator's original postmortem purpose.

Typical of court regard for the testator's specific intent is the 1973 case of *DePew* v. *Union Free School District.*[101] The *DePew* court, in a remarkably hidebound decision, gives the dead hand firm control by ruling that the trial court should attempt to discover whether the testator had a general intent to benefit education in a particular school district or whether he wished the benefit to be limited to the use of the bequeathed land as a school. Thus, in order to discern the actual intent of the testator, the trial court was instructed to consult school minutes and diaries dating from the time the bequest was made in 1852. Had it taken the time, the DePew Court would likely have echoed sentiments expressed by the Wyoming Supreme Court in another 1973 decision construing a charitable trust:

> The clearly expressed intention of the settlor should be zealously guarded by the courts, particularly when the trust instrument reveals a careful and painstaking expression of the use and purposes to which [his assets] shall be devoted. A settlor must have assurance that his solemn arrangements and instructions will not be subject to the whim or suggested expediency of others after his death.[102]

Perhaps more surprising is the recent use of "general charitable intent" to prevent application of cy pres in the jurisdiction which gave the doctrine its first substantial life.[103] In *First Church of Somerville (Unitarian)* v. *Attorney General,* the Supreme Judicial Court of Massachusetts refused to find any general intent to benefit the Unitarian religion in the will of the testator despite the pleas of the appellant Unitarian Universalist Association:

> On the contrary, we conclude that the intent of the testator in this case was to support the particular Unitarian church which he had helped establish and, in the alternative [via a "gift over"], to support Unitarian education at Harvard and the poor of McLean Asylum.

Since the gift over was to take effect if the church changed its religious tenets and ceased to inculcate a liberal religion, it become effective when, by dissolving, the church "ceased to inculcate any religion."[104]

Despite the result, a progressive facet of the decision involves the court's apparent willingness to consider cy pres application despite the existence of a gift over. The general American rule has been that the mere existence of a gift over automatically blocks cy pres application.[105] This rule serves to "hold the line" against the free use of cy pres which might be made possible by any loosening in the basic general charitable intent requirement. Its rationale is that the existence of any gift over shows there is no general charitable intent, only primary and alternative specific intents. Whether a gift over which is void because it may go to a private individual beyond the period of the Rule against Perpetuities (but is nonetheless expressive of testator's intent) would also block cy pres application has not been tested under the American rule.

The opposite rule, allowing cy pres application to the primary charitable gift, regardless of the existence of a gift over, appears to be in force in England.[106] Because of the greater flexibility it provides the court, this doctrine seems preferable; however, only the World War II California case of *Society of California's Pioneers* v. *McElroy*[107] applies it in America. Nonetheless, the more recent Massachusetts case of *Trustees of Dartmouth College* v. *City of Quincy* applies equitable deviation—a doctrine allied to cy pres—where there is a gift over.[108] Apparently, this case provided the basis for the *First Church* court's willingness to *consider* cy pres application despite the gift over. Since *Dartmouth College*, unlike *First Church*, actually blocked the gift over in this situation, it is worth discussing in detail here.

The case arose when the beneficiary of the gift over, Dartmouth College, petitoned in equity to stop the City of Quincy, Massachusetts, as trustee from admitting to a girls' school established under the will of a Dr. Woodward in 1869, any girl not from Quincy. Dartmouth's gift over was to be triggered if Quincy failed to "comply with the words and intent of the will" or "used the fund for any other purpose." The trustee had formulated a plan to save the school from dissolution by admitting non-Quincy girls (in violation of Dr. Woodward's wishes) at a higher tuition and without scholarship aid from the trust itself.

The Supreme Judicial Court was faced with a situation where it might be said that the trust purpose had become impractical, thus raising the possibility of cy pres. Admitting that cy pres and equitable deviation had not been clearly delineated in Massachusetts decisions (and thus suggesting that its ruling would apply whichever doctrine was used), the court chose to apply equitable deviation. It claimed that it was modifying administrative details of the trust in allowing the Quincy plan—not changing the trust's purpose, as was necessary for cy pres.

The court decided that if Quincy's proposed violation of Dr.

Woodward's condition were allowed to trigger the gift to Dartmouth, this would result in *forfeiture,* which was within the court's equitable power to avoid. This was an imaginative use of the forfeiture doctrine, which has previously been applied to save failed charitable bequests from going back to the testator's estate via a "resulting trust" where no gift over had been made."[109] But in *Dartmouth College* it was being used to block testator's expressed secondary intent to make a gift over!

Citing a cy pres article in the *Boston University Law Review,* the court decided to preserve testator's dominant intention, rather than diverting funds to his secondary, though laudable, purpose of helping Dartmouth. Its important reasoning follows:

> A gift over should be resorted to only when it appears that more benefit to the community would be derived from the alternative disposition and nobody would be substantially damaged by terminating the original trust [for the girls' school].[110]

With the *Dartmouth College* case as precedent, the *First Church* court could not simply rule that the gifts over to Harvard Theological School and for the poor of McLean's Asylum blocked application of cy pres to the original gift to the First Church. Instead it concentrated on whether the testator had revealed any general intent to benefit the Unitarian religion aside from the Church, as the appellant Unitarian Universalist Association claimed. Since testator had been a founding member, chairman of a standing committee of the Church, and had been instrumental in getting the Church's debts paid after an 1852 fire, the court concluded his intent was confined to helping this particular church.

Further, though testator knew of the Universalist Association's predecessor, he had left nothing to it. Moreover, his gifts over were important to him and not really "secondary" in the *Dartmouth College* sense. Thus the court stressed that the gift to Harvard Theological School (which admitted no non-Unitarians until 1880) was consistent with his religious beliefs; also he and his wife were longtime employees of the McLean Hospital.

Had the gifts over in *First Church of Somerville* been to private individuals rather than charities, they would have been subject to the Rule Against Perpetuities (which does not apply to charitable trusts).

Since the church might have stopped "inculcating a Liberal Religion" at any time after testator's death, one could not be certain that the gift over would vest, if at all, within human lives in being plus twenty-one years (the period of the Rule). With the gifts over thus void the court would not have had the choice presented by the case itself upon the church's demise: applying cy pres to the original gift or funding secondary charitable beneficiaries. Instead, the void gifts over would have forced a choice between cy pres application and the unattractive alternative of intestate succession (via "resulting trust") for testator's heirs.

Since the *First Church* court insists that "each case turns on the intent of the particular testator," it might well have decided that allowing intestate succession to unknown heirs a century and a quarter after the date of testator's bequest defies that intent more than does the use of cy pres. The application of the doctrine to benefit, for example, the Unitarian Universalist Association, at least gives life to the primacy placed by testator on leaving the fund for charitable purposes.

While *First Church* takes a step backward in finding no general charitable intent, it expressly leaves open the *Dartmouth College* court's willingness to consider cy pres or equitable deviation where the will reveals a gift over. Taken together, then, the cases open up an entire new area in which cy pres can be considered under United States law. One can hope for more general application of the new rule precisely because Massachusetts has long been a leader in doctrinal changes in trust law—particularly in the uses of cy pres.

The new rule might be formulated thus: a gift over, whether (1) to individuals and in violation of the Rule Against Perpetuities, or (2) to individuals but duly limited to the perpetuities period, or (3) to an alternative charity should not block cy pres application to the original charitable gift. The testator or settlor has expressed that his primary purpose is charitable. The courts should thus apply cy pres as a matter of social policy, regardless of secondary dispositions. Allowing the gift over to take effect when the dominant charitable purpose of the donor can be protected by cy pres can realistically be seen as forfeiture, as the *Dartmouth College* court stressed.

c. Legislative Use of the Cy Pres Power   It has sometimes been suggested that legislatures instead of courts should apply cy pres because of their political accountability and the doctrine's public policy implications. For example, the Massachusetts legislature recently asked the Supreme Judicial Court whether it now had the authority to order that the care, custody, management, and control of the Franklin Institute (established by applying the cy pres power to a fund left by Benjamin Franklin to help young artisans get a financial start in business)[111] be transferred from the Franklin Foundation to Boston University and the City of Boston when the trust establishing the foundation expires in 1991.[112] The court determined not only that the legislature had no authority to use the cy pres power, but that no one had the right to ask the courts to apply that power to purposes chosen by designated beneficiaries [e.g., the City of Boston] now, since the terms of Franklin's will contemplate distribution by the city government in 1991 for purposes to be *chosen* in 1991.[113] Thus, not only was cy pres to remain outside the power of the publicly-elected legislature, but it could not be exercised in advance in violation of Benjamin Franklin's expressed intent. Perhaps the Massachusetts courts have understood that once they cease to be the guardians of the testator's intent, their claim to use cy pres at all will be in jeopardy; once the initial question becomes not *whether* to apply the doctrine, but *how* to apply the fund in question for the public good, one has moved into a traditionally legislative area of decision making.[114]

As indicated, a number of small foundations are now likely to fail after the death of donor and friends. I would suggest that the fact of increasing numbers of individual cases requiring cy pres application militates against legislative usurpation of the power. Rather, if courts can shed the remnants of outworn doctrines, they are better equipped institutionally to make the individual decisions required. Though judicial political accountability is less direct than that of the legislature, it has developed sufficiently to handle such public policy tasks.

d. Proposals for the Future   Unfortunately, shedding doctrinal inhibitions has proven difficult. The progress made by the courts since the 1950s in applying cy pres has come to a standstill in the 1970s due to the persistence of the general charitable inherent requirement, a remnant of the stress on individual property rights so prevalent in Anglo-American common law. If, as has been suggested in previous chapters, dead hand control over property passing to individual heirs might be limited to providing a comfortable but not luxurious living to the initial takers, and little if anything to subsequent heirs, why not limit the testator's control over charitable giving by giving effect only to the initial charitable bequest? The delicate balance between property rights and the common good can justifiably be tilted in favor of the public when testator's dead hand control seeks to extend beyond the initial disposition. Once the original charitable bequest fails, courts should feel free to apply the cy pres whether or not there is a gift over and whether or not this gift over is to a charitable or individual beneficiary.[115] After all, as Lawrence Friedman suggests, cy pres may give testator the kind of control he sought while at the same time satisfying current public needs.

One may argue that society can also be protected by doing what the *First Church* court did: denying cy pres application to the original bequest where the gift over is charitable. If they limited denial to this situation, courts could still apply cy pres where a valid gift over is noncharitable. Still, for the sake of both doctrinal consistency and ease of administration, it would seem preferable to impose an across-the-board limitation on the remoteness of dead hand control over the gift's specific purpose. This should be done whether the failed bequest is followed by no gift over, by a noncharitable gift over void under the Rule, by a valid noncharitable gift over, or even by a charitable gift over. Once the testator expresses the primacy of his intent via the original charitable gift, one may argue that he has put the gift in the public realm. Then a court should be empowered, upon failure, to apply it for a related purpose, regardless of any secondary dispositions he may have made.

Under the above formulation, courts can preserve the testator's charitable intent by choosing as an alternative a viable charity as near as possible to the one originally chosen by testator. However, in doing so, courts should be aware that they are functioning as distributive, not commutative, decision makers; they are directing the particular distribution of wealth desired, rather than serving as a mere referee, allowing the principles of law and economy to determine "who gets what."[116] They should not be too shy about performing government's role in wealth distribution when it is directed at providing more equal starting places.

Though American courts have often sought distributive ends tacitly, they are not always comfortable doing so explicit. One hopes they will remember Karl Llewellyn's Legal Realist dictum: "Covert tools are never reliable tools.[117] As a 1939 commentator in the *Yale*

Law Journal wrote: "Courts in reaching results which obviously show the impact of social considerations should not continue to couch their decisions in the outmoded terminology of the eighteenth century."[118]

Thus, in applying the cy pres doctrine to failing foundations, courts should explicitly recognize the element of social welfare in the doctrine to avoid the impression of "judicial hypocrisy." In doing so they should reach beyond extension of the settlor's dynastic purpose in the Friedman sense; a charitable memorial to the donor can do him honor without excessive obsequiousness to the guidance of his dead hand.[119] Facing as they do both overwhelming social needs and an overtaxed, even rebellious citizenry,[120] courts will best serve society's interest in foundation survival by applying cy pres widely and openly as a matter of public policy, regardless of notions of individual intent developed under previous social conditions.

CONCLUSION

The process of inheritance ultimately provides at least 50% of foundation assets. Thus, inheritance reform necessarily makes certain impacts on foundations themselves. In assessing what would be done about these impacts, it is necessary to assess the value of foundations as an institution.

After examining the pros and cons of foundations, I have concluded that, despite their limited financial resources, these institutions provide a valuable alternative to government monopoly of grant-making. Thus their funding should be kept at least at current levels. This means that any reform of the estate tax should be tailored to allow at least the present levels of bequesting.

Finally, since many small foundations and some larger ones are in danger of failing, I have argued for a greatly expanded use of the judicial cy pres power to save their funds for charitable purposes directed toward equal opportunity goals.

6

The Perpetuation of
Dynastic Trusts

While discussing the concentration of personal wealth, we noted that the high degree of inequality shown by estate tax figures was greatly underestimated, largely because most wealth held in trust escapes inclusion in these returns. Trusteed wealth is concentrated in very high wealth brackets; put another way, the concentration of trusts is greater than the concentration of individual wealth.[1]

CONCENTRATION AND PROTECTION OF TRUST ASSETS

Every year since the end of World War I the amount of trusteed wealth has increased at a remarkably high rate. By the end of 1972, roughly $800 billion in trust investments were being managed by corporate and individual fiduciaries.[2] Assuming a 5% rate of return at the time, this would have produced about $40 billion in trust income in one year. Although no more recent estimates are available, it would not be unreasonable to assume that the recent inflation alone could have doubled trust assets by 1982. At a present return conservatively estimated at 10%, this $1.6 trillion in assets would now be producing $1.6 billion in income per year.

Nearly all of the enormous wealth represented by these figures is "manacled by spendthrift-trust clauses."[3] These provisions seek to void the power of the beneficiary to "anticipate" his right to income, and often to principal. Since the beneficiary's power to anticipate is restricted, there is a corresponding restraint upon involuntary transfers to creditors (by legal process) which have the effect of anticipation. Spendthrift clauses do not restrain the use of income or principal once it is *received* by the beneficiary, nor does attachment by creditors at that time. Spendthrift clauses impose a direct restraint on alienation of the property involved.[4]

Closely related in effect to the spendthrift trust are two other types: "discretionary" and "support" trusts. In a pure discretionary trust, the trustee has absolute discretion over whether to pay anything at all to the beneficiary. If the beneficiary tries to transfer his interest (a mere expectancy), or if his creditors seek to take it before the trustee has made the decision to pay, the transferee or creditor has no remedy. Thus a discretionary clause imposes an indirect restraint on alienation in that it discourages attempts at voluntary alienation and efforts by creditors to reach the beneficiary's interest. Few will be willing to purchase the "expectancy" of the beneficiary, because whether it ripens into a benefit depends on the uncontrolled discretion of the trustee.[5]

If a trustee is directed to pay or apply trust income or principal for the benefit of a beneficiary, but only to the extent necessary to *support* him (and only when the disbursements will accomplish support), the nature of the beneficiary's interest makes it neither transferable nor subject to the claims of creditors. Payments to an assignee of the beneficiary or to his creditors would not result in *supporting* the beneficiary. These support clauses, like the discretionary ones, indirectly prevent alienability of the beneficiary's interest. All three types of clauses can be combined to give the maximum possible protection to trust income, and often, to principal.[6]

The resultant "protective trusts" (as the English call them) serve largely dynastic ends. This contrasts with the purposes of the "caretaker" trust, as Lawrence Friedman has explained them. Caretaker trusts are usually short-term (one lifetime or less) and are meant to protect or serve the needs and interests of one or more particular beneficiaries: generally minor children, incompetents, the elderly, or those with little business experience. Dynastic trusts, on the other hand, commonly exhibit a chain of lifetime interests, paying income to each successive beneficiary until the Rule Against Perpetuities causes the interests of relatively remote descendants to fail. These are less common than caretaker trusts, but they usually share some caretaker features. Their main characteristic is the evident concern with "the hunger for vicarious immortality" of the trust settlor, protecting his dynasty via dead hand control.[7]

The dynastic trust could have been discouraged in America by a tax system which taxed an estate at the death of each beneficiary or set of beneficiaries. Instead, such generation-skipping trusts were allowed to escape taxation. Although the Tax Reform Act of 1976 reached certain of these transfers, the prototypical one—T by will to trustee, income to T's children for life, then to the grandchildren— is not subject to the new tax at all until trusts assets exceed $250,000.[8]

Generation-skipping trusts offer a significant subsidy to the rich. As economist Gerald Jantscher found in examining estate tax returns from 1957–1959, taxation of successive transfers would primarily reach the millionaire rather than the person of moderate means. In gross estates of $1 million or more, trust use was much greater than in estates of smaller size. In the millionaire group alone, widows bequeathed nearly two-thirds as much property in generation-skipping trusts as they did outright to their families. Millionaire divorcees bequeathed more property in generation-skipping family trusts than they did in outright legacies. Thus decedents with gross estates greater than $1 million frequently bequeathed property in generation-skipping family trusts to distant descendants with income to intervening generations.[9]

Since the 1976 Act's complicated provisions eliminated a number of commonly encountered dispositions from the purview of the act,[10] they have not made a significant dent in the power of the wealthy to keep money in the family for generations. This leaves the ancient Rule Against Perpetuities as the main weapon against the perpetuation of dynastic trusts.

The rapid validation of the spendthrift trust in the United States in the late years of the nineteenth and early years of the twentieth century ran counter to British repudiation of the doctrine. Friedman sees this validation as a response to the spread of the dynastic trust during that period. Owners of the great "paper" fortunes produced in that era felt the psychological need to protect their wealth in an era of "boom and bust" market conditions. They succeeded in limiting trustees to a conservative, "prudent investor" standard in managing trust assets to protect them against market fluctuations, and they established the spendthrift clause to secure the trust against the whims of particular beneficiaries. Judges of the period accepted the behavior of their own social class in trying to consolidate their economic power. They acted in a period when "values were being called into question" and when the affluent had an overwhelming urge for safety "in an economic order increasingly beyond the individual's grasp."[11]

The dynastic urge of the new wealth holders also gave rise to the *Claflin* doctrine, based on the Massachusetts case of *Claflin* v. *Claflin*.[12] This case established the principle that, even if all beneficiaries consented to termination of a trust, the trust cannot be ended prior to the time set by the settlor, if termination is contrary to settlor's purpose. Courts found such destruction of a trust to be contrary to settlor's purpose where, for example, a spendthrift, discretionary, or support trust (usually a dynastic trust) had been created. Since these trusts expressed the settlor's desire to protect the estate over generations instead of serving the needs of particular beneficiaries, this dynastic purpose was to be protected. *Claflin*, like the spendthrift trust, violated English law, giving overweening importance to the vanity of a settlor in seeking to extend his control beyond the grave.[13]

This chapter focuses on the remarkable propensity of American law to extend the concept of individual rights over property beyond a settlor's lifetime by means of the spendthrift and *Claflin* doctrines. These doctrines form an important part of the institution of inheritance. Because of their use primarily to protect the estates of the very wealthy, the creation of spendthrift trusts (as protected by *Claflin*) even during the life of a settlor heavily involves inherited wealth. Because of their express purpose of outliving the settlor, spendthrift trusts also form an entirely inherited body of wealth upon his death. Further, such trusts are testamentary substitutes and may in certain cases be treated by the law as testamentary in fact.[14]

Reform in inheritance practices through elimination of these doctrines will have substantial impact on the wealth distribution problems we have been discussing. In general, the removal of protection now given to dynastic trusts should eventually force this enormous store of protected wealth back into the competitive marketplace. Trusteeing of wealth under conservative investment standards and with spendthrift protection against its presumptive beneficiaries has led to increased concentration of wealth, at the same time hindering the innovative use of "risk capital." Here is how this works:

Trustees are generally permitted to engage only in capital investments like bonds, mortgages, and "blue chip" stocks. Though the trustee often has the power of sale over trust assets, the trust device also makes possible long periods of continuous management, facilitating concentration of low-risk forms of wealth. Actual security ownership is divorced from effective managerial control by an elite group of trust officers, whose boards of directors often interlock with those of the very corporations whose stocks, bonds, and mortgages they hold.[15]

According to Simes, this freezes too much wealth in the form of capital concentrations, largely unavailable for use in risk ventures. Also this wealth, if it had been distributed directly rather than trusteed, would have caused its recipients to buy consumer goods, providing jobs and stimulating the economy. Nevertheless Simes sees the necessity—in neoclassical terms—for national saving and he is not overly disturbed by the other social consequences. He sees the problem as basically one of balancing the rights of the living against those of the dead.[16]

A recent commentator goes beyond the dead hand control issue, arguing that trusteeing of wealth should be attacked on broader grounds. This view emphasizes the fulfillment of social goals like lessening wealth concentration, increasing consumer expenditures, and keeping property unfettered for productive investment. This is seen finally as more important than Simes' emphasis on the determination of rights of different generations of individuals.[17]

The irony of the trusteeing and protection of America's great wealth is that those who benefited from the relatively free and open market of the immediate post-Civil War period evidently had little faith in the abilities of their children. Most modern conservatives continue to talk glibly about their desire for a free market, when in fact what they want is a continuation of "big money" control with the economic stagnation this produces. In fact, breaking up large concentrations of wealth and power, and the return to a relatively free market, may be the first step in achieving the productive growth which libertarians claim so avidly to seek. At the same time, the breakup of such unhealthy concentrations is a step toward the redistributive goals stressed throughout this book.

THE SPENDTHRIFT TRUST IN ENGLAND

The ancestor of the modern spendthrift trust evolved because of the unjust restrictions the English common law imposed on the property rights of married women. Until the nineteenth century, all personal property acquired by a married woman immediately became subject to the dominion of her husband. Though equity, as opposed to law courts, recognized separate property in the wife after 1600, the husband could still acquire the benefit of that property through marital pressure. Sometime after 1700, in an attempt to nullify that pressure by the more business-wise husband, equity began to allow fathers to stipulate in a trust for a married daughter that she could not anticipate (to her husband or his creditors) her income interest.

This restraint on the daughter's interest was allowed—not as recognition of settlor's control over trust property nor as protection of the wife from her folly—but to cripple the husband's power of dominion. The common law, then as now, prohibited direct restraints on the alienation of *legal* interests (i.e., absolute or fee simple interests) in property. However, the more flexible equity courts, having determined that a trust with a restraint on voluntary alienation was the only practical way to give a married woman property without in reality giving it to her husband, allowed an equitable (trusteed) interest to be so restrained.

English courts refused to extend this protection against voluntary alienation to the husband and his creditors or to involuntary alienation by the wife to her creditors. They also refused to extend it to mentally defenseless persons in general, with respect to either voluntary or involuntary alienation. Today certain trusts protective of beneficiaries (though not spendthrift trusts themselves) are permitted in England, but only insofar as to avoid the "deleterious social consequences inherent in American spendthrift trusts."[18]

SPENDTHRIFT TRUSTS IN THE UNITED STATES

In the United States up to 1875, the majority of cases involving spendthrift trust restraints followed the English rule.[19] Thus, it must have surprised many when the United States Supreme Court in that year announced in *Nichols* v. *Eaton*[20] that a spendthrift trust could be valid. The case involved a discretionary trust in which a bankrupt beneficiary had attempted to assign his expected "interest." Justice Miller, in invalidating the assignment because the beneficiary had merely an expectancy and no legal interest to assign, took the occasion (citing scant and weak authority) to declare that he did not accept the English rule on spendthrift trusts. Though this language was not necessary to the decision and was thus *dictum* (having no value as binding precedent), later courts used it as the foundation upon which to build the American spendthrift trust doctrine.[21]

As spendthrift trusts gained acceptance, the courts lost sight of the original reason for allowing such trusts: protection of the beneficiary. They focused instead on the settlor's *right* to dispose of the trust corpus as he wished and on the duty of the courts to execute his desires. By 1919, the compilation called *Ruling Case Law* was declaring that this was the primary reason for sustaining the doctrine. It said that the law was concerned neither with beneficiaries' rights in general nor with the propensity of a particular beneficiary to dissipate the property.[22] What had begun in the married woman's trusts as a narrow exception to the rule against restraints on alienation in favor of beneficiaries defenseless at law, and had been expanded, particularly in the United States, to the mentally defenseless, now blossomed into a doctrine under which anyone, regardless of sanity or economic stability, could qualify as the beneficiary of a spendthrift trust.[23]

Almost from the beginning, great legal scholars like John Chipman Gray saw what was happening and raised alarum cries. In the preface to the second edition of his *Restraints on Alienation of Property,* the formidable Gray took spendthrift trusts directly to task. He wrote: "If there is one sentiment, which it would seem to be the part of all in authority . . . particularly . . . judges to fortify, it is the duty of keeping one's promises and paying one's debts."[24] Judges who entertained the doctrine were therefore undermining capitalism "by that spirit . . . of paternalism, which is the fundamental essence alike of spendthrift trusts and of socialism."[25]

Gray felt he should show "that spendthrift trusts have no place in the system of Common Law." Still, he could not predict whether the future would bring socialism and a further reduction in the role of the common law, under which individual enterprise had flourished:

> But I am no prophet, and certainly do not mean to deny that [spendthrift] trusts may be in entire harmony with the Social Code of the next

century. Dirt is only matter out of place; and what is a blot on the escutcheon of the Common Law may be a jewel in the crown of the Social Republic.[26]

To many, the effects of the spendthrift trust doctrine were disastrous for the successful continuation of America's free-enterprise economy. Amid the economic chaos of 1931, Frederick J. Stimson, Massachusetts lawyer, diplomat, and author, wrote:

The most notable cause of Boston's commercial ... decline is the "spendthrift trust" decision of Massachusetts courts ... that a man could tie his children's inheritance up, either by deed or will, so that they could not spend or risk the principal. ... Immense wealth had been accumulated in Boston in the first sixty years of the republic; instead of trusting their sons and sending them out at their own risks ... they distrusted their ability ... and had them all trusteed. No new enterprise could be undertaken by them, for under the court decision, they had no capital to risk. Perforce they became coupon cutters—parasites, not promoters.[27]

Perhaps the popularly elected legislature would be an answer to self-serving rules promulgated by socially elite judges. Not so, wrote Gray: "If the remedy is like that applied in New York, it is, if not worse, more disgusting than the disease." What perturbed him was the "station-in-life" rule the courts wrote into the New York reform statute. This statute provided that the surplus of income given in trust beyond what was "necessary" for the education and support of the beneficiary was reachable for his debts. The education and support necessary for the "gentleman of leisure," however, was interpreted to be so costly that the statute became of little use to creditors.

In blunt terms, Gray pilloried this rule:

To say that whatever money is given to a man cannot be taken by his creditors is bad enough; at any rate, however, it is law for rich and poor alike. But to say that from the sum which creditors can reach, one man, who has lived simply and plainly, can deduct but a small sum, while a large sum may be deducted by another man because he is "of high social standing" or because "his associations are chiefly with men of leisure" ... is to descend to a depth of a shameless snobbishness as any into which the justice of a country was ever plunged.[28]

Still the station-in-life rule became what it was in New York largely because of its interpretation by the courts, not its enactment by the legislature. By the 1960s state legislatures had used various means to limit the settlor's power of restraint. They limited the amount of income exempt from alienation (a set weekly or annual dollar amount), the permissible beneficiaries (direct descendants or actual spendthrifts), the purpose for which the restrained income could be spent (usually support and education only), and allowed certain creditors to reach all income despite the trust provisions.

In the 1940s, when Dean Erwin Griswold of Harvard took up Gray's fight against the spendthrift trust, he used not only a common law treatise, but a model state statute to do it.[29] His model spend-thrift trust act, now adopted with various modifications in energy-rich Oklahoma and Louisiana, is stricter than the statutes of other states. The model act so severely limits the restraints on voluntary and involuntary alienation that the amount of income guaranteed to the beneficiary provides little more than a minimal subsistence, parallel-ing the exemption laws for wage garnishment. All income above $5000 per year can be voluntarily or involuntarily alienated and general creditors can reach 10% of all income exceeding $12 per week. Also, several classes of creditors—those who furnish support for the beneficiary, his spouse, or child, or who furnish necessaries to the beneficiary, and tort creditors—can reach all income.[30]

Eventually state courts, like legislatures, began to restrict the settlor's powers to restrain alienability. They have permitted the following kinds of creditors to reach trust income before the benefi-ciary: wife or child of beneficiary, during marriage or after divorce; the beneficiary's attorney; doctor rendering necessary medical ser-vices; executor of settlor's estate; the trustee for expenses; the benefi-ciary's trustee in bankruptcy. Creditors have also been allowed to reach income for necessaries and, upon limited authority, to collect on tort judgments.[31]

A few states, indeed, never accepted the spendthrift trust doc-trine. New Hampshire voided such trusts by statute and by case law. Rhode Island has decided that the restraints violate fundamental rules of property and unfairly harm creditors, while Ohio voids these trusts because they violate judgment execution laws.[32]

Still, by-and-large, spendthrift trusts are allowed in America. Despite the three states mentioned that ban the doctrine and five others (Alaska, Idaho, New Mexico, Utah and Wyoming) in which the question is undecided, court decisions or statutes exist in the other

41 states and District of Columbia indicating that spendthrift trusts are legally enforceable, either without qualification or subject to certain limits.[33] Coupled with the recent extension of the doctrine to trust principal, this acceptance suggests a persistence of dead-hand control very similar to that which has hindered the judicial use of cy pres.

Extension of spendthrift protection to trust principal has been accomplished most notably in the New York Court of Appeals case *Matter of Vought's Will.*[34] Dean Niles of New York University Law School noted that this decision "upset the statutory system" in New York rendering interests of income beneficiaries partially assignable and more vulnerable to certain claimants. This resulted, writes Niles, in a "tighter grip by the dead hand," which made the trusts "more restrictive" and altered "the trend toward more control by the living."[35]

Chance Vought Jr. had a vested remainder in property left by his father which was first to be held in trust for his mother during her life. The issue was simple: could Chance Jr. assign his remainder while his mother lived despite testator's express direction that "principal" was not to be assignable? (The income interest was nonassignable by statute.) In his later life Chance Jr. had been in dire need of money and had therefore sought funds from companies that make a business of buying shares at a heavy discount in the expectant interests of heirs and devices. He executed four assignments of interest in his remainder totaling more than $1 million, but he received only a small fraction in return. At the death of his mother, Chance Jr.'s interest in the trust principal was worth about $900,000. If the assignments were valid, then Chance's widow and children would receive nothing.[36]

Affirming the decisions of lower courts, Judge Breitel for the Court of Appeals, ruled for the widow and children. While noting the conflict of authority, Breitel followed what he believed to be the weight of modern trust law in favor of permitting Chance Sr.'s disabling restraint on a remainder after an income trust for life. Though recognizing the general policy of the law against restraints on alienation and conceding that a disabling restraint could not be imposed on a vested remainder after a *legal* life estate, he found there were no definite rules with respect to entrusted (equitable) life estates. He therefore concluded that "absent strong policy reasons to the contrary," these restraints should be valid. Though the statutes governing equitable interests were deliberately designed to parallel those governing legal estates, Breitel came out for the right of Chance Sr. to do what he wanted with the property within the bounds of social policy, despite the injury to legal symmetry.[37]

Chief Judge Fuld in dissent argued first that Chance Jr.'s remainder was not merely equitable but *legal* (it became an absolute, fee simple interest on the mother's death), and thus inalienable under long-established principles. Moreover:

> The policy considerations in favor of permitting a restraint upon the alienability of property until such time as the beneficiary is believed to be equipped to manage it wisely do not operate where a remainderman is given an absolute and unqualified right to dispose of the property as he chooses, subject only to the prior life estate of another. [it was not, e.g., given to Chance, Jr. in trust][38]

The case may be just an example of judicial sympathy (often called "Widow's Law") but the precedent unfortunately concretizes the right to restrict alienability in an area long subject to dispute. The *Restatement of Property* provides that *remainders* are alienable and subject to the rights of creditors. Likewise the first *Restatement of Trusts* states that disabling restraints on "principal" are invalid. Judge Breitel had instead relied on the second *Restatement of Trusts* —which he felt reflected the "current weight of authority." There, at least some restraints on alienation of trust principal are said to be valid, but no reference is made to remainders as such. Thus, Chance Jr.'s interest, if its status as a remainder is emphasized, would have been alienable under the *Restatement of Property.* However, if we look at the interest as "trust principal," it *may* be subject to a disabling restraint, at least under the second *Restatement of Trusts.*[39]

Though Dean Niles and Professor Powell (in a separate article)[40] discuss the legal basis of the decision in detail, it is sufficient here to note the influence of this decision by a respected judge in a very important jurisdiction. In a case that could have gone either way, Judge Breitel, in the name of the widow and children, established a powerful precedent for enlarging dead hand control.

POLICY CONSIDERATIONS CONCERNING THE SPENDTHRIFT TRUST

From the perspective of this book, it is obvious that spendthrift trusts should be eliminated in order to provide more equal starting places. This follows the Gray-Griswold approach that the doctrine is inconsistent with an equal opportunity capitalist system. As such, it protects the rich man's estate, allows the spendthrift heir to incur debts he does not pay, and locks up money that could be circulating in a free and competitive economy. Further, the spendthrift's position raises "equal protection" issues under the Fourteenth Amendment to the Constitution when his debt-free status is compared with that of those who earn a living.

Another traditional argument against the doctrine involves dead hand control. Though the original aim of spendthrift clauses was protection of the beneficiary, the extreme individualism of late Nineteenth-century America perverted this purpose, utilizing the doctrine to extend control of private property beyond the grave. In this guise the spendthrift trust protected not the beneficiary (who could not deal with the property in the market), but the estate and "will" —the dynasty—of the settlor. That vast amounts of wealth should be thus hindered from free competition in the marketplace in order to salve the vanity of the settlor seems ridiculous from the equal opportunity perspective.

Certainly, the beneficiary often suffers rather than benefits from spendthrift protection. His freedom of action is hampered; great financial need, coupled with his inability to reach trust assets, may drive him into a bad bargain with creditors, as in *Vought.* His character may also suffer, his protected status encouraging idleness and dissipation.

It is difficult to imagine, moreover, how there can be anything like free enterprise when a *class* of people who have benefited from economic competition hoards its wealth, "refusing to play" anymore. Despite the obvious point that the living are better able to take account of changing circumstances than the dead, their dead parents have sought to protect them from the very competition that produced the wealth. Not only does this serve to eliminate the risk taking necessary for production, it damages society in another way: if the spendthrift is not to pay his creditors, then the public must. While creditors might have been able to get some notice of spendthrift provisions when most wealth was in real property and thus recorded in land registries, they are now totally unable to protect themselves and society. The funding of spendthrift trusts is now largely in intangible personal property like stocks and bonds, whose ownership appears in no central, public, register. Moreover, many spendthrift trusts now are established *inter vivos,* not by will, and thus do not appear in probate records. Even if all were testamentary, it is ridiculous to suppose that creditors will make the complicated search of probate records necessary to reveal if anyone they do business with is a "spendthrift heir."[41]

Some have suggested that viewing spendthrift trusts from the equal opportunity perspective is too narrow and even obsolete, given the mixed nature of the modern American economy. They suggest that the protective function of spendthrift trusts is important. They believe that no matter how "fair" the free enterprise system is made, many must still suffer. It thus follows that there is a legitimate need for protecting those disadvantaged in the competition and that spendthrift principles, far from being socially destructive, can be made to serve this need.[42]

According to Costigan, modern spendthrift trusts originated in response to inadequate legislation for establishing guardianship over persons incapable of managing their own affairs.[43] Even Gray admitted that a spendthrift trust for an actual incompetent was socially beneficial. Seen from this perspective, the problem today involves incapacity falling short of complete incompetence. Though guardianship is available for the totally incapacitated, eccentric, gullible, elderly or irresponsible heirs must defend themselves (and the estate) unaided. Thus the role of the spendthrift clause as a private means of providing protection for these persons should be stressed more fully than has been possible under a doctrine where characteristics of the beneficiary are irrelevant to the settlor's right to use the clause.[44]

Under this view, guardianship principles could be extended to the marginally competent; this could be coupled with necessary reforms in spendthrift doctrine. Thus, the spendthrift trust beneficiary would clearly be liable for the same obligations as an incompetent under guardianship—those to legitimate creditors such as tort claimants.[45]

The abuses of present spendthrift trust law, from this perspective, are not central to the true protective purpose of the doctrine. This is why modern courts and legislatures have already made substantial inroads on the aspects of the doctrine that smack more of privilege than of protection. For example, restraints on voluntary alienation have been relaxed in a number of states already, and in practice the efforts of legitimate creditors to recover have sometimes proved successful despite the apparent existence of the doctrine.[46]

Extending the spendthrift doctrine's emphasis on protection rather than on settlor's rights to *classes* of disadvantaged persons is already widespread in American society. Social Security laws and many private pension plans create funds which cannot be reached either by settlor or creditors before retirement or death.[47]

Thus, while in many states the anomaly still exists of a creditor able to garnish a wage earner's salary but not the income of a spendthrift heir,[48] at the same time the "employee benefit trust," based on spendthrift principles, has become the "fastest growing sector of trust investment."[49] This new trend makes these principles look less like instruments that can be used to exploit workers and more like ones useful for their protection. If we take these examples a few steps further, we can see that spendthrift protective principles can be made to serve the purposes of "ends-equality" and socialism.

Ends-equality theorists usually view class, privilege, and exploitation as inevitable outgrowths of capitalism. If this is true, breaking up spendthrift trusts as the equal opportunity thinkers suggest merely "reshuffles the deck." If most capital eventually reverts to government, that government essentially becomes the trustee of a giant spendthrift trust which protects its citizens against alienation of their "property" either by themselves or by others. By holding wealth "in trust" for those classes of citizens who need protection, the "cards" in the economy are not reshuffled for another competition, but put "face up" on the table. Thus the ends-equality thinker writes:

> The damnation of the spendthrift trust is largely a pronouncement from the past, a pronouncement of dubious validity for modern society. The views of John Chipman Gray belong to the nineteenth century in which they were written. The fundamental social and economic theories popular, if not axiomatic, sixty years ago, fundamentally differ from those that hold sway today. Gray lived in an era when 'sacredness of contract' and individual 'liberty' were used to defeat wages and hours legislation. . . . Certainly, these ideas are less convincing at a time when social security and unemployment insurance are accepted facts. . . .[50]

Though penned during the Great Society euphoria of the 1960s, such thoughts pose a genuine challenge to the position I have taken in this book. Indeed a recent commentator has identified the important Employee Retirement Income Security Act of 1974 (ERISA) as a gigantic and necessary extension of spendthrift principles to the pensions of numerous groups of beneficiaries.[51] Thus, the spendthrift idea can be viewed as a sound one today, at least in the pension area. Here is how the Act works:

Most pension plans maintained by employers to provide their employees with retirement benefits are funded by means of trusts. Typically, the plan calls for the employer (and sometimes participating employees as well) to make periodic contributions to the trust. The trustee then invests the contributions and, as each participant retires or otherwise becomes eligible for a benefit, he makes distributions in accordance with the plan's provisions. Since the interest of each trust beneficiary is "property" and thus liable for the beneficiary's debts (unless exempted by direction of settlor or statute) there is danger that funds in a pension trust might be appropriated by his creditors.[52]

Congress responded to this problem under §206 (d) of ERISA by requiring that every pension plan (with certain unimportant exceptions) must prohibit the assignment or alienation of plan benefits. In addition, ERISA amended the Internal Revenue Code to impose a similar requirement on all pension plans intended to secure tax benefits pursuant to I.R.C. §401 (a), whether or not such plans are covered by ERISA §206 (d). Hence practically every pension trust is now a spendthrift trust. Paralleling developments in individual spendthrift trust law, exceptions to protection are being allowed for such claims as alimony, support, and federal taxes.[53]

FUTURE APPLICATION OF SPENDTHRIFT PRINCIPLES

It is possible to steer a course between the Scylla of unrestrained libertarianism and the Charybdis of socialism, both of which are at work in the spendthrift trust field. This can be done by eliminating the doctrine with respect to private individuals (unless they are actually in need of "guardianship-like" protection) and by keeping the notion with respect to classes of people such as workers or Social Security recipients. In doing so, no emphasis need be given either to desires for individual privilege and dead hand control, or to wishes for greatly expanded classes of individuals to be "protected" by government.

On one hand, it should be made impossible for a settlor to lock up a portion of his estate for the benefit of someone not actually in need of protection. Nor should those actually in need of such protection have more set aside for them than is necessary for adequate care and maintenance. The model spendthrift trust act drafted by Dean Griswold and adopted (with modifications) in Louisiana and Oklahoma goes in the right direction.[54]

At the other end of the spectrum, government, corporations, and unions have already identified classes of people who are in need of spendthrift-type protection for pension benefits. I see no reason why worker or union benefit trusts should not continue their protective function, while government provides similar functions for the poor, the elderly, or the unemployed. Allowing the poorer classes to take advantage of spendthrift protective (rather than privilege-creating) provisions should also help redistribute wealth and further the creation of more equal starting places. In fact, allowing workers' organizations to amass large amounts of investment capital in pension trusts will help alleviate any productivity declines which would result from the gradual breakup of large individual estates. This notion is discussed further in the final chapter.

TERMINATION OF TRUSTS BY BENEFICIARIES UNDER ENGLISH AND AMERICAN LAW

The dynastic urge of individual settlors should be given no more credence as respects the time of trust termination than in preventing free alienation. The living, providing they are legally interested parties and can all agree, should be able to bring to an end an individual's estate plan when it no longer suits them, unless there remains some need for "guardianship-like" protection. Since spendthrift principles when applied to *classes* of individuals serve solely a protective function and not the dynastic purpose of a settlor, these classes do not need termination as a counterweight to wishes of the fund's creator. For the protection of all, each in the class can reasonably be expected to surrender his individual right to reach his death or retirement benefits before they become payable.

Though English courts have been lenient as regards termination of a private trust by its beneficiaries, *Claflin* v. *Claflin*,[55] disallowing this when contrary to the intention of the settlor, states the majority rule in the United States. This 1889 Massachusetts case involved a trust providing that $10,000 should be paid to the beneficiary at age 21, $10,000 at age 25, and the balance of the fund at age 30. In denying a beneficiary's petition for termination, the court said:

> The existing situation is one which the testator manifestly had in mind and made provision for; the strict execution of the trust has not become impossible; the restriction on plaintiff's possession and control is, we think, one that the testator had a right to make; other provisions for the plaintiff are contained in the will, apparently sufficient for his support, and we see no good reason why the intention of the testator should not be carried out.[56]

Thus arose the rule that if termination will defeat a material purpose of the trust, it will not be permitted. Material purposes contrary to termination were found in the above kind of clause and in those producing discretionary, support, and spendthrift trusts. American courts reasoned that these types of trusts would not have been created in the first place had their settlors wished to allow for termination.

Predictably, Gray was outraged. To him, *Claflin* was as indefensible as the spendthrift trust. In fact, the two went arm-in-arm: if spendthrift trusts were terminable by their beneficiaries, testator's dynastic intent would prove futile. Despite Gray's cries of protest, American courts of the late Nineteenth century pursued their dynastic fervor by flirting with indestructible spendthrift trusts of unlimited duration. All that stood in the way of such perpetual trusts was the ancient, mysterious, and often unfathomable Rule Against Perpetuities.[57]

The Rule—it is usually capitalized out of respect by lawyers— was discussed briefly in chapter 5. While it may have grown up to encourage reasonably timely dispersal of trust assets, the Rule was concerned with only the remoteness of vesting a future interest and had nothing directly to do with disbursement of trust assets. Thus if an interest will vest, if at all, within the period of the Rule, that interest may be kept alive by *Claflin*.

Since the Rule does not force timely dispersal of properly vested trust assets, the federal estate tax has no "taxable event" on which to levy until distribution finally occurs. Thus it allows transfers via the multigeneration trust to escape the estate taxes imposed on outright bequest. "The generosity of the Rule merges with the generosity of the tax structure in a happy coincidence for the rich and powerful."[58]

This "coincidence" has been heightened by the recent tendency of courts to defeat even application of the orthodox Rule, through devices such as "waiting to see" if a future interest, invalid at creation under the Rule, will *actually* vest within the perpetuities period. The result has been that sophisticated testators can avoid estate taxes, not only for the possible 80–100 years before the orthodox Rule would declare an interest void, but also until the death of a remainderman perhaps some 50 years later. Thus modern courts in applying the Rule have failed to protect the public welfare against the "predatory rich" who can afford good legal advice, while imposing forfeiture upon those whose estate plans suffer from "poor draftsmanship."[59]

As a remedy, Van Doren suggests a Federal Rule against Perpetuities providing that "no interest [in property] is good unless it (1) must vest in possession, rather than interest not later than 21 years after some life in being at the creation of the interest and (2) must vest in possession, if at all, within 50 years of the creation of the interest." This latter period should be "progressively shortened" as experience with the new Rule dictates.[60]

Some courts, at the behest of scholars, have already taken steps toward requiring early disbursement by limiting the *Claflin* doctrine. Under this approach, the time for termination is limited to the time specified for vesting under the orthodox Rule, thus requiring not only vesting, but disbursement within the perpetuities period. However, this rule is by no means "settled."[61]

Another suggestion for reform is to shorten the period of trust indestructibility to less than the period of the Rule—to the lives of the beneficiaries in being, or in the alternative, to 21 years. While this does not necessarily limit trust duration, full alienability of the interest in insured by declaring a spendthrift provision (or other provision ensuring indestructibility under *Claflin*) void after the prescribed period. This result is consistent with the rule against restraints on alienation on present vested interests.[62] Since the less radical alternative of limiting indestructibility to the potentially longer period of the Rule has not yet been completely accepted, a move this extreme would surely require legislation.

Both spendthrift and other "indestructible" trusts involve serious restraints on alienation. A spendthrift trust restrains alienation by definition; any other indestructible trust, under *Claflin,* does so by practical effect. Theoretically a beneficiary may be *able* to alienate his interest under an indestructible trust that is not spendthrift, but there is no adequate market for such an interest. The enforced permanent separation of ownership and control of principal from the right to receive income facilitates the accumulation in all these trusts of vast property in a few hands, retarding normal commercial intercourse.[63]

In their acceptance of the *Claflin* doctrine, as in their championing of the spendthrift trust, American courts have attached overweaning significance to the wishes of the settlor, rather than to the interest of beneficiaries. This contrasts with the English view on both counts. As discussed earlier, this great reverence for settlor's rights is noticeable in charitable trusts as well, making it harder in America to apply cy pres in certain cases.

The situations which test these doctrines most often occur after the settlor's death. In comparable situations where the settlor is alive, no such preference is given to the settlor's intent. For example, the donee of an annuity may elect to take its price, despite the donor's expressed preference that he take the annuity itself. Likewise, when realty is given to a trustee to be sold and the proceeds are to be paid to a beneficiary, the beneficiary may choose the realty instead of the sale price.[64] Thus, it may be seen again in the context of trust settlors that the American preference for individual property rights is stronger after death of the property-owner than during life—an outgrowth of the dynastic urge.

It should be noted that even dead hand control by the settlor under *Claflin* has not been given complete sway by the courts. In Pennsylvania, for example, courts have often disregarded a settlor's specific intent on indestructibility and searched for a general underlying intent which would support termination.[65] This cy pres-like analysis has greatly undermined the effect of the doctrine in that state. In other states, such as Missouri, courts have looked carefully at the facts of each case—particularly to the needs of the particular beneficiaries—in deciding for or against termination. This has produced apparently contradictory results. In Missouri *St. Louis Union Trust Co.* v. *Conant* (1973)[66] holds that a settlement agreement cannot eliminate a spendthrift trust established by testator's will for his daughter, in seeming conflict with *Commerce Trust Co.* v. *Fast* (1965).[67] Such case-by-case decision making leads to doubts that *Claflin* will automatically be applied in such states.[68]

Most surprising perhaps is the turn taken by the same Massachusetts court which announced the *Claflin* doctrine. In *Budin* v. *Levy* (1962) the Supreme Judicial Court approved compromise agreements designed deliberately to eliminate trusts, even the spendthrift trusts which Massachusetts had gone to such great lengths to uphold. It reasoned that, as a matter of contract, not trust law, such agreements (if validly executed) should be given effect, even if contrary to the testator's intent.[69]

Finally, *Claflin* has application only if the trustee, beneficiary, or someone else with standing complains about the termination or petitions the court for instructions. Thus extrajudicial terminations are possible despite the doctrine. If the trustee transfers the property to the beneficiaries and obtains releases of liability from them, the trust is terminated by merger and no one has standing to complain.[70]

CLAFLIN AND SPENDTHRIFT PENSION TRUSTS

A last question which arises is whether, given the detrimental effects of *Claflin* on private beneficiaries' rights, pension trusts should also be made indestructible by the beneficiaries. Under the spendthrift protection of the Social Security Act, beneficiaries have no such right of termination.[71] The situation under private pension plans is somewhat more complicated, but the effect is largely the same.

Section 4041 of ERISA gives the employer or employee organization the right to terminate a pension plan upon giving proper notice to the government. Although the plan thus terminates, the trust in which assets are held for participating beneficiaries ordinarily continues until their benefits are paid. Such decisions on termination are usually made by a board of directors of the plan who are removed from any control by the beneficiaries once the plan is under way. Generally, their power of termination is written into the plan's governing documents.

The one really feasible instance where beneficiaries of such a plan might move to terminate it would involve a union pension plan under which the plan's administrators were subject to removal or direction by the vote of the membership. Arguably, the membership could then vote termination of the plan. Whether distribution of plan assets in violation of spendthrift principles could then be demanded is an open question. Under common-law principles, the trust (as opposed to the plan) with its spendthrift provision might be held nonterminable. Thus the assets already paid into the plan might be held for dispersal to workers upon death or retirement. However, where no dynastic interest of the settlor is to be considered, it might be inappropriate to apply a *Claflin*-like rule. The dominant interest to be considered in such situations is the protection of the beneficiaries and their families. Thus, if the union as settlor-trustee and its members as beneficiaries decide such protection is best served by immediate distribution of assets, this should be allowed.

Still, such ability of beneficiaries to terminate and disperse a pension fund, thereby destroying its spendthrift protective features, would be highly unusual. Even if exercised, giving the beneficiaries freely-alienable assets, this power would be like that under individual trusts, where beneficiaries can accomplish this result with the consent of other interested parties, including the court.

CONCLUSION

Dead hand control of trust assets through spendthrift-type clauses and the early termination prohibited by *Claflin* is destructive of living beneficiaries' rights. Such control should be extensively curtailed, except where it serves to protect a needy beneficiary. The beneficiary-protective function of pension trusts is already the sole consideration there.

Though one is tempted to find a gradual emergence from the dead hand control position of a century ago to one giving preference to the living, there is little evidence of such a change in the courts. In its decisions on spendthrift trusts and under *Claflin*, as well as in its ambivalence about cy pres, the American judiciary continues to imbue with remarkable strength individual control extended beyond the grave. Thus, the idea of dynastic continuation of an individual's control over property—whether exercised over heirs or through the settlor's favorite charity—is a fixture of the American institution of inheritance. Dead hand control can be eliminated only if the majority of Americans vote their true interest in productivity and wealth distribution by legislatively curtailing its continuing sway.

7

The Impact of Inheritance Reform on Property Crime

This chapter examines questions in an area not usually associated with inheritance—property crime. In doing so it rekindles themes associated with envy, a concept central to chapter 4.

RELATIVE DEPRIVATION AND RELATED CONCEPTS

Relative deprivation is a concept similar to, but more inclusive than, envy. Some scholars view relative deprivation from a sociological perspective: the statistics they produce measure the actual, statistical deprivation of some groups as compared to others. Studies like those of Eberts and Schwirian and the Council on Municipal Performance have identified these differences. They mark as particularly crime-prone those "border" geographical areas where the relatively rich live near the relatively poor.[1]

As I have used the term elsewhere, relative deprivation takes on a psychological rather than a sociological aspect.[2] The psychological approach attempts to explain the effects of relative deprivation on the individual personality. Cook, Crosby, and Hennigan have recently specified four components which combine to produce these *feelings* of relative deprivation in individuals: (1) not having something, (2) wanting it, (3) comparing oneself to similar others who have it, and (4) feeling that its attainment is possible. Feeling entitled to the object and feeling no responsibility for not possessing it can channel relative deprivation into anger against those persons or circumstances preventing someone from getting what he wants.[3]

When we compare the term envy with the above description of relative deprivation, it clearly involves the first three factors: not having an object, desiring it, and comparing oneself to others who have it. The fourth point—the feeling that attainment of the object is possible—is not necessarily related to envy as we know it. Likewise, the two mechanisms that channel relative deprivation into anger are not necessary to a concept of envy. It should be noted, however, that when economists write about the Pareto-optimal reduction of envy (see chapter 4), they are also talking about reducing its nonutilitarian *effects.* Chief among those is the anger directed against those possessing desired objects like money. Thus, inheritance reform may be expected to reduce not only envy and the more complicated feeling of relative deprivation, but also the Pareto-inefficient anger this produces. One way this anger manifests itself is in property crime, including, most obviously, its more violent forms.

Our discussion will center around individual responses to relative wealth differentials whether or not these differences are seen as inherited. However, as we have discussed in chapter 4, great wealth is at least 50% due to inheritance; thus the institution is always intimately involved where there are large wealth differentials. Further, I think it reasonable to assume (as the economists do about envy) that inherited wealth is resented more than earned wealth. This relates directly to the second of those mechanisms which translate relative deprivation into anger: a feeling of lack of personal responsibility for not possessing the inherited wealth which is coveted.

All of this suggests that social problems associated with relative deprivation are more severe in a society permitting much inherited wealth than in one permitting relatively little. Thus if we wish to reduce these social problems, reforms in the institution of inheritance are relevant. This chapter concentrates on the connection between inheritance and the problem of property crime; why nonproperty crime is excluded will be discussed in the following section.

Naturally, feelings of relative deprivation and associated anger do not influence all those who possess them to commit property crime. Even within the social groups who contribute most heavily to crime (at least as it is defined by middle- and upper-class lawmakers), individuals vary enormously in the extent to which they internalize those community standards proscribing criminal behavior. Thus it should be understood that the phenomena under discussion make more likely the commission of property crime by a given individual, but in no way determine it. Many individuals channel feelings of relative deprivation (and even associated anger) into socially-accepted acts such as entrepreneurship. In the circumstances outlined here, however, such channeling becomes relatively less likely.

POVERTY, RELATIVE POVERTY, AND PROPERTY CRIME

The link between poverty and criminal behavior is not a new thought. According to British criminologist Leon Radzinowicz:

> Several references . . . to poverty as a contributory cause of crime were made by Xenephon, Plato, Aristotle, Virgil, Horatio, by moral and religious philosophers such as Sir Thomas More, by the French encyclopedists, and by social enquirers of one kind or another.[4]

Modern data in the United States appears to support this link. In 1976, for example, the National Defender Survey, using thirteen finance-related factors as indicators, estimated that 65% of all misdemeanor defendants were poor.[5] What is more, blacks, who are grossly overrepresented in the poorer classes,[6] comprised 26.4% of those arrested for major felonies in 1978 though they represented only 11.4% of the population. For the feared property crime of robbery (taking by force or threat of force), blacks comprised a staggering 58.7% of those arrested in that year.[7]

The vast majority of misdemeanors and felonies are property-related.[8] This is consistent with the entire Western experience, in which crime is usually committed against our society's basic institution. Thus, the use of others' generalizations about "crime" in this chapter are always relevant to property crime. Since property crime can be more directly linked with feelings of relative deprivation than other forms of crime, this slightly more limited term is used in the course of my own analysis.

Modern non-Marxian theorists have tended to view relative, rather than absolute poverty as the crucial variable, whether discussing property or other crime. Most agree with British social scientist Barbara Wootton, who observes that those in desperate poverty (mainly the old, the sick, the widowed, and deserted wives) contribute least to the statistics of crime. Since, *inter alia,* "the old are poorer than the young," and "women are usually poorer than men," then, "if by poverty we mean sheer lack of worldly wealth," it "seems to be positively correlated with honesty." Perhaps, Wootton suggests, this lack of correlation between absolute poverty and (property) crime could show why the welfare state in Britain has not reduced crime (though she admits it has not eliminated poverty either).[9]

Obviously, many thieves are middle class. In essence, however, their stealing is related to the same factors as that of the lower class: their perception of relative deprivation. "Poverty is always in part a subjective condition, relative to what others have, rather than any simple objective fact of the presence or absence of a certain amount of property or other measure of wealth."[10]

Still, the evidence of a correlation between relatively poor (if not desperate) circumstances and recorded criminality seems solid. Drawing on both British and American data, Wootton concludes that it "would be a mistake to underrate the economic element in crimes against property":

> Convictions for dishonesty are most frequent in the poorer than in the richer quarters of our cities. . . . If it is the richer members of the poorer classes who chiefly practice thieving ("I was short of money"), this may well be because in an acquisitive society in which wealth is most unequally distributed, it is this group which is peculiarly sensitive to the shortage of money. One must not assume that the horizons of the poorer classes are bounded by the social environment in which they find themselves.[11]

Several points should be made about Wootton's perceptive comments. First she is careful to base her generalizations on "convictions," rather than on unrecorded criminality. It is clear to most criminologists that, by and large, it is the richer classes (most prominently the upper-middle class) who define what behavior is to be officially regarded as *criminally*-deviant. This is true despite differing concepts of deviance among the classes, and among various of their constituent groups. Thus criminality such as robbery and burglary which is most accessible to the poorer classes provides the bulk of criminal statistics. More sophisticated crimes such as embezzlement, bribery, computer-fraud, and price-fixing may be recognized in varying degrees as "crime," but they often shade off into marginally acceptable "business practices." Since those who make and administer the laws are more tolerant of their own practices than those of other classes, it is not surprising that most convictions for property crimes occur among the poorer classes.

A number of authorities support this view. As Michael Schwartz notes: "Deviance ... is representative of [the view] held by those with the power to label, that is by the middle class. Deviance is whatever the labelers (that is, the powerful) say it is." Generally, the powerful also allow for a nondeviant, stable lower-class life for those who do not enter the middle-class system and win at this game.[12]

J. B. Mays has pointed out a similar middle-class control of the definition of criminality in England, by citing Wootton's comment: "The prevalence of criminality among the lower classes is ... easily demonstrated by the use of definitions which automatically exclude those crimes to which the upper classes are most likely to be addicted."[13] He feels that the deeds of organized criminals are similar to those of the business world. Thus, the freedom enjoyed and desired by criminals matches the freedom enjoyed and desired by honest men.[14]

Another point worth mentioning is that Wootton's comment appears directed at *who* is convicted (the relatively poor), rather than to *where* that criminality occurs. The relative deprivation theories mentioned earlier find that criminality is highest either in cities (Council on Municipal Performance) or in areas within cities (Eberts and Schwirian) where rich and poor are mixed. Thus, in cities or in areas within them where the relatively poor are surrounded chiefly by those of their own class, criminality is relatively low.

If one concentrates on lower-class criminality, one sees in Wootton's comments the seeds of a theory of psychological relative deprivation. The "horizons" of the poorer classes are "not bounded by" their own social milieu partially because of contact with wealthier individuals, but even more important, in my view, because of their access to images of success via advertising and the media.

Much of the discussion that follows focuses on the connection between the relative deprivation of the poorer classes and their criminality. As this progresses, one should keep in mind that relative deprivation is not confined to these groups: it is prevalent in all classes, leading to anti-social acts throughout the social strata. Differences in recorded criminality may lead most commentators to discuss lower-class criminality, but it should be recalled that much of this phenomenon is explained by wealthier groups' control of criminal justice. It may also be associated with relatively different opportunities to express the feeling of deprivation in "legitimate" (that is, middle-class) ways.

Dutch criminologist William Bonger saw the criminogenic nature of twentieth-century capitalism early in the century. He theorized that in times of prosperity the perception of the growing contrast between the standard of living enjoyed by the rich and that endured by the poor stimulates the desires of those who are relatively deprived, creating an impulse to achieve a higher standard even if the only realistic means are illegitimate.[15] More recently (1968), Sir Leon Radzinowicz noted: "The sources of crime in an increasingly prosperous society must be sought not in absolute poverty or wealth or even welfare, but in relative feelings of content or discontent, satisfaction or dissatisfaction, the extension of artificial needs and the over-stimulation of aspirations."[16]

The key factor in both comments is that the *perception* of relative deprivation is an increasing contribution to crime. Radzinowicz's remarks obviously take account of the effects on this perception of two institutions which have expanded enormously since Bonger wrote: the media and advertising. As Ramsey Clark put it in the American context:

> As if through a one-way mirror, the urban poor watch the outside world speed by in expensive automobiles. They see steel and glass skyscrapers of affluent America rise from the slums where they used to live. Television reminds them all day long that most opportunity is barred to them. They see out from the slums, but few see in. The first generation to suffer poverty in the midst of plenty, they are the first to be stigmatized by poverty. In the past nearly all were poor. Now in America the poor are a small minority. The frustrations arising from this fact not experienced by the poor heretofore, compound the anguish of the interdependence of urban life.[17]

While much of the deprived feeling which Clark describes is based on actual relative deprivation, modern communication techniques often create an illusion more potent than the reality behind it. Thus, it is the *perception* of relative deprivation which should be examined. Such a perception, fanned by the advertising and the media, is further strengthened (and made more criminogenic) by the belief that differences are unfair and unrelated to effort: this belief is significant to any study of the effects of inheritance, and of the wealth differentials it so strongly influences.

Psychologists have recently attempted to delineate the facets of the complex of feelings surrounding perceptions of "unfairness." A 1976 Chicago survey by Hennigan and Cook found that three types of unfairness were perceived by its respondents: personal, fraternal (peer), and double. Low-income groups felt personal unfairness more strongly than did middle-income groups. Low-income groups resented lack of financial resources most, whereas middle-income groups felt their lack of opportunities was most unfair. Only 16% of all respondents felt that unfairness was directed primarily at their fraternal group. Many blacks and the poor, however, reported feelings of double unfairness: their perceived deprivations were of objects both themselves and their peers lacked. The study also found that lack of respect was perceived as a source of relative deprivation by middle-income groups more often than their lower-income counterparts because poorer respondents, unlike the relatively wealthy, did not feel relatively deprived compared to their peers.[18]

It would not be a long leap from the conclusions of the Chicago study to the hypothesis that much of our recorded crime is the ultimate result of perceptions of "personal" or "double" unfairness by those who are poor and black, in regard to their material desires. Feelings of unfairness plus the transformation of perceived relative deprivation into property crime may work roughly as follows: Through the media and interpersonal contact, members of the lower class are constantly made aware of the high standard of living which everyone in our society can supposedly achieve. Juveniles are especially vulnerable to the power of these success images, having, on the average, less internalized resistance to them than do adults. Moreover, the media and other socializing agencies like schools seldom counterbalance these images with reality training about structural economic inequalities which may pose insurmountable barriers to the relatively deprived.[19]

Ironically, by perpetuating the success myth beyond the bounds of reality, the socializing institutions designed to reduce deviance both create and intensify the frustrations which may cause members of poorer groups to commit a disproportionate rate of property crime. The increasing levels of violence associated with property crime also seem to be associated with the increasing gap between real and perceived possibilities of success brought about by failures in these socializing institutions.[20]

The generalizations made in this chapter are more accurate when applied to property crime than to crime in general. Any relationship between the frustration of the relatively deprived and their propensity for committing property crimes is better subject to empirical verification than is the case with other crimes. Why a relative economic deprivation perceived at, say, $20,000, leads to an impulse to acquire this difference through theft is more readily ascertainable than why the same perception might lead to an assault or murder.

If a given crime is a violent one, the link with perceived relative deprivation would be clearer if it is property-related (e.g., armed robbery) than if, for example, it is an aggravated assault unrelated to property. Still, we would want to know what factors lead one person to violent theft and another to nonviolent theft in response to a similar level of economic frustration. Presently, these answers are beyond the data we possess.

PERCEIVED AND ACTUAL RELATIVE DEPRIVATION: THEIR RELATION TO PROPERTY CRIME

Two key studies of the effects of relative deprivation take somewhat different approaches to the problem: the first, by Eberts and Schwirian, takes a sociological approach to the question and then "reasons down" to the psychological. The second, by the Council on Municipal Performance, is strictly sociological.[21]

Eberts and Schwirian studied actual as opposed to perceived relative deprivation in 200 metropolitan communities. In doing so they used general crime rates, which are largely synonymous with those for property crime. Using a model developed by Henry and Short,[22] the authors began with these assumptions: (1) most criminal acts are aggressive responses to induced frustrations; (2) such frustrations come from, *inter alia,* relative social positions in specific status hierarchies; and (3) people in the lower class are oriented toward immediate rather than deferred gratification and have higher crime rates as reported in the Uniform Crime Reports.

The authors postulated that in communities with more people in the highest income category relative to those in the lowest income categories, the economic aspirations of those in the lowest classes are raised so that frustrations are more keenly felt. This produces aggressive behavior, some of which is visible in higher crime rates. The corollary of this is that crime rates will be lower where there is a balance of wealthy and poor people in one community.

Eberts and Schwirian, after comparing the data from 200 communities with painstakingly controlled variables like race, density, and region, found that their hypothesis is borne out: that greater status disparities in a social system, particularly those affecting the lower-class population, will produce greater frustrations or relative deprivations in the lower-class population, resulting in greater anti-social and criminal behavior (as indicated by higher rates of crime). They found, as expected, that crime rates were highest in the metropolitan areas where relatively successful whites (in regard to occupation) and relatively unsuccessful nonwhites lived. In areas where both whites and nonwhites were unsuccessful, crime rates were lowest. The authors' explanation of this is simply that no relative deprivation exists where there is no drastic contrast in wealth levels.

A comparative study of crime in the nation's 30 largest cities by the Council on Municipal Performance produced similar results. Some of the conclusions reached were as follows: crime rates are not explained by absolute poverty[23] but rather by differences in income inequality. Cities with the greatest income inequality (or the largest percentage of wealthy residents) have the most reported crimes. For example, compared with other cities, Los Angeles and Boston have a high incidence of property crime although a relatively small proportion of families in these cities live in "poverty." On the other hand, Baltimore and Philadelphia have relatively little property crime although a relatively high proportion of families in those cities live in poverty. Further, there is a significant statistical correlation between inequality and both violent and property crime: the greater the inequality, the higher the crime rate. Thus the report found that poverty in the sense of *not having as much as the next person* is related to crime.

Actual relative deprivation need not, however, coincide with what is perceived. Aspiring members of the lower classes may feel more deprived in contrast to those who ostentatiously display their wealth than in contrast to those of equally advantageous position who live more conservatively. In fact, media presentation of lifestyles may be a more important factor in producing crime than physical proximity to higher standards of living. Whatever the actual inequalities within a city or a district, all the relatively poor are constantly made aware (by television and cinema, for example) of the differences between themselves and wealthier people, wherever those people may live.

If, then, it is really the visibility of wealth differentials that is the key, studies such as those just cited may be inadequate. Stressing physical propinquity of classes and crime rates within this physical space, they ignore some other factors:

1. Living near wealthier people and having contact with them may show the relatively deprived that wealth differentials are often earned through the struggles of real people not so unlike themselves. By contrast, the media usually presents only the glamourous side of these people's lives.

2. In real life the distinctions between lifestyles may not be as sharp as those depicted by television, the movies, and advertising. Some wealthy people choose to live without ostentation.

3. The urban criminal, according to the Uniform Crime Reports, is increasingly committing his crimes in the suburbs against those who are symbolic of his relative deprivation, rather than against his immediate neighbors.

In their study of the levels of aspiration of different classes of American juveniles, Cloward and Ohlin look at both absolute and relative aspirations.[24] After examining the empirical evidence,[25] they conclude that there are definite class differentials in absolute aspiration but that these divisions disappear when the discussion turns to relative aspiration: the height to which one aspires in relation to current status. Hyman reports that the poorer one is, the greater the proportionate increase in income he desires, and Empey finds that poorer high school seniors aspired to surpass the occupational positions of their fathers by a far greater margin than did wealthier seniors with respect to theirs. From this and other evidence, Cloward and Ohlin conclude that since their relative aspirations are higher, lower-class persons experience greater discontent with their status than do other classes.

The authors further find from the collected research that the level of aspiration may be a function of a desire for both a change in economic position and a shift to a different normative reference— a different social class. This is summarized in the following typology:

Orientation among Lower-Class Boys

Type of Lower-Class Boy	Toward Middle-Class Membership	Toward Economic Improvement
I	+	+
II	+	−
III	−	+
IV	−	−

After Cloward and Ohlin, *supra* note 24, table 3–2 at 140

Type I and II boys are what Whyte[26] called "college boys." They seek to become "middle class" whether or not they seek a change in economic position. Type III boys are most likely to become delinquent because their desire for more money is not matched by the willingness to play the middle class "game"; they tend to make up their own rules. Type IV would be Whyte's "street corner boys," content to stay in their present situation: they seek neither class nor economic advancement.

Cloward and Ohlin point out the many cultural, educational, and economic barriers that face the lower-class boys who wish for legitimate opportunities to advance their status through conventional channels. The only legitimate alternative avenues are occupations in sports or entertainment, which are, realistically, unattainable for the majority of them. This leaves illegitimate avenues: crime and delinquency. Referring to Merton,[27] the authors note that when a society extols, virtually above all else, certain common success goals for the whole population at the same time that the social structure restricts or completely closes access to approved modes of reaching these goals for a considerable part of the same population, then deviant behavior will occur on a large scale.[28]

Do such scholarly conclusions actually explain the motive force behind the deviant behavior of an individual from the lower class? Roger Feldman and Glenn Weisfeld have reported an interview with a white, 24-year-old former gang leader named "Tom," then on parole after serving a year in jail for involuntary manslaughter—one in a long list of violent and property crimes for which he had been arrested.[29]

Tom is clearly a Type III individual according to the Cloward and Ohlin typology. He is desperately envious of moneyed people "in the suburbs." However, he has no desire to adopt a middle-class lifestyle to gain the economic reward he seeks. In his view, everyone in all classes steals, albeit in different ways; there is no perception that hard, honest work may bring middle-class economic status (or perhaps Tom merely realizes that for him this road is blocked). There are just big criminals and little criminals and the big exploit the little. The wealthy (big criminals) deserve to get "ripped off" because they treat the poor with less than decent respect.[30]

Tom's understanding of "the system" is supported by criminologists Edwin Sutherland and J. B. Mays, who note the contrast between the crude and physical type of slum crime and the highly sophisticated subtleties of upper-income people. Mays writes that the people of the business world are probably more criminalistic than slum dwellers but, because of their indirect, devious, anonymous methods, they do not feel the resentment of their victims.[31] While one need not believe that this is generally true, there are certainly enough examples of business-class dishonesty to fuel the seething resentments of men like Tom.

Just as Eberts and Schwirian might predict, unequal distribution of wealth in Tom's area induces him to more crime. He feels that stealing from the poor is irrational since, like him, they have nothing.[32] It is the differentials in wealth he sees all about him which incite Tom to strike back at those who have more than he has; it is clear from the entire interview that, were things as bad for everyone as for him, he would not be the criminal he has been.

REDISTRIBUTION OF WEALTH AND PROPERTY CRIME

In Western nations what is deviant and labeled as crime is defined by the middle class with reference to its own norms.[33] Thus, when those who run Western society attempt to reduce crime, they are in fact trying to make the less powerful lower classes conform to their own values. Despite the middle-class socializing agencies of school, courts, church, and family (supported by the professions and numerous other institutions), the wealthier classes have failed in this attempt.

First of all, the lower class seems to maintain its own norm structure.[34] It would be unprofitable to enter here the controversy as to whether its members strive for or reject middle-class values.[35] It should be admitted, however, that through television, radio, newspapers, magazines, advertisements, and interpersonal contact, members of the lower class are constantly made aware of the existence—and, probably, the relative societal importance—of middle-class value structures. Surely they know who runs things and what the basic lifestyles and value structures of (at least some of) these "rulers" are.

Perhaps middle-class attempts to socialize the lower class through the schools, administrative bodies, and legal codes have failed chiefly because of insurmountable differences in wealth and opportunity between the classes. Even assuming they want to become "middle class," most members of the lower classes have no means to attain the middle-class lifestyles so relentlessly paraded before them. The middle class has, in turn, reasoned that keeping its own values, lifestyles, and relative affluence is more important than submerging itself in a communistic worker-oriented social system, even if such a change would mean a substantial decrease in crime.

As long as wages are sufficient to provide workers with a stable or slightly improving living standard, bourgeois society may, with reason, simply wish to accept crime, poverty, hunger, and other social ills—to issue a few palliatives but basically to "let it be." Crime, as defined, compiled, and reported by the official organs of middle-class society, is largely a lower-class phenomenon and will continue to be so as long as the middle class determines the dominant, not variant, morality. Once one accepts this fact, is there any way in which crime can be effectively reduced while the basic bourgeois orientation of Western society is maintained? Is any method of structural change which will act to reduce crime a practical one in the light of what we know to be Western values?

One way is to emphasize what remains positive about Western bourgeois culture including hard work, saving, future orientation, and an emphasis on individual rights and self-fulfillment, while removing the destructive elements, many of which stem from inequalities of wealth and opportunity. A substantial portion of these inequalities stems from our excessive tolerance for the transfer of accumulated wealth from generation to generation. Many invidious distinctions in our society, much conspicuous consumption, and many tensions based on the lack of equal social and economic opportunity can be traced to wealth differentials significantly influenced by this factor. The compromise made by Western societies between the conflicting ideals of liberty and equality[36] postulates liberty and *equality of opportunity,* not actual equality, as their ultimate goal. It is precisely the nonfulfillment of this compromise goal that has caused much of the friction between classes in the West. By removing excess inherited wealth, we remove a major stumbling block to the achievement of both the reality and the perception of equal opportunity. These achievements should in turn substantially reduce property crime.

This process would work gradually and on a number of levels. The most immediate effect of enacting the changes already discussed in this book (supplemented by other tax measures proposed in the final chapter) would be symbolic. If estate tax revenues were doubled, dynastic uses of protective trusts eliminated, and net worth taxes imposed, the relatively deprived would perceive "the system" as fairer. When coupled with tangible decreases in the income taxes of workers and increases in government payments to the poor, this perception would be strengthened. All the while the actuality of more equal economic starting places would be increasing; if the Rignano principle were implemented, this process would be accelerated.

More equal starting places will not necessarily produce greater equality of end results. They will, however, allow both the reality and the perception of increased social mobility. Great wealth differentials will still exist, but different people will enter the "relatively rich" and the "relatively poor." What will be reduced is the anger and frustration of being relatively deprived through no fault of one's own; this is what channels relative deprivation into social ills like property crime.

Advertising and media cannot be expected to stop bombarding the relatively deprived with success images. Thus, the impression and reality of greater social fairness is crucial. Those who are poorer must perceive both that they have had and continue to have a chance at attaining the achievements of others. Only in this situation are rationalization and ultimate acceptance of one's position possible.

Since there are many sources of unfairness in our society, why focus on material inheritance? One reason is practical. As sociologist Melvin Tumin writes, cultural ideology in America defines inheritance of material advantage as not quite morally legitimate, despite its legality.[37] An example of this ambivalent attitude surfaced during Nelson Rockefeller's vice-presidential confirmation hearings held by Congress after Spiro Agnew's resignation. The questions raised throughout these hearings, especially those concerning Rockefeller's lavish gifts to public officials, point up the uneasiness with which Americans view great inherited wealth, particularly in times of economic and moral crisis.[38]

As Tumin observes, the American ideological tendency is toward a "society based upon achievement rather than ascription." In India, by contrast, the caste system makes the inheritance of special privilege not only legally acceptable but expected. While America, like India, erects no legal barriers to the passing of advantages from one generation to the next, it has pervasive cultural norms that make the exploitation of such advantages less respectable than in India.[39]

Thus, if the majority of Americans can face realistically their tiny chances of either leaving substantial wealth or winning the inheritance lottery, the changes I propose should be politically feasible. In saying this, the writer is aware of the 1980 Republican platform proposal, which has significant popular support, to eliminate all taxes on inheritance. The proposal resulted in sweeping changes in the estate and gift tax law passed by Congress in the summer of 1981. The new law represents a successful attempt by the wealthy to increase their hegemony and that of their families. It is an example—all too familiar in American life—of the tendency of those who have "made it" to "pull up the ladder," denying a similar chance to others. As such it is inconsistent with much that our nation has stood for.

One can only hope that a majority of voters will see the self-serving nature of such proposals. Unfortunately, those who have "made it" have disproportionate access to the propaganda organs capable of disseminating their message. A good example appears in an advertisement by W. R. Grace & Co.:

There is a word for a country that lets every man become all that he can become. Free. It is almost axiomatic that those who succeed in this society praise the system; those who don't condemn it. Whether or not one succeeds is not the issue. Too many factors enter into the outcome: talent, drive, ability, motivation, perseverance—even luck. The point is: *one has the opportunity.*[40]

On the contrary, the point is precisely that no such opportunity exists for many of our people; the "outcome" often depends more on the inheritance of some form of special privilege than it does on one of the virtues discerned through the special glasses of Madison Avenue. Instead of facing the reality that is the widening gulf between rich and poor in this nation, industry continues to parade values far more appropriate to a nation with an open frontier than to a nation containing Watts, Bedford-Stuyvesant, the South Bronx, and Roxbury.

The problem remains basically the same as it has throughout the century:

There is the relentless pressure exerted by modern industry toward the stimulation of new needs, through the countless forms which advertising may take . . . [Thus] there is the [constant] example of a leisure class openly enjoying all the advantages of modern society [because] democracy has broken down the caste lines which formerly cut an individual off from the privileges of the class above him. The modern individual does not wish to be simply a spectator at the feast of others. . . . He interprets the democratic theory to mean that all men are born with an equal right to enjoy the good things in life. What cuts him off is no inherent inferiority but merely a lack of money.[41]

ARE MORE REVOLUTIONARY MEANS NECESSARY?

Numerous observers, including J. B. Mays (who is British) and Americans such as E. H. Sutherland and Daniel Bell believe that preaching equal opportunity without its fulfillment has made the American social structure powerfully criminogenic.[42] Likewise, as Donald Taft has noted, the results of unequal opportunity are made all too obvious: "American culture is, even if decreasingly, the embodiment of materialism. The dollar is dominant if not almighty. The symbol of success is still what Veblen called conspicuous consumption." Writers like Mays and Taft view a socioeconomic system based on both free enterprise capitalism and the protection of special privilege as positively criminalistic both in the way it is organized and in the attitudes of mind, such as the hope of "something for nothing," that it characteristically produces."[43]

Libertarians may not like the anticapitalist style of such critiques, but they seldom deny America's severe crime problem. Since they tend to believe that all are "free," they blame the individual criminal alone, disregarding societal influences. When not promulgating "Band-Aid" measures such as more police and police hardware, the libertarians, if pressed, may argue that their emphasis on production—which should increase overall societal wealth—inevitably reduces social ills like property crime.

Lester Thurow, for one, disputes that such increases for all are any longer possible. Thus, in his *Zero-Sum Society,* he views our society chiefly as one in which any gains made by one segment of society must now come at the expense of another.[44] Whether or not things are really this bleak, it can be said both that the American frontier has long been closed and that opportunities for truly dynamic growth of our economy have largely disappeared.

Even if we accept the libertarian model of a society more dynamic than static, it is difficult to swallow the idea that increasing wealth levels will reduce crime. As Mays has written:

> Prosperity, far from allaying the necessity for crime tends to exacerbate it further in a society which has institutionalized the goals of financial reward and free enterprise.... We can look forward to rising crime rates ... unless we decide to undertake a substantial revision of society as a whole. Skilled social work techniques may help to contain, but they will never reduce, the problem for the simple reason that they do not touch the heart of the matter.[45]

Mays locates "the heart of the matter" directly: "Crime is intimately bound up with the social structure." Therefore:

> If we seriously want to eliminate, or greatly reduce its incidence, then we must alter the social system. We must create a new society. But the price we will have to pay to achieve so vast and comprehensive a change may be too high for many of us to contemplate. Revolution is not an easy or comfortable experience. So much good may be lost in order to avoid some of the evils of crime that we may well decide, on balance, that it must be to some degree accepted.[46]

Is such a gloomy prognosis justified? A report from the Center for Policy Research at Harvard suggests that it indeed may be.[47] The report observes that the present character of crime in America flows almost inevitably from the structure of our social and economic institutions: most property crime represents perfectly rational responses to the conditions of competition and inequality fostered by capitalism. Therefore, it is unlikely that the crime problem can be solved without first effecting a radical redistribution of wealth and power in society.[48]

The report indicates that class boundaries are created by capitalism and that the system promotes inequality of opportunity for fear that otherwise true equality might exist. Those who become members of the lower class turn to crime as a means of survival in a society in which survival is never assured. The resultant crimes of the lower class are personal and direct and are often publicized by the media, whereas the crimes of the upper class are so gradual and sophisticated that no one person or group is instantaneously and brutally victimized. Clearly implicit in the report is the need for some type of revolution in our institutions if crime is to be halted.

The reporter's anger with American hypocrisy is understandable; however, "sweeping solutions" may throw out much that America has achieved, while causing social turmoil and dislocation. The precedent for government intervention established in the 1930s should be used, but used to restore rather than destroy market mechanisms. Capitalism can work reasonably well, but not without periodic adjustments of its excesses.

It is doubtful that reductions in property crime, and therefore in overall crime, can be achieved without opening opportunity channels through government interventions such as those proposed in this book. Government intervention on the order necessary to create more equal starting places will of course require additional bureaucrats to implement it. Ideally fewer and fewer of these will be required as the prescribed opportunity measures begin to have the desired effects. However, once in place these individuals, if experience is a guide, will seek not only to preserve their role but to expand it. "Finding things to do" has often lead American bureaucracy over the crucial line between "means-equality" and "ends—equality"—a step many (including the author) do not favor taking.[49]

The first answer to this problem is to put these new bureaucrats in an existing agency, preferably a generally successful one like Internal Revenue. Some of the work, however, will have to be assigned to welfare agencies like Social Security in order to administer those grants to the poor who cannot be accommodated under the income tax system (e.g., via a negative income tax). The main hope is that by moving toward flat, uniform grants to the poor, rather than grants given or withheld on the basis of complex formulae, such agencies can perform these new tasks without adding personnel.[50] Still, forming more bureaucracies will always be a problem with broad new programs. Given a certain amount of political will, however, it is a manageable one. In this case it seems necessary to the creation of more equal starting places.

Another difficulty involves my position that unfairly blocked upward mobility is behind much of the crime problem. Does it follow then that the mere opening of middle-class opportunities to the lower classes will reduce property crime? No, because criminality is practiced, though with varying degrees of sophistication and subtlety, throughout the social strata.[51] There is, therefore, a gap between the standards which the middle class sets for society and those which its own members practice. This may be one reason why the middle class has failed in most of its institutional attempts to force the lower class to behave according to these standards.

In fact, a significant reduction in criminality will require not only the movement into the middle class of those now in the lower classes and their acceptance of middle-class values, but also adherence to the professed norms of the middle class by all levels of American society. As tax and other programs reduce differences in starting places between typical members of each class, feelings of unfairness about their relative deprivations will decrease. This should lead to more normative behavior among the advantaged classes, just as it has among the relatively disadvantaged. Thus, as ruling classes begin practicing the real values they profess, their crimes of embezzlement, stock manipulation, and violations of business regulations will decrease alongside larceny, auto theft and burglary.

8

Inheritance Reform in Modern Society

In the course of this book, a number of problems have been addressed concerning the institution of inheritance and other societal institutions with which it interacts. These include the contribution of inheritance to: unequal material starting places in life, low socioeconomic mobility, the favoring of the rights of the dead over thoses of the living, idleness, the removal of trusteed wealth from competitive markets, and social ills connected with feelings of relative deprivation. On the positive side, inheritance is associated with charitable foundations and gifts and may provide—through its ability to concentrate wealth—more investment capital, managed more efficiently than small scattered holdings could be. I have tried to show that the problems surrounding the institution are grave and that, even if substantially reformed, its few positive side effects may be achieved in other ways.

What remains is an inquiry into how the institution can be reformed consistent with the major socioeconomic problems our society now faces. John Stuart Mill's proposals detailed in chapter 2, may serve as a starting point: (1) allow intestate succession only to lineal heirs; (2) limit these heirs "reasonable amount" of property; (3) and allow those taking under a will only an amount affording "the means of a comfortable independence." The first of these reforms might be achieved now through changes in state intestacy statutes; the second and third through reforms in state and federal death taxation. Eventually we may want all these taxes levied on the heir and not the estate. Net worth and consumption taxes may also be advisable as a supplement. There is little to suggest that the market can achieve wealth redistribution without these taxation reforms.

A problem which has arisen since Mill's day — the perpetuation of dynastic trusts — is also subject to reforms through taxation. Likewise, Van Doren has summarized ways in which a reformed Rule Against Perpetuities would help in this area. While both Mill's approach to intestate succession (disinheriting collaterals) and Van Doren's suggestion of a federal Rule against Perpetuities seem sound, the discussion which follows is focused on taxation as a way of solving the distribution and equity problems associated with inheritance.

PRESENT ECONOMIC PROBLEMS

America now faces severe economic problems, symbolized by both slow growth and inflation. The heart of these problems is productivity — output per man-hour. If productivity does not increase, our money income can rise but individuals have no more real purchasing power. During the period 1972–1978, industrial productivity rose only 1% per year in the United States, compared to nearly 4% in West Germany and over 5% in Japan. Until the low productivity/high inflation syndrome is arrested—which may mean stopping automatic cost-of-living increases for wage earners and linking their wages to productivity—government redistributions of wealth may be useless and may themselves feed inflation.[1]

The libertarian solution to "stagflation" is familiar: liberate free enterprise, reduce social expenditures, and shift taxation to favor the rich (who save) rather than the poor (who consume). Specifically, these goals would be achieved by (1) eliminating government rules and regulations which hinder business; (2) reducing further the tax on capital gains already reduced in 1978; (3) ending the "double taxation" of dividends by the personal and corporate income taxes; and (4) freezing income transfer payments to the poor and elderly.[2] Although federal estate and gift taxes were weakened substantially by the Economic Recovery Tax Act of 1981, they were not eliminated as proposed in the 1980 Republican party platform. These taxes are now so weak that their removal would hardly seem a high priority item for a libertarian, save possibly in a symbolic way.

Libertarians generally believe that increases in the great disparities of wealth and income which now exist are short-term necessities on the way to a utopia of higher growth. However, the West Germans are far more productive than the Americans with 36% less inequality than we now have, and the Japanese are even more productive with 50% less inequality. As for the benefits of getting government "off the backs" of business and freezing transfer payments, it should be noted that government is "bigger" in many countries than in the United States. While government absorbs 30% of our GNP, the figure is higher in 15 other countries, rising to over 50% in West Germany.[3]

It is true, as libertarians charge, that our investment is low as compared with more productive countries: 10% of GNP, compared to 15% in West Germany and 20% in Japan. However, to increase our investment 5%–10% relative to GNP, taxes must be raised on the poor while lowering taxes on savers.[4] This is because the rich are able to save more than the poor, who must "consume" almost all their income. Thus, to achieve this increased investment we may have to engage in a pure "zero-sum game," where each gain for one group results in an equivalent loss for another. This is always a politically difficult task and, when the losers are to be the poor, it raises a severe ethical dilemma.

Despite the closing of the American frontier, with its nearly limitless potential for development, many economists continue to believe there are ways to accelerate economic growth significantly. Like taxation changes however, these methods may involve a zero-sum element: for example, discouraging investement in failing industries may increase growth, but it puts wage-earners out of work.[5] Still, economists like Lester Thurow believe such changes are possible, if those who lose in the market can find surcease in a much fairer system of taxation than we have today.[6]

Some thinkers have proposed a policy of "zero economic growth" to avoid depletion of nonrenewable resources and to reduce pollution. Under this approach, productivity but not production would increase through the attainment of greater efficiency. The difficulty is that this reduces employment and only the preferred and better-off workers remain employed.[7] As Thurow writes, "it is difficult to make society work with a substantial zero-sum element." Thus, "it is difficult to believe that we could make a society that was a pure zero-sum game work at all." Partially, this is because a stagnant economy produces more, not less "cutthroat competition."[8] With zero economic growth, "every increase in income, every promotion and every advancement would require someone else to go give up everything he had."[9]

If we accept this proposition, economic growth still appears to be necessary. I have discussed the outlines of a taxation scheme which takes from the rich, lessens taxation on the middle class, and increases transfer payments to the poor in order to provide more equal starting points. Can such a scheme contribute to economic growth, at least at a reasonable rate? Economic analysis — on the face of it — makes this appear unlikely.

Despite direct redistribution schemes which now go beyond merely preventing extreme deprivation, we have not solved our wealth and income distribution problems. In 1978, direct transfer payments accounted for $224 billion in annual spending. Thus over 10% of GNP was devoted to taking income from one private individual and giving it to another. Yet income inequality continued to increase.[10]

Thurow believes the "delicate political balance" we have achieved since World War II is being quickly eroded by the increasing inequality produced by our current economic problems. Until now the rich have had their tax loopholes; the middle class their parks, schools, roads, and government-stimulated jobs; and the poor their transfer payments. Inflation creates the demand to cut back government, but this will result in increased economic pressures on the poor (fewer transfer payments) and the middle class (fewer good jobs and public amenities). Thus, our slow economic growth dictates further tax cuts for rich capitalists to encourage savings and investment, but this will necessitate increased taxes for the middle class, as will the demand for increased tranfer payments by the poor.[11] Is there a way out of this dilemma?

CAN REDISTRIBUTION BE
RECONCILED WITH ECONOMIC GROWTH?

As we have discussed, the rich rather than the middle class should bear the brunt of redistribution aimed at reversing the trend toward greater inequality. Within this group, the increased tax burden should fall to the extent possible on inherited rather than earned wealth. Income taxes on earnings, particularly at middle levels, should be held steady and, if possible, be decreased. To offset any reductions these changes make in the investment capital of the wealthy, we should consider unfettering the wealth now locked in protective trusts, as suggested in chapter 6.

To the extent their income taxes can be decreased, high salary earners can increase savings to help counteract lowered savings of the rich. Still, a savings and investment shortfall might be expected. Individually, lower wage and salary earners would have little with which to replace this capital. To cure this, their capital available for savings might be pooled in cooperative investment associations, much as their retirement capital now is in pension funds. A large number of these associations would be necessary, however. This is because ten $100,000 (after tax) earners would earn $1 million in a year of which, say 50%, or $500,000, could be put in savings, while one hundred $10,000 (after tax) earners might be able to set aside only 10 percent or $100,000.

The overall notion is to carry on and even increase investment despite significant taxation of the rich. This could be accomplished if the assets of the wealthy were somewhat reduced, and some of their unprotected capital were available for investment. A somewhat wealthier group of middle to high salary earners would contribute, and investment cooperatives would add the savings of low wage earners. With reasonable economic growth thus assured, more money would be available for the very poor in the form of transfer payments. Although Thurow does not envisage precisely such a scheme (and feels anyway that taxation is a less important redistributive mechanism than the market), he agrees "that one of the basic ingredients of future progress is a tax system that can raise substantial amounts of revenue fairly." At present "our tax system is so unfair that it is simply not capable of doing what is demanded of it."[12] Finally, as stressed in this book, "the great current loophole in American taxation is that great wealth can be generated, controlled, spent and passed to one's children without ever being subject to the levels of taxation faced by modest wage-earners."[13]

Despite what the libertarians may call "confiscatory" inheritance taxes, U.S. gift and inheritance taxes, even before the reductions of 1981, amounted to a levy of only 0.2% on net worth.[14] For all practical purposes, the current estate and gift tax system has no impact on the distribution of wealth. If you are very rich and want to hand your assets on to your own children, "nothing stops you from doing so."[15] Estate and gift levies are, as George Cooper calls them, in effect a "voluntary tax."[16] A brief examination of the current coverage of the tax should convince us of the need for reform.

CURRENT FEDERAL ESTATE AND GIFT TAXES

The 1976 Tax Reform Act attempted to make federal estate and gift taxes more effective, primarily by (1) imposing a new tax on generation-skipping transfers, (2) making the gift tax rate as high as that on estates, and (3) under certain circumstances, making the heirs of anyone dying after 1979 take the value at which decedent acquired an asset as its basis for figuring a capital gain. Under prior law the executor had been able to "step up" the basis in an appreciated asset to its value at decedent's death, a move which lowered capital gains taxes for the heirs.

Of these reforms, the first — the new generation-skipping transfer tax —imposes essentially the same burden on intervening generations of trust beneficiaries as if they had been given the property outright. As to rates, gift and estate taxes are now the same (formerly a gift was taxed at three-fourths the estate rate). A bequest is treated, in effect, as the last of a series of lifetime gifts.[17] Until repealed in 1980 by a rider to the Windfall Profits Tax (P.L. 96–223), the carryover basis rule worked as follows: for all those dying after 1979, the heirs carried over decedent's basis in the property and paid a capital gains tax on all post-1976 appreciation.[18] Even had the carry-over basis rule survived, the act as a whole would not have significantly increased tax liabilities.[19]

The reasons for this can be found both in the provisions of the 1976 act itself and in the plentiful opportunities for avoiding the tax still available to the rich and powerful. For example, by increasing the standard exemption from $60,000 to the equivalent of $175,625, and allowing a $250,000 marital deduction if this much property was left to the spouse, the Act was made applicable only to the richest 1%–2% of decedents rather than to the top 6%–7%.[20] This meant that by 1981, about 56,000 estates were being taxed annually.

The Economic Recovery Tax Act of 1981 will result in a massive decrease in estates subject to the tax when its provisions are fully implemented. By 1986, only about 6,500 estates will be taxed annually. One would expect this to greatly increase the pressure on those few still subject to the tax to make up the huge loss in tax revenue, thus resulting in even more emphasis on tax avoidance in their estate planning. However, the act made clear that their estates will not be expected to make up much of the shortfall. Major tax breaks in the act include raising the amount of exempted assets in stages to $600,-000, and providing an unlimited marital deduction for bequests to a spouse. Congress appears ready to accept at least a $5.6 billion loss to the Treasury in fiscal 1986.[21]

That Congress could pass such an act indicates the weakness of any popular constituency for limiting inheritance. It also points up the lack of any coherent political theory among liberals which can stem the ideological push by the Reagan administration to benefit the wealthy. This can be seen in the curious rush of the Democrat-led House Ways and Means Committee to weaken the tax even further than had the administration proposal.

Apparently, the Democrats are convinced that small closely held businesses and family farms need more help than has been provided for them by special valuation procedures for their real estate in the 1976 and 1981 acts. The family businessman, faced with little market for his closely held stock, which he usually wants to keep in the family anyway, had been buying large amounts of life insurance so that his heirs could pay the tax. Since his farmland, when used in agriculture, could not generate the revenues to pay the tax and because he usually didn't want to sell part of the farm, the family farmer was doing the same. Although special valuation procedures probably help these groups sufficiently, if more help were needed it should have been targeted to their peculiar liquidity problems. Nonetheless, because of pressure from these interests, Congress gave scarcely a thought to other political and economic consequences of across-the-board actions such as those involving exempted property and the marital deduction.

One aim of this book is to bring about a discussion and an understanding of what this nation seems to be acquiescing to: a government of, by, and for the prosperous, based in part on the hope of "trickle-down" benefits to the poor. This change can be viewed as one of radical selfishness by those in power, with ominous consequences for future social harmony. A final step in the inheritance field may even be the repeal of estate and gift taxes, beginning with the tax on generation-skipping transfers mentioned in chapter 6. Until that point is reached planners for the extremely rich will continue to use a number of tax avoidance techniques to make sure that their clients provide even less revenue to the nation than Congress intends.

One tax avoidance method involves the use of increasingly sophisticated asset valuation techniques, resulting in lower asset figures, particularly with regard to closely held stock in "family" corporations. Once the assets are valued, a number of other avoidance schemes are possible. The most important of these follow.

Lifetime gift-giving still provides tax benefits, and most ordinary gifts no longer have to be made more than three years before death to avoid capture in the estate.[22] Lifetime gifts are taxed at the same rate as estate assets.[23] This is because the estate tax base includes amounts later used to pay the tax, while the gift tax is imposed only on the net amount of the gift. Still, this difference exhibits only a slight preference for lifetime giving.[24]

Much more important for avoidance purposes is the $20,000 annual exclusion available for gifts from a married donor to each donee.[25] Assuming a $3.5 million (adjusted) estate, such a donor with two married children and four grandchildren can, by giving $20,000 gifts each year to the children, their spouses and their grandchildren, reduce his estate by $1.6 million over ten years with absolutely no tax cost. By then bequeathing $1.3 million tax free to his spouse, he reduces his estate to $600,000; assuming the 1981 Act's exemption of assets has reached its $600,000 goal for 1987, that will result in no estate tax due at all.

The gift tax exclusion can also be used to transfer hundreds of thousands of life insurance to heirs completely free of tax. The previously allowable $6,000 annual exclusion for married people could buy more than $300,000 in ordinary life and even greater amounts of term insurance (often paid for by an employeer) for a 45-year-old man. Under the 1981 law this amount of course is much higher. By assigning all "incidents of ownership" in this insurance to the prospective heirs or to a trust on their behalf, such an individual excludes the entire "face amount" of the insurance from his estate and pays no gift tax on the excluded premium payments. The latter technique has been under challenge by the I.R.S., which calls such insurance premiums an "indirect gift" from the donor.[26]

Another possibility is a private annuity contract between the donor and his child. The donor can transfer a lump sum to the child tax-free in exchange for the child's promise to pay back this amount plus, for example, 12% over a set number of years. If the donor dies reasonably soon, he has passed the principal amount minus the annuities received tax-free to his child without inclusion in his estate.[27]

Another method is the charitable-lead annuity trust in which property is held to pay a fixed sum annually to a charity for a fixed period of time. At the end of that time, full ownership of the property and the income therefrom revert to noncharitable beneficiaries, such as the heirs of the trust creator. When property is placed in such a trust, the creator receives a charitable deduction for the actuarial value of the front-end annuity interest, determined under Internal Revenue Service tables.[28]

The "charitable lead" technique can best be shown by an example. If a wealthy person puts $10 million in trust to pay $800,000 per year to charity for 24 years, the estate tax charitable deduction computed under the tables is $10,040,320—slightly more than the full amount of $10 million given to the trust. This is because a $10 million trust paying an 8% annuity is the equivalent of a $13,333,333 trust paying the 6% annuity built into the tables. Thus it is possible in this case to claim a charitable deduction for the full amount of trust property even though the charity is being given only a temporary interest in the property and the full amount of property is eventually going free and clear to one's heirs.

Moreover, consider the income tax effects of this device. Had he absorbed the income himself rather than making the charitable gift, before 1982 the donor in the above example would have paid 70% of $800,000, or $560,000 in income taxes to the government while keeping only $240,000 per year for himself. Thus, out of every dollar donated, the Treasury has been losing 70 cents for each 30 cents the maximum-bracket taxpayer is actually sacrificing. However, under the Economic Recovery Tax Act of 1981, the 70% bracket is reduced to 50% as of 1982. Therefore, until the maximum rate is changed again, the Treasury will be "forgiving" an amount of revenue exactly equal to what this taxpayer is himself sacrificing when he makes a gift to charity. Though the reduction in maximum bracket (which has also occurred in the estate and gift tax) is expected to reduce all forms of charitable giving by very rich taxpayers, the estate tax savings mentioned above may continue to make the charitable-lead trust attractive to a number of them.[29]

Of course, given the political will to use them, strategies exist for closing many of the remaining loopholes in the tax. These include: (1) further restraint on generation-skipping transfers by imposing a special additional tax on any transfer of property (whether outright or in trust) to the grandchildren (such direct transfers are now exempt); (2) reduction of the $20,000 annual gift exclusion (available via gift-splitting for a married person) to $10,000, and/or imposing a reasonably low *lifetime* limit on the amount of such transfers; and (3) an *actual* tax on capital gains occurring during the decedent's life, assessed on the heir's income. At present the law merely fixes a valuation basis from which to compute capital gains made by the heir upon sale of the inherited property.[30]

In his valuable book, *A Voluntary Tax?*, Cooper also includes various technical reforms for problems associated with valuation, the charitable lead annuity trust, and the private annuity.[31]

Even before its reform, the estate tax was "clearly not striking terror into the hearts of the very wealthy."[32] In addition to its ineffectiveness, it is economically wasteful. Allowable avoidance schemes involve manipulations in the form of property ownership rather than the reasoned choice of particular investment schemes. This ties up property in trusts and holding companies, effectively reconcentrating wealth while providing phony assurances to the poor that the rich are being heavily taxed.[33]

Even "reforms" like the short-lived carry-over basis may have had negative effects on the collection of the estate tax, in that case because of the pressure to make lifetime gifts. Under the stepped-up basis rule revived in 1980, there is a great advantage in submitting property to the estate tax rather than attempting to escape its grasp through *inter vivos* transfers. Only by waiting until his own death can a testator obtain the reward of passing on a stepped-up basis to his heirs. Thus if an oft-suggested reform—the imposition of an *actual* capital gains tax on assets held until death (making death rather than later sale the taxable event)—were passed, the pressure to make lifetime gifts would increase, causing estate tax avoidance to rise in the same way as would a carry-over basis.[34]

REFORM OF THE AMERICAN SYSTEM OF WEALTH TAXATION

In the discussion that follows, the reader should remember that the debates about the so-called "natural right" of inheritance are largely over. Constitutional problems may remain as to a net worth tax because it is not an excise on transfer, but a direct tax which must be apportioned according to population.[35] However, legislators may paint with a broad brush in the field of estate, gift, and inheritance taxation. The privilege of passing on or receiving wealth at death may be substantially curtailed or altered in exchange for society's allowance of it in the first place. Thus the modes of reform are multiple. However, as with changes in any institution, one must weigh carefully associated effects on the other institutions and practices.

Initially, the egalitarian reformer is given pause by Cooper's skeptical view. Cooper sees the attempted reform of the estate and gift tax as relatively useless given the power, desires, and influence of the very rich. As a replacement, he recommends a periodic net worth tax. In doing so, Cooper notes that the purpose of the estate and gift tax is not to tax death transfers *per se*, but to tax wealth accumulations, consistent with social policy.[36] This view disregards the role of the tax in establishing the rights of the living as superior to those of the dead.

In any event, the periodic net worth tax might serve to redistribute wealth. It will produce more revenue than the estate and gift tax, and because it customarily has taken a small, gradual "bite," will be more easily accepted by the wealthy. As Cooper admits, however, the tax has its own problems—chiefly practical ones, like the working of periodic property valuations and the monitoring of compliance with its wealth disclosure requirements. These problems caused the Japanese to abandon such a tax. Add to this the possible constitutional problem already mentioned and questions of invasion of privacy, and one can sense reasons for not moving pell-mell toward enactment of the tax.[37]

However, few taxes deplete existing assets as effectively as a net worth tax. It would also eliminate the problem that some wealth is accumulated and spent and is therefore unavailable for death taxation. Such a tax might, therefore, avoid present forms of accumulation in which capital is often conservatively invested. This would compel the more productive use of capital.[38]

Since the net worth tax has both genuine social and revenue value, one suspects that an effort could be mounted which would solve many of the practical problems associated with the tax. For purposes of this book, the chief problem of the net worth tax is that it sweeps in self-produced wealth as well as the inherited kind. This is true even though big earners probably will conserve less on which to impose taxation than those whose assets are already accumulated. Because of the nonetheless significant burden on earnings, which are not touched by estate and gift taxes, equal opportunity values dictate the relegation of net worth taxes to a supplementary rather than replacement role in wealth taxation. This is the approach which has been taken in West Germany and Sweden.[39]

One problem with effective death and wealth taxes, however, is that individuals—assuming they want to maintain previous levels of consumption—will save less, thus reducing funds for investment. Thus, Thurow and others have suggested that an important facet of any viable wealth taxation policy would be a consumption tax which is more highly progressive than net worth and death taxes. Such a tax would counter inducements to reduce savings under restrictive inheritance and wealth accumulation policies. There is little doubt that a sufficiently progressive tax on one's yearly purchases could overwhelm any such incentives to reduce savings.[40] Libertarians, of course, want neither the net worth nor the consumption tax.[41]

Several years ago a debate about the consumption tax between Professors Warren and Andrews occupied a number of pages in the *Harvard Law Review.* Their point of departure, was the question of replacing the current tax on personal income with one on consumption or "cash flow." They discussed the forms such a tax might take and its effect on other elements of taxation policy.[42] Particularly interesting for our purposes was Andrews' conclusion that disparities in wealth should be dealt with not by the income tax (whether or not modified to include either accretions of wealth or consumption), but "by strengthening the estate and gift tax."[43]

New forms of taxation to supplement present death taxes form only one aspect of a reform strategy. Many theorists believe the present federal tax on estates should be eliminated and death taxes imposed on the heir, as is done now in most states. This would direct attention away from whatever right a decedent may have to the expectation of leaving property as he chooses, toward a more important question for our purposes — how much of an inherited "head start" each of his beneficiaries should be allowed.

If the focus of federal death taxation is shifted to the beneficiary, one reason will probably be that society wants beneficiaries who are already "better off" than others to pay more tax. The Soviet Union applies a means test to inheritance; those needing it are favored over those who do not. To measure such "deep-pocket ability" in our system, inheritance proceeds could be treated as a form of income to be added to the income tax base of recipients. In this way, society can ecourage the decedents themselves to redistribute asserts among a number of less wealthy legatees in order to avoid the heavier tax these assets would bear under progressive taxation if given to a wealthier beneficiary.[44] To avoid legacies to "straw" individuals, such as the poorer wife of a favored son, the taxable unit under such a plan could be the household, not the individual.[45]

Most state inheritance taxes now ignore the deep-pocket ability of the beneficiary. Via a levy separate from that on income, they tax at low progressive rates the size of the individual bequest received. The only way the individual recipient is classed is by relation to the decedent, not by his income or wealth.[46] If a federal tax were structured on these lines it would of course be at much higher progressive rates. As to their magnitude, Thurow goes so far as to suggest: "If society really believes its rhetoric that no one should start life with a substantial head start, the inheritance tax might have only two rates, zero on amounts up to $100,000 and 100 percent over that amount."[47]

Although Thurow's remark is at least partially "tongue-in-cheek," it shows how far removed he is from the libertarian thinking exhibited by Wagner. Wagner believes that inheritance taxes on a bequest, if imposed at all, should be levied at proportional rates to help stimulate wealth accumulation. Thus neither the size of the gift nor the depth of the beneficiary's pocket would add progression to the tax. Libertarians apparently believe such techniques are sufficient to assure that "the game is fair, and that the lowest returns [in the game] attain some minimum level."[48] On the other hand, one may be just skeptical enough to believe that Wagner's willingness to accept a proportional tax on inheritances shows his understanding of just how ineffective any death tax has proved to be.

Nonetheless there are a number of Americans, especially prominent ones, who agree more-or-less with Wagner. Thus, although the change required to ensure a fairer social system must be substantial, it should not be cataclysmic. I see no likelihood that this society is now or will soon be willing for the state to take over nearly all of the means of production as a result of an escheat of all inherited assets over $100,000.

As Shultz pointed out in the 1920s, the escheat of great amounts of property to the state, even if it could be accomplished without violent revolution, would make enormous changes in the way our society operates. A significant number of payments of such a tax would have to be made "in kind," and both land and business property would become socially owned.[49] This would mean a dramatic shift from the present economy of concentrated private wealth to an economy of concentrated public wealth managed by a public bureaucracy.[50]

Even as to less global, more feasible measures than a 100% tax over $100,000, society might look askance at an increased government role in making redistributions. One concern is that even if concentrations of wealth can be reduced by greater taxation, the government itself will eventually defeat this effort by returning this revenue to the powerful and wealthy segment of the population from which it came. Even without such a betrayal, many feel that government can still be expected to use new tax revenues wastefully and/or corruptly.[51]

Is it desirable to use the government, over which the rich and powerful have substantial control, as the vehicle for wealth redistribution? As Van Doren writes:

> The answer to such concerns lies in the belief or hope that citizens will utilize the democratic process to make the state responsible. Measures to achieve such responsibility ... [include] strong and seriously enforced, financial disclosure laws; conflict of interest restrictions; public financing of political campaigns; and improved access to government functions. Redistribution subject to such checks and pressures would indeed reduce the vulnerability of government and [its] officials to control by [the rich]. It is at least possible that wealth and power could be redistributed to those presently "disenfranchised," and that democratic controls could be maintained and exercised.[52]

In part this argument can be used to rebut Cooper's fears that estate and gift tax reform would necessarily result in more — and effective — tax avoidance by the rich. It is an optimistic scenario, but one in the best traditions of American democracy. As Van Doren concludes:

> At present, only minimal controls are exercised over the private oligarchy that runs this country's enterprises. The situation could be no worse if wealth were held by government, which is subject to at least some checks. Unless the political process alters the distribution of wealth, wealth and power will become more concentrated. Aggregating wealth in the state is not a cure-all, but it is an initial step that must be taken.[53]

I would only add that such concentration should—and indeed must—proceed slowly and have limits.

EQUAL OPPORTUNITY THROUGH GOVERNMENT REDISTRIBUTION OF WEALTH

In his book, *The Zero-Sum Society,* Lester Thurow asks two provocative questions of his fellow equal opportunity theorists. In answering them, he pushes beyond an "equal starting places" position in the direction of ends-equality. The questions are: (1) what economic game is to be played by those with "equal" opportunity—capitalism, socialism, or some mixture? and (2) more important, whatever game is played, what is to be the distribution of economic prizes to those who win or lose?[54] An investigation of various possible answers follows.

1. THE LIBERTARIAN GAME   The idea of a "libertarian" society is currently enjoying great success with the American people, perhaps due largely to its nostalgic appeal. Its postulates include a relatively unrestrained individualism, largely free from egalitarian limits on economic incentive and individual liberty. This liberated economic incentive would, it is hoped, produce great rewards for the successful and these rewards would spill over into society as a whole through increased wealth production. Unlike Mill, the libertarians focus on production as the creator of wealth and let consumption take a back seat.

Libertarians tend to view wealth as unlimited because of man's inventiveness. There is a longing here for the open frontier of the early nineteenth century; surely almost everyone then had a chance at wealth. Even if resources are now far more limited than in Jefferson's time, the libertarians retain a nearly utopian belief in the power of enlightened self interest (Adam Smith's term) to do enough with what remains to continue enlarging the economic pie. In this way they can cheerfully ignore direct redistribution issues.

Given a vast continent to develop, capitalism worked well and there was little need for governmental regulation of the market and redistributions of wealth. Issues like inheritance — which formerly concerned chiefly real estate — could be avoided because land was plentiful. When it became necessary to face the inheritance problem, this posed a substantial paradox for the libertarians. Beneficiaries of inherited wealth had no part in the success to which they had been born; once wealthy, they rushed to protect that wealth. The "freedom" preached by libertarians has become a metaphysical abstraction, unsupportable in the empirical world of increasingly unequal starting places.

Thus the libertarians really have two games — a genuine one between capital oligarchies each trying to protect its own interests and a fantasy game between millions of "free" individuals. This is not to say that an altered social structure would be incapable of giving substance to some libertarian dreams. In fact individual liberty on a broad scale is a central concern of this book.

At present, however, libertarian society appears likely to have the following characteristics. Giving free rein to their desire for free capital formation would result in the hoarding of wealth by the relatively few, producing "boom/bust" economic cycles for the economy as a whole, dependent on the whims of the wealth holders. Further concentration of wealth would also produce an increased concentration of political and economic power, cumulatively hindering equal opportunity. While productivity can be increased through technology, production itself my become stagnant or decrease, due to decreased demand from consumers who are out of work. Such a situation may conserve resources in a world where wealth is limited, but can hardly produce the "bigger pie" for all which libertarians promise.

The "game" might become very grim indeed. Once wealth (assuming it has recognizable limits) is distributed mostly among the few, the incentive to compete for major financial reward would begin to disappear. Once it became clear that opportunities for advancement were infinitesimal, the majority would turn its competition inward for what wealth remained. In a world of finite wealth, such competition could only be socially damaging.

2. THE EQUAL OPPORTUNITY GAME American "liberals" or equal opportunity theorists are basically pragmatic individualists in the tradition of William James. They are "responsible capitalists" realizing that limits must be placed on economic incentive to preserve that incentive for the majority. There is a more pessimistic view of human nature in this group. They do not believe in the possiblity of unlimited economic growth; thus to maintain incentives for all, large accumulations of wealth must be prevented in order to insure equal opportunity and class mobility. Human greed and callousness, they believe, may well affect the policies of the large accumulators.

These theorists view wealth hoarding as detrimental, stifling the flow of capital and investment and potentially spurring large-scale depression. With Keynes, they believe that capital must be kept moving. This dictates an emphasis on large-scale government social and economic programs to assure a minimum flow of capital from capitalists to consumers; it also dictates some controls on big business and big money.

A primary goal of the liberal program is to redistribute privately held wealth to the extent necessary to assure opportunity and capital flow. Thurow, for one, believes the majority of the public favors both this and other limited redistributive goals. Most can be achieved by market adjustments and the creation of a fairer tax scheme.

The effects of such a program might be to bring the rich and the poor closer together economically. The prizes are smaller in the liberal or equal opportunity game, but they are more widely shared.

Can this game work? One problem with the liberal approach lies in the tension between their beliefs in limits to wealth and the necessity of encouraging consumption to keep capital flowing and redistribute wealth. If resources are indeed limited, consumerism may mean wasteful use of resources. The overproduction it causes also leads to inflation, which may put the more equal distribution of prizes out of reach.

One way inflation can be cured is through price and wage controls.[55] Associated ecological waste through overproduction can be cured by increased productivity. But one may respond that increased productivity (and Thurow's book provides many ways to achieve it) will only slow down resource depletion. The real trouble is with Keynesian growth economics in a world of limited wealth. The traditional equal opportunity game may not be able to produce more equal prizes for the majority in such a world.

3. THE SOCIALIST GAME   Like the liberals, socialists aim at the utilitarian goal of the greatest good for the greatest number. However, they feel that in a world of limited wealth, even enlightened individualism will fail to reach this result. Hence they favor state control of wealth for the benefit of society as a whole. Unlike the liberals who attempt to encourage consumption, thus running up against the limits of wealth, the socialists would regulate and restrict unnecessary consumption.

The roots of socialism can be found in the thought of Plato and Marx.[56] Both advocate collectivization as a means of effecting impartiality and equality. However, for Plato this is an ideal form of social organization; for Marx it is a historical necessity. Where socialism thus becomes the end in itself rather than the means of effecting equality and impartiality, it may lead to totalitarianism.

The individual in such a society may play only a limited game. In effect, the state becomes the only capitalist; competition between its component parts is socially wasteful. Production thus is forced to fill the needs of the state rather than the desires of individuals to amass wealth.

The socialist state, as holder of capital, is in a good posiiton to minimize the impact of production on resources by regulating capital flow. Its goal is high productivity through concentrated state investment. However, centralized capital control eliminates individual economic incentive, thus slowing or eliminating the progress expected.

In such a "gray" society, the prizes sought are largely political, not economic. As in the West, such political prizes are often achieved through conformity rather than initiative. Since all power—economic and political—becomes concentrated in the state, the curtailment of individual liberties is likely. In the West these liberties are protected to a certain extent by walls of individual property, edifices sure to crumble under effective socialism.[57]

4. WHY THE BEST GAME ELUDES US   One reason no consensus has yet been reached on what game is to be played, lies in a fundamental economic dilemma. One horn arises from the need to form capital and the other from the need to redistribute wealth to prevent extreme wealth inequality. The benefits of capital formation and redistribution can be diagramed roughly as follows:

Capital Formation	Redistribution
conservation of resources	equal opportunity
technological progress	elimination of poverty
high productivity	government supervision of
economic liberty (for	the economy
the successful)	

The problem is to have the advantages of both sides of the diagram to whatever extent is possible.

The libertarian program may score lowest overall because it gains benefits only on the capital formation side while paying only lip service to the benefits of distribution. It may substitute economic for political tyranny.

The equal opportunity program holds government power in balance by diffusing its underlying economic basis throughout society. Capital formation is limited by government. Consumerism and inflation are encouraged, fostering low productivity and waste. For this reason, the scheme is basically inconsistent with a limited wealth view.

Socialism scores on both sides of the diagram by favoring both redistribution and capital formation. The problem is that in using the state for capital formation, socialism concentrates both political and economic power there, curtailing liberty. If liberty is our key goal, socialism may fail despite its successes on other fronts.

What society requires is some other system which encourages both. While consensus, at least in America, must wait for a new system which combines limited capital formation with limited redistribution, it is still possible to define the equity goals we desire, regardless of the precise character of the game we ask our players to play. Reaching such goals in absence of a defined game can only be achieved through trial-and-error methods. In time it is hoped these may yield an ideologically consistent game in which actions will have predictable results.

5. THE DISTRIBUTION OF ECONOMIC PRIZES Whatever economic game is to be played, we cannot escape the problem of what economic prizes are to be distributed to those who win or lose. Thus a goal of equal starting places would not seem enough. In either the libertarian or liberal contexts, an examination of inheritance leads to the question of what constitutes an equal start economically. In the socialist context, where political power can be "inherited," an equal start politically would be of more concern. Since the basic American tension is between playing the libertarian and the equal opportunity game, I focus here on whether a definite range of prizes must be decided upon in advance.

Thurow's argument that we must is a forceful one. It goes more or less as follows: History decides the unequal starting point of each individual economic runner. He can give the "baton" to whomever he pleases at whatever time he chooses. The race never starts over. "Once a duke, always a duke."[58]

Leaving aside the starting score and the problem of how often you start over, how can we decide whether the rules of a game in progress are fair? Since, e.g., American women who work full-time the year round have earned less than 60% of what their male counterparts earn ever since we began recording such statistics 40 years ago, the rules of our game are either unfair or women are inferior. Similar statistics could be produced showing sustained inequality by social class, not sex. Since none of these groups are inherently inferior, Thurow believes "it is not possible to retreat to the position that we should specify the rules of a fair economic game and then let this game determine the fair distribution of purchasing power."[59]

The reason is that "many fair games that produce many different distributions or prizes could be construed." In order to pick which fair game we wish to play, we must decide which distribution of prizes we want. There is no escape from having make explicit equity decisions."[60]

Thurow is not saying we must all become ends-equality theorists. In fact the ends he suggests are decidedly unequal: we should establish a goal for a distribution of earnings for everyone "no more unequal than that which now exists for fully employed white males."[61] Still, Thurow feels we must decide on *an* end for our economic game. Presumably our degree of success in reaching it determines the relative fairness of our game.

Clearly, Thurow is concerned with the emptiness of much of our "equal opportunity" rhetoric, particularly as it has been preached by the libertarians. What he seeks is a standard for American performance on distributional issues. In choosing the standard of earnings distribution among fully employed white men, he feels he has come closest "to our ideal vision of [the results of a] natural lottery" of abilities. Such white males "do not suffer from the handicaps of discrmination, lack of skills, or unemployment." Further, if "we look at their *earnings* rather than their *income* [emphasis added] inherited wealth plays a relatively small role in their current position."[62]

Although reasonable, the choice of this or any explicit equity goal would seem unnecessary. It even may be politically unwise. Since the creation of an adequately administered net worth tax would provide us with good data on *wealth* differentials within the population, it might be preferable to concentrate on reducing *these*, rather than earning disparities, through the kinds of tax programs outlined herein. This looks at the problem dynamically, instead of statically. It involves movement in a fairer *direction*, rather than toward a fixed goal on which it would be more difficult to achieve political consensus.

Thurow's new emphasis on fairness in the distribution of earnings may be a departure from his previous concern with the distribution of wealth. In his *Impact of Taxes on the American Economy* (1971) and "Tax Wealth, Not Income" (1976),[63] Thurow called for stronger death taxes, a net worth tax, and a highly progressive consumption tax. While *The Zero-Sum Society* (1980) makes passing reference to the unfairness of present death taxation policy, it focuses on the corporate income tax as that area in which reformers should concentrate.[64]

As to taxation in general, Thurow's book seems to put more emphasis on horizontal equity (equal tax for equals) than on vertical equity (the correct distribution of tax burdens between the rich and the poor).[65] Perhaps this is due to a heightened concern to stimulate investment in our lagging economy. Though unobjectionable in itself, this focus does not confront the wealth redistribution problems Thurow so brilliantly addressed in his past work—problems which have not gone away. Are we to assume that the increased need for investment has now overwhelmed the need for more effective redistribution through wealth and inheritance taxation?

There is another possible explanation for Thurow's new reluctance to discuss inheritance reform. Perhaps he has caught a dose of Cooper's skepticism about the ability of the Treasury to police tax avoidance by the rich. It is true that a direct and forceful emphasis on taxation of wealth, rather than income or its earned component, will further encourage the wealthy to avoid taxes. The present estate and gift tax still leaves a number of avenues for such avoidance; a net worth tax may present even more opportunities, particularly in the valuation and disclosure areas. Still, for the reasons expressed in this book, the effort must be made. Though both investment reduction and tax-avoidance are real issues in inheritance reform, it is hoped that this book has suggested methods of addressing them in pursuit of the overriding aim of reducing inequality.

Thurow, like many economists, puts primary emphasis on achieving a system of market earnings that is equitable and would use progressive taxation to move toward the goal only to the extent that the present distribution of market earnings remains "unfair."[66] Given limited resources and inflation, it seems likely, however, that the market cannot guarantee economic equity. Thus the role of government as redistributor must be faced at the outset. Once accepted, this role would be to set a direction for the economy (including the reduction of wealth differentials) and move toward it via the tax and transfer system. The distributive scheme produced by this system could, with periodic adjustments, ensure relatively open competition in the market.

RELATIVE DEPRIVATION, POLITICS, AND INHERITANCE

At the botton of the demand for specific equity goals is the problem of "unsatiated wants." Libertarians and Marxists alike have stumbled on this difficulty in their attempts to avoid making explicit equity decisions. Both describe a utopia of superabundance and satiated wants—though their utopias are of course reached by different routes. In utopia there is plenty for everyone and equity problems disappear. Unfortunately our demonstrated ability to generate new wants has eliminated the possibility of ever being able to satisfy everyone's desires.[67]

A person's psychological wants differ markedly from his absolute physiological needs. The former often are generated artificially by society through advertising and the media. Though this is an extreme problem in Western countries because of the necessity for advertising to differentiate consumer goods, wants never seem to be satisfied in Communist countries either. This is partly true because of the ability of modern communications to beam images from the West across their borders. Also, it may be true because socialist and communist media necessarily show the differential status of their own political elites. Still, Communist nations stimulate nowhere near the demand for goods and resources that Western nations do; if their problem of unsatiated wants is similar, it is because their production of goods and services falls so far below the lower levels of aspirations generated in their population.

In the Western context, this discussion brings us back to the relative deprivation issues raised in chapter 7. American society, failing even to approach the tremendous wants generated through its media, has had to settle for attempting to satisfy physiological needs at some minimal level.[68] This has not helped the perceived relative deprivation problem which feeds off ever-increasing psychological wants.

Studies have shown that individuals have a very strong feeling that economic benefit should be proportional to "costs" such as effort and talent. Equal costs then should provide equal benefits. People look around to see whether they are being treated "relatively equally and proportionally." However, they are most concerned with doing well within their own reference group rather than in relation to the entire population. This explains the immense anger of working people toward those on welfare and their relative equanimity toward those at the very top who may likewise pay no cost for their enormously greater wealth.[69]

This explanation, if sound, has disturbing implications for many of the directions taken in this book. If the working class is concerned mainly with its own reference group, their resentment will be unavailable as political incentive for redistributing inherited wealth. Though the "costs" of effort and talent are zero in the cases of both the welfare recipient and the inheritance recipient, the disparity of reward involved should, in the absence of the reference group effect, direct worker frustration toward the very rich, rather than toward those on welfare.

The strength of this reference group effect is doubtful in a society with as much media penetration as ours. Surely the relative lack of working- and lower-class support for wealth redistribution, even of wealth from inherited sources, can be explained in other ways. The very rich are much harder targets than the welfare recipients. Their ways, unlike those of welfare recipients, are often only dimly understood by those in a different milieu. Also, welfare recipients may be disliked for racial reasons not applicable to the very rich.

I have shown that substantial resentment against the wealthy exists among the poor and that it is showing up in the accelerating rate of both violent and non-violent property crime. As I have discussed, these crimes usually are committed against the relatively rich, rather than against persons similar to the perpetrator in economic status. This is the only way that the relatively disadvantaged *can* strike back at the rich, given current social realities. By contrast, their political efforts are far more easily directed at welfare recipients.

For furthering the ambitions of the lower classes, the efforts of workers against welfare recipients are useless. One is reminded of the situation in the South early in this century when rich whites continually exploited racial differences to turn poor whites against poor blacks. The same effect is observable all over the country today, although the welfare chiseler has replaced the "lazy" black as a key figure in elite propaganda.

In order for government to become the redistributor of wealth which can move Americans toward more equal starting places, a majority of the electorate will have to recognize its own self-interest. If many areas of American life are becoming a "zero-sum game," then this majority will have to discern from whom their own gains must come. Inheritance is as unrelated to effort and ability as is welfare, and it is usually unrelated to absolute need. Thus, as the dream of an ever-expanding economic pie fades, Americans should vote their interest in inheritance reform.

Still Dostoevski's *Grand Inquisitor* may have been right, even about Americans. A world with more equal starting places provides less excuse for failure and little reason for our lives to be ruled by others. Certainly, it is a less secure world than the utopia of ends-equality. These factors may render more equal starting places a difficult choice to make.

Even if this choice is made and redistribution is squarely faced, its consequences must be viewed with circumspection. While inheritance is not "natural right," many perfectly decent people have formed expectations of entitlement to it; like people losing in any economic exchange, they should be treated with respect and understanding. For their part, the wealthy must realize that unless they, like the rest of us, are ready to accept reasonable sacrifices, even a modified capitalism may not survive.

Notes

1. INTRODUCTION

1. F. H. Allport, *Institutional Behavior* 134 (1933).
2. A. M. Rose (ed.), *The Institutions of Advanced Societies* 30 (1958).
3. Webster's *New World Dictionary* 730 (2d college ed. 1970). When legal scholar Karl Llewellyn was asked to define institution, a concept he considered central and most important in social science, he generally referred to one employed by economist Walton Hamilton:

> Institution is a verbal symbol which for want of a better word describes a cluster of social usages. It connotes a way of thought or action *of some prevalence and permanence* [emphasis added] which is embedded in the habits of a group or the customs of a people. In ordinary speech it is another word for procedure, convention or arrangement. [*Enc. Soc. Sci.* 84 (1932), quoted in W. Twining, *Karl Llewellyn and the Realist Movement* 176 (1971)]

4. D. A. Martindale, *Institutions, Organizations and Mass Society* 123, 126 (1966).
5. See J. K. Fiebleman, *The Institutions of Society* 143 (1960).
6. *Id.* at 20.
7. L. E. Davis and D. C. North, *Institutional Change and Economic Growth* 10 (1971).
8. Projector and Weiss, *Survey of Financial Characteristics of Consumers*, 96, 136 (1966). See also L. C. Thurow, *Generating Inequality* 14 (1975).
9. J. A. Brittain, *Inheritance and the Inequality of Material Wealth* 4 (1978), citing Smith and Franklin estimates reported in U.S. Bureau of the Census, *Statistical Abstract of the United States: 1975* 410 (1975). See generally Smith and Franklin, "The Concentration of Personal Wealth 1922–1969," 64 *American Economic Review* 162 (1974), which discusses the consistency of wealth concentrations over time.
10. Brittain, *supra* note 9, at 4; see also A. Tait, *The Taxation of Personal Wealth* 5 (1967).
11. Brittain, *supra* note 9, at 21–22.
12. See R. E. Wagner, *Inheritance and the State: Tax Principles For a Free and Prosperous Commonwealth* 2 n.2 (1977). At the federal level, an estate tax is imposed. See Internal Revenue Code §2001 *et seq.* All states except Nevada have enacted death taxes; fifteen use estate taxation and thirty-four tax the inheritance received by the beneficiary. See generally Wagner, *supra*, at 89–95.
13. See L. C. Thurow, *The Impact of Taxes on the American Economy* 127 (1971), discussed in Chester, "Inheritance and Wealth Taxation in a Just Society," 30 *Rutgers L. Rev.* 62 (1976). See also J. A. Brittain, *The Inheritance of Economic Status* 6 (1977).
14. See Thurow, *supra* note 13.

15. See Brittain, *supra* note 9, at 4, 22.

16. Wagner, *supra* note 12, at 24–31.

17. *Id.* at 34, 38.

18. See D. C. McClelland, *The Achieving Society* 234–35 (1961). McClelland found that the lower classes respond chiefly to differential monetary incentives because of financial need; on the other hand, in the business classes, where need for achievement is higher, individuals use money only as a symbol of achievement. See generally Chester, *supra* note 13, at 88–89.

19. A study by Seymour Fiekowsky concludes that large estates do not appear to be held by persons motivated to accumulate large fortunes for their heirs:

> The belief held by such writers as Taussig and Stamp that the mainspring of accumulations of great private fortunes is domestic affection and family ambition has no empirical validity in 20th century American capitalism: The large fortunes held by individuals who came into their possession sometime after 1900 ... were managed by their owners in a way not calculated to best preserve the interest of their successors (i.e., they did not, on the whole, make inter vivos transfers at the lower gift tax rates to escape estate tax)." [Fiekowsky, "On the Economic Effects of Death Taxation in the United States" 370–71 (unpublished doctoral dissertation, Harvard University 1959)]

20. Thurow, *supra* note 8, at 147–50. See Ch. 4 *infra*.

21. See A. Tait, *The Taxation of Personal Wealth* 141–54 (1967). Tait proposes a "Pay-As-You-Accumulate" tax to prevent tax avoidance through shelter devices.

22. Sweden, Norway, Finland, Denmark, Iceland, Germany, the Netherlands, Luxembourg, Austria, some Swiss Cantons, and the Republic of Ireland have net worth taxes of various types. See C. Sanford, J. Willis, and D. Ironside, *An Annual Wealth Tax* 29–32 (1975).

23. R. DeLone, *Small Futures: Children, Inequality, and the Limits of Liberal Reform* 250 n.28 (1979).

24. *Id.* at *ix.*

25. *Id.* at 14.

26. *Id.* The quotation is from S. Thernstrom, *The Other Bostonians: Poverty and Progress in the American Metropolis 1880–1970* (1973); see chapters 5 and 9 especially. See also P. Blau and O. D. Duncan, *The American Occupational Structure* (1967).

27. DeLone, *supra* note 23, at 15.

28. S. Lebergott, *The American Economy: Income, Wealth, and Want* 162, 175 (1976).

29. DeLone, *supra* note 23, at 15.

30. C. Jencks et al., *Who Gets Ahead? The Determinants of Economic Success in America* 82 (1979).

31. *Id.* at 83.

32. *Id.*

33. DeLone, *supra* note 23, at 10.

34. A sophisticated egalitarian view of inheritance is expressed by philosopher John Rawls:

[I]nheritance is permissible provided that the resulting inequalities are to the advantage of the least fortunate and compatible with liberty and fair equality of opportunity. . . . [F]air equality of opportunity means a certain set of institutions that assures similar chances of education and culture for persons similarly motivated and keeps positions and offices open to all. . . . It is these institutions that are put in jeopardy when inequalities of wealth exceed a certain limit; and political liberty likewise tends to lose its value, and representative government to become such in appearance only. The taxes and enactments of the distribution branch are to prevent this limit from being exceeded. [J. Rawls, *A Theory of Justice* 278 (1971)]

35. See generally Tullock, "Inheritance Justified," 14 *J. Law & Econ.* 467 (1971) and Tullock, "Inheritance Rejustified," 16 *J. Law & Econ.* 425 (1973). For a summary of the debate these articles spawned, see Chester, *supra* note 13, at 96–98.

36. See F. A. Hayek, *The Constitution of Liberty* 90–91 (1960) and R. Nozick, *Anarchy, The State, and Utopia* 235–38 (1975).

37. For a fascinating account of the revolt of Veblen and John Dewey, his counterpart in philosophy, against formalistic, a priori learning, see M. G. White, *Social Thought in America* 11–27 (1966). White emphasizes the heavy debt these and other antiformalists owed to Charles Darwin.

2. INHERITANCE IN WESTERN EUROPEAN THOUGHT

1. McMurry, "Liberty of Testation," 14 *Ill. L. Rev.* 96, 99–100 (1919).

2. 32 Hen. 8, C. 1.

3. See F. Coleman, *Hobbes and America* 68–69 (1977). Coleman's analysis seems rooted in the assumptions of Max Weber about the connections between Protestantism and commercialism.

4. See generally J. Locke, *Two Treatises of Government* (Laslett ed. 1970); see also J. Plamenatz, *The English Utilitarians* 18 (1958).

5. See Coleman, *supra* note 3, at 82–83, 69–70.

6. Locke, *supra* note 4, *Second Treatise,* §§190, 192–194.

7. See *id., First Treatise,* §93.

8. J. W. Gough, *John Locke's Political Philosophy* 86 n.4 (1950). Locke did not recognize the testamentary power as a natural right. See *supra* note 4, *Second Treatise* at §65.

9. See *id., First Treatise* at §88. Cf. *First Treatise* §93.

10. See Coleman, *supra* note 3, at 105.

11. *Id.* As to Locke's acceptance of the unequal distribution of property see Locke, *supra* note 4, *Second Treatise,* §50.

12. *Id., Second Treatise,* §§27, 124, 131; see 3 *Classics of Western Thought: The Modern World* 125 *et seq.* (C. Hirschfeld ed. 1968).

13. See Gough, *supra* note 8, at 84–85.

14. C. E. Vaughan, *Studies in the History of Political Philosophy . . .* 172 (1960).

15. See C. J. Czajkowski, *The Theory of Private Property in Locke's Political Philosophy* 90 (1950).

16. See *id.* at 95. The quote is from Locke, *supra* note 4, *Second Treatise,* §138.

17. T. Aquinas, 2 *Summa Theologica* pt. II-II q.32a.5 at 1327–28(1947); see Czajkowski, *supra* note 15, at 102.

18. See Gough, *supra* note 8, at 90.

19. John Rawls, philosopher and author of *A Theory of Justice* (1971), made this point in lecture at Harvard University, November 14, 1975.

20. See D. Baumgardt, *Bentham and the Ethics of Today* 47 (1952).

21. See Plamenatz, *supra* note 4, at 17.

22. J. Bentham, *A Fragment on Government* Ch. 1 para. 38 (Montague ed. 1891); see Baumgardt, *supra* note 20, at 81.

23. *Id.* at 135.

24. J. Bentham, *Supply Without Burthen, or Escheat vice Taxation* (Essay Two) 24 (1795). Bentham noted that Cocceij, author of the Code Frederick, was for abolishing inheritance altogether. However, Bentham felt that if a man were allowed no power at all over what property he left behind him he would, in many instances, either be indifferent about getting it or transfer it to some "happier clime," thus destroying a great deal of the value of all property. However, merely limiting inheritance as Bentham proposed would not "preclude a man from changing his estate, from changing the nature of it, or from giving or spending it in his lifetime." *Id.* at 7, n.7, 9.

25. J. Bentham, "Principles of the Civil Code," in *Theory of Legislation,* Pt. 1, Ch. 12, at 122 (Ogden ed. 1931).

26. See P. Miller, *The Life of the Mind in America from Revolution to Civil War* 224 (1965).

27. W. Blackstone, *Commentaries* 10–12 (St. George Tucker ed. 1803).

28. *Id.*

29. A. Smith, *The Theory of Moral Sentiments* Pt. VI, §288 (1882).

30. See E. Ginzburg, *The House of Adam Smith* 242 (1934); see also *Classics, supra* note 12, at 193, 207.

31. Ginzburg, *supra* note 30, at 35.

32. *Id.* at 85.

33. A. Smith, *The Wealth of Nations* bk. 5. Ch. 2, app. to arts. I&II (1776).

34. Ginzburg, *supra* note 30, at 161–3.

35. D. Ricardo, *The Principles of Political Economy and Taxation* Ch. 8, 133–34 (Gonner ed. 1927).

36. These were the *Critique of Pure Reason,* the *Critique of Practical Reason,* and the *Critique of Judgment.*

37. I. Kant, *Political Writings* 3 (H. Reiss ed. 1970).

38. See *id.* at 3–4.

39. See *id.* at 11.

40. See *id.* at 26.

41. Kant, "On the Relation of Theory to Practice in Political Right (Against Hobbes)," *id.* at 75.

42. See *id.* at 14.

43. See *id.* at 10, 27.

44. See *id.* at 11.

45. I. Kant, *The Metaphysical Elements of Justice* ix (J. Ladd ed. 1965).

46. Kant, *supra* note 37, at 19.

47. See Kant, *supra* note 45, at xvii.

48. Kant, *supra* note 37, at 21.
49. See Kant, *supra* note 45, at xxviii–xxx.
50. See *id.* at xxiv; see also *The Age of Ideology* 33 (H. Aiken ed. 1956).
51. *Id.* §1, at 52–53; see *id.* §7, at 63–64.
52. I. Kant, *The Philosophy of Law* §34 136 (W. Hastie trans. 1887, 1974).
53. *Id.* at 248–49 (Supplementary Principle VII).
54. *Id.* at 138.
55. *Id.* at 248.
56. See Kant, *supra* note 37, at 136.
57. *Id.* at 149.
58. "Metaphysics of Morals" §48, *id.* at 141.
59. *Id.* at 75.
60. "General Remarks on the Legal Consequences of the Nature of the Civil Union," *id.* at 153.
61. See W. J. Shultz, *The Taxation of Inheritance* 169 (1926).
62. See R. Stourm, *Systèmes Généraux d'Impôts* 224–225 (1905).
63. *Id.* at 228–230.
64. *Classics, supra* note 12, at 307.
65. See *Age of Ideology, supra* note 50, at 139–141.
66. *Id.* at 146, 148.
67. J. S. Mill, *On Liberty* 109 (1955).
68. J. S. Mill, *Three Essays on Religion* 14, 16–17 (1884).
69. *Id.* 18–19, 62.
70. *Id.* at 65.
71. J. S. Mill, *Principles of the Political Economy,* bk. 2, Ch. 2 §4 (1929).
72. *Id.* §1.
73. *Id.* §3; see H. Maine, *Ancient Law* (1861), cited with approval by Mill.
74. Mill, *supra* note 71, §3.
75. *Id.*
76. *Id.* §4.
77. *Id.*, bk 5, Ch. 9, §1.
78. *Id.* bk. 2, Ch. 2, §4.
79. *Id.*
80. *Id.*
81. *Id.* bk. 5, Ch. 2, §3.
82. *Id.*
83. See J. Kennedy, *Herbert Spencer* 109 (1978).
84. Spencer, "Replies to Criticisms on *The Data of Ethics,*" 6 *Mind* 82, 93 (1881). For a sympathetic portrayal of Spencer and his work, see Aiken's treatment, *supra* note 50, at 163 *et seq.*

3. INHERITANCE IN EARLY AMERICAN THOUGHT

1. Letter from Thomas Jefferson to James Madison, September 6, 1789, in 5 *The Works of Thomas Jefferson,* 115, 116 (P. L. Ford ed. 1895). See A. Koch, *Jefferson and Madison: The Great Collaboration* 64 (1964).
2. Letter, *supra* note 1, at 116.
3. Letter from Thomas Paine to Thomas Jefferson, probably February or May, 1788, in 1 W. Van der Weyde, *The Life and Works of Thomas Paine,* 175, 176 (1925); see Koch, *supra* note 1, at 83.

4. See Koch, *supra* note 1, at 73.

5. 1 *The Complete Writings of Thomas Paine* 251 (P. Foner, ed. 1945). Paine proposed a plan to deal with the problem of poverty by providing for taxation of accumulated capital to permit the state to give each man and woman £15 per year at age 21 and £10 per year at age 50. Since society made possible the existence of private property, he felt that society was entitled to the surplus that men accumulated beyond their own labor. His "social insurance" scheme was to be paid for from graduated inheritance taxes and ground rents. *Id.* at 605.

6. Quoted in Koch, *supra* note 1, at 86.

7. *Id.* at 90.

8. *Id.* at 92.

9. See D. Boorstin, *The Lost World of Thomas Jefferson* 242 (1963).

10. *Id.* at 164–165.

11. Letter from Thomas Jefferson to James Earle, Sept. 24, 1823, 15 *The Writings of Thomas Jefferson,* 470–471 (A. E. Bergh ed. 1907).

12. 55 Va. 526, 14 Grat. 422 (1858).

13. 14 Grat. at 427, 430.

14. See, *e.g.,* Knowlton v. Moore, 178 U.S. 41 (1900), discussed in text accompanying notes 97–100 *infra.*

15. 14 Grat. 422, at 430–431.

16. See P. Miller, *The Life of the Mind in America from Revolution to the Civil War,* 109–118, esp. 118 (1965).

17. The most famous and influential American edition was by Jeffersonian editor St. George Tucker (1803).

18. See Kennedy, "The Structure of Blackstone's Commentaries," 28 *Buff. L. R.* 209, 372–3 (1979).

19. See F. Coleman, *Hobbes and America: Exploring the Constitutional Foundations* 105 (1977).

20. See W. Blackstone, 1 *Commentaries on the Laws of England* 55 (1803); see also Kennedy, *supra* note 18.

21. Miller, *supra* note 16, at 164.

22. *Id.* at 165.

23. See *id.* at 117–118.

24. See *id.* at 224.

25. *Id.*

26. J. Kent, 2 *Commentaries on American Law* 263 (1971).

27. *Id.*

28. See, *e.g.,* Brownson, "The Descent of Property," 3 *Bost. Q. Rev.* 472 (1840), discussed in detail in text accompanying notes 66–78 *infra.* See also Chester, "Inheritance and Wealth Taxation in a Just Society," 30 *Rutgers L. Rev.* 62, 86–87 (1976).

29. Kent, *supra* note 26.

30. *Id.*

31. *Id.* at 263–264.

32. *Id.* at 265.

33. *Id.* at 266.

34. *Id.*

35. See G. E. White, *The American Judicial Tradition* 14 (1976).

36. See *id.* at 18.

is so satisfactorily displayed as in the researches of political economy. [Quoted in S. Mead, *The Lively Experiment: The Shaping of Christianity in America* 150 (1963)]

For a reference to the influences of Protestant Christianity and Social Darwinism on Roosevelt, see D. H. Burton, *Theodore Roosevelt: Confident Imperialist* 133–34 (1968).

5. G. P. Watkins, *The Growth of Large Fortunes* 160–3 (1907).

6. Fisher, "Some Impending National Problems," 24 *J. Pol. Econ.* 694, 711 (1916).

7. H. Read, *The Abolition of Inheritance* (1919). The influence of Protestant Christianity was also strong in Read. See *id.*, esp. 119–22.

8. McMaster, "The Federal Estate Tax: A Brief Defense . . . ," in 17 *National Tax Ass'n* at App. 57 (1924).

9. See text accompanying notes 72–75, Ch. 3, *supra.* See also Plato, "The Republic," in *1 Dialogues of Plato* 727 (Jowett ed. 1892) discussed in the material wealth context by R. E. Wagner, *Inheritance and the State* 20 (1977).

10. E. Rignano, *The Social Significance of the Inheritance Tax* 14 (W. Shultz trans. & adapt. 1924).

11. *Id.* at 18.

12. *Id.* at 21, 18.

13. *Id.* at 19.

14. *Id.* at 24.

15. *Id.* at 21–22.

16. *See id.* at 83–84.

17. *Id.* at 36–37.

18. *Id.* at 21–22.

19. *Id.* at 21–22.

20. *Id.* at 63.

21. H. D. Henderson, *Inheritance and Inequality: A Practical Step* 5 (1926). Henderson was also editor of *The Nation* and eventually earned knighthood; his inheritance monograph had the general agreement of John Maynard Keynes.

22. *Id.*

23. *Id.* at 12–13.

24. *Id.* at 5–6.

25. The annuity amount would be based on the prevailing interest rate paid by government securities.

26. Henderson, *supra* note 21, at 19–21.

27. *Id.* As equitable as this may appear in the case of B's children's estates, it nonetheless seems inequitable that B's grandchild, assuming he was one of five, should pay the same tax on his smaller legacy as does one child of B's brother in a family of three. If a similar scheme were adopted today, I would recommend that rates be set according to the size of the particular legacy of each of A's grandchildren.

28. *Id.* at 21, 23–24. See, e.g., the discussion of Andrew Carnegie at text accompanying notes 84, 86–88 to Ch. 3, *supra.*

29. Rignano, *supra* note 10, at 84.

30. *Id.* at 112–13.

31. *Id.*

32. *Id.* at 116.

33. *Id.*

34. *Id* at 119.

35. *Id.* at 119–120.

36. Editorial, *Chicago Tribune,* Aug. 24, 1915.

37. The speech was published in Montgomery, "The Inheritance Tax and the Constitution," 10 *Ill. L. Rev.* 633 (1916).

38. *Id.* at 637.

39. Quoted in *id.* at 641.

40. *Id.* at 643–44.

41. 1919 *Miss. State Tax Comm. Ann. Rep.* 32, quoted in Shultz, *supra* note 3, at 167.

42. See 170 U.S. 283, 288 (1898).

43. Rignano, *supra* note 10, at 96.

44. *Id.* at 96–97. See Knowlton v. Moore, 178 U.S. 41 (1900).

45. Rignano, *supra* note 10, at 97.

46. See *id.* at 98; see also Gleason and Otis, *Inheritance Taxation* 67 (1919).

47. Winston, "State and Federal Relations in Inheritance Taxation," in 17 *Proceedings of the National Tax Association* 246, 249 (1924).

48. See Rignano, *supra* note 10, at 119.

49. See, *e.g.,* Chester, "The Effects of a Redistribution of Wealth on Property Crime," 23 *Crime & Delin.* 272 (1977).

50. See L. Thurow, *The Impact of Taxes on the American Economy* 15, 80, 127, 153, (1971). All wealth taxes (including the estate and gift tax) are levied at an effective rate of 4.5 percent for those with negative net worths; this rises to 31.1 percent for those with net worths between $20,000 and $49,999, but most of the progression comes before net worths of only $5,000. "For the very wealthy, tax rates begin to fall just as they do in the income tax. Thus the group with over $500,000 in net worth has an effective tax rate of only 27.2%." *Id.* at 76–77.

Estate and gift tax collections varied from 1.5 percent of income for those with incomes under $3,000 in 1965 to 5.3 percent of income for those with incomes over $15,000, with an average rate of 1.7 percent of total income. N.Y. Tax Foundation, *Tax Burdens and Benefits of Government Expenditures by Income Class (1961, 1965)* 20 (1967).

51. J. Brittain, *The Inheritance of Economic Status* 1 (1977); see A. Okun, *Equality and Efficiency: The Big Trade-off* (1975).

52. Brittain, *supra* note 51, at 29.

53. *Id.* at 4, 5.

54. *Id.* at 6.

55. *Id.* at 6, 7.

56. *Id.* at 7.

57. *Id.* at 30.

58. J. Brittain, *Inheritance and the Inequality of Material Wealth* 13 n.31 (1978).

59. *Id.* at 31.

60. See R. Hofstadter, *Anti-Intellectualism in American Life* 51 (1963).

61. Brittain, *supra* note 58, at 8.

62. J. Wedgwood, *The Economics of Inheritance* 164 (1929).

63. Smith, "The Fifty-Million-Dollar Man," *Fortune* 176 (November 1957); Louis, "America's Centimillionaires," *Id.* 152 (May 1968); Louis, "The New Rich of the Seventies," *Id.* 170 (September 1973).

64. For a discussion of the technique, see Internal Revenue Service, *Statistics of Income-1972, Personal Wealth Estimated from Estate Tax Returns* 37, 39 (1976).

65. See R. Lampman, *The Share of Top Wealth-Holders in National Wealth 1922–26,* esp. 224, chart 36, 228 (1962).

66. Smith & Franklin, estimates reported in U.S. Bureau of the Census, *Statistical Abstract of the United States, 1975,* at 410 (1975).

67. Brittain, *supra* note 58, at 4.

68. See A. B. Atkinson, *Unequal Shares: Wealth in Britain* Ch. 3 (1972).

69. L. C. Thurow, *Generating Inequality: Mechanisms of Distribution in the U.S. Economy* 129 (1975).

70. Brittain, *supra* note 58, at 11.

71. See Thurow, "Tax Wealth, Not Income," *New York Times Magazine,* Apr. 11, 1976, §6, at 32–33.

72. *Id.* at 33.

73. See *id.* at 33, 102; see also Thurow, *supra* note 69, at 151, 153–54; see also Brittain, *supra* note 58, at 13.

74. Thurow, *supra* note 71, at 102.

75. Brittain, *supra* note 58, at 14.

76. *Id.* at 14–16.

77. See *id.* at 16–19. Included in this criticism but not discussed here are Barlow, Brazer, and Morgan, *Economic Behavior of the Affluent* Ch. 7 (1966); and Lampman, *supra* note 65, at 218.

78. S. Lebergott, *The American Economy: Income Wealth and Want* esp. 166–67 (1976).

79. See generally Lampman, *supra* note 65.

80. Brittain, *supra* note 58, at 20.

81. See Sussman, Cates, and Smith, *The Family and Inheritance* (1970).

82. Wagner, *supra* note 9, at 5. Actually, Mill regarded nature as setting limits on the technical manipulations which man could make in production while there were no such natural limits on man's manipulation of society. Thus production was, to some extent, alterable.

83. Shown on WGBH, Boston, Feb. 20, 1980. See also M. and R. Friedman, *Free to Choose* (1980).

84. F. A. Hayek, *The Constitution of Liberty* 91 (1960). Doubt is cast on Hayek's assertion that material inheritance produces situations of "equal value to the community" compared with other types of advantage when one considers, e.g., Stewart Mott's unwelcome meddling with Rep. John Anderson's 1980 Presidential campaign. Mott, a wealthy General Motors heir, reportedly makes $2 million per year from his assets; however his political advice proved much less weighty than his financial muscle.

85. *Id.* For confirmation of this point, see Smith, "How the Soviet Elite Lives," *Atlantic Monthly,* Dec. 1975, at 39, which points out how the Soviet elite are able to provide for their children despite the supposed escheat to the state of all a decedent's property beyond a moderate allowance for his immediate family. *Id.* at 50. *See* Shultz, *supra* note 3, at 97; and H. Smith,

The Russians 47–48 (1976). Smith, Moscow bureau chief for the *New York Times,* notes that the argument that the Russians have no classes has "some validity" in a society where privilege and status purportedly do not follow their owner after termination of his employment. This is especially true in contrast to the czarist practice by which the nobility inherited titles estates and all the trappings of official status. However:

> [By] placing their children and grandchildren in the most prestigious institutes and using their influence to get them jobs and careers in select agencies and organizations, the new leaders are providing long term status for the next two family generations. Moreover, in science and in culture, high-ranking fathers do succeed in passing on private wealth and property such as dachas, apartments, cars, and money as well as career opportunities and status, to their offspring. *Id.* at 50.

86. R. Nozick, *Anarchy, the State, and Utopia* 235–38 (1975).

87. See note 83, *supra*.

88. Nozick, *supra* note 86, at 160.

89. The philosophical and practical objections that follow are distilled largely from Wagner, *supra* note 9, esp. at 84–5, though numbers 10 and 11 of the latter are from Tullock, "Inheritance Justified," 14 *J. Law & Econ.* 465 (1971).

90. Vilfredo Pareto, Italian sociologist and economist, introduced Pareto optimality (as it was subsequently called) in his *Manuel D'Economie Politique* Ch. 6, §53 and App. §89 (1909). This point of maximum "efficiency," as it is termed by John Rawls in *A Theory of Justice* 66–75 (1971), is really the point of "maximum equal distribution" at which one cannot give more to C without taking from A and B.

91. See R. E. Wagner, *Death and Taxes: Some Perspectives on Inheritance, Inequality and Progressive Taxation* 49 (1973). Wagner is referring to Mill's "On Liberty," in *Utilitarianism, Liberty and Representative Government* 75 (1859). Perhaps invigorated by the libertarian air of the Free Enterprise Institute, Wagner is considerably harder on the "envy" ruminations of "welfare economists" when he takes up the topic again in Wagner, *supra* note 9, at 83–84.

92. Tullock, *supra* note 89, at 466.

93. Green, "Inheritance Unjustified?" 16 *J. Law & Econ.* 417, 418 (1973); see also Ireland, "Inheritance Justified: A Comment," *Id.* at 421. Tullock replies that envy of inherited wealth is simply not as important as Green believes. Tullock, "Inheritance Rejustified," *Id.* at 425, 426.

94. M. Tumin, *Social Stratification* 11 (1967).

95. Ireland, *supra* note 93.

96. Rawls, *supra* note 90, at 278.

97. *Id.*

98. *Id.*

99. Tait, "The Taxation of Wealth at Death: A New Proposal," 9 *Scot. J. Pol. Econ.* 38–39 (1962).

100. See Wagner, *supra* note 9, at 83.

5. THE IMPACT OF INHERITANCE
REFORM ON FOUNDATIONS

1. Commission on Foundations and Private Philanthropy (Peterson Commission), *Foundations, Private Giving and Public Policy* 247, Table A-35, (1970).

2. *Id.* at 33–34.

3. M. Katz, *The Modern Foundation: Its Dual Character, Public and Private* 7 (1968).

4. See, *e.g.,* Peterson Commission Report, *supra* note 1, at 39.

5. J. Nason, *Trustees and the Future of Foundations* 31 (1977).

6. Foundations Library Center, *Foundation Directory* xvi (7th ed. 1979). Whenever I refer to $1-million-plus foundations in this chapter, I am referring to those in this category in the Foundation Directory; it should be understood that these may include some foundations under $1 million in assets which make at least $100,000 in annual gifts.

7. *Id.*

8. American Association of Fund-Raising Counsel, *Giving USA: A Compilation of Facts Related to Philanthropy* (1979 Annual).

9. Katz, *supra* note 3, at 10.

10. See *id.*

11. L. Friedman, *A History of American Law* 223 (1973).

12. M. Horwitz, *The Transformation of American Law* 254 (1977). See Chester, "Cy Pres: A Promise Unfulfilled," 54 *Ind. L. J.* 407 (1979).

13. 17 U.S. (4 Wheat.) 1 (1819).

14. See Fisch, "American Acceptance of Charitable Trusts," 28 *N.D. Law.,* 219, 225 (1953).

15. H. Miller, *Legal Foundations of American Philanthropy, 1776–1844,* at 42 (1961).

16. *Id.*

17. *Id.* at 42–43.

18. *Id.* Edward I engineered passage of the Statute of Mortmain in 1279 to prevent the Church from owning more land. This statute declared that all land thereafter conveyed to the Church or monasteries would be forfeited to the king. The clerics subsequently evaded this statute by developing the "conveyance to uses," a forerunner of the modern trust.

Despite Story's protests, the Statute of Mortmain was never held applicable in America. Nevertheless, the fear of vast wealth held in perpetuity caused legislatures in some states to pass statutes restricting transfers to charity by gift, conveyance, or will. Typical of these prohibitions are the restrictions remaining in seven states on the percentage of the estate which can be left to charity and the making of such bequests within a short time before death. See J. Dukeminier and S. Johanson, *Family Wealth Transactions* 340–41 (2d. ed. 1978).

19. Review, "Reports of Cases Adjudged in the Court of Chancery of New York," 11 *N. Am. Rev.* 140, 147 (1820), unsigned but attributed to Justice Story by Miller, *supra* note 15, at 43–44.

20. Miller, *supra* note 15, at 47.

21. *Id.* at 49.

22. 43 U.S. 127 (1844). The testator was a native of France who emigrated to the United States before 1776 and settled in Philadelphia. He became a prominent banker and philanthropist, and died a widower without issue in 1831, leaving real and personal property valued at approximately $6,700,-000. See *id.* at 128. The case held that Girard's devise to the city of Philadelphia of real and personal property in trust to establish and support a college for poor orphan boys was valid and not inconsistent with public policy.

23. See, *e.g.,* Fifield v. Van Wyck's Ex'r, 94 Va. 557, 27 S.E. 446 (1897); Holmes v. Mead, 52 N.Y. 332 (1873); Wilderman v. Mayor of Baltimore, 8 Md. 551 (1885).

24. See Troutman v. De Boissiere Odd Fellows' Orphans Home & Indus. School Ass'n., 64 P. 33 (1901), *rev'd on other grounds* 66 Kan. 1, 71 P. 286 (1903).

25. See, *e.g.,* Russell v. Allen, 107 U.S. 163 (1882).

26. 130 N.Y. 29, 28 N.E. 880 (1891). See Ames, "The Failure of the 'Tilden Trust,'" 5 *Harv. L. Rev.* 389 (1892).

27. The 35th article of the Tilden will directed his executors and trustees to procure the incorporation of the "Tilden Trust" with capacity to establish and maintain from the residue of his estate a free library and reading room in New York City. If incorporation was not achieved or if the trustees and executors deemed it "inexpedient" to convey the residue to the trust, then they were directed to apply it to "such charitable, educational and scientific purposes as . . . will render the said . . . property most widely and substantially beneficial to the interests of mankind." 130 N.Y. at 44–45, 28 N.E. at 881.

The Court of Appeals found this article an invalid disposition of the residue because the object and subject of the trust were "indefinite and uncertain." The court stated that where the power is given to the trustees to select a beneficiary, the class in whose favor the power may be exercised must be designated by the testator with such certainty that a court can ascertain the objects of power. Furthermore, cy pres could not be used to uphold a gift to indefinite beneficiaries as had been done in England for the doctrine "has no place in the jurisprudence of this state." 130 N.Y. at 45, 28 N.E. at 882.

28. Tilden Act, ch. 701, §1 (1893). Current version at N.Y. Est., Powers & Trusts Law §8.1–1(a) (1967).

29. Friedman, *supra* note 11, at 370.

30. Pound, "The Spirit of the Common Law," 18 *The Green Bag,* 17, 24 (1906).

31. See, *e.g.,* Carnegie, "Wealth," 148 *N. Am. Rev.* 653 (1889); Carnegie, "The Best Fields for Philanthropy," 149 *N. Am. Rev.* 682 (1889). See generally Chester, "Inheritance and Wealth Taxation in a Just Society," 30 *Rutgers L. Rev.* 62, 88–89 (1976).

32. See, *e.g.,* Wachovia Banking & Trust Co., v. Ogburn, 181 N.C. 324, 331, 107 S.E. 238, 242 (1921); see also Dickey v. Volker, 321 Mo. 235, 11 S.W. 2d 278 (1928); *cert. denied,* 279 U.S. 839 (1929).

33. *In re* Estate of Browning, 165 Misc. 819, 829, 1 N.Y.S. 2d 825, 833 (Sur. Ct. 1938), *aff'd* 281 N.Y. 577, 22 N.E. 2d 160 (1939).

34. *In re* Estate of Dean, 167 Misc. 238, 240, 3 N.Y.S. 2d 711, 713 (Sur. Ct. 1938).

35. See M. Cuninggim, *Private Money and Public Service: The Role of Foundations in American Society* 11–12 (1972).

36. See Katz, *supra* note 3, at 13.

37. See U.S. Treasury, *Report on Private Foundations* issued on Feb. 2, 1965, submitted to Committee on Finance, U.S. Senate, 89 Cong., 1st sess, pp. 6–10; see also Foundations and the Law Symposium, 13 *U.C.L.A. L. Rev.* 933 (1966); see also Katz, *supra* note 3, at 16.

38. See J. Dukeminier and S. Johanson, *Family Wealth Transactions* 956 (1st ed. 1972).

39. See U.S. Treasury Report, *supra* note 37, at 2, 10.

40. See generally *Tax Reform Act of 1969,* P.L. 91–172 (1970) discussed in Dukeminier and Johanson, *supra* note 38, at 957. Approximately two-thirds of the Act dealt with the problems of charitable foundations.

41. *Id.* See also Fremont-Smith, "The Impact of the Tax Reform Act of 1969 on State Supervision of Charities," 8 *Harv. J. of Legisl.* 537, 539 (1971).

42. *Id.*

43. See Dukeminier and Johanson, *supra* note 18, at 185–6, 1315–16.

44. Cuninggim, *supra* note 35, at 194–95.

45. See Parrish, "The Foundation 'A Special American Institution'" in *The Future of Foundations* 7, 17 (F. Heimann, ed. 1973).

46. R. Friedman, "Private Foundation—Government Relations," *Id.* at 163, 166.

47. *Id.* at 165.

48. See *Giving USA, supra* note 8, at 6; see generally May 1980 edition.

49. See *Foundation Directory, supra* note 6, at xxiv and *U.S. Budget in Brief Fiscal 1981,* charts at 44, 47, 50, and 53.

50. See *Foundation Directory, supra* note 6, at 13, xvi.

51. See Katz, *supra* note 3, at 20–21.

52. See *id.* at 23, 25–26.

53. See *Tax-Exempt Foundations and Charitable Trusts: Their Impact on our Economy* (Patman Report) 33 (1962).

54. See *Congressional Record,* Dec. 5, 1969, pp. S15755–15760; see also Cuninggim, *supra* note 35, at 75–76.

55. Kirstein, "Philanthropy: The Golden Crowbar," *Nation,* Sept. 16, 1968, at 239.

56. Curti, "Creative Giving: Slogan or Reality?" *Foundation News,* November 1962, at 8; but see J. Hart, "Foundations and Social Activism: A Critical View," in *The Future of Foundations, supra* note 45, at 43. Both the Kirstein and Curti articles are quoted in Cuninggim, *supra* note 35, at 100–101.

57. Report of the Peterson Commission, *supra* note 1, at 84, quoted in Cuninggim at 102.

58. Appearing on the "Donahue" segment of the *Today* show, August 4, 1980, were two "children of great inherited wealth," George Pillsbury and Peggy Stern, who participate in the Funding Exchange and Haymarket People's Fund respectively. These are organizations pooling the resources of wealthy youth who do not feel "the system is working" and are concerned about maldistributions of wealth. In the case of the Funding Exchange, the pooled assets are turned over directly to a community board which, apparently independent of donor control, decides how to distribute the funds.

59. See Lipton, "Significant Private Foundations and the Need for Public Selection of their Trustees," 64 *Va. L. Rev.* 779 (1978).

60. James, "Perspectives on Internal Functioning of Foundations," in *The Future of Foundations, supra* note 45, at 193.

61. "Women's Groups Assail Low Level of Grants from Foundations," *New York Times*, July 23, 1979, at A14.

62. See *id.*

63. See, *e.g.*, Mooney, "The Ministry of Culture," *Harper's*, August 1980, at 23.

64. Commission on Private Philanthropy and Public Needs, *Giving in America*, 172 (1975); see Report of Peterson Commission, *supra* note 1, at 45–46.

65. Report of Peterson Commission, *id.* at 46.

66. Nason, *supra* note 5.

67. Commission on Private Philanthropy, *supra* note 64, at 148–49. The Commission attributes the figures to Martin Feldstein.

68. See *id.* at 149.

69. See generally W. Nielsen, *The Big Foundations* (1972); see also Heimann, "Foundations and the Government: Perspectives for the Future," in *The Future of Foundations, supra* note 45, at 264.

70. See generally Nason, *supra* note 5.

71. See Heimann, *supra* note 69, at 272, 260–62.

72. The libertarian position is summarized in R. Wagner, *Inheritance and the State* 58 (1977). See generally W. A. Niskanen, *Bureaucracy and Representative Government* (1971).

73. Wagner, *supra* note 72, at 48–49. The Economic Tax Recovery Act of 1981 phases down the 70% bracket to 50%.

74. *Giving USA, supra* note 8, at 11–12.

75. Wagner, *supra* note 72, at 57–58.

76. See, *e.g.*, Dukeminier and Johanson, *supra* note 18, at 186–88. One change I would make in the 1976 marital deduction would have no effect on our hypothetical estate because of its large size. Until the 1976 Reform Act, the deduction was given for the actual amount bequeathed to the survivor up to one-half of the estate. Under the Tax Reform Act of 1976, if one-half is given and this is less than $250,000, the deduction is still $250,000. I see no reason to go beyond the tax equity principles discussed in the text in order to enlarge the deduction for smaller estates. In these cases we should go back to the pre-1976 laws and allow a deduction only for the actual amount bequeathed to the spouse.

77. See Boskin, "Estate Taxation and Charitable Bequests," 5 *J. Public Economics* 27 (February 1976).

78. See 1981 Budget of the United States (1980). For the 1981 figures, see *New York Times*, July 16, 1981, at D17.

79. See text accompanying and immediately following notes 1–2 *supra*.

80. See *Foundation Directory, supra* note 6.

81. See J. Ritchie, N. Alford, and R. Effland, *Decedents' Estates and Trusts*, 590–91 n.2 (5th ed. 1977).

82. Amer. Law Institute, 2 *Restatement of Trusts* Intro. Note at 1093 (1935). See St. Joseph's Hospital v. Bennett, 281 N.Y. 115, 22 N.E. 2d. 305 (1939); Sherman v. Richmond, 230 N.Y. 462, 130 N.E. 613 (1921); Matter of Scott, 8 N.Y. 2d. 419, 208 N.Y.S. 2d. 984, 171 N.E. 2d. 326 (1960); see also Holt v. College of Osteopathic Physicians & Surgeons, 61 Cal. 2d. 750, 40 Cal. Rptr. 244, 394 P. 2d. 932 (1964):

It is true that trustees of a charitable corporation do not have all the attributes of a trustee of a charitable trust. They do not hold legal title to corporate property and are not individually liable for corporate liabilities. Individual trustees, however, are the ones solely responsible for administering the trust assets and in both cases are fiduciaries in performing their trust duties . . . The rules governing charitable trusts ordinarily apply to charitable corporations.

But see YWCA v. Morgan, 281 N.C. 485, 189 S.E. 2d. 169 (1972) holding that a gift to a charitable corporation could be used for general corporate purposes, despite specific restrictions on its use.

83. See, *e.g.*, Moore's Heirs v. Moore's Devisees & Ex'rs, 34 Ky. (4 Dana) 354, 366 (1836); see also DeClerico, *Cy Pres: A Proposal for Change*, 47 *B.U. L. Rev.* 153, 167 (1967).

84. E. Fisch, *The Cy Pres Doctrine in the United States* 115 n.1 (1950).

85. For an example of an outrageous use of prerogative cy pres, see Da Costa v. De Pas, 27 Eng. Rep. 150 (Ch. 1754) in which a legacy left by a Jew to establish a Jesuba (an assembly for reading the law and instructing people in Judaism) was held illegal because it promoted a religion contrary to that of the established church. It was within the power of the Crown, the court held, to dispose of the bequest for the instruction of foundlings in the Christian religion.

86. Fisch, *supra* note 84, at 56.

87. See Jackson v. Phillips, 96 Mass. (14 Allen) 539 (1867). Favoring of charity over the "dead hand" of the testator was not, however, extended in Massachusetts to include so-called semisecret trusts in favor of a charity.The leading case is Oliffe v. Wells, 138 Mass. 221 (1881).

88. Friedman, "The Dynastic Trust," 73 *Yale L. J.* 547, 589–90 (1964).

89. 69 Mass. (3 Gray) 280 (1855); see also Merrill v. Hayden, 86 Me. 133, 29A. 949 (1893).

90. First Congregational Soc'y v. City of Bridgeport, 99 Conn. 22, 37, 121 A. 77 (1923). For a ringing defense of this philosophy, see Willard, "Illustrations of the Origin of Cy Pres," 8 *Harv L. Rev.* 69, 91–92 (1894).

91. *In re* Estate of Browning, 165 Misc. 819, 829, 1 N.Y.S. 2d. 825, 833 (Sur. Ct. 1938), *aff'd* 281 N.Y. 577, 22 N.E. 2d. 160 (1939).

92. *In re* Estate of Dean, 167 Misc. 238, 240, 3 N.Y.S. 2d. 711, 713 (Sur. Ct. 1938).

93. Fisch, *supra* note 84, at 123. See, *e.g.*, Thatcher v. Lewis, 335 Mo. 1130, 76 S.W. 2d. 677 (1934), noted in 35 *Colum. L. Rev.* 467 (1935). See also Blackwell, "The Charitable Corporation and Charitable Trust," 24 *Wash. U. L.Q.* 1 (1938).

94. See Fisch, *supra* note 84, at 120, n.16. For examples of this favorable tax treatment, see Revenue Act of 1926, ch. 27 §303(b)(3), 44 Stat. 73 (1926). Current version at I.R.C. §2055 (estate tax deduction); *id.* §214(a)(10), 44 Stat. 27–28 (1926). Current version I.R.C. §170 (income tax deduction).

95. See Fisch, *supra* note 84, at 128, 139. For cases eliminating the first requirement see, *e.g.*, *In re* Estate of Walter, 150 Misc. 512, 269 N.Y.S. 400 (Sur. Ct. 1933) and Read v. Willard Hosp., 215 Mass. 132, 102 N.E. 95 (1913).

96. Fisch, *supra* note 84, at 150–51.

97. *Pa. Stat. Ann.* tit. 20, §301.10 (Purdon 1947), now appearing at 20 *Pa. Cons. Stat. Ann.* §6110 (Purdon 1975).

98. See, *e.g.*, Roberds v. Markham, 81 F. Supp. 38, 41–42 (D.DC 1948).

99. Fisch, *supra* note 84, at 393. One requirement that had apparently been eliminated—that a valid charitable *trust* be in existence—has been rescuscitated by the Supreme Court of Alabama in Baxley v. Birmingham Trust Nat'l Bank, 334 So. 2d. 848 (Ala. 1976).

100. G. G. Bogert and G. T. Bogert, *Trusts and Trustees,* §436 at 527 (rev. 2d ed. 1977).

101. 41 App. Div. 2d. 308, 342 N.Y.S. 2d. 560 (Sup. Ct. 1973).

102. First Nat'l Bank & Trust Co. v. Brimmer, 504 P. 2d. 1367, 1371 (Wyo. 1973). This action was brought by the trustee of a fund which provided scholarships for children from Cheyenne and Casper, Wyoming, for attendance at either the University of Wyoming or Casper Community College. The trustee sought to apply the fund to children from these communities who wished to attend Laramie County Community College. Since the original trust purposes had become neither impossible nor impractical to fulfill, the trustee sought the alteration via the doctrine of equitable deviation. See *infra* note 118. Even this modest change was denied by the court for the reason stated in the quotation to which this note refers.

103. See Jackson v. Phillips, 96 Mass. (14 Allen) 539 (1867). More recently, the Massachusetts Supreme Judicial Court had little trouble finding the general charitable intent necessary to cy pres in Wesley United Church v. Harvard College, 366 Mass. 247, 316 N.E. 2d. 620 (1974).

104. 78 Mass. Adv. Sh. 1443, 1449–50, 376 N.E. 2d. 1226, 1230 (1978).

105. See, *e.g.*, Simmons v. Parsons College, 256 N.W. 2d. (1977).

106. See Hanbey's Will Trusts [1955] 3 All. E.R. 874, 879 (stating the rule and citing previous cases to that effect); see also Bogert and Bogert, *supra* note 100, §431 at 496–99 and n.28 thereto.

107. 63 Cal. App. 332, 146 P. 2d. 962 (1944).

108. Trustees of Dartmouth College v. City of Quincy, 357 Mass. 521, 258 N.E. 2d 745 (1970). Under this doctrine, it is not the purpose of the trust which has failed—requiring the funds to be put to an allied use (cy pres)—but the mechanics of the trust which are inadequate, requiring changes in the trust's administration.

109. The forfeiture doctrine itself has not been generally applied in cy pres cases. In 1970 the Rhode Island Supreme Court let a gift to a defunct nursing home fail, finding that it had been made solely in appreciation for the care given by the home to testator's father, and not with the more general intent of helping the ill and elderly. Industrial Nat'l Bank of R.I. v. Glocester Manor, Free Pub. Library, 107 R.I. 161, 265 A. 2d. 724 (1970).

110. 357 Mass. at 521, 258 N.E. 2d at 753.

111. Franklin established virtually identical funds for the cities of Philadelphia and Boston. For the history of the Philidelphia fund and the refusal of the Pennsylvania Supreme Court to allow trust income to accumulate or to apply cy pres to the trust, see Benjamin Franklin's Estate, 27 W.N. 545, 48 Leg. Int. 136 (1891), *aff'd,* 150 Pa. 437, 24 A. 626 (1892). The tale of the Boston fund is still unwinding; for a summary of Massachusetts' allowance both of accumulation and cy pres, see Franklin Foundation v. Attorney General, 340 Mass. 197, 163 N.E. 2d. 662 (1960), recounted in Dukeminier and Johanson, *supra* note 18, at 1358–59.

112. Order No. 6664 of the Massachusetts House of Representatives, October 12, 1977.

113. Opinion of the Justices of the Supreme Judicial Court: Transfer to the City of Boston of Assets of the Franklin Institute in 1991 by Legislation, 78 Mass. Adv. Sh. 1 (1978).

114. Nonetheless, legislatures in 25 states now give the power to their Attorneys General, if written consent cannot be obtained from the donor (because of death or other causes) for removal of restrictions on a charitable fund whose purpose has failed, to bring an action for removal of the restriction. "If the court finds the restriction is obsolete, inappropriate or impractical, it may by order release the restriction in whole or in part. . . . This section does not limit the application of the doctrine of cy pres." Uniform Management of Institutional Funds Act, 7A *Uniform Laws Ann.* §7(b)(d) (Master ed. 1978).

115. If the event divesting the initial charitable gift in favor of individual beneficiaries must happen within the period of the Rule Against Perpetuities, or is vested at the time of creation of the trust, or must vest, if at all within the period, the gift over to individual beneficiaries is valid. 4 A. Scott, *Trusts* §401.6 (3d ed. 1967). See, *e.g.,* Holsey v. Atlantic Nat'l. Bank, 115 Fla. 604, 155 So. 821 (1934).

116. "Distributive" and "commutative" justice were terms first used by Aristotle and Thomas Aquinas. F. A. Hayek, *The Constitution of Liberty,* 441 n.11 (1960). Hayek has discussed the modern meaning of the terms in the following way:

> The restrictions which the rule of law imposes upon government . . . preclude all those measures which would be necessary to insure that individuals will be rewarded according to another's conception of merit or desert rather than according to the value that their services have for their fellows—or what amounts to the same thing, it precludes the use of distributive, as opposed to commutative justice. Id. at 232. . . . In Aristotelian terms . . . liberalism aims at commutative justice and socialism at distributive justice. [*Id.* at 440 n.10.]

117. Llewellyn, Book Review, 52 *Harv. L. Rev.* 700, 703 (1939).

118. Note, "A Revaluation of Cy Pres," 49 *Yale L. J.* 303, 322 (1939).

119. See *id.* at 323.

120. See, *e.g.,* the famous California Initiative Measure, "Proposition 13," approved by the people June 6, 1978, *Cal. Const.* art. 13 A.

6. THE PERPETUATION OF DYNASTIC TRUSTS

1. See R. Wagner, *Inheritance and the State* 4–6 (1977).

2. Given the paucity of data, reaching this figure requires some extrapolation. By December 31, 1972, $403 billion in trust investments was being handled by corporate fiduciaries. Wicker, "Spendthrift Trusts," 10 *Gonz. L. Rev.* 1,2 (1974). An expert in the field estimates that at least as many trusts were being handled by individual fiduciaries. R. Powell, *Cases and Materials on Trusts and Wills* 12–13 (1960).

3. See Bushman, "The (In) Validity of Spendthrift Trusts," 47 *Ore. L. Rev.* 304 (1968). See also G. G. Bogert and G. T. Bogert, *Trusts and Trustees* §222 *et seq.* (rev. 2d ed. 1979).

4. See J. Ritchie, N. Alford, and R. Effland, *Cases and Materials on Decedents' Estates and Trusts* 458 (1977).

5. See Bogert and Bogert, *supra* note 3, at §228.

6. *Id.* at §229.

7. See Friedman, "The Dynastic Trust," 73 *Yale L. J.* 547, 548 (1964).

8. See Van Doren, "Redistributing Wealth by Curtailing Inheritance . . ." 3 *Fla. St. L. Rev.* 33, 49 (1975); see also J. Dukeminier and S. Johanson, *Family Wealth Transactions* 228 (2d ed. 1978). For Code sections imposing the generation-skipping transfer tax, a separate tax from estate and gift levies, see I.R.C. §2601 *et seq.*

9. See G. Jantscher, *Trusts and Estate Taxation* 57–59, 128–29, 157 (1967), recounted in Van Doren, *supra* note 8, at 49–50.

10. Dukeminier and Johanson, *supra* note 8.

11. Friedman, *supra* note 7, at 572, 583.

12. 149 Mass. 19, 20 N.E. 545 (1889).

13. See Friedman, *supra* note 7, at 586; see also Dukeminier and Johanson, *supra* note 8, at 960. Cases announcing the doctrine are collected at Bogert and Bogert, *supra* note 3, at §1007–1008 and at 4 A. Scott, *Trusts* §337–337.8 (3d ed. 1967).

14. See Friedman, "The Law of the Living, the Law of the Dead: Property, Succession, and Society," *Law & Society Reprint #8* at 14. See generally L. Simes, *Public Policy and the Dead Hand* (1955).

15. See Van Doren, *supra* note 8, at 54, 35.

16. See Simes, *supra* note 14, at 60–61.

17. Van Doren, *supra* note 8, at 54–55.

18. The discussion of English doctrine is based on Bushman, *supra* note 3, at 305.

19. *Id.* at 306.

20. 91 U.S. 716 (1875). Apparently this overruled the position taken by the United States Supreme Court in Nichols v. Levy, 72 U.S. (5 Wall) 433 (1867).

21. See Bushman, *supra* note 3, at 306–307.

22. 25 *Ruling Case Law* §4 (1919), citing Wagner v. Wagner, 244 Ill. 101, 91 N.E. 66 (1910), the first case to declare this thesis. Apparently misconstruing the meaning of other cases, the Wagner court offered this view as dicta, citing no authority.

23. See Bushman, *supra* note 3, at 307.

24. J. Gray, *Restraints on the Alienation of Property* iii (1895).

25. *Id.* at ix.

26. *Id.* at x.

27. F. Stimson, *My United States* 76–77 (1931); but see Friedman, *supra* note 7, at 575. Stimson (1855–1943) graduated from Harvard College and Law School. At first a conservative railroad lawyer in the firm of the Boston Lowells, he eventually became a Democrat crusading for justice, labor, and the American Indian. Most of his writings made reference to his lifelong opposition to government interference with individual liberties and property rights.

28. Gray, *supra* note 24, at xi. In current form, the statute appears at 17B

Cons. Laws of N.Y. §7–3.4 (Supp. 1979). For a case construing the "station in life" rule, see *In re* Brown's Estate, 35 N.Y.S. 2d 646, *aff'd* 264 App. Div. 824, 35 N.Y.S. 2d 738 (1941).

29. See E. Griswold, *Spendthrift Trusts* (2d ed. 1947). The model act is set out at section 565.

30. See Bushman, *supra* note 3, at 308. Griswold's suggested limitations are due for a substantial increase because of recent inflation.

31. See *id.* at 309. For a recent case proclaiming the exceptions for doctors' bills and necessaries, see Estate of Caroline P. Dodge, Supreme Ct. of Iowa Adv. Sh., Sept. 4, 1979, 281 N.W. 2d 447 (1979).

32. See Bushman, *supra* note 3, at 308. Kentucky courts had for a long time construed a state Code provision (§381.180) as negating spendthrift protection attempted by a settlor. See, *e.g.,* Keith v. First Nat'l Bank & Trust Co. 256 Ky. 88, 75 S.W. 2d 747 (1934); Fidelity Trust & Safety Vault Co. v. Walker, 116 Ky. 381, 76 S.W. 131 (1903). However, a 1966 amendment to the statute specifically exempted spendthrift trusts from those trusts covered by the free alienability provisions of §381.180. It now appears that spendthrift protection is valid in Kentucky due to the amended statute.

33. Wicker, *supra* note 2, at 45.

34. 25 N.Y. 2d 163, 250 N.E. 2d 343, 303 N.Y.S. 2d 61 (1969).

35. Niles, "Matter of Vought's Will: A Tighter Grip by the Dead Hand," 45 *N.Y.U. L. Rev.* 421 (1970).

36. See *id.* at 422–423.

37. 25 N.Y. 2d at 173–74, 250 N.E. 2d at 348, 303 N.Y.S. 2d at 69. See Niles, *supra* note 35, at 424–25.

38. 25 N.Y. 2d at 175, 250 N.E. 2d at 349, 303 N.Y.S. 2d at 70.

39. See Niles, *supra* note 35, at 425–427. See *Restatement of Property* §162 and comment (d) to §162(1) (1936); *Restatement of Trusts* §151 (1935); and *Restatement (Second) of Trusts* §153 (1957).

40. Powell, "The Rule Against Perpetuities and Spendthrift Trusts in New York," 71 *Colum. L. Rev.* 688 (1971); for another relevant article by Powell, see "Freedom of Alienation—For Whom?" 2 *Real Prop., Prob., & Trust J.* 127 (1967).

41. See Bushman, *supra* note 3, at 317.

42. See Note, "A Rationale for the Spendthrift Trust," 64 *Colum. L. Rev.* 1323, 1327 (1964).

43. Costigan, "Those Protective Trusts Which are Miscalled 'Spendthrift Trusts' Reexamined," 22 *Calif. L. Rev.* 471, 483 (1934).

44. See Note, *supra* note 42, at 1327.

45. See *id.* at 1327–28.

46. See *id.* at 1325.

47. See Friedman, *supra* note 7, at 582.

48. Callahan, "Trusts and Succession," 22 *Wayne St. L. Rev.* 692, 693–695 (1976).

49. Wicker, *supra* note 2, at 2.

50. Note, *supra* note 42, at 1335.

51. See Sherman, "Spendthrift Trusts and Employee Pensions: The Problem of Creditors' Rights" 55 *Ind. L. J.* 247 (1980).

52. *Id.* at 248. That benefits like employee pensions are considered a new form of property, see Reich, "The New Property," 73 *Yale L. J.* 733 (1964).

53. See generally Sherman, *supra* note 51.

54. See Wicker, *supra* note 2, at 15.

55. 149 Mass. 19 (1889).

56. *Id.* at 24. See Comment, "Trusts—Duration and Indestructibility," 24 *Tenn. L. Rev.* 1021, 1024 (1957).

57. See Note, "Trusts Restraints on Alienation: Duration of Indestructible and Spendthrift Trusts," 23 *Cornell L. Q.* 629, 630 (1938).

58. Van Doren, *supra* note 8, at 40. Some of these transfers are now caught by the generation-skipping transfer tax; see note 8, *supra* and accompanying text.

59. *Id.* at 48.

60. *Id.* at 51.

61. See Comment, *supra* note 56, at 1028–1029.

62. Note, *supra* note 57, at 634. See also Leach, "Perpetuities in a Nutshell," 51 *Harv. L. Rev.* 638, 668 (1938); L. Simes, *The Law of Future Interests* 440–443 (1936).

63. See Note, *supra* note 57, at 632–33.

64. See Ritchie et al., *supra* note 4, at 569.

65. See Wright, "Termination of Trusts in Pennsylvania—Some Current Trends," 115 *U. Pa. L. Rev.* 917 (1967).

66. 449 S.W. 2d 761 (1973).

67. 396 S.W. 2d 683 (1965).

68. See Dukeminier and Johanson, *supra* note 8, at 965–966.

69. 343 Mass. 644, 649, 180 N.E. 2d 74, 77 (1962); noted at 39 *B.U. L. Rev.* 274 (1959).

70. See Ritchie et al., *supra* note 4, at 569. See also Comment, "Termination of Trusts," 46 *Yale L. J.* 1005 (1937).

71. See 42 U.S.C.A. §401–433 (supp. 1980).

7. THE IMPACT OF INHERITANCE REFORM ON PROPERTY CRIME

1. See Eberts and Schwirian, "Metropolitan Crime Rates and Relative Deprivation," 5 *Criminologia* 43 (1967–68), and "City Crime: Report of Council on Municipal Performance," 9 *Crim. L. Bull.* 557 (1973).

2. Chester, "Perceived Relative Deprivation as a Cause of Property Crime," 22 *Crime & Del.* 17 (1976).

3. See Cook, Crosby, and Hennigan, "The Construct Validity of Relative Deprivation" in *Social Comparison Processes: Theoretical and Empirical Perspectives* 307 (J. Suls and R. Miller eds. 1977).

4. L. Radzinowicz, "Economic Conditions and Crime" paper presented to the National Commission on the Causes and Prevention of Violence (1968), reprinted in 1 *Crime and Justice: The Criminal in Society* 429 (Radzinowicz and Wolfgang eds. 1971).

5. U.S. Gov't, Dep't of Justice, *Sourcebook of Criminal Justice Statistics* 580 (1976).

6. In 1977 black families had a mean income of $8,422 compared to $14,272 for whites. Furthermore in 1978 blacks had an unemployment rate of 13.1% compared to 6.2% for whites. U.S. Gov't, Dep't of Commerce,

Bureau of Census, *Statistical Abstracts of the United States* 449, 396 (1978). The percentage of blacks in the total population is on page 28.

7. U.S. Gov't, Dep't of Justice, *Uniform Crime Reports: 1978,* at 198 (1979).

8. See, *e.g.,* R. Clark, *Crime in America* 24 (1971). After examining the Uniform Crime Reports of the FBI, the former attorney general notes that seven of eight "serious crimes" are against property and that many crimes against persons are incidental to property crimes.

9. B. Wootton, *Social Science and Social Pathology* 79–80 (1959). An experimental study by G. M. Stephenson and J. H. White found, contrary to Wootton's expectations, that absolutely deprived boys actually cheated more than boys who were relatively deprived in comparison with more privileged groups. Stephenson and White, "An Experimental Study of Some Effects of Injustice on Children's Moral Behavior" 4 *J. Exp. Soc. Psych.* 460 (1968). However, a follow-up study showed that these and other results in the first study were characteristic only of introverted and not extraverted boys. Stephenson & Barker, "Personality and the Pursuit of Distributive Justice: An Experimental Study of Children's Moral Behavior" 11 *Brit. J. Soc. & Clin. Psych.* 207, 219 (1972).

10. G. Vold, *Theoretical Criminology* 173–74 (1958).

11. Wootton, *supra* note 9, at 103.

12. Schwartz, "Education, Poverty and Juvenile Delinquency" in *Poverty: New Interdisciplinary Perspectives* 180, 204 (T. Weaver and A. Magid eds., 1969).

13. J. Mays, *Crime and the Social Structure* 41 (1963).

14. *Id.* at 203.

15. W. A. Bonger, *Criminality and Economic Conditions* 87 (Eng. trans. 1916).

16. Radzinowicz, *supra* note 4, at 437.

17. Clark, *supra* note 8, at 40.

18. See Hennigan and Cook, "A Comparison of the Prevalence, Intensity and Distribution of Feelings of Personal, Fraternal, and Double Unfairness" (Unpublished manuscript, Northwestern University.)

19. Alternative schools both in the United States and Britain are attempting to counteract this problem through development of a positive working-class consciousness. An example in the United States is The Group School in Cambridge, Massachusetts.

20. See the discussion of frustration from blocked social and economic mobility and its link to violent acquisitive crime in the United States Nat'l Comm. on Causes & Prevention of Violence, *Commission Statement on Violent Crime: Homicide, Assault, Rape and Robbery* (1969).

21. Eberts and Schwirian, "Metropolitan Crime Rates . . ." and "City Crime," *supra* note 1.

22. See Henry and Short, *Suicide and Homicide* (1964).

23. Those living in "poverty" were families earning a low income (adjusted for the cost of living) using the federal government's measure of city poverty. For a complete definition and discussion of the concept of poverty, see Dentler, "Poverty," in *Basic Social Problems,* 106–122 (Dentler ed. 1971).

24. Cloward and Ohlin, "Social Class, Aspirations and Economics" in *Juve-*

nile Delinquency: A Reader 136 (J. Teele, ed. 1970). See also R. Cloward and L. Ohlin, *Delinquency and Opportunity* (1961). A British view is related in L. MacDonald, *Social Class and Delinquency,* esp. 51–52 (1969).

25. See, *e.g.,* Hyman, "The Value Systems of Different Classes" in *Class, Status and Power* 432 (Bendix & Lipset eds. 1953); Empey, "Social Class and Occupational Aspiration" 21 *Am. Soc. Rev.* 706 (1956).

26. See generally W. Whyte, *Street Corner Society* (1955).

27. Merton's theory of anomie is basic to much of the discussion in this and surrounding paragraphs. See generally R. Merton, *Social Theory and Social Structure* (1957).

28. See Cloward and Ohlin, *supra* note 24. For other important articles in the field see: Erickson and Empey, "Class Position, Peers and Delinquency," 49 *Soc. & Soc. Res.* 268 (1963); Reiss and Rhodes, "Status Deprivation and Delinquent Behavior" 4 *Soc. Q.* 135 (1963); Clark and Wenninger, "Socioeconomic Class and Area as Correlates of Illegal Behavior Among Juveniles," 27 *Am. Soc. Rev.* 826 (1962). Reiss and Rhodes, "The Distribution of Delinquency in the Social Class Structure," 26 *Am. Soc. Rev.* 720 (1961); Dentler and Monro, "Social Correlates of Early Adolescent Theft," 26 *Am. Soc. Rev.* 733 (1961); and Nye and Short, "Socioeconomic Status and Delinquent Boys," 63 *Am. J. Soc.* 381 (1958).

29. Feldman and Weisfeld, "An Interdisciplinary Study of Crime," 19 *Crime & Del.* 150 (1973).

30. Samples of Tom's view:

> Every kid that lives in this neighborhood hates people that live in the suburbs. . . . They hate all suburbs, man . . . They hate anybody that got more than they do. . . . I'm a roofer, but when I go out there to do one of the roofs . . . they sit there on the patio . . . and drink Pepsi-Cola, Jack, when you're sweating your ass off, man, and they look at you like you're some kind of creep, man, and they stick up their nose in the air. If you ask them a question—one time one girl told me, "Don't talk to me, talk to my husband.' I went to talk to him and he just walked away. They're creeps, man. They get a little bit of bread and then they move out to some little-bitty suburb and then they act like they're some kind of president or something. Too good to talk to anybody . . . I don't like nobody with money anyway . . . Most of them own businesses . . . The way they got up there, man, they robbed people, right? But they robbed them in a way where they couldn't get arrested for it. Only they're good people. To society they're good people. [*Id.* at 156.]

31. Mays observes that Sutherland, as well as Shaw and McKay, felt that the entire American social structure with its norm of corruption and "the fix" was powerfully criminogenic. Mays, *supra* note 13, at 201. See generally Bell, "Crime as an American Way of Life," 13 *Antioch Rev.* 131 (1953).

32. Feldman and Weisfeld, *supra* note 29, at 156–57. "You don't want to burglarize someone that ain't got nothing. You want to go out and burglarize someone that got something. What are you doing, just running around for tricks, just burglarizing to find out what was happening?"

33. This essentially is a relativistic view of deviance, i.e., that deviance is not pathological or innate, but rather a function of failure to follow the

dominant group's norms. See generally E. Lemert, *Human Deviance, Social Problems and Social Control* 63–72; 74–76 (1967); L. Wilkins, *Social Deviance* 46-50 (1964); M. Becker, *Outsiders* 1–18; 121–34 (1963).

34. The basic works proclaiming this thesis are: Miller, "Lower Class Culture as a Generating Milieu of Gang Delinquency," 14 *J. Soc. Iss.* 6–13 (1958); T. Morris, *The Criminal Area* (1957); and A. Cohen, *Delinquent Boys: The Culture of the Gang* (1955).

35. See Hood and Sparks, "Subcultural Gang Delinquency," in *Key Issues in Criminology* (Hood & Sparks, eds. 1970); D. Matza, *Delinquency and Drift* (1964).

36. See chapters 1 and 4 *supra.* Attempting to reconcile the two competing concepts was a common theme of European political philosophers during the late eighteenth and the nineteenth centuries. See, *e.g.,* J. Rousseau, *The Social Contract* (trans. 1954); Marx and Engels, *Basic Writings on Politics and Philosophy* (Doubleday ed. 1959).

37. M. Tumin, *Social Stratification* 49 (1967).

38. Chester, "The Effects of a Redistribution of Wealth on Property Crime," 23 *Crime & Del.* 272 (1977).

39. Tumin, *supra* note 37.

40. *New York Times,* July 18, 1976. Emphasis in the original.

41. Ploscowe, "Some Causative Factors in Criminality," *Report on Causes of Crime,* Vol. 1, Part 1 of 13 *Report of Nat'l Comm. on Law Observance and Law Enforcement* 115–16 (1931). The original quotation is from C. Jacquart, *Essais de Statistique La Criminalité Belge 1868–1909* 117 (1912).

42. See, *e.g.,* Bell, *supra* note 31.

43. Mays, *supra* note 13, at 201–202.

44. See generally L. Thurow, *The Zero-Sum Society* (1980).

45. Mays, *supra* note 13, at 201.

46. *Id.*

47. Gordon, "Capitalism, Class and Crime in America," 19 *Crime & Del.* 163 (1973).

48. See *id.* See also Dentler, *supra* note 23, at 118–119.

49. See generally M. and R. Friedman, *Free to Choose* 140–146 (1980). Milton Friedman and I agree on this point, but our views of what constitute "equality of opportunity" are widely divergent. In short, he believes this exists in a truly capitalist society and I do not.

50. Considering the power of the civil service, apparently the only way these agencies can be reduced in size is through attrition coupled with no new hiring. This is an unlikely but not impossible prospect.

51. See Bell, *supra* note 31.

8. INHERITANCE REFORM IN MODERN SOCIETY

1. L. C. Thurow, *The Zero-Sum Society* 5, 71 (1980). The paradox is that such solutions help the rich (who get more valuable money) more than the wage earner (who loses his automatic cost-of-living raise). Such problems may explain Thurow's "go slow" approach to redistribution in this book.

2. See *id.* at 7.

3. See *id.* at 5.

4. *Id.* at 101.

5. *Id.* at 77.

6. See *id.* at 94.

7. See *id.* at 115.

8. *Id.* at 117.

9. *Id.* at 120.

10. See *id.* at 155–156.

11. See *id.* at 158.

12. *Id.* at 193–194.

13. *Id.* at 171.

14. U.S. Gov't, Dept. of Commerce, *Survey of Current Business* 59, No. 7 at 39–40 (1979).

15. Thurow, *supra* note 1, at 172.

16. See generally G. Cooper, *A Voluntary Tax?* (1979). Cooper was my teacher at Columbia and really is—though he may not know it—the creator of my interest in inheritance problems. An outstanding teacher, Cooper has sown some of the seed for this book, but is in no way to blame for the harvest.

17. See *id.* at 2 n.3.

18. See *id.* at 11. Carry-over basis rules were described in I.R.C. §1023. The stepped-up basis is detailed in I.R.C. §1014.

19. *Id.* at 2.

20. See *id.* at 90.

21. See *The Wall Street Journal,* July 16, 1981, at 27 and the *New York Times,* July 16, 1981, at D17. Some estimates put the revenue loss in fiscal 1986 at $6 billion. See *Newsweek,* July 13, 1981, at 59.

22. I.R.C. §2035, as amended by the Economic Recovery Tax Act of 1981.

23. I.R.C. §2001(c)

24. See Cooper, *supra* note 16, at 13.

25. I.R.C. §2513. The "gift-splitting" provision of the tax allows a spouse double the normal annual exclusion of $10,000 under §2503(b).

26. I.R.C. §2042(2). See Cooper, *supra* note 16, at 34–35. I.R.S.'s ruling subjecting employer-funded group term insurance to the gift tax is at Rev. Rul. 76–490, 50 I.R.B. 28 (1976).

27. See Cooper, *supra* note 16, at 41–43.

28. See *id.* at 59–60. The Code provision allowing the charitable lead trust is I.R.C. §2055(e)(2)(B). The deduction itself is determined under the tables at I.R.C. Regs. §20.2031–10(f), Table B.

29. See Cooper, *id.* at 60–61. Income tax rates are found at I.R.C. §1and estate and gift tax rates at I.R.C. §2001.

30. See *id.* at 94, 96, 82.

31. See *id.* at 83–89, 91–92, 93, 94.

32. *Id.* at 81.

33. See *id.* at 81–82.

34. See *id.* at 11.

35. *U.S. Const.* Art. 1., sec. 8.

36. See Cooper, *supra* note 16, at 107.

37. See *id.* at 110 n.69. For detail on the Japanese problems with the tax see R. W. Thomas, *Net Wealth Taxation* 8, 80 (Unpublished manuscript, Harvard-Chile Tax Project, 1966).

38. See Van Doren, "Redistributing Wealth by Curtailing Inheritance …"3 *Fla. St. L. Rev.* 33, 61 (1975).

39. See Bale, "Whither Death Duties ..." 1974 *Pub. L.* 121, 123.

40. See L. C. Thurow, *The Impact of Taxes on the American Economy* 132 (1971); See also Chester, "Inheritance and Wealth Taxation in a Just Society," 30 *Rutgers L. Rev.* 62, 69 (1976).

41. R. E. Wagner, *Death and Taxes: Some Perspectives on Inheritance, Inequality and Progressive Taxation* 52 (1973).

42. See Warren, "Fairness and a Consumption-Type or Cash Flow Personal Income Tax," 88 *Harv. L. Rev.* 931 (1975); Andrews, "A Consumption-Type or Cash Flow Personal Income Tax," 87 *Harv. L. Rev.* 1113 (1974).

43. Andrews, *id.* at 1172.

44. See Van Doren, *supra* note 38, at 60–61; see also Chester, *supra* note 40, at 69–70.

45. See Tait, "The Taxation of Wealth at Death: A New Proposal," 9 *Scot. J. Pol. Econ.* 38, 44–45 (1962).

46. See, *e.g.*, discussion in J. Dukeminier and S. Johanson, *Family Wealth Transactions* 232 (2d ed. 1978).

47. Thurow, *supra* note 40, at 158.

48. Wagner, *supra* note 41, at 52.

49. W. Shultz, *The Taxation of Inheritance* 198 (1926).

50. See Van Doren, *supra* note 38, at 62.

51. See *id.* at 61–62.

52. *Id.* at 62.

53. *Id.*

54. Thurow, *supra* note 1, at 195.

55. *Id.* at 66–68.

56. For a socialist view of inheritance, see E. Rignano, *The Social Significance of the Inheritance Tax* (Shultz trans. & adapt. 1924). Rignano's views are discussed at length in chapter 4, *supra*.

57. The libertarian/equal opportunity/ends-equality (socialist) triad in political economy has a rather neat analogue in legal theory: formal, procedural, and substantive models of justice. For an excellent discussion of the latter see R. Unger, *Law and Modern Society* 194–200 (1976).

58. Thurow, *supra* note 1, at 196.

59. *Id.*

60. *Id.*

61. *Id.* at 201.

62. *Id.*

63. *New York Times Magazine,* Apr. 11, 1976, §6 at 32.

64. Thurow wants to eliminate that tax and to replace it with a personal income tax levied on dividends *and* earnings retained by the corporation, as allocated to the individual shareholder. Thurow, *supra* note 1, at 97–99. As to problems which elimination of this corporate "double tax" would cause for enforcement of the estate and gift tax, see Cooper, *supra* note 16, at 83.

65. See *id.* at 97–99, 143.

66. See Thurow, *supra* note 1, at 207.

67. *Id.* at 197.

68. See *id.* at 198.

69. See *id.* at 199.

Bibliography

Aiken, Henry D., ed. *The Age of Ideology: The 19th Century Philosophers.* New York: New American Library, 1956.

Allport, Floyd H. *Institutional Behavior.* Chapel Hill: The University of North Carolina Press, 1933.

American Association of Fund-Raising Counsel. *Giving U.S.A: A Compilation of Facts Related to Philanthropy.* New York: 1979.

American Law Institute. *Restatement of Trusts.* St. Paul: American Law Institute Publishers, 1935.

Ames, James B. "The Failure of the Tilden Trust," *Harvard Law Review,* vol. 5 (March 15, 1892).

Andrews, William D. "A Consumption-Type or Cash Flow Personal Income Tax," *Harvard Law Review,* vol. 87 (April, 1974).

Aquinas, Thomas. *Summa Theologica.* New York: Benzinger Brothers, 1947.

Atkinson, A. B. *Unequal Shares: Wealth in Britain.* Baltimore: Penguin, 1974.

Bale, Gordon. "Whither Death Duties," *Public Law,* Summer 1974.

Barlow, Robin. *Economic Behavior of the Affluent.* Washington D.C.: Brookings Institution, 1966.

Baumgardt, David. *Bentham and the Ethics of Today.* Princeton: Princeton University Press, 1952.

Bell, Daniel. "Crime as an American Way of Life," *Antioch Review,* vol. 13 (Summer 1953).

Bellamy, Charles J. *The Way Out.* New York: G. P. Putnam Sons, 1884.

Bentham, Jeremy. *A Fragment on Government.* Oxford: The Clarendon Press, 1891.

———. "Principles of the Civil Code." In *Theory of Legislation,* edited by C. K. Ogden. New York: Harcourt, Brace, 1931.

———. *Supply Without Burthen, or Escheat Vice Taxation.* London: J. Debrett, 1795.

Blackstone, William. *Commentaries on the Laws of England.* Oxford: Clarendon Press, 1803.

Blackwell, Thomas E. "The Charitable Corporation and Charitable Trust," *Washington University Law Quarterly,* vol. 24 (December 1938).

Blau, Peter M. *The American Occupational Structure.* New York: Wiley, 1967.

Bogert, George G., and Bogert, George T. *The Law of Trusts and Trustees.* rev. 2d ed. St. Paul: West, 1980.

Bonger, Willem A. *Criminality and Economic Conditions.* Boston: Little, Brown, 1916.

Boorstin, Daniel J. *The Lost World of Thomas Jefferson.* Boston: Beacon Press, 1963.

Boskin, Michael J. "Estate Taxation and Charitable Bequests," *Journal of Public Economics,* vol. 5 (February 1976).

Brittain, John A. *Inheritance and the Inequality of Material Wealth.* Washington, D.C.: Brookings Institution, 1978.

――――. *The Inheritance of Economic Status.* Washington, D.C.: Brookings Institution, 1977.

Brownson, Orestes A. "The Descent of Property," *Boston Quarterly Review,* vol. 3 (October 1840).

Burton, David H. *Theodore Roosevelt: Confident Imperialist.* Philadelphia: University of Pennsylvania Press, 1968.

Bushman, Willard M. "The (In) Validity of Spendthrift Trusts," *Oregon Law Review,* vol. 47 (April 1968).

Callahan, Kenneth R. "Trusts and Successions," *Wayne Law Review,* vol. 22 (January 1976).

Carnegie, Andrew. "The Best Fields for Philanthropy," *North American Review,* vol. 149 (December 1889).

――――. "The Gospel of Wealth," *North American Review,* vol. 148 (June 1889).

Chester, C. Ronald. "Cy Pres: A Promise Unfulfilled," *Indiana Law Journal,* vol. 54 (Fall 1979).

――――. "The Effects of a Redistribution of Wealth on Property Crime," *Crime and Delinquency,* vol. 23 (July 1977).

――――. "Inheritance and Wealth Taxation in a Just Society," *Rutgers Law Review,* vol. 30 (Fall 1976).

――――. "Perceived Relative Deprivation as a Cause of Property Crime," *Crime and Delinquency,* vol. 22 (January 1976).

"City Crime: Report of the Council on Municipal Performance," *Criminal Law Bulletin,* vol. 9 (No. 7, 1973).

Clark, John P., and Wenninger, Eugene P. "Socioeconomic Class and Area as Correlates of Illegal Behavior Among Juveniles," *American Sociological Review,* vol. 27 (December 1962).

Clark, Ramsey. *Crime in America.* New York: Simon and Schuster, 1970.

Cloward, Richard, and Ohlin, Lloyd. *Delinquency and Opportunity.* New York: Free Press, 1961.

――――. "Social Class, Aspirations and Economics." In *Juvenile Delinquency: a Reader,* edited by J. Teele. Itasca, Illinois: F. E. Peacock, 1970.

Cohen, Albert K. *Delinquent Boys: The Culture of the Gang.* Glencoe, Ill.: Free Press, 1955.

Coleman, Frank M. *Hobbes and America: Exploring the Constitutional Foundations.* Toronto: University of Toronto Press, 1977.

Commission on Foundations and Private Philanthropy (Peterson Commission). *Foundations, Private Giving and Public Policy.* Chicago: University of Chicago Press, 1970.

Commission on Private Philanthropy and Public Needs. *Giving in America.* Washington, D.C.: The Commission, 1975.

Cook, Thomas; Crosby, Fay; and Hennigan, Karen. "The Construct Validity of Relative Deprivation." In *Social Comparison Processes: Theoretical and Empirical Perspectives,* edited by J. Suls and R. Miller, Washington, D.C.: Hemisphere, 1977.

Cooper, George A. *A Voluntary Tax? New Perspectives on Sophisticated Estate Tax Avoidance.* Washington, D.C.: Brookings Institution, 1979.

Costigan, George P., Jr. "Those Protective Trusts Which Are Miscalled 'Spendthrift Trusts' Reexamined," *California Law Review*, vol. 22 (July 1934).

Cuninggim, Merrimon. *Private Money and Public Service: The Role of Foundations in American Society.* New York: McGraw-Hill, 1972.

Curti, Merle, "Creative Giving: Slogan or Reality," *Foundation News*, November 1962.

Czajkowski, Casimir J. "The Theory of Private Property in Locke's Political Philosophy." Ph.D. Dissertation, University of Notre Dame, 1941.

Davie, Maurice R. *Sumner Today: Selected Essays of William Graham Sumner.* New Haven: Yale University Press, 1940.

Davis, Lance E., and North, Douglass C. *Institutional Change and Economic Growth.* Cambridge, England: University Press, 1971.

DeClerico, Joseph A., Jr. "Cy Pres: A Proposal for Change," *Boston University Law Review*, vol. 47 (No. 2, 1967).

DeLone, Richard H. *Small Futures: Children, Inequality and the Limits of Liberal Reform.* New York: Harcourt, Brace Jovanovich, 1979.

Dentler, Robert A. *Basic Social Problems.* Chicago: Rand-McNally, 1971.

Dentler, Robert A., and Monroe, Lawrence J. "Social Correlates of Early Adolescent Theft," *American Sociological Review*, vol. 26 (October 1961).

Dukeminier, Jesse, and Johanson, Stanley. *Family Wealth Transactions.* Boston: Little, Brown, 1972. Also 2d ed., 1978.

Eberts, Paul, and Schwirian, Kent P. "Metropolitan Crime Rates and Relative Deprivation," *Criminologica*, vol. 5 (February 1968).

Emerson, Ralph W., *Essays and Journals.* Edited by L. Mumford. New York: Doubleday, 1968.

———. *Nature.* Boston: Osgood, 1865.

Empey, Lamar T. "Social Class and Occupational Aspiration in America," *American Sociological Review*, vol. 21 (December 1956).

Erickson, Maynard L., and Empey, Lamar T. "Class Position, Peers, and Delinquency," *Sociology and Social Research*, vol. 49 (April 1965).

Feibleman, James K. *The Institutions of Society.* London: Allen and Unwin, 1956.

Feldman, Roger, and Weisfeld, Glenn. "An Interdisciplinary Study of Crime," *Crime and Delinquency*, vol. 19 (April 1973).

Fisch, Edith L. "American Acceptance of Charitable Trusts," *Notre Dame Lawyer*, vol. 28 (Winter 1953).

———. *The Cy Pres Doctrine in the United States.* Albany, N.Y.: Bender, 1950.

Fisher, Irving. "Some Impending National Problems," *Journal of Political Economy*, vol. 24 (July 1916).

Foner, Philip S., ed. *The Complete Writings of Thomas Paine.* New York: The Citadel Press, 1945.

Ford, Paul L., ed. *The Works of Thomas Jefferson.* New York and London: G. P. Putnam's Sons, 1904–5.

"Foundations and the Law." Symposium in *UCLA Law Review*, vol. 13 (May 1966).

Foundations Center, New York. *The Foundation Directory.* 7th ed. New York: The Center, 1979.

Fremont-Smith, Marion R. "The Impact of the Tax Reform Act of 1969 on State Supervision of Charities," *Harvard Journal of Legislation,* vol. 8 (May 1971).

Friedman, Lawrence M. "The Dynastic Trust," *Yale Law Journal,* vol. 73 (March, 1964).

———. *A History of American Law.* New York: Simon and Schuster, 1973.

———. "The Law of the Living and the Law of the Dead: Property, Succession, and Society," *Wisconsin Law Review,* vol. 1966 (Spring 1966).

Friedman, Milton, and Friedman, Rose. *Free to Choose: A Personal Statement.* New York: Harcourt, Brace Jovanovich 1980.

Ginsberg, Eli. *The House of Adam Smith.* New York: Columbia University Press, 1934.

Gleason, Lafayette B., and Otis, Alexander. *A Treatise on the Law of Inheritance Taxation.* 2d ed. Albany and New York: Bender, 1919.

Gordon, D. M. "Capitalism, Class and Crime in America," *Crime and Delinquency,* vol. 19 (April 1973).

Gough, John W. *John Locke's Political Philosophy.* Oxford: Clarendon, 1960.

Gray, John C. *Restraints on the Alienation of Property.* 2d ed. Boston: Boston Book Company, 1895.

Green, Kenneth V. "Inheritance Unjustified?" *Journal of Law and Economics,* vol. 16 (October 1973).

Griswold, Erwin N. *Spendthrift Trusts.* 2d ed., Albany and New York: Bender, 1947.

Hayek, Friedrich A. *The Constitution of Liberty.* Chicago: University of Chicago Press, 1960.

Heimann, Fritz F., ed. *The Future of Foundations.* Englewood Cliffs, N.J.: Prentice-Hall, 1973.

Henry, Andrew, and Short, James. *Suicide and Homicide.* Glencoe, Ill.: Free Press, 1954.

Hirschfeld, Charles, ed. *Classics of Western Thought: The Modern World.* vol. 3. New York: Harcourt, Brace and World, 1968.

Hofstadter, Richard. *Anti-Intellectualism in American Life.* New York: Knopf, 1963.

Hood, Roger G., and Sparks, Richard. *Key Issues in Criminology.* London: Weidenfeld and Nicolson, 1970.

Horwitz, Morton J. *The Transformation of American Law, 1780–1860.* Cambridge, Mass.: Harvard University Press, 1977.

Hyman, Herbert H. "Values Systems of Different Classes." In *Class, Status, and Power,* edited by R. Bendix. Glencoe, Ill.: Free Press, 1953.

Ireland, Thomas R. "Inheritance Justified: A Comment," *Journal of Law and Economics,* vol. 16 (October 1973).

Jacobson, Augustus. *Higher Ground.* Chicago: A. C. McClurg, 1888.

Jacquart, Camille. *Essais de Statistique Morale de Belge.* Brussels: A. Dewit, 1908.

Jantscher, Gerald R. *Trusts and Estate Taxation.* Washington, D.C.: Brookings Institution, 1967.

Jencks, Christopher, et al. *Who Gets Ahead? The Determinants of Economic Success in America.* New York: Basic Books, 1979.

Kant, Immanuel. *The Metaphysical Elements of Justice.* Edited by J. Ladd. Indianapolis: Bobbs-Merrill, 1965.

————. *The Philosophy of Law.* Translated by W. Hastie, Edinburgh: 1887.

————. *Political Writings.* Edited by H. Reiss. Cambridge, England: University Press, 1970.

Katz, Milton. *The Modern Foundation: Its Dual Character, Public and Private.* New York: Foundation Library Center, 1968.

Kennedy, Duncan. "The Structure of Blackstone's Commentaries," *Buffalo Law Review,* vol. 28 (Spring 1979).

Kennedy, James G. *Herbert Spencer.* Boston: Twayne, 1978.

Kent, James. *Commentaries on American Law.* 4 vols. New York: Da Capo, 1971.

Kirstein, George G. "Philanthropy: The Golden Crowbar," *Nation,* September 16, 1968.

Koch, Adrienne, *Jefferson and Madison: The Great Collaboration.* New York: Oxford University Press, 1964.

Leach, W. Barton. "Perpetuities in a Nutshell," *Harvard Law Review,* vol. 51 (February 1938).

Lebergott, Stanley. *The American Economy: Income, Wealth and Want.* Princeton, N.J.: Princeton University Press, 1976.

Lemert, Edwin M. *Human Deviance, Social Problems and Social Control.* Englewood Cliffs, N.J.: Prentice-Hall, 1967.

Lipscomb, Andrew E., ed. *The Writings of Thomas Jefferson.* Washington, D.C.: Thomas Jefferson Memorial Association, 1905.

Lipton, David A. "Significant Private Foundations and the Need for Public Selection of Their Trustees," *Virginia Law Review,* vol. 64 (October 1978).

Llewellyn, Karl N. "Book Review," *Harvard Law Review,* vol. 52 (February 1939).

Locke, John. *Two Treatises of Government.* Edited by P. Laslett, Cambridge, England: Cambridge University Press, 1970.

Louis, Arthur M. "America's Centimillionaires," *Fortune,* May 1968.

————. "The New Rich of the Seventies," *Fortune,* September 1973.

McClelland, David C. *The Achieving Society.* Princeton, N.J.: Van Nostrand, 1961.

MacDonald, Lynn. *Social Class and Delinquency.* London: Faber, 1969.

McMaster, John L. "The Federal Estate Tax: A Brief Defense . . .," *Proceedings of the National Tax Association* at App., vol. 17 (Sept. 1924).

McMurray, Orrin K. "Liberty of Testation and Some Modern Limitations Thereon," *Illinois Law Review,* vol. 14 (June 1919).

Maine, Sir Henry S. *Ancient Law.* London: J. Murray, 1861.

Martindale, Don A. *Institutions, Organizations and Mass Society.* Boston: Houghton Mifflin, 1966.

Marx, Karl, and Engels, Friedrich. *Basic Writings on Politics and Philosophy.* Garden City, N.Y.: Doubleday, 1959.

Matza, David. *Delinquency and Drift.* New York: Wiley, 1964.

Mays, John B. *Crime and the Social Structure.* London: Faber, 1963.

Mead, Sidney E. *The Lively Experiment: The Shaping of Christianity in America.* New York: Harper and Row, 1963.

Merton, Robert K. *Social Theory and Social Structure.* Glencoe, Ill.: Free Press, 1957.

Mill, John Stuart. *On Liberty.* Chicago: Henry Regnery Company, 1955.

————. *Principles of Political Economy.* London: Longmans, 1929.

————. *Three Essays on Religion.* New York: H. Holt and Co., 1884.

Miller, Howard S. *Legal Foundations of American Philanthropy.* Madison: Wisconsin State Historical Society, 1971.

Miller, Perry. *The Life of the Mind in America from Revolution to Civil War.* New York: Harcourt, Brace, and World, 1965.

Miller, Walter B. "Lower Class Structure as a Generating Milieu of Gang Delinquency," *Journal of Social Issues,* vol. 14 (May 1958).

Mooney, Michael M. "The Ministry of Culture," *Harper's,* August 1980.

Morris, Terence. *The Criminal Area.* London: Routledge and Paul, 1958.

Nason, John W. *Trustees and the Future of Foundations.* New York: Council on Foundations, 1977.

Nielsen, Waldemar A. *The Big Foundations.* New York: Columbia University Press, 1972.

Niles, Russell D. "Matter of Vought's Will: A Tighter Grip by the Dead Hand," *New York University Law Review,* vol. 45 (May 1970).

Niskanen, William A., Jr. *Bureaucracy and Representative Government.* Chicago: Aldine, Atherton, 1971.

Nozick, Robert. *Anarchy, The State, and Utopia.* New York: Basic Books, 1974.

Nye, F. Ivan; Short, James F.; and Olson, Virgil J. "Socioeconomic Status and Delinquent Behavior," *American Journal of Sociology,* vol. 63 (January 1958).

Okun, Arthur M. *Equality and Efficiency: The Big Tradeoff.* Washington, D.C: Brookings Institution, 1975.

Pareto, Vilfredo. *Manuel D'Économie Politique.* Paris: V. Giard and E. Brière, 1909.

Plamenatz, John P. *The English Utilitarians.* Oxford: Blackwell, 1958.

Plato. "The Republic." In *I Dialogues of Plato,* edited by B. Jowett. 3d ed. rev. New York and London: Macmillan, 1892.

Ploscowe, Morris. "Some Causative Factors in Criminality," in *Report on Causes of Crime.* 2 vols. Washington, D.C.: U.S. Government Printing Office, 1931.

Pound, Roscoe. *The Formative Era of American Law.* Boston: Little, Brown, 1938.

————. "The Spirit of the Common Law," *The Green Bag,* vol. 18 (January 1906).

Powell, Richard R. *Cases and Materials on Trusts and Estates.* St. Paul: West, 1960.

————. "Freedom of Alienation—For Whom?," *Real Property, Probate and Trust Journal,* vol. 2 (Summer 1967).

————. "The Rule Against Perpetuities and Spendthrift Trusts in New York: Comments and Suggestions," *Columbia Law Review,* vol. 71 (April 1971).

Projector, Dorothy S., and Weiss, Gertrude S. *Survey of Financial Characteristics of Consumers.* Washington, D.C.: Federal Reserve Board of Governors, 1966.

Radzinowicz, Sir Leon. "Economic Conditions and Crime." In *Crime and Justice,* edited by L. Radzinowicz and M. E. Wolfgang. 3 vols. New York: Basic Books, 1971.

Rawls, John A. *A Theory of Justice.* Cambridge, Mass.: Belknap Press of Harvard University Press, 1971.

Read, Harlan E. *The Abolition of Inheritance.* New York: Macmillan, 1919.

Reich, Charles A. "The New Property," *Yale Law Journal,* vol. 73 (April 1964).

Reiss, Albert J., Jr., and Rhodes, Albert L. "The Distribution of Delinquency in Social Class Structure," *American Sociological Review,* vol. 26 (October 1961).

———. "Status Deprivation and Delinquent Behavior," *Sociological Quarterly,* vol. 4 (Spring 1963).

Ricardo, David. *The Principles of Political Economy and Taxation.* Edited by E. C. K. Gonner. London: G. Bell, 1927.

Rignano, Eugenio. *The Social Significance of the Inheritance Tax.* Translated and adapted by William J. Shultz. New York: Knopf, 1924.

Ritchie, John; Alford, Neill H., Jr.; and Effland, Richard W. *Cases and Materials on Decedents' Estates and Trusts.* 5th ed. Mineola, N.Y.: Foundation Press, 1977.

Rose, Arnold M. *The Institutions of Advanced Societies.* Minneapolis: Minnesota University Press, 1958.

Rousseau, Jean J. *The Social Contract.* Translated and with introduction by W. Kendall, Chicago: H. Regnery Co., 1954.

Schwartz, Michael. "Education, Poverty, and Juvenile Delinquency." In *Poverty: New Interdisciplinary Perspectives,* edited by T. Weaver and A. Magid. Mimeographed. 1969.

Scott, Austin W. *The Law of Trusts.* 3d ed. Boston: Little, Brown, 1967.

Sherman, Jeffrey G. "Spendthrift Trusts and Employee Pensions: The Problem of Creditors' Rights," *Indiana Law Journal,* vol. 55 (Winter 1980).

Shultz, William J. *The Taxation of Inheritance.* Boston: Houghton, Mifflin, 1926.

Simes, Lewis M. *Public Policy and the Dead Hand.* Ann Arbor: University of Michigan Law School, 1955.

———. *The Law of Future Interests.* St. Paul: West, 1936.

Smith, Adam. *An Inquiry into the Nature and Causes of the Wealth of Nations.* London: W. Strahan and T. Cadell, 1776.

———. *The Theory of Moral Sentiments.* London: G. Bell and Sons, 1880.

Smith, Hedrick. "How the Soviet Elite Lives," *Atlantic Monthly,* December 1975.

———. *The Russians.* New York: Quandrangle, 1976.

Smith, Richard A. "The Fifty-Million-Dollar Man," *Fortune,* November 1957.

Spencer, Herbert. "Replies to Criticisms on the Data of Ethics," *Mind,* vol. 6 (January 1881).

Stephenson, Geoffry M., and Barker, John. "Personality and the Pursuit of Distributive Justice: An Experimental Study of Children's Moral Behavior," *British Journal of Social and Clinical Psychology,* vol. 11 (September 1972).

Stephenson, Geoffry M., and White, J. H. "An Experimental Study of Some Effects of Injustice on Children's Moral Behavior," *Journal of Experimental Social Psychology,* vol. 4 (October 1968).

Stimson, Frederic J., *My United States.* New York, London: C. Scribner's Sons, 1931.

Story, Joseph, *Commentaries on the Constitution of The United States.* 3 vols. Boston: Hilliard, Gray, 1833.

Stourm, René. *Systems Généraux d'Impôts.* 2d ed. rev. Paris: Guillaumin, 1905.

Sussman, Marvin B., Cates, Judith N., and Smith, David T. *The Family and Inheritance.* New York: Russell Sage Foundation, 1970.

Tait, Alan A. *The Taxation of Personal Wealth.* Urbana: University of Illinois Press, 1967.

———. "The Taxation of Wealth at Death: A New Proposal," *Scottish Journal of Political Economy.* vol. 9 (February 1962).

Tax Foundation, Inc., New York. *Tax Burdens and Benefits of Government Expenditures by Income Class, 1961 and 1965.* New York: 1967.

Thernstrom, Stephen. *The Other Bostonians: Poverty and Progress in the American Metropolis, 1880–1970.* Cambridge, Mass.: Harvard University Press, 1973.

Thurow, Lester C. *Generating Inequality: Mechanisms of Distribution in the U.S. Economy.* New York: Basic Books, 1975.

———. *The Impact of Taxes on the American Economy.* New York: Praeger, 1971.

———. "Tax Wealth, Not Income," *New York Times Magazine,* April 11, 1976.

———. *The Zero-Sum Society.* New York: Basic Books, 1980.

Tullock, Gordon, "Inheritance Justified," *The Journal of Law and Economics,* vol. 14 (October 1971).

Tumin, Melvin M. *Social Stratification: The Forms and Functions of Inequality.* Englewood Cliffs, N.J.: Prentice-Hall, 1967.

Unger, Roberto M. *Law in Modern Society: Toward a Criticism of Social Theory.* New York: Free Press, 1976.

U.S., Congress, House, Select Committee on Small Businesses, *Tax-exempt Foundations and Charitable Trusts: Their Impact on our Economy,* Installment I (Patman Report). Washington, D.C.: U.S. Government Printing Office, 1962.

U.S., Department of Commerce, *Survey of Current Business.* Washington, D.C.: U.S. Government Printing Office, 1979.

U.S., Department of the Treasury, *Report on Private Foundations February 2, 1965.* Submitted to Committee on Finance, U.S. Senate. Washington, D.C.: U.S. Government Printing Office, 1965.

U.S., Internal Revenue Service, *Statistics of Income—1972, Personal Wealth Estimated from Estate Tax Revenues.* Washington, D.C.: U.S. Government Printing Office, 1973.

U.S., National Commission on Causes and Prevention of Violence, *Commission Statement on Violent Crime: Homicide, Assault, Rape and Robbery.* New York: G. Braziller, 1967,

Van der Weyde, William M., ed. *The Life and Works of Thomas Paine.* New Rochelle, N.Y.: Paine National Historical Association, 1925.

Van Doren, John W. "Redistributing Wealth by Curtailing Inheritance: The Community Interest in the Rule against Perpetuities and the Estate Tax," *Florida State University Law Review,* vol. 3 (Winter 1975).

Vaughn, Charles E. *Studies in the History of Political Philosophy Before and After Rousseau.* Edited by A. G. Little. New York: Russell, 1960.

Vold, George B. *Theoretical Criminology.* New York: Oxford University Press, 1958.

Wagner, Richard E. *Death and Taxes: Some Perspectives on Inheritance, Inequality and Progressive Taxation.* Washington, D.C.: American Enterprise Institute, 1973.

―――. *Inheritance and the State: Tax Principles for a Free and Prosperous Commonwealth.* Washington, D.C.: American Enterprise Institute, 1977.

Warren, Alvin C. Jr. "Fairness and a Consumption-Type or Cash Flow Personal Income Tax," *Harvard Law Review,* vol. 88 (March 1975).

Watkins, George P. *The Growth of Large Fortunes.* New York: Macmillan, 1907.

Wedgwood, Josiah. *The Economics of Inheritance.* London: G. Routledge, 1929.

Whicher, George F., ed. *The Transcendentalist Revolt against Materialism.* Boston: Heath, 1949.

White, G. Edward. *The American Judicial Tradition.* New York: Oxford University Press, 1976.

White, Morton G. *Social Thought in America: The Revolt against Formalism.* Boston: Beacon Press, 1963.

Whyte, William F. *Street Corner Society: The Social Structure of an Italian Slum.* 2d ed., Chicago: University of Chicago Press, 1955.

Wicker, William H. "Spendthrift Trusts," *Gonzaga Law Review,* vol. 10 (Fall 1974).

Wilkins, Leslie T. *Social Deviance: Social Policy, Action, and Research.* London: Tavistock, 1964.

Willard, Joseph, "Illustrations of the Origin of Cy Pres," *Harvard Law Review,* vol. 8 (May 25, 1894).

Winston, Garrad B. "State and Federal Relations in Inheritance Taxation," *Proceedings of the National Tax Association,* vol. 17 (September 1924).

Wootton, Barbara, *Social Science and Social Pathology.* London: Allen and Unwin, 1959.

Wright, Minturn T. "Termination of Trusts in Pennsylvania—Some Current Trends," *University of Pennsylvania Law Review,* vol. 115 (April 1967).

Index